Threescore Years and Ten

Threescore Years and Ten

An Anecdotal Autobiography

William R. Russell

Threescore Years and Ten
An Anecdotal Autobiography

by

William R. Russell

ISBN 978-1-887730-57-0

Photo credits: Front cover—© 1996 Karen Rodgers Photography

"Young, handsome, bearded prophet" on p. 188—© 1978 William Notman

Printed in the United States of America.

Published 2019 by THE INTERMUNDIA PRESS LLC

The days of our years are threescore years and ten;
and if by reason of strength they be fourscore years,
yet is their strength labour and sorrow;
for it is soon cut off, and we fly away (Ps 90:10).

IN MEMORIAM

ELIZABETH ANN TROTTER RUSSELL
June 2, 1942–August 5, 2002

I have written this book

for
Tori, Will, Abbi and Ryan
who light up my life . . .

and for
Sarah, Kirk and Rebecca
who probably wish I hadn't . . .

and, finally, for
Sherri
who insisted!

CONTENTS

FOREWORD

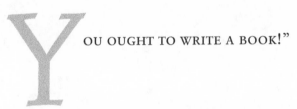Y OU OUGHT TO WRITE A BOOK!"

How often have we rambling raconteurs heard that tempting tribute to our storytelling skills? For years—decades, in fact—I have resisted every admonition to "record for posterity" the anecdotes and incidents that have punctuated my full and fascinating (at least to me!) life and ministry.

Now, well into my seventh decade, with one book published and one wife insisting, I realize that "posterity" is closing in on me, and, if I am ever going to do what so many have been urging me to do for so long, I had better start doing it now. And when better to start than on my birthday?

I am thinking of "an anecdotal autobiography"—an informal retelling of the life stories I have loved to tell lo these many years, and I would love to have my grandchildren (and maybe even great-grandchildren) know more about me and about their late grandmother Ann, whom they have never known and who would have loved them so, and about their "Nana Sher," whom they do know and who does love them so, and about their parents and aunts and uncles who may not want them to know some of the stories I am about to tell but who also love them each and every one ever so much.

William R. Russell
The Plantation
Ponte Vedra Beach, Florida
September 10, 2011

THE
FORTIES

I WAS BORN ON SEPTEMBER 10, 1939, the day Canada entered World War II by joining with Great Britain and eventually most of the British Empire in declaring war on Germany . . . then Italy . . . and, eventually, Japan.

Technically, this was not yet the forties, and of course I remember nothing from those last four months of "the Thirties," but there are (or were) some oft-told tales from that brief period that I think are worth retelling once more.

I was named William Ray, after my two grandfathers. My mother, *née* Marion Rae Kenyon, allegedly wanted her surname to be my middle name but that was thought to sound too pretentious for the Russell family. Much later in my life, when I began my ministry at the Fifth Avenue Presbyterian Church in New York City, where all Manhattan's prestigious pulpiteers had very distinguished-sounding triple names, how I wished I could have been William Kenyon Russell!

My father, "Bill Jr." to everyone in the extended Russell family, was not actually a junior at all. He was just plain William Russell, thanks to the insistence of his father, William

Henry Clow Russell, who was frequently heard to complain that having three given names was at least one too many, so he would give his son but one to even the score!

"William" was and still is an historic family name. My great-grandfather, born at Tintock, Kirkintilloch, Scotland, on September 27, 1861, had been just plain William. But his wife, my great-grandmother, Jane Baird Clow, born on April 13, 1863, also in Kirkintilloch, was (ironically) the daughter of William Henry Clow, which was the full name they bestowed on their first surviving son, born on March 27, 1890. What proud satisfaction I take in the William, son of William tradition that has continued unbroken through the naming of my only son William Kirk and my elder grandson William Ronald!

My mother, Marion, was very ill when I was born; in fact, she had to have her gall bladder removed immediately after my birth and remained in hospital for some significant period of time before returning home. My father, who always loved cars, was at that time the proud owner of a Ford coupe with a "rumble seat," which he never let me forget he had to sell to pay the hospital bill to bring my mother home to care for me.

The story goes that the first morning she was home from the hospital, she put out her usual sort of note in an empty milk-bottle—milk, cream, butter, probably—only to find one quart of unhomogenized milk on the doorstep with a note from the milkman: "Lady, don't you know there's a war on?" Of course, she did not; no one had thought to mention it to her during her illness.

Since their marriage on September 22, 1937, my parents lived in a prewar triplex in Linwood Place in Windsor. Ever the entrepreneur, my father had bought it as an income-producing investment property, but my mother apparently found the ever-so-helpful neighbors on either side of the shared front porch a bit much, on top of the equally willing-to-help mothers, grand-mothers, aunts, and nieces all living nearby, so my father "traded up" early in 1940 to a typical Windsor prewar two-bedroom brick bungalow on Sunset Avenue, where the central steam plant of the University of Windsor stands today.

Of this home, I do have some vague memories—or are they the vestiges of more of those oft-told tales from my childhood?

* * * * *

SOMETIME IN THE EARLY 1940S, my parents undertook a do-it-yourself project to "finish" the bungalow's attic, turning it into living space to provide a temporary home for a Scottish émigré cousin, Tom Cunningham, and eventually his wife Mary. Why they came to live with us I never knew, but they were relatives on my paternal grandmother's side, and their stories of the "auld country" opened my heart and mind to the realization that there was a family heritage back in Scotland of which my paternal grandfather (and therefore his children) would never speak. One of the first things I clearly recollect my Grampa Russell saying to me in response to my insistent childish queries about Scotland was, "Wullie, dinna press!"

And I didn't, at least not until the mid-1970s, when I was privileged to visit my grandmother's two sisters still living in Scotland—Aunt Annie Brown and Aunt Crawford and her husband, Uncle Matthew Murdoch—and learned so much about the Browns and the Russells and the Clows and the Bairds.

I remember that there was a used car lot down the block from our little house, at the corner of Wyandotte Street probably, and my father, though painfully lame, would take me for early evening walks to "kick the tires" and teach me how to recognize the various makes and models of the prewar automobiles on the lot. There was a Peerless Dairies ice cream parlour along the block, and we would occasionally go and sit on one of the long wooden benches inside and lick "sinnle dip" cones.

My brother, Thomas Edward—"Tommy," named, I think, for the Scottish cousin still living upstairs on Sunset Avenue— was born on April 6, 1944. His arrival made our little bungalow crowded, I remember, and I suspect that it was not long before my father started looking for another real estate opportunity in which to house our little family of four more comfortably.

And I very clearly remember V-E Day, May 8, 1945, the date declared as the official end of World War II in Europe. My mother sent me out into the street, along with every other kid on the block, to bang together two metal saucepans to celebrate "Victory in Europe!"

Sometime that summer, we moved out of the city proper to an area then known as "South Windsor," to one of two sub-stantial two-story brick homes that had been built in 1929 as "model homes" for an ambitious new, planned subdivision that, unfortunately, became one of the first victims of the Great Depression. It was a beautiful home, vaguely Dutch Colonial in design, probably small and meager by today's standards but seemingly quite grand back then, with formal living and dining rooms and a kitchen on the first floor, three bedrooms, and a bath upstairs and a full basement below.

But, for me, Randolph Street was always a lonely place to live. It intersected the rural Third Concession along which the 1929 development had been planned, with still-nonexistent streets and roads marked off by trees planted sixteen years be-fore and now maturing in weed-filled acreage extending as far as the eye could see. The neighborhood offered but one set of neighbors, an elderly couple living in the model home across the street, before it petered out into a gravel strip along which a sort of shantytown had sprung up during the war.

I first experienced that loneliness in an unforgettable way. On August 14, 1945, when Japan surrendered to the Allies and World War II seemed to be over, my mother got out the dented saucepans and sent me out to bang them in celebration. There was no one in the street but me. Three weeks later, when Japan formally signed the terms of surrender on what came to known as V-J Day, my mother wanted to send me out yet again, which I steadfastly refused to do—my first recognized and remembered act of defiance against a parent!

There was no public elementary school in the area. But there was a Roman Catholic parochial school about a mile away, considered in those days within easy walking distance, where my father's youngest sister, Isabel, had been attending since her father had bought a peach orchard farm property about another mile farther along Third Concession from our new home. So in September 1945, just about to turn six, I was enrolled in Grade 1 at École Notre Dame de Bon Secours, a four-room multi-purpose building on the site of the as-yet-to-be-built Christ the King Roman Catholic Church, where, serendipitously, I was much later invited to assist at the wedding of my best friend Lex McCrindle's son in 1988!

Most of the teachers were French-speaking nuns of the Order of the Holy Names of Jesus, Mary, and Joseph, and they lived in St. Mary's Academy, a girls' convent-school nearby. My father strictly abjured them from "proselytizing" his strictly Presbyterian little boy; and to give the sisters credit, they never overstepped that admonition in the six years I was in their classrooms, although in an Easter pageant when I was in Grade 4 they did cast me as Doubting Thomas!

The following spring, on June 17, 1946, to be precise, when Tommy was a toddler and I was still six, our exurban way of life was torn to shreds by an F4 tornado, the worst ever to hit Windsor, Ontario. It was a sultry early summer afternoon, and my brother and I were cavorting in our underwear under a lawn sprinkler in the front yard, when the skies darkened to a gray-ish-yellowish-greenish hue and the atmosphere became deathly still. Coming from the kitchen to the front door to see what the weather was doing, our mother spotted an ominous funnel cloud a mile away and began to scream at us to come inside, dripping wet—a "no-no" if ever there was one in our house! Terrified and uncomprehending, we were herded down the basement stairs and told to sit on the cement floor up against the big old coal furnace. Suddenly, our father remembered that our little dog, Blackie, was tied to his doghouse in the backyard. As disabled as he was, he began to run for the basement stairs, only to be tackled by our mother, screaming and pleading "No, Bill, no! You'll be killed too!"

The tornado hit our home a glancing blow, knocking a huge hole in the roof, shattering the glass in all the upstairs windows, unaccountably shearing in half a pussy willow tree planted at one of the back corners of the house, and lifting our free-standing wood-frame garage off its footings and collapsing it onto Blackie's doghouse fifty feet away. We survived, in shock but otherwise unscathed. Even Blackie was found unharmed in his sturdy doghouse beneath the rubble of the garage. Upstairs, in Tommy's crib, a section of the roof with a vicious spike protruding from one end had impaled my baby brother's pillow. When I saw it, I wept uncontrollably at my first real recognition of the fragility of life, the finality of death, and the significance of our family's faith in the risen Lord Jesus Christ that had made little or no sense to me till then.

The tornado wiped out the shantytown at the end of our street, killed at least one of our unknown neighbors, and unleashed an insurance-fueled redevelopment of our neighborhood with street upon street of cookie-cutter housing and all the incipient evils of inadequate infrastructure and under-regulated construction.

We could not live in our house in its damaged condition, so we moved immediately and temporarily to Amherstburg, where our mother's parents lived in the huge once-upon-a-time Presbyterian manse. DeeDee and Poppy Kenyon made a home for us that very night. I finished out the school year with my Kenyon cousin, JayAnne. I made a few new friends and spent the summer playing on the historic grounds of the Fort Malden Museum and Battlefield. Tommy cried himself to sleep every night, and so did I, probably, although I have no clear memory of it, but our mother repressed her traumatic experience by clenching her teeth so tightly while she slept that eventually she had to have them all extracted, in great discomfort and at a relatively young age.

By the time we returned to Randolph Street for the start of a new school year, our neighborhood was already "in transition," and a new kind of loneliness began. We were suddenly strangers, living in one of the two homes that had withstood the tornado and were now surrounded by burgeoning suburbia and new neighbors. Many of them proved to be Pentecostals in their religious affiliation, choosing to live near their little Assemblies of God chapel a mile or so away on Huron Church Line—"Holy Rollers" we called them in an age of innocence long before correctness of any kind. I just remember that they were arrogantly "holier-than-thou" and rigorously judgmental about almost everything we Presbyterians did or thought or believed.

Farther along Third Concession in the opposite direction and closer to the parochial school, almost all of the new homeowners were, not surprisingly, Roman Catholic but remarkably more belligerently so than the folks I remembered from my first year at Bon Secours. My Aunt Isabel had graduated and gone to high school, and I felt overwhelmingly alone.

The next summer, I discovered a potential playmate living across Third Concession in a dilapidated farmhouse almost hidden from view by its overgrown shrubbery. Brian's family were not Holy Rollers. They were born-again Christian fundamentalists who disapproved of me and my family every bit as vehemently as did the Pentecostals! But Brian and I forged a furtive friendship of sorts that summer, climbing trees, sleeping under the stars in a new-mown hayfield, catching polliwogs in the little creek that gurgled its way through their property. One day, about a week before school started up again, Brian's older brother took us to his "secret place" further up the creek bed and tried to teach us how to "get a hard-on" by fondling ourselves through our corduroy pants while thinking about girls. Brian and I were bewildered, embarrassed, and sworn to secrecy before we were allowed to go home. By unspoken mutual consent, we never played together again, and I didn't figure out what Lorne had been talking about for probably another decade!

I think of my only other playmate from that period every time I watch the movie classic, *A Christmas Story*. Bobby was not a bully like Scut Farcas, but he was sly and sneering and sinister. His family had lived in the shantytown before the tornado and had returned to a government-built house down where Randolph Street still petered out into gravel. They were, of course, Pentecostals and disapproving, but not above encouraging their little boy to make our Presbyterian lives miserable. Once in a while, cycling past our house on his way home from his school, Bobby would offer an occasional olive branch of friendship, invariably to turn it into a scourge of criticism and cruelty.

One day as we stood arguing on our side lawn, he said something truly unforgivable about our mother—I did not say "unforgettable" because I have completely forgotten whatever it was! But I lost it! Enraged, I grabbed Bobby, threw him to the ground in a muddy puddle, straddled him, and began to beat on him with my fists. My little brother, Tommy, bless his heart, ran to "tell Mommy," who came out and with surprising strength pulled me off Bobby and dragged me, sobbing uncontrollably by now, into the house. Like Mother Parker, she never said a word to my father, at least not in my presence, and the episode was never mentioned again—ever!

But, from then on, Bobby looked neither to left nor right as he cycled past our house on his daily trek to and from school. To the best of my recollection, we never spoke again.

And I was lonely.

My "saving grace" in those years and for many years thereafter was St. Andrew's Presbyterian Church in downtown Windsor. At that time the largest Presbyterian congregation in Canada and certainly the most distinguished congregation of any Protestant denomination in Windsor, St. Andrew's was our family church home. Our Russell grandparents had been married there in 1914; both our parents had been baptized, confirmed, and married there as had (or would eventually be) my brother and myself and our wives. Our father was elected at a surprisingly young age to the board of managers and then to the session, where he served actively until his death, becoming in due course the senior elder of the congregation. Our mother was a Sunday school teacher and then superintendent of the kindergarten department; a Brownie, Girl Guide, and Ranger leader; and an active member and several times president of the women's guild.

The church's immensely popular minister was the Reverend Dr. Hugh Mortimer Paulin, a short, stocky Scot with an infectious grin and a powerful pulpit presence. One of his classic preaching techniques I remember particularly well: he always kept a white linen handkerchief balled up in the sleeve of his pulpit robe, and at the climactic moment of his message he would pause, pull out his hankie, wipe his sweaty brow, and hurl the soggy missile underneath his preaching desk.

Because our parents had so many different responsibilities in the congregation, they were often caught up in conversations with other church leaders in the sanctuary at the end of worship. One of my most precious—and frequent—memories is of Dr. Paulin coming down our aisle after he finished shaking hands at the church door. Every so often, he would pick me up bodily and hold me over his head, glaring at me as he intoned more prophetically than he knew: "Billy Russell, when you grow up, I want you to be a minister like me!"

Even more precious are the memories of the friendships I made there, some lasting to this very day! In my Sunday school classes were boys and girls of my own age and of my own—however juvenile—belief system. There was no bullying, no criticizing, no judgmentalism, no ostracism. How I looked forward to Sunday school and Mission Band and Children's Day and the annual Dominion—now Canada—Day church picnic excursions cruising down the Detroit River on one of the "Bob-lo" boats to that magical island amusement park!

One last brief memory of the forties: As the family painting business—William Russell & Sons—prospered in postwar Windsor, our father acquired a second vehicle, which allowed much more freedom and flexibility in our trips into the city for church events. Early on Sunday mornings—but never quite as early as planned—our mother would drive herself, Tommy, and me downtown in time for Sunday school. I can still hear her muttering to herself as she sped down Victoria Avenue toward the church, "I can just see the headline in tomorrow's *Star*: 'Sunday School Teacher Arrested in Mad Dash through Town!'"

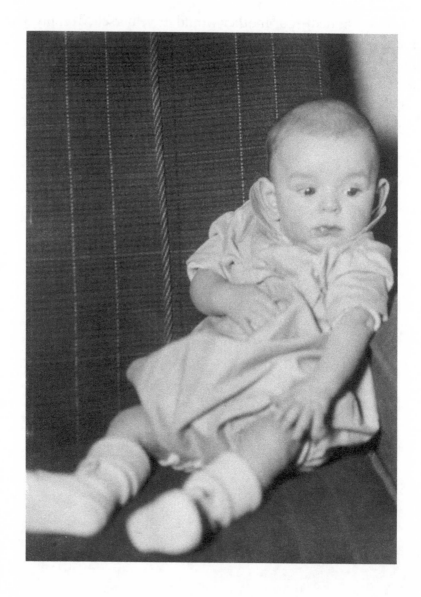

Christmas 1939
Linwood Place, Windsor, Ontario
My first Christmas

Summer 1940
Linwood Place, Windsor, Ontario
With my mother Marion

Autumn 1941
Sunset Avenue. Windsor, Ontario
A natty dresser even then!

Easter Sunday, April 6, 1947
Randolph Street, South Windsor, Ontario
Home from church with a lily

Summer 1949
Hidden Valley Lodge, Huntsville, Ontario
Adventuring with my brother Tommy

THE FIFTIES

I N JUNE 1951, I GRADUATED FROM Grade 8 at Notre Dame de Bon Secours. Over the course of my six years there, I had "skipped" Grade 3—easily accomplished since Mme. Potvin taught Grades 3 and 4 in the same room—and then combined Grades 7 and 8 in my final year under the tutelage of a very demanding Sister Principal. I was eleven years old.

My parents wisely recognized that though academically I seemed sufficiently proficient to enter high school, I was no-where near physically or socially mature enough to handle being plunged into high school. At that time, Victoria Avenue was considered one of Windsor's most desirable residential ad-dresses, and the educational institution that bore its name was certainly the most desirable public elementary school in the city. Given that the family business owned property on Riverside Drive downtown and that my Russell grandparents lived about six blocks from the school, my father was somehow able to get me admitted to the Victoria Avenue School to *repeat* Grade 8, thus putting off entering high school for another year.

Some of Windsor's most prominent and successful families lived on Victoria Avenue. Many of my classmates in Miss Golden's Grade 8 class were gifted, privileged, competitive, and sophisticated, and I was in over my head from the first day of school. Fortunately, one of the first students I met was a good friend from St. Andrew's Sunday School, Lex McCrindle, who lived just over a block away on Dougall Avenue. He and his younger brother Archie had lots of friends in the neighbourhood, and they helped ease my way in socially.

Academically, things were almost overwhelming. I had never had an art or music lesson, never been in a science lab or an auditorium or a gymnasium or even a manual training shop. I was very good at the three R's, but I had learned a very French Roman Catholic version of Canadian history, and I had been schooled in a very didactic and nonparticipatory approach to education in general and soon realized that I was not *repeating* Grade 8 at all but was experiencing it in a whole new way and at a whole new level.

My father drove me into the city to school every morning. I walked to and from Grampa and Grandma Russell's house for lunch each day and returned there every afternoon to do my homework and wait for my father to pick me up for the trip back to South Windsor. I felt as though I was straddling two different worlds and wasn't really at home in either of them. Meanwhile, Tommy was attending Notre Dame de Bon Secours and experiencing the dreaded *Why can't you be more like your big brother Bill?* reaction from insensitive teachers who never stopped to notice how fundamentally different we were from one another. Thus were sown the seeds of a sense of estrangement between us that persisted to one degree or another for over fifty years.

One prescient memory from that year was the visit to Windsor (and the rest of Canada) by HRH the Princess Elizabeth and her handsome husband, HRH Prince Philip, Duke of Edinburgh. On cool day outings, the heir apparent to the throne was often photographed wearing a Christian Dior-inspired fitted chocolate brown wool coat with a large and lavish beaver shawl collar. Our mother had and was joyfully wearing almost exactly the same coat, and with her diminutive size and rich brown curly hair she attracted a lot of double takes, especially on the day the princess was actually in Windsor.

I said "prescient" because totally unknown to me until twenty-five years later, one of my brother's and my little friends from St. Andrew's Sunday school, Elizabeth Ann Trotter, was among Windsor's Brownies chosen to audition for the privilege of presenting a bouquet to Her Royal Highness at some point during the visit. Apparently, Ann did not curtsy well enough to win the privilege, something she never told me until in May 1976 as my wife she remembered the incident with a secret smile as she curtsied very satisfactorily indeed to the princess's mother, HM Queen Elizabeth the Queen Mother in Her Majesty's own drawing room at Clarence House! But that, again, is a story for a later chapter.

In June 1952, our father surprised us boys with the purchase of a house at 1484 Victoria Avenue, just a block away from the Victoria Avenue School and within walking distance of Kennedy Collegiate. A modest Dutch Colonial stucco home very similar to our old house on Randolph Street but without a garage, it boasted a bright sunroom and a beautiful backyard. We Russells lived there very happily for the next decade.

Later that month, I graduated from the Victoria Avenue School, standing twentieth in my class, despite my *repeating* Grade 8! During the year, I had developed a good friendship with a boy named Ross Dixon, the son of a Windsor bank manager. He was the only one of my classmates to end up in the same class with me as we entered Grade 9 at Kennedy Collegiate. Unfortunately, his father was soon transferred to the main branch of his bank in Hamilton, Ontario. Our hit-and-miss friendship survived into our university years and then petered out, only to be renewed decades later when we both worshiped at Yorkminster Park Baptist Church in Toronto.

The Hon. W. C. Kennedy Collegiate Institute boasted a highly sophisticated and competitive student body. Nevertheless, at Kennedy, incoming Grade 9 students were assigned at random to one of at least eight homerooms. Mine was 9E. It was not an easy adjustment from the intensely academic and socially sophisticated atmosphere of the one and only Grade 8 class at Victoria Avenue School. Students from many different parts of the city and from various social, economic, racial, religious, ethnic, and intellectual backgrounds were all lumped together in a class grouping that traveled from classroom to classroom and subject to subject through eight periods every day for a whole school year.

It was not a particularly happy school year for me, and I have few memories of it, pleasant or otherwise; however, by far the most significant memories from that first year of high school involve the death of Dr. Paulin, the minister of St. Andrew's Church for thirty-seven years. A hale and hearty Scot, he was on his way out the manse door to play golf, when he was felled by a massive heart attack. My family, our congregation, and the whole city of Windsor mourned his passing. His was the first funeral I ever attended, and its size and magnificence had a profound effect on me. Over and over during it all, I kept hearing Dr. Paulin saying to me: *"Billy Russell, when you grow up, I want you to be a minister like me!"* In truth, my career path and life destiny were sealed in that tragic and tearful week in

October 1952, and I never really wavered from them over the next sixty years.

I also remember taking a classmate to Kennedy's annual pre-Christmas "Snowball" prom, although I don't remember her name. She was a new Canadian immigrant from England, in some ways as much a fish out of water as I was—taller than I, skinnier, too, as I remember—and one of the only girls in our class not to have a date as the prom night neared. I guess I felt as sorry for her as I did for myself, so I invited her and she accepted and we went. She wore a horrible pale green net formal with a huge hoop skirt that she did not know how to manage very well, and I presented her with a horrible, single white carnation-with-green-fuzzy-things corsage that clashed with the dress, of course!

I don't remember the dance *at all*. I do remember that afterward we went with a group of classmates to get something to eat and drink at Mario's, a pizza-and-burger restaurant a few blocks from the school. Then I walked her home a few more blocks in the opposite direction. There was snow on the ground, or at least icy patches on the sidewalk, and she was wearing high-heeled open-toed dancing slippers. We navigated the treacherous sidewalks almost all the way to her house, where, alas, on a dimly-lit street corner her feet became entangled in some binding-wire cuttings left behind by a careless paperboy, and she fell to the sidewalk, grazing her knees, tearing her dress, and scratching her ankles. Humiliated that I was too young to drive and too proud to have asked my father to come to Mario's and drive her safely home, I helped her limp the rest of the way to her house and decided then and there that I was *too young* to date!

In that winter of 1953, our parents undertook to make a midwinter vacation trip to Florida, an extravagance of incred-

ible significance! They requested permission to take Tommy and
me out of school for two weeks or so. No problem for my
brother, now a student at Victoria Avenue School. Not so for
me: Kennedy's principal, the formidably unpopular A. F. S. Gilbert, took exception to such an unjustifiable undertaking and
refused to approve my absence. We went anyway, and thus
began a lifelong love for Florida within both Tom and me and
our respective families later on. But Principal Gilbert had his revenge. When the end-of-year final exams took place in June,
most of my friends and classmates were excused from sitting
exams in the subjects for which they had demonstrated competence throughout the school year. I may have been recommended to be excused by my teachers, but the principal
demanded that I sit every single final exam that year!

The coronation of Queen Elizabeth II took place on June 2,
1953, and Kennedy's cadet corps marched in Windsor's Coronation Day parade down Ouellette Avenue to the riverfront. I
marched with the school's drum-and-bugle band, resplendent
in a scarlet tunic, navy trousers with a red stripe down each leg,
and a huge white pith helmet with a shiny brass pointed finial.
I thought I was pretty hot stuff that day and remembered it
wryly decades later when I was privileged to march with the
pipes and drums of the Black Watch—Royal Highland Regiment—of Canada on Sherbrooke Street in Montreal.

Grade 10 at Kennedy Collegiate was like another world.
Students were grouped in classes according to their academic
abilities and interests. The brightest students, excelling in history, literature, and languages, were all assigned to 10A. Our
counterparts with strengths in mathematics and sciences were
in 10B, and so on down the line. Lex ended up in 10B; I, of
course, landed in 10A. What a difference it made to be among
like-minded and like-gifted classmates! I began to make friends,

primarily, as I look back on it now, among Jewish boys and girls, many of whom lived in my neighborhood. In fact, there were so many students from Jewish families that Kennedy was known derisively as "Hebrew Heights."

I have very few memories of that year. I began the study of Latin and loved it, never suspecting what an asset mastery of that classical language would prove to be in my later studies in philosophy and theology. I met my first girlfriend—Elaine some-body-or-other—and I started working on Saturday mornings in the family painting and decorating store on Riverside Drive, downtown. I began to attend the PYPS (Presbyterian Young People's Society) at St. Andrew's Church on Sunday evenings after worship.

Our father had by now designed and built a two-bedroom cottage on leased Crown land in Rondeau Provincial Park on the north shore of Lake Erie, about an hour's drive east of Windsor. The "Little Pink Palace" became our summer home from the day school let out late in June until nightfall on Labour Day in early September. So many of my most vivid teenaged memories cluster around the time I spent at Rondeau. I had a summer job at Mr. Biddle's Bayview Inn, both before it burned down and after it was rebuilt as the Bayview Market. I stocked shelves and swept floors and, best of all, scooped ice cream cones at an open-air window on weekends.

Life at the Little Pink Palace was spartan at best. We had two bedrooms, a small living room, an even smaller kitchen, a still smaller sunroom, and a still-smaller-yet two-piece bath-room, almost one half of which was taken up with the pump and water tank of our sand-point well system. An oil stove for heat when it got chilly—but no hot water, no laundry facilities, no closets, no telephone, no television—nothing but the simple joys of *just being there*!

Our well water was so hard that our mother used to have Tommy and me haul buckets of water up from the lake to wash her hair or our clothes. She heated a big galvanized tub of water on the oil stove and then carried it out to a sturdy picnic table in the backyard to do the laundry. For the first few years, we had no car except on weekends when our father would drive out from Windsor. But we wanted for nothing: milk, bread, ice, meat, and dry cleaning were brought to our door by mobile vendors from the neighboring towns of Blenheim and Ridgetown, and, of course, there was always the Bayview Market at the park gates and the Trading Post at the traffic circle near the Government Dock and the Yacht Club.

I remember the summer my beloved great-grandmother—Nana—spent a month or so with us, striving to recover from a stroke. She was determined to learn to walk again, and a neighboring nurse spent her vacation showing us how to help Nana as best we could. Her second husband, Grandad Sunderland, was a sour, self-centered old man who refused to take any part in his wife's rehabilitation. He would get up in the morning, pour cold water over a Muffet cereal biscuit, then leave for the day to sit on a bench with a bunch of other old codgers in front of the Bayview Market.

In the summer of 1954, Dad bought a sailboat, an old shallow-draft, single-masted gaff-rigged "Lark" and hired its original builder, "Pop" Weir, to teach me to sail, which he did in a gruff and knowing manner that brooked no nonsense from a thirteen-year-old boy from the big city. Larks were the racing craft of choice on Rondeau Bay, with the Erieau Yacht Club miles away eastward near the Lake Erie mouth of the bay and the Rondeau Yacht Club next to the Government Dock at the west end. Although "Pop" Weir had designed the original Larks (of which mine was one), his brother and chief competitor, Al

Weir, had refined the design somewhat to narrow the cockpit and reduce the freeboard, thus making *his* boats lighter, faster, and therefore more popular.

I didn't care! "Pop" taught me to sail not for speed but for joy, and I truly enjoyed every moment I spent on the bay during those early and idyllic Rondeau summers. I painted my Lark coral and gray and white, the colors on my favorite Chrysler Forward Look models, introduced in 1957, and Dad had his Uncle Henry Russell hand-paint "SH-BOOM" nameplates for both sides of the boat just forward of the mast's guy wires. I never raced "SH-BOOM," but I transported a lot of family and friends back and forth across the bay or on longer voyages to picnic and sunbathe on the relatively private point beaches at the far end.

For us teenagers, social life at Rondeau centered first around the old dance pavilion on the beach near the park traffic circle and later included the new dance hall built on the bay just outside the park gates. It was truly the innocent idyllic existence of the '50s, portrayed in the silly beach movies of the era. Summer romances flourished for two months, only to wither and die when we all went back to school. My first real summer love was one Margaret Ann Downie, the older daughter of a Detroit lawyer with a cottage on the bay near the Government Dock. We dated all summer and into the fall, when she went back to Grosse Pointe, then Detroit's most affluent and exclusive suburb. My father was adamant that I could not drive the family car in the USA—too many crazy American drivers! So, he would drive me to the Canadian end of the tunnel, whence I would board a bus to the American side, where Margaret Ann and her father would be waiting to pick me up. At the end of our date, our fathers and we would reverse the procedure, a pattern that left little room for romance and tired us of one another by

Christmas.

For most of my high school summers, I had a part-time job, usually at the Bayview Market. But the summer I was to turn eighteen and go away to university, my parents decreed that I should have the summer off to prepare myself for this awesome turning point in my life. Dad insisted that I put the time to good use by learning to type! He gave me a big, old Underwood upright machine and a do-it-yourself book of instructions, and I did it myself. I can still remember sitting at the picnic table in the backyard under one of those huge old oak trees, learning touch typing, a skill I mastered that summer and have used every year of my life since!

In Grade 13, I joined my friend, Lex, to sing in the Kennedy Collegiate octet. Our conductor and coach was Harvey Ward, one of the school's Latin teachers. He was a perfectionist, but he brought out the very best in each of the eight of us as singers to the point that our group was invited to participate in a province-wide music festival in Toronto's Massey Hall during the Easter vacation that year. For the occasion, my father managed to secure a room for Lex and me in one of the residence halls of Knox College, the Presbyterian church in Canada's theological college, conveniently located on the university's main quadrangle, just around the corner from University College.

It had long been my intention to apply for admission to the newly-established Assumption University of Windsor for my post-secondary education. A fledgling institution formed by the secularization of Windsor's old Roman Catholic Assumption College the year before, it would be almost a decade before it became a "real" university, the University of Windsor; but back then it seemed a safe and comfortable destination for a still very young and naïve Bill Russell.

Everything changed during that April week spent on the

campus of the University of Toronto. Established in 1827 by royal charter as a collegiate university, it had faculties in almost every academic discipline and a system of (then) four semi-autonomous liberal arts colleges, the oldest and most secular of which was and still is University College, the most prestigious undergraduate institution in Canada. By the end of the week, I knew that my world had been turned upside down. I returned home to confide to my parents that I had my heart set on an honours degree in philosophy from University College of the University of Toronto if I could get in!

In those days, the culmination of Grade 13 involved sitting the departmental exams prepared by the Ontario Department of Education to be taken anonymously by all students of whichever subject at the same hour of the same day all over the province and then marked collectively by panels of secondary school teachers recruited from across the province. Each year's results were released in the first or second week of August and published throughout the province by each community's local newspaper. In effect, no one knew how she or he fared on the departmentals and whether or not she or he would be accepted to one or more of the province's few universities and community colleges until the grades came out.

I still remember riding up to the Bayview Market on my bicycle day after day in early August to buy a copy of the *Windsor Star* to see whether or not it contained those results. Because I was an arts major and had sat double exams (one for grammar and another for literature), for four languages (English, French, Latin and German), plus two for biology (botany and zoology), and one for history thrown in for good measure, I would have eleven marks reported in all, only the top eight of which would count for grade averages and university admission.

When the results were finally published, my eight best grades made me Kennedy Collegiate's top student for the year. Then the *Star* contacted my father to obtain a picture of me to publish as one of the top three students in the City of Windsor. I was truly astonished, but my real excitement was the assurance that I would be admitted to the Class of 1961 at University College of the University of Toronto.

However, in the next couple of weeks, I received no news from Toronto. The Labour Day weekend was looming, and our family was committed to driving to Montreal and back for the annual national convention of the Kinsmen Clubs of which our father was the retiring president of the Windsor club. So anxious was I for news from U of T that I persuaded our parents to get off the 401 at the Bloor Street exit at the far western edge of metropolitan Toronto and then to let me drive into the city for miles and miles and miles of stop-and-go traffic to the university campus, where we located the registrar's office, and I was finally assured, verbally at least, that I had been accepted and would find a letter waiting at home upon our return from Montreal!

To my amazement and my parents' delight, not only was I admitted to University College, but because of my departmental grade average, I was awarded a full scholarship named in honour of the late wife of the university's chancellor. I had just two weeks to arrange for room and board in the aforementioned Knox College and then to pack everything I would need in a metal steamer trunk my parents bought for me, plus a small, suitcase-sized fiberboard laundry box in which I was to ship my dirty laundry home by train to my mother every other week and in which, on its return, I would find a packet of fresh-baked cookies from Mom and a little something on the side from Dad.

Only two other members of my Kennedy graduating class had been admitted to U of T that year, and neither of them were particular friends, so eventually I headed off to Toronto alone on the train, my mother on the station platform weeping copiously, my father trying mightily *not* to cry, and my heart in my mouth in realization of the enormity of the unknown adventure I had chosen for the next phase of my life.

* * * * *

I MAY HAVE BEEN A GOOD STUDENT IN HIGH SCHOOL, but University College quickly revealed to me how sheltered, idyllic, and "provincial" my upbringing had been and how much I needed to learn about the ways of the world. I had chosen University College and honours philosophy in particular because I wanted to be prepared to confront intellectually a world I knew to be skeptical of or even downright hostile to my Christian faith. Not surprisingly, on my first day, in my first class, the first person I talked to was a student from St. Hilda's College, the women's half of Trinity College, the Anglican Church-related liberal arts institution on campus. We exchanged names, brief bios, and aspirations. When I mentioned that I planned to become a Presbyterian clergyman, she exclaimed, "Oh, goodie, I'm an atheist!"

That first year at University College was truly tough on me. Learning had always come easily to me, and I had not had to work very hard at it. But the sheer volume of reading expected and the intensity of full professors lecturing to small classes of first-year philosophy students and the tutorial system of weekly give-and-take involved in most of my courses had me in way over my head. Living in Knox College did not really help. No one in the whole residence had ever been a philosophy major; in fact, as I look back I do not remember there being even one other University College student in the whole place!

The happiest part of my life that year involved the Dovercourt Road Presbyterian Church and its minister, the Reverend Dr. Ross K. Cameron, a former moderator of the PCC's General Assembly and a frequent guest preacher at St. Andrew's Church, Windsor, during the long vacancy following the death of Dr. Paulin. Dr. Cameron had struck up a friendship with my father, and on learning that I was attending the University of Toronto and living in Knox College he contacted me and suggested that I become his student assistant for the years of my undergraduate education.

One of my Sunday morning responsibilities was offering a children's sermon to the handful of youngsters in regular attendance at worship. I borrowed a couple of volumes of such material from the Knox College library and got a bright idea that I soon regretted. The message involved some ice cubes floating in a glass of water. I had noticed that there was always a fresh glass of water hidden on a shelf—usually untouched—behind the pulpit. Without saying a word to Dr. Cameron, I slipped a few ice cubes into the glass of water before the service began.

During the singing of the first hymn, Dr. Cameron began to cough and continued to do so through the prayer of invocation. As we sat down at the end of the prayer and I reached out for the glass of water to begin my children's sermon, Dr. Cameron grabbed it first, took a healthy drink of the ice-cold water, and bellowed for all to hear, "Who the hell put *ice* in my drinking water?"

The next summer's romance involved another American girl, Mary Lou Sanford, whose family spent their summers in a little cabin in the middle of Rondeau Provincial Park. Mary Lou and I had a wonderful summer together until we went back to our respective universities, and she immediately took up again with the boyfriend she had broken up with in June.

I was well and truly heartbroken until one of the girls in several of my classes took me in hand and pointed out all the other possibilities on campus. Her name was Debbie Schwartz, a Jewish debutante from Ottawa who became my best female friend for our remaining time at U of T. She encouraged me to date Brenda Harris, a daughter of the Harris half of the Massey-Harris farm implement manufacturing family, whose uncle was then governor general of Canada; and Cynthia Creighton, whose father was then head of the university's history department; and Mary Fleming, whose father was at that time Canada's minister of finance. Interaction with them and their families certainly broadened my horizons socially and politically as well as intellectually and played a significant role in making me the man I became.

During the autumn and early winter of 1959, my mother's voluminous correspondence made frequent mention of a girl of whom she was particularly fond, one Elizabeth Ann Trotter, the only daughter of Kinsmen friends of my parents and fellow worshipers at St. Andrew's Presbyterian Church, both of which facts made my mother sure that I must remember Ann from various church and social encounters in years past.

Apparently, Ann had been injured during a particularly rough water polo game at Kintail, a Presbyterian Church-related summer camp on the shores of Lake Huron on Labour Day weekend. She spent much of the fall in hospital in Windsor, and, for some reason, my mother started sending me weekly updates on Ann's medical progress.

The first time I encountered Ann in this context was at a PYPS (Presbyterian Young People's Society) Christmas week house party. She appeared to be fully recovered from her head injury, so I asked her to dance, and she accepted. My friend, Lex, tells me that I danced only with her for the rest of the evening until he warned me to back off because I was tiring her out. Then he offered to drive her—and me—home from the party.

Ann lived about six blocks in one direction from the house where the party had been held, and I lived about six blocks in the opposite direction. By then, Lex was dating another girl from St. Andrew's, Ann Rutherford, whose home was miles away just off Riverside Drive near the Ambassador Bridge. I thought it odd that Lex drove *her* home first rather than last, but all became clear as he was driving *us* home and casually mentioned the Essex Golf and Country Club post-Christmas dance to which most of our group were invited each year by one of our PYPS friends, Markie McFarlane. "Are you going, Ann?" he asked.

"No," she replied.

"Are you going, Bill?" came next.

"No," I, too, replied.

"Well, then, why don't you go together?" Lex asked ever so innocently. Which we did.

It was, as always, a gala event, and we had a great time together. At the end of the party, the club released the customary flock of huge red balloons from the ceiling. I remember capturing one, protecting it from all those who wanted to puncture it, and getting it out to my car, where I slyly put it in the front passenger seat, planning to escort Ann to the driver's side door, where she would be forced to sit close to me on the ride home. All went as planned until Ann got into the front bench seat from the driver's side and promptly lifted the big red balloon over her lap and deposited it exactly where I had had visions of her sitting all the way home!

During the course of the evening, talk around our table had eventually turned to plans for Lex's annual New Year's Eve party in the basement of his parents' new home on Dougall

Road. Once again, Lex ever so innocently managed the conversation to the point where I had to agree to escort Ann to the party, whether I wanted to or not, which I definitely did not.

Summer 1952
Victoria Avenue, Windsor, Ontario
I had the hat long before I got the boat!

Summer 1955
On Rondeau Bay, Ontario
Sailing my Lark the summer I named it "SH-BOOM"

October 1955
Windsor, Ontario
*With my parents, brother, step-great-grandfather
and great-grandmother Sarah Lucretia White Kenyon Sunderland
on her eightieth birthday*

THE SIXTIES

I HATE NEW YEAR'S EVE AND, therefore, New Year's Eve parties, and I truly did not want to attend the one that ushered in the sixties, even with Ann Trotter as my date. I was stone broke, and my father had had such a bad year in business that there had been no "little something on the side" that Christmas. Plus, I had an enormous amount of heavy reading of philosophy texts to complete before classes resumed in a few days. I agreed, grudgingly I suppose, to pick Ann up at 10:00 p.m. to escort her to Lex's party.

By the time I did so, she was in as foul a mood as I was, so it was not surprising that we did not enjoy ourselves. At midnight, she refused to kiss me—little wonder, I realize, looking back—and we left as soon as we could thereafter. When I took her home, her parents' own festivities were still going full force, and I was not so very gently dragged into the house by her father to be introduced as "Ann's new boyfriend!" It was a painful experience for both of us, and I left as soon as I reasonably could with nothing said between us but, "Good night!"

Nevertheless, I could not get the idea of being Ann's new

boyfriend out of my mind. I wrote to her a couple of times in January and casually mentioned that I would be returning home for a long weekend in mid-February, which just happened to be the weekend of Kennedy Collegiate's annual girl-ask-boy semi-formal. To this day, I do not know why I entertained a hope that she would ask *me*, right up to my arriving in Windsor on the weekend of the dance and learning that she had invited an old boyfriend whose family had moved to Toronto the previous summer. Well, that was that!

That spring, I was surprised to be invited to participate in a leadership development tour of central and western Canada, sponsored by the National Federation of Canadian University Students (NFCUS). Shortly after the end of the academic year, half a dozen University of Toronto third-year students joined two dozen or so students chosen from all the universities in eastern and central Canada for a train ride across the country and back. We were billeted in single "roomettes" in two sleeper coaches, wherein we traveled from city to city overnight and from which, by day, we visited Thunder Bay, Winnipeg, Saskatoon, Calgary, Lake Louise, Vancouver, and Victoria. At each stop, we toured another example of Canadian industry and met with local politicians, executives, and entrepreneurs, each offering us a personal slant on the state of social, economic, political, and cultural leadership in "our home and native land."

As the only potential cleric in the group, my introductions were heavily among cultural leaders in the arts, along with occasional bishops and distinguished clergy. We attended a symphony concert in Calgary, enjoyed a touring company performance of *The Music Man* in Vancouver, and behaved ourselves during high tea at the historic Empress Hotel in Victoria. I remembered to buy Ann a souvenir to assure her that I had been thinking of her while I was sharing a sleeping car with a dozen Canadian coeds; in the Birks store in Vancouver, I found a charmingly modest sterling silver charm bracelet and had its first charm, a miniature replica of a native totem pole, soldered onto it. On returning to Windsor, I was not best pleased to learn that while I had been gone, my best friend's younger brother, Archie McCrindle, had been trying to woo and win Ann during my absence!

For the summer of 1960, instead of returning to Rondeau to work for the Department of Lands and Forests as I had the two past two summers, I accepted an offer to intern with the Board of Home Missions of the Presbyterian Church in Canada, conducting a survey/study of the potential impact of Toronto's new crosstown subway system on the West Toronto Presbytery's congregations, whose houses of worship lay along the TTC's announced route. It was quite a summer! I roomed in a small house in the Swansea area and visited the half a dozen churches to be studied. I made frequent trips to the Metro Toronto and TTC planning departments and an unforgettable trip by train to Montreal to interview the staff of Tyndale House, a community service model I thought might be appropriate for at least two of the congregations back in Toronto. I say "unforgettable" for two reasons: one, I stayed at the downtown Montreal YMCA and came face-to-face with the gay lifestyle that I had not hitherto known existed; and two, I ate borscht for the first time at a smart little bistro across the street from the Y and suffered twenty-four agonizing hours of nausea for it!

At the end of the summer, my final report was not received favorably by the powers that be in the presbytery or the Board of Home Missions. In essence, I reported my research, indicating that the dwellers of the high-rise condominiums and apartments expected to be built at the various entrances and exits of the subway system would not be attracted to the timeworn premises of the Presbyterian churches *in situ* but would more likely ride the convenient subway trains to attend worship at larger and more upscale places of worship, like Timothy Eaton United Church or Yorkminster Park Baptist Church or even the downtown St. Andrew's Presbyterian Church. I urged the congregations of the aging and dreary Dovercourt Road and Dufferin Street churches to amalgamate and sponsor a community-focused social service ministry akin to the Tyndale House mission model that I had studied in Montreal.

Ironically, decades later, when I became a member of the West Toronto Presbytery as a result of being appointed general secretary of the Canadian Bible Society, my report surfaced again and was widely hailed as having been visionary at the time and was lamented for not having been acted upon before the very things I had foreseen had come to pass!

On most weekends that summer, I took the train home, or at least to Chatham, to be picked up by one parent or the other to spend the weekend at the lake house. On several of those weekends, I ended up with pulpit supply responsibilities at one or another of the small Presbyterian congregations in the area.

One such was the two-point charge of Duart and Turin. My father had just bought a brand-new metallic blue and white Chrysler hardtop coupe, which he offered to me to drive to my Sunday morning appointments. The earlier service was in Duart, the later a few miles away in Turin. When I arrived for the second service, the congregation had already begun worship. I parked Dad's car at the far end of the parking strip, hurried inside, and joined the service. When it was over, the elders gathered around the communion table to count the offering, only to discover that there was not enough money in the plates to pay their portion of the required preacher's stipend. I distinctly remember their fishing in their pockets for enough small bills to make up the difference and unceremoniously handing the full amount to me. Then we walked outside. One of the elders glanced down the road to where I had parked. "Is that your car?" he asked. "Yes," I replied without thinking. "Well," he muttered, "it looks as though you ought to be paying *us*!"

The most memorable experience of that summer, though, was the arrival in Toronto one Friday afternoon of Lex McCrindle and a carload of PYPS friends on their way to the new home of Bev Kipp, whose family had moved to Aurora, then a small suburban town north of Toronto. On their way, they stopped by the national offices of the Presbyterian Church in Canada to say hello, and I was surprised to see Ann Trotter in their midst. She was not Aurora-bound, however, but on her way to spend the weekend with the family of the boy who had been her February dance date. Almost immediately, I suspected Lex's fine hand in this visit somehow.

On Saturday afternoon, I headed up to Aurora and joined the group for a barn dance somewhere, which I left fairly early to return to Toronto. To my surprise, on Sunday morning I got a phone call from Ann—could I possibly come to see her at the home of her mother's best friend, where she was staying for the weekend? When I got there, she was in a state! Apparently, during the preceding evening her old boyfriend had become exceedingly and forcefully amorous, and she broke off their relationship for good. I am to this day not quite sure what she expected from me, but what she got was some TLC and a lot of reassurance that the breakup was neither her fault nor her undoing. But from then on, I well and truly became her new boyfriend.

Fourth-year honours philosophy at University College was a grueling year of which I have very few memories. I think that Ann traveled by train to Toronto for the Knox College spring dance, but I am not sure. By then, she was in Grade XIII at Kennedy Collegiate and in a pretty grueling academic program of her own with those dreaded departmentals looming in June.

One of my most cherished college memories was of the inauguration in 1961 of the University of Toronto Student Administative Council's Honour Society, a sort of gold medal awards program of which I was one of the initial recipients. Debbie Schwartz and Brenda Harris were the other two awardees from University College, and we were thrilled to be among the twenty-four recipients of this unique universitywide distinction.

My parents generously invited Ann to travel with them to Toronto for my graduation, and she came even though her Grade XIII departmentals were only a few weeks away. My folks took a two-bedroom suite at the Park Plaza Hotel on Bloor Street just across from the university main campus, where, one evening, they entertained virtually everyone who had been hospitable to me during my four years in Toronto. I was amazed—and so were they—to realize how many friends I had made.

At the graduation ceremony, Ann and my parents sat with their longtime friends, the Honorable Paul Martin and his wife, Nell. The Martins had been customers on my Sunday paper route in South Windsor years before, and their son Paul Jr. was graduating from St. Michael's College at the same event. If I remember correctly, Mr. Martin was then Canada's secretary of state for external affairs. Later in his career, he became a senator, then leader of the government in the senate, and eventually Canada's high commissioner to the court of St. James in the United Kingdom. In retirement, he, a childhood victim of polio like my father, became one of Dad's regular golfing partners along with Senator Keith Laird—a distinguished threesome indicative of the level of respect to which my father had risen from his humble beginnings as a lame housepainter!

* * * * *

THE SUMMER OF 1961 SAW MY return to working for the Department of Lands and Forests at Rondeau, running the park office at the Point campgrounds I had helped design and lay out in previous summers. It was, as I look back, an idyllic season of rest and relaxation, the last such that I would enjoy for another forty-some years. Ann and I continued to see each other fairly often. Brenda Harris drove her father's huge white Lincoln Continental convertible down from Toronto for a few days, which threw my mother into an uncharacteristic tizzy of hospitality *cum* chaperonage, and I felt my way into my chosen profession with a number of supply preaching assignments.

I really wanted to pursue a master's degree in philosophy before entering into the study of theology, and I had high hopes of securing a Rockefeller Foundation grant to finance a year at another university. I considered Cornell—why I do not remember—and made a trip with Ann to Ann Arbor, Michigan, to scout out the University of Michigan. Then came word that the Rockefeller Grant, intended to encourage students to *consider* studying for Christian ministry, would not be mine because I was already *committed* to a career in ministry and under the care of the Presbytery of Chatham of the Presbyterian Church in Canada. It was a bitter disappointment, made even harder to take by the realization that my father was in no position financially to fund a postgraduate year *and* that I would have to return to Knox College where I had given up my beloved dorm room under the eaves of West House.

I was miserable as a student at Knox College. Looking back,

I recognize and admit that I was an academic snob: I held an honours degree in philosophy from the University of Toronto, and no one else in my class even had a four-year degree from any other university. When the first-term grades were posted, I had straight A's when there were only three other individual A's in the whole class. I was restless, bored, and in trivial trouble with the faculty most of the time. The one saving grace of the fall semester was that I had been elected to represent Knox College on the University's Students Administrative Council, where I was assigned to organize and run the annual university homecoming parade.

That was fun! A local alumnus auto dealer provided me with a little old MG sportscar as parade marshal, and my across-the-hall neighbor in West House, Randy Vandermark, served as my driver. The parade was to be the kickoff for the inauguration of the university's Varsity Fund, whose cochairs, one a senator and the other a bank president, were to be the parade judges along with the university's president, Claude Bissell. The parade floats were, for the most part, just awful, but the three judges and I had a hilarious time on the reviewing stand, and Dr. Bissell and I became good friends for the rest of the academic year.

Recognizing early on that returning to Knox had been a big mistake, I concocted a plan to apply for admission to New College in Edinburgh and was almost immediately accepted as a midyear transfer to begin classes in January 1962. Again, I gave up my room in West House, packed up all my worldly goods, and went home to Windsor for Christmas, intending to fly to Scotland just after New Year's. My mother was so excited by this prospect that, as I remember, all of my Christmas gifts were chosen with an eye to my using them in Edinburgh. Ann, as I remember, was not nearly as enthusiastic.

I shall never forget Boxing Day, 1961, when my father sat me down and told me that there was no money for this adventure, not even enough to purchase the airfare to get me to Scotland and that I would have to "tuck my tail between my legs"—his words, not mine) and return yet again to Knox College. I am not sure who was more heartbroken—my mother or me—but I do remember that Ann was not at all disappointed.

Returning to Toronto, I was even unhappier than before, and I acted it! I contrived to spike the punch for the annual Knox College dance, and I joined with several other rebellious types to drape a huge black brassiere over the ample bust of the white marble statue in the college's main rotunda depicting a Scottish Covenanter, "Margaret," being drowned at the stake, complete with a placard that read, "I dreamt I was martyred in my Maidenform bra!"

Knox's principal, Dr. J. Stanley "Snuffy" Glen, was furious. Summoned to his office, I was shown a shelf full of seminary academic catalogues worldwide and invited: "Pick one," he challenged me, "any one, and I will get you admitted to study there next year!" Glancing through the options, I glibly chose Princeton Theological Seminary, and the rest, as they say, is history!

Ann had come to Toronto for the annual Knox residence dance and was staying again at the home of her mother's college friend. Our relationship had blossomed into love even though we both knew that marriage would have to be another three years away. Nevertheless, on that Saturday we somehow found ourselves shopping on Toronto's Yonge Street in Birks Jewelers no less and trying on diamond rings. Fortunately, Ann's taste in jewelry ran to simple and tasteful because the next day I asked her to marry me.

Sometime before, I had foolishly promised that if ever I were to propose, I would get down on one knee to do it. So, that Sunday morning I took her to worship at the Rosedale Presbyterian Church, a traditionally high church congregation where many people prayed on kneelers attached to the pews. In the middle of the long pastoral prayer, I whispered my proposal on bended knee, Ann accepted, and the old biddy at the other end of the pew shushed us up!

For the summer of 1962, I had planned to accept a Board of Home Missions three-month appointment to one of those Presbyterian Church in Canada's small, struggling, and mostly rural congregations that had been promised back in 1925 that if they stayed with the denomination rather than joining into the United Church of Canada, they would be provided with ministerial support. My one stipulation was that I be assigned to a charge within reasonable access of a university library. As a measure of the regard in which I was then held by the denomination, I was assigned to conduct Vacation Bible Schools up and down the Alaska Highway in British Columbia!

My dismay was almost immediately alleviated by the Knox College librarian, the retired minister of Ann's grandmother's congregation in Woodstock, Ontario. In a casual conversation whilst I was volunteering in the library one day, he mentioned that he knew of a newly vacant congregation that was looking for summer student supply. Would I be interested? Of course!

The charge turned out to be in Southampton and Elsinore, a small town-and-crossroads pair of churches on Lake Huron at the southern edge of the Bruce Peninsula, less than five miles from Port Elgin, where Ann's extended family always rented a pair of cottages for their three-week summer vacation. It was a wonderful opportunity for me, and I jumped at the chance!

On the first Sunday in August, I joyously informed the congregation of St. Andrew's Church, Southampton, that I had not only been accepted into the middler year at Princeton Theological Seminary but had also been awarded a full academic scholarship. Ann's aunt, Norma Williamson, was in the congregation, having arrived at their rental cottage in Port Elgin the day before. She was so excited for me: "Now you and Ann can afford to get married!" she cried.

When Ann finally got to Port Elgin that Sunday afternoon, we went for a long drive in my little old red Volkswagen Beetle and had a long talk about love and marriage and her studies at the University of Western Ontario and my opportunity to study at Princeton. Love, marriage and Princeton won out, but when we broke the news to her parents that evening that we wanted to be married in early September before heading off to New Jersey, Ann's parents were anything but happy. "Do you *want* to, or do you *have* to?" asked Ann's father. I was so nonplussed that I hardly comprehended what he meant! "I can't put a wedding together in a *month*!" complained Ann's mother, and Ann started to cry.

Eventually, Ann's Granna Currah spoke up. "Bill is a fine young man, and he will make a very fine minister. You should be proud to welcome him into this family. I am!" So then we got down to the business of actually planning a wedding at St. Andrew's Church, Windsor, for the weekend of American Thanksgiving in November. And a month later, I left, alone, to drive my beetle to Princeton, packed with all my worldly goods and such a goodly number of Ann's that we had to take the back seat out of the VW and leave it in the Trotters' garage.

Princeton Theological Seminary is situated almost next door to the main campus of Princeton University in a beautiful college town only a few minutes away from the New Jersey state capitol, Trenton. The seminary's main quadrangle is bordered by Alexander Hall (the oldest building on campus), Miller

Chapel, the President's Office, and Hodge Hall, an open V-shaped residence built in the nineteenth century to house male students only. But by the time I arrived in the fall of 1962, many of the two- and three-room suites had been given over to married students of which I was about to become one.

Number 207 Hodge Hall boasted two tiny rooms, one non-functioning fireplace, a sturdy oak desk and matching dresser, an obscenely sagging double bed, and a magnificent view out over the back campus toward Springbank, the official residence of the seminary president. I had brought from Rondeau a pair of coral pink vinyl-and-aluminum folding lawn chaises, and they comprised the creature comforts of my new dorm home. The married women residents shared bathroom facilities on the second and fourth floors; the men, single as well as married, used facilities on the third floor and in the basement. There was one telephone for the whole dorm, situated on the wall outside #209 next door. To say that life in Hodge Hall was spartan at best would be putting the most generous possible description on it!

All dorm students were required to take their meals in the student center next door, which was fine, since there were no cooking or dishwashing facilities in Hodge Hall, save for one aged and overcrowded refrigerator in the basement. The catering service provided ample food, but much of it was so starchy and sweet that I had already developed dental problems by the time I flew home in November to get married.

Prior to that, though, I went shopping at Bamberger's department store in the local mall and ordered a Simmons BeautyRest sleep sofa to be delivered while I was away so that Ann and I would have something decent to sleep on when we returned from our honeymoon in New York City.

I have very few memories of those first two months at PTS.

I started classes, made a few friends, and began my fieldwork appointment at Bethel Presbyterian Church in East Orange, New Jersey. The pastor was Dutch Reformed in background and personality: rigidly self-righteous and obsessively domineering, he was everything I determined not to be in ministry. One of my first weekends at Bethel was World Communion Sunday, and I was astonished to hear Pastor Burggraff refer to the contents of the Communion chalice as "grape juice!"

My main responsibility was, of course, youth work, which there was precious little of—not one iota of which did the pastor want any part. I was paid $25.00 a weekend, which included a Sunday morning Bible class and a Sunday evening youth group meeting.

Because the church was almost an hour away up the Garden State Parkway, and there were occasional Saturday afternoon or evening activities I was expected to attend or even organize, I very often spent Saturday night in East Orange, usually sleeping on a sofa in the church parlor while the Burggraffs enjoyed a huge old manse next door. There was a seventy-five-cent toll to use the Garden State Parkway, and I was so strapped for cash that I had to be careful to keep $1.50 in my pocket each week in order to get to my fieldwork and back and earn that wretched $25.00! How I thought Ann and I were going to manage on so little money I cannot imagine; I guess I really believed the old adage that two can live as cheaply as one.

The biggest excitement at PTS that fall was the scheduled visit in the week of Thanksgiving by none other than Karl Barth, the world-renowned German theologian and author of the monumental thirteen-volume *Church Dogmatics magnum opus* that was at that time re-shaping postwar Christian thinking. My professors—and even some of my fellow students—were appalled that I was planning to miss the Barth lecture series to go home to Canada to get married.

But I went anyway, much to Ann's relief, for she eventually confessed that she had entertained some doubts that I would turn up for the wedding after such a brief engagement and even briefer planning period. Nevertheless, the wedding went off without a hitch—more or less. St. Andrew's minister, Bill Lawson, had known both of us for almost a decade, but his typically Presbyterian wedding ceremony was conducted with a total lack of any personal reference or acknowledgment. I was "William" throughout, Ann was "Elizabeth" always, and there was not a word said to either of us that was not printed in the Book of Common Worship. On our wedding night, as we snuggled into bed, Ann said to me: "Promise me that when you are a minister, you will never do *that* to any couple you marry!" And I never did.

Our wedding reception was held at the Norton Palmer Hotel diagonally across Victoria Avenue in downtown Windsor. In those days, most people brought their wedding gifts to the reception rather than sending them ahead of time. I must have arranged for the hotel staff to carry all of the gifts, plus the two huge floral arrangements of white-and-yellow pompom and Fiji mums, to the Bridal Suite, where we postponed as long as possible the inevitable loss of our mutual virginity by opening and admiring our wedding gifts and ordering a midnight snack from room service.

Our wedding night locale was a well-kept secret. After the reception, in a shower of confetti we left the hotel and drove around Windsor for an hour until all our guests would be gone and then returned to the Norton Palmer in my mother's tissue paper flower-bedecked car with a huge cardboard "Just Married" sign on the back bumper.

The Bridal Suite was truly awful. Its two small dingy rooms

filled with faux-finished brown metal-framed furniture were stuffy and faintly smoky, and any ventilation was provided by large open transom windows above the doors. When we finally went to bed, we could clearly hear people passing by in the hallway. "Please, Bill," Ann whispered, "can we *not* 'do it' tonight? Anyone out in the hall could hear us!" So we *didn't* "do it" after all!

The hotel manager had kindly arranged to hide our vehicle overnight in his private garage. The next morning, we retrieved our car and our "going away" luggage and drove out to Detroit's Metropolitan Airport to fly to New York City for our few days' honeymoon. By prior arrangement, our parents all showed up at the airport to see us off. In those days, the terminal concourses were open to everyone, so our folks escorted us right to the departure gate. Ann's mother had armed herself with a bag of confetti, with which she liberally doused us as we neared the gate. Feeling incredibly shy and exposed, we boarded the plane and walked the full length of the aisle to our seats in the back, all the while streaming confetti from hats, coats, and carry-on luggage.

Without learning of it until much later, we were avenged. Ann's mother had come to the airport wearing her fur jacket and wedding corsage. When our four parents went to retrieve my mother's car from the terminal parking lot, bedecked as it was, everyone driving by assumed that "GB" was the bride and honked and hooted and shouted congratulations to this middle-aged lady who had finally snagged her man!

Meanwhile, soon after take-off, the stewardesses on board our aircraft came processing down the aisle carrying a candlelit cake and singing "Congratulations to you! . . ." We shyly asked that the cake be set aside and served after dinner to the people sitting around us. Unfortunately, the flight was so turbulent that they never served dinner, let alone our cake, so that when we deplaned, one of the stewardesses handed us the cake, securely boxed, to add to our carry-on luggage and the other eight bags we had checked through to LaGuardia.

It took us what seemed like *forever* to flag a taxi, load ourselves and our worldly goods in it, and make the drive into midtown Manhattan and the Waldorf-Astoria Hotel, where we were to spend our four-night honeymoon. Ann was so overcome by the grandeur of the hotel's main lobby and so shy about actually registering as "Mr. and Mrs. Russell" that she insisted on sitting behind a palm tree while I got in line to sign in. As the very large African-American man ahead of me finished his registration, he turned, looked me up and down, and boomed for all to hear: "Aren't you the *newlywed* from Dee-troit?"

We honeymooned at the Waldorf because I had discovered that it offered a special discounted room rate to college students, which made it one of the most economical places to stay in Manhattan. The grandeur of the lobby was offset somewhat by the size of our room: not much bigger than a broom closet, with just enough room for a double bed and dresser. *Great*, I thought, *Ann will be getting used to what she will live like in Hodge Hall!*

Apart from a few touristy things, we did very little during our four-day honeymoon. Two memories stand out. First, we took the subway north one evening to 125th Street and walked over to Riverside Drive to visit a U of T classmate, Edgar Coxeter, and his bride "Perf" at International House, where they were living while he studied at Union Theological Seminary. On the way back downtown, Ann realized that she had lost one of her beautiful trousseau cream-colored kid gloves, possibly in the subway station. So we retraced our steps back up into Harlem, and sure enough we found the glove on the iron mesh catwalk connecting both sides of the subway station. Blissfully, we rode the subway back downtown, naïvely oblivious to the fact that we had just been prowling around in one of New York City's most racially charged and dangerous neighborhoods!

The other honeymoon memory I cherish involved the Delegates Dining Room at the United Nations where, we learned during a tour of the UN building on Manhattan's East Side, the public could eat lunch on weekdays after 2:00 p.m. We thought that that would be memorable, and it was. Feeling very sophisticated and worldly, we ordered pre-luncheon cocktails: a dry martini for me and a Manhattan for Ann because, of course, we were honeymooning in *Manhattan*! She took one sip of the sweet maraschino cherry, rye, and whiskey combination and immediately demanded that we switch drinks, which we did. I remember nothing else about the lunch or how we got back to the Waldorf or how long we slept away the rest of the afternoon and evening, but I do remember drinking the worst cocktail ever that day!

Our idyll at the Waldorf was to end on Thanksgiving Day. I took the train out to East Orange to retrieve my little red VW Beetle, parked behind the church where I did weekend fieldwork, drove back into Manhattan to pick up Ann and our eleven pieces of luggage and then started out for Princeton. My stash of cash was running very low—a serious problem in those ancient days before credit cards and ATMs—so I opted to follow Route 1 through northern New Jersey rather than pay the tolls for the New Jersey Turnpike or the Garden State Parkway. The trip through Jersey City and over the Pulaski Skyway was daunting, to say the least: gray skies, grim slums, gritty oil dumps, God knows what odors, were all we could see—or smell. By the time we neared Newark's International Airport, Ann was threatening to make me drop her off curbside and let her go home to her mother!

I prevailed, and eventually we made it to Princeton. Having bought gas and a snack of sorts on the road, I was left with exactly $10.00 in my pocket: just enough to buy a full-course Thanksgiving dinner for two at the beautiful old Nassau Inn in the heart of town across the street from Princeton University. When I went to pay the bill, I was humiliated to realize that I had no money for a tip, for which I apologized fulsomely to our waitress, who, in the spirit of the day, was graciousness itself.

At last, it was time to introduce Ann to her new home at 207 Hodge Hall. How I dreaded her first sight of our two meager little rooms with no "mod coms" and that dreadful double bed with its sagging sleeping indentation. However—bless my soul!—the Simmons BeautyRest sleep sofa I had ordered from Bamberger's had been delivered in my absence, and a couple of my Hodge Hall friends had gotten rid of the old double bed and rearranged the "front" room to hold the sofa, plus a table and two beat-up but sturdy chairs. "This isn't nearly as bad as you said it would be!" was Ann's first reaction, and indeed it wasn't!

Because we would be living in student dormitory housing, many of our wedding presents were cash gifts, and we had a delightful time buying an area rug for our "front" room, some café curtains, an electric frying pan, and a set of dishes so that we could make, serve, and eat our own meals on the weekends. Eventually, we realized that, as Ann put it, we were "frittering away" our wedding gift cash and would have nothing substantial to show for it. So we went out and bought a big console Magnavox stereo radio-record player and a few LP records. One of my happiest memories of that first year in Hodge Hall is of opening the windows overlooking the playing fields behind the residence and blaring out an album of Georg Philipp Telemann's baroque *Heldenmusik* for all the world to hear and know that we had the biggest and best stereo system on campus!

We quickly learned that two *cannot* live as cheaply as one, and money was tight from the very beginning. Ann had promised her parents that she would resume her college education once we were settled in Princeton and so she registered for the spring semester at Douglass College, at that time the women's college of Rutgers University in New Brunswick, New Jersey, less than an hour's drive north from Princeton. The added costs of her tuition, books, travel expenses, and other sundries were more than I had counted on, and at the end of many weeks we were reduced to pocket change until we could drive up to East Orange and collect and cash my $25.00 fieldwork check!

Before our wedding, Ann had begun taking birth control pills. They never agreed with her, often causing cramps and nausea until the inevitable happened, and she vomited several doses in succession and eventually discovered that she was pregnant. She was thrilled, and I was horrified! She dropped out of Douglass College and began sewing maternity dresses. Sadly, at the end of her third month of pregnancy, she miscarried, lost the baby, and ended up in the hospital for a few days. In the bad old days before any form of health insurance, a hospital stay was a financial disaster, and we ended up a little over $1,200.00 in debt.

I was truly desperate. My father had generously agreed to continue my $100.00-a-month allowance after we got married, so I did not feel that I could ask him for anything more. And I would certainly *not* ask Ann's still-unapproving parents for anything at all. However, the seminary offered a number of small cash prizes and scholarships each year and so I set out to win as many of them as I could. I memorized all 107 questions and answers of the *Westminster Shorter Catechism* (1646–1647 AD); I won the middler preaching prize for that year; and I consulted my faculty mentor, Professor Donald Macleod, about any and all other financial opportunities for which I might be qualified and able to win.

Then, one day just before the end of term, I was summoned to President McCord's office to meet with his administrative assistant, Roy Pfautch, who later in life became a very well-known Washington political consultant. Roy began by asking me some very pointed questions about my desperate financial situation and how deeply in debt I actually was. He confided that Professor Macleod had spoken about my plight to President McCord, who had delegated Roy to "deal with it!" Apparently, I was regarded as one of the "brightest and best" students on campus and therefore should not be burdened by financial worries when I should be studying instead. A check for $1,500.00 was almost immediately forthcoming, so I quickly paid off the $1,200.00 hospital bill and gave up trying to win every middler prize in sight.

For the summer of 1963, I was assigned to a student internship at the Hamilton Presbyterian Church on Harford Road in Baltimore, Maryland. It was, in many respects, a very fine posting, but Ann and I were sort of like fish out of water in its rigidly conservative milieu. We lived in a tiny third floor walk-up apartment tucked under the eaves of a big old house, owned by one of the parishioners. Like Pastor Siddons and his wife, the congregation was defined more by its negatives than its positives: no smoking, no drinking, no dancing, no makeup for the women, no fun for the men! That summer, the United Presbyterian Church in the United States of America (UPCUSA) was roiled by the arrest at a Baltimore amusement park on July 4 of the stated clerk of the General Assembly, Eugene Carson Blake, in a civil rights demonstration that got out of hand. In retrospect, this event, more than any other, marked the beginning of the shift away from middle-of-the-road theological and social positions in the denomination and the increasingly strident activist positions that still perturb the Presbyterian Church (USA) to this very day. Bloodied but unbowed, Dr. Blake later went on to become the president of the National Council of Churches and then the general secretary of the World Council of Churches. The Hamilton church and its pastor eventually left the denomination to help found the Presbyterian Church in America (PCA) in 1973.

Before leaving Princeton for Baltimore, Ann and I had been elected as the dorm presidents of Hodge Hall for the next academic year. With the help of the seminary custodian, Tom Bryan, we were able to secure the use of #209, the three-room apartment at the center of crescent-shaped Hodge Hall, for the summer as well as the next year. We made several trips back and forth between Princeton and Baltimore that summer, painting the apartment, installing floor-to-ceiling wall-to-wall unbleached muslin drapes for the three large windows in the center room of the unit, and acquiring odds and ends of other furniture to make the place habitable. Our trip on the fateful weekend of Dr. Blake's arrest was fateful for us too. My little old red VW Beetle literally gave up the ghost in the inside-most lane of the toll plaza at the Delaware end of the New Jersey Turnpike. We had to push the car across every lane full of July 4th travelers and wait for hours until the little old engine cooled down enough that it would start again and then drive all the way back to Baltimore in second gear!

The next week, we went shopping for a new car, armed with that $300.00 left over from the seminary's generosity the month before. Fortunately, the VW registration was in the name of

William Russell (my father); but I was "William Russell," too, and able to persuade a Baltimore car dealer to take the vehicle in trade on a brand-new little Dodge Dart convertible, all white with a red leather interior! By then, we had determined that we were going to apply for permanent resident alien status in the USA at the end of the summer, primarily so that Ann could get a job—which, legally, she could not do on a wife-of-a-foreign-student visa—and thereby be able to make the payments on the car once we returned to Princeton in the fall.

For reasons that I did not fully comprehend at the time—but which became much more comprehensible to me later in life when I had children of my own, financially dependent on me!—my father was furious that I had traded away his VW without any consultation or by-your-leave. He threatened to stop sending me my monthly allowance and made good on that threat through the summer but relented when . . . no, that is a story for later!

Three memories stand out from that summer. The first involved the death of President and Mrs. Kennedy's newborn baby and Ann's brief prayer for the bereaved family at the Hamilton Church's midweek prayer meeting. "Doncha know they're *Catholics*?" some of the women hissed at Ann. "We don't pray for *Catholics*!"

The second standout memory happened at the end of the very next week's prayer meeting. As the attendees were making their way from the church past the manse where the Siddons and their two teenaged sons lived, a commotion broke out on the second-floor balcony over the manse sunroom. Two figures were seen struggling violently on the balcony until one succeeded in toppling the other over the railing and down onto the shrubbery below, from which were then heard heartrending cries of pain and anguish. Terrified, I ran to the shrubbery to determine the extent of the poor victim's injuries, only to find a lifesized and very realistic *dummy* and the younger Siddons boy making all that pathetic noise! Needless to say, I was furious, but I got my revenge.

Ann and I gathered up the dummy, put him in the back seat of our convertible, and drove off without another word. Then, late on Sunday evening, after everyone had left the church building for the night, we carried the dummy into the church office and placed him in the doorway between the church secretary's desk and the minister's study. When the exceedingly prim and proper church secretary arrived for work the next morning and saw what looked for all the world like a dead man on the floor next to her desk, she fled the office and called the police. Within minutes, a patrol car pulled up outside the church, and the officers rushed in to investigate and, of course, find the dummy! The whole incident had every indication of being a nasty prank by young Master Siddons, who got all the blame and a tongue-lashing from the church secretary and finally a long and severe grounding from his father!

The third memorable event was not funny at all and troubles me to this day. Over the Labor Day holiday weekend, it was my responsibility to take the congregation's teenagers and a few adult chaperones to a church camp on the outskirts of Baltimore. The camp had effectively closed down for the season, but the camp cook had stayed on to feed us with the help of a young African-American boy to serve and bus our tables. On the Sunday afternoon after our morning's diet of worship and Bible study, we all went to the camp swimming pool for an afternoon of fun. Soon after all our young people were in the pool, having a grand time, our African-American server sauntered down to the pool to join in the fun. As he dove into the water, everyone in the pool clambered out and stood around the pool staring at the boy. Realizing that he had made a gross error in judgment, the boy climbed out of the pool, toweled off, and went back into the cookhouse, whereupon my teens and adults jumped back into the water to resume their fun.

I was stunned. As a Canadian growing up in a racially integrated community and school system, I had never seen, let alone experienced, the kind of cruel and mindless racial prejudice that I had just witnessed. After a few minutes to compose myself and clarify my thoughts, I ordered my entire group out of the water and into the dining hall, where I excoriated them one and all for the way they had treated a young man who was there on his holiday weekend to work at making our stay as pleasant as possible. I do not remember all that I said; but at one point I told them all that there would be no more swimming in the pool for the duration of the camp. "If that boy so contaminated the water by getting into the pool that you all felt the need to get out, then it was—and still is—just as contaminated once he got out, and I will not allow you to endanger your own health and well-being by swimming in that water again!"

Clearly, neither the teens nor the adults comprehended what I was upset about. Their hearts and minds and lives were so riddled with racial prejudice that they could see nothing untoward in what had happened except that I was making a big deal out of something that was no big deal at all. The adult chaperones did their best to calm me down and explain to me a few of the facts of life in Baltimore and in the Hamilton Presbyterian Church, and I eventually relented and allowed everyone to go swimming for an hour on Monday before we left. That weekend marked the end of my summer internship and so Ann and I packed up and set out for Canada and the process of applying for permanent resident alien status in the USA without ever seeing or speaking to anyone in the congregation again. No one ever wrote to us or telephoned us after that weekend; it was as though it—and we—had never happened.

* * * * *

THE FIRST WEEKS OF SEPTEMBER 1963 were hectic for us as we gathered the documentation and medical test results required to support our application for resident alien status in the USA. Mid-month, Ann and I were driving past Grampa and Grandma Russell's house on Janette Street in Windsor, when Grampa happened to be out on the front stoop. We waved, then stopped, and he came to the curb to chat with us. Eventually, the conversation got around to our applying for US residency, which fact was proving *not* to be popular with most of our Windsor relatives and friends—in fact, Ann and I were quite distressed by the hostility we sensed whenever anyone spoke to us about emigrating! To my amazement, Grampa Russell told us how strongly he approved of our decision and the future it would open for us and asked pointedly how much it was costing us financially to put the application documents together. I knew the amount almost to the dollar—$1,000.00—at which Grampa pulled his chequebook (sic) out of his pocket and wrote out a cheque for that amount!

When my father learned of Grampa's strong support and unwonted generosity, he quickly began to change his tune not only about our emigrating but also about his resuming my $100.00-a-month allowance. From then on, I felt particularly close to the grandfather figure almost everyone else in the Russell family feared and resented, so much so that decades later, when I was about to become a grandfather, I made it known to my family that I, too, wanted to be known as "Grampa Russell!"

Another clutch of memories from that month of waiting for our US visas to be approved and issued cluster around the invitation I had received some months earlier to return to St. Andrew's Church, Southampton to help celebrate the centennial of the congregation. The weekend in question was also the occasion for Jay-Anne, my eldest Kenyon cousin, to be married in St. Thomas, less than an hour's drive from the Little Pink Palace at Rondeau Provincial Park. Ann had already arranged for us to spend the weekend with Granna Currah in Woodstock when it was decided that we could very easily drive from Woodstock to St. Thomas and back on Saturday and then to Southampton and back the next day.

So we went to Jay-Anne's wedding, Ann wearing a beautiful gold silk shantung dress-and-jacket outfit (very Jackie Kennedy-ish!) that we had bought at the historic Woodward and Lothrop department store during one of our summer outings to Washington, DC. She was also wearing a brand-new hat—a high-crowned fez of little beige-and-gold feathers Granna had bought after insisting on taking Ann to London that very morning to shop at her own milliner. Our little Dodge Dart convertible, as much fun as it was, was proving to be very wearying on long highway trips, and Dad had just bought Mom a brand-new bright yellow Buick convertible, which she *hated*, and which somehow he insisted we drive to Woodstock and then to Southampton and back, while he and my mother drove our car back to Rondeau where we would pick it up again on Monday.

When we awoke in Woodstock on Sunday morning, the weather had turned unexpectedly cold overnight, and of course we had only our lightweight Sunday-go-to-church clothes with us. Granna had nothing warm in her closet that fit Ann except her gorgeous pastel mink stole, which looked even more gorgeous (if possible) over the gold silk shantung outfit! So off we went to Southampton, arriving early enough (thank goodness) to discover that I was *also* expected to preach the regular Sunday morning service in the little Elsinore congregation that was part of the two-point charge. We hurried on up the road and dashed into the sanctuary as the service was beginning without us, I in my black Brooks Brothers suit and Ann resplendent in her gold dress, feathered fez and mink stole.

At the end of the service as he exited the sanctuary and saw the yellow Buick convertible sitting in the parking space reserved for the minister, the curmudgeonly Elsinore Clerk of Session said aloud what everyone else was thinking in stunned silence: "You've sure come a long way in a year!"

With permanent residents' visas in hand, we returned to the Seminary for the fall term. Ann immediately began to look for work and very quickly found a position as administrative assistant to the Princeton University Archivist, Dr. M. Halsey Thomas, working in the basement of the university library, just a short walk from Hodge Hall, where we were living. It was a very happy and rewarding time for her, especially after the assassination of President John F. Kennedy who, unbeknownst to many, had actually begun his university career at Princeton! Interest in any memorabilia connected to Kennedy skyrocketed, and Ann got to handle virtually every request.

My fieldwork assignment for the 1963–1964 academic year was at the First Presbyterian Church in Red Bank, affectionately known as "the Church atop Tower Hill," where I was responsible for portions of the youth program, particularly the large group of eighth graders in that year's confirmation class. We loved the Red Bank congregation, and they seemed to love us in return. The senior pastor was Dr. Charles "Charlie" Webster, a golden-tongued orator with an almost authentic Scottish accent and a pulpit presence that attracted larger and larger attendances at Sunday morning worship.

I learned a lot from Dr. Webster, who, to my amazement, also drove a white convertible and unforgettably advised me: "Bill, always buy a *used*—never a *new*—car from a local dealer. Tell him who you are and where you preach and that if he sells you a 'lemon,' you will use him as a sermon illustration on Easter Sunday!" Charlie was famous for his "tear-jerker" illustrations; every sermon had one at about three minutes before the inevitably funny end of the message because, he explained, "If they leave with a tear in their eye and a smile on their face, they'll love you for your preaching!"

A few years after my graduation, Dr. Webster unaccountably accepted a call to the Moorings Presbyterian Church in Naples, Florida. It was a small, struggling congregation then, but Charlie saw the potential for growth in the Naples area and rode the wave of it to tremendous and long-lasting success. Ironically, our paths crossed a number of times during my years in ministry as church members spent their winters in Naples and invited Ann and me to visit them from time to time.

Our senior year at the seminary was largely focused on preparing for and actually landing a job for after graduation. At the beginning of the fall term, I gave job hunting little thought. I was almost assured of winning the annual "traveling" scholarship, and Ann and I looked forward to (finally!) going to New College, Edinburgh, for a year of postgraduate study. We stayed in Princeton over Christmas and New Year's and were unexpectedly excited to receive a query letter from a friend of a friend in Canada, asking if I might be interested in becoming the Chaplain at St. Andrew's College, a very prestigious boys' preparatory school, sponsored by the United Church of Canada. The *caveat* was that I must be eligible for ordination in either the United Church of Canada (UCC) or in the Presbyterian

Church in Canada (PCC).

It turned out that the UCC had some pretty rigorous time-lines regarding membership in the denomination and preparation for ordination, and I could not qualify in a timely manner in order to secure the position. I was still a member of the PCC and under the care of the Presbytery of Chatham but that denomination had a longstanding tradition of requiring graduating theologians to accept a two-year mission appointment to one of the myriad of small, struggling congregations that had been promised regular and continuing ministries if they agreed *not* to enter the Church Union of 1925 and remain within the PCC. There was no way my lifelong denomination would be willing to exempt me from that requirement, *even* (perhaps even *particularly*) to take such a prominent position in the UCC establishment!

I don't remember whether I was more heartbroken or disillusioned. I poured my heart out to Charlie Webster, who immediately offered to fast track my membership in and qualification for coming under the care of the Presbytery of Monmouth of the UPCUSA. Within a month, Ann and I were members of the Red Bank congregation, and I was on Monmouth Presbytery's list to sit the annual standardized ordination examinations of the United Presbyterian Church (USA).

All the while, I was feeling more and more drawn to pastoral ministry rather than to theological academia. I began to participate in the job-hunting frenzy but without much success, since I was such an unknown quantity in the UPCUSA. My closest friend and classmate, Jim Bain, and I both interviewed for the plum appointment of the year, an assistantship at the Hollywood Presbyterian Church in Los Angeles, which he eventually won. Right about then, Ann realized that she was pregnant (again), and any lingering thoughts about spending a study year abroad came to an end. I began to apply myself in earnest to the job hunt without any encouraging results, let alone a job offer!

Mid-May, Professor Donald Macleod, my faculty mentor and fellow Canadian, called me to his office to inquire whether or not I might be interested in a position that had not yet been posted: that of assistant to the new minister of the Fifth Avenue Presbyterian Church in midtown Manhattan, Dr. Bryant M. Kirkland. Would I? Why not? An interview on campus with Dr. Kirkland was quickly arranged and from that came an invitation to travel into New York City to meet with a search committee of elders and trustees from one of the great avenue churches in America. "Wear a suit and tie," Dr. Kirkland commanded, "we'll be having dinner at the University Club."

The day in question dawned hot and humid, and the only suit I owned was a heavy pick and pick tweed outfit my father had had custom tailored for me for the previous Christmas, which, of course, I wore on the bus trip into Manhattan. As I was leaving, the last bit of advice Ann gave me was, "Watch the silver; we're in America, you know!"

When I arrived at the Port Authority of New York bus terminal, there was not a taxi to be had, so I set off on foot from Eighth Avenue and 42nd Street, walking to the church on Fifth Avenue at 55th Street. By the time I got there, I was soaking wet with sweat and in no fit condition for a formal interview. Dr. Kirkland was not impressed. "Didn't you have anything *lighter* you could have worn?" But he led me to his private bathroom adjacent to his study on the seventh floor of the Fifth Avenue church house, and I refreshed myself as best I could.

I shall never forget the interview over dinner at the University Club. The main dining room is a magnificent two-story space of paneling and paintings with white-linen-drapery around tables for eight, each place setting featuring at least eleven pieces of sterling silver. Wine and the conversation flowed freely throughout the meal, and I thought that I had the job in the bag until dessert was served with tiny demitasse cups of coffee, and I realized that the only piece of silver I had left at my place was a great big soup spoon! Needless to say, I drank my coffee black! Years later, let me add parenthetically, I was reminiscing with one of the elders who had been in attendance at that dinner. We had become good friends, and I mentioned my glaring *faux-pas* to him and my fear that it might have cost me the job. "I can assure you, Bill," he told me, "not one of us even noticed!"

Ironically, Dr. Kirkland called to offer me the position officially just as Ann and I were heading out the door of 209 Hodge Hall to attend my graduation banquet, making me one of the *last* members of my class to have secured a church placement that year. As I began to tell people about it at the banquet, I was startled to realize that it was not a *popular* placement: the positions most admired by my classmates were in the East Harlem Protestant Parish and similar urban/ghetto locations across the country. Given my friendship with Jim Bain who was going to Hollywood Pres, then the largest Presbyterian congregation in the world, our classmates began to tease us about being "the bishops of the East and West Coasts!"

As I graduated from Princeton Seminary, Ann, still pregnant, was suffering greatly from morning-sickness. Once I had the Fifth Avenue appointment, I needed to find living accommodations in Manhattan, but Ann was too ill to accompany me. In fact, she actually needed hospitalization for acute dehydration as a result of her frequent nausea, so while she was in hospital in Princeton, I went into Manhattan for a day and found our little two-bedroom apartment at 531 East 88th Street on the fourth floor of a five-story renovated old brownstone with a tiny balcony overlooking Gracie Mansion and the East River. The building was actually right across the street from the side entrances of Doctors Hospital, a detail that would play a significant part in our lives later on!

A funny thing happened on the day of my oral ordination examination before Monmouth Presbytery. That morning's edition of the *New York Times* featured a front-page article announcing that the Fifth Avenue Church was going to spend about two million dollars to repoint and repair its front façade and main entrance. The very first question I was asked from the floor of the Presbytery was: "How can you justify accepting an invitation to serve in a church that is about to spend over two million dollars on a facelift?" Without thinking, I began to reply: "Well, I wasn't on staff when that decision was made." Amidst an unexpected outbreak of laughter, the poser of the question shouted: "I move that the examination be arrested and the candidate be approved for ordination!" And so it was.

I began work as an *assistant* to the minister at Fifth Avenue early in June, occupying an office on the seventh floor of the church house next door to the sanctuary along West 55th Street. Across the hall was Dr. Kirkland's associate, Rev. Kenneth Jones, and around the corner was my personal secretary, Miss Booth, a Jehovah's Witness. Her stock response to any comment or correction from me was, "Well, I'm not a Presbyterian; how am I supposed to know?"

Less than three weeks after I began work in June, Dr. Kirkland left for his two-month summer vacation on Lake Michigan. At the end of July, Ken Jones also left on vacation, and there I was: unordained and seven weeks into my profession, all alone ministering to the Fifth Avenue congregation. It was a heady experience!

One of the best things about that summer and the summers to follow was that I was responsible for hosting the weekly succession of distinguished guest preachers from all over America: George Docherty, Peter Marshall's successor at the New York Avenue Church in Washington, DC; Elam Davies, the silver-tongued Welsh preacher at Fourth Church in Chicago; Edward L. R. Elson, the chaplain of the United States Senate; Ernest Campbell, who later became the senior pastor of the great Riverside Church in New York City; Harold DeWindt from the Kirk in the Hills in Bloomfield Hills, Michigan (where, many years later, I was for several summers a guest preacher myself); and on and on. I learned so much from each and every one of them — things to do and things *not* to do — for which riches I shall always be grateful.

An anecdote I have shared many times: for the first Sunday George Docherty was to preach, he had not yet arrived in town from a vacation in Scotland by early Saturday evening. I was beginning to brush up an old sermon from seminary days when he called from the Warwick Hotel, the church's putting-up place for visiting clergy, asking me to come to his room as soon as possible. Since I was at home some forty blocks away, I took a cab to the hotel and presented myself at his room door. He opened the door clad only in his underpants and proceeded to question me closely about every aspect of the next day's services, before finally letting me go home sometime after 10:00 p.m.

The next morning, he arrived at the church earlier than I had expected and closeted himself with me in the formal vestry, where the session customarily met for prayer with the clergy before every Sunday morning service. "Do you have a sheet of stationery?" he asked; and then, "What about a pair of scissors?" Receiving both, he proceeded to cut out a reasonable facsimile of a pair of preaching tabs of the sort many traditional Presbyterian clergy (myself included) wore with their gowns and hoods. After he stuffed this creation into his shirtfront under his clerical collar, I reached over to try to straighten it for him. "Don't," he commanded, "they look more real if they're a bit crooked!"

Dr. Campbell unwittingly channeled a memory from my University of Toronto days serving as Dr. Ross Cameron's student assistant. Before preaching his Sunday afternoon sermon, Ernie asked me for a glass of water while robing in the vestry. Without thinking, I hurried up the back stairs to the second-floor kitchen and returned with a large glass of ice water. "Don't you know *never* to drink *ice* water before you preach? What do they teach you these days at Princeton?" he groused. And true to form, as often as we met in years to come he never let me forget that gaffe!

In the polity of the United Presbyterian Church in the USA at that time, assistants were invited and appointed to serve solely at the pleasure of the senior pastor: no call, no installation, no job security. However, I had been approved for ordination by the Presbytery of Monmouth, which graciously agreed that I should be ordained by the Presbytery of New York City in the Fifth Avenue Church, which I duly was on Sunday, September 27, 1964.

As Ann and I settled into our new digs on Manhattan's Upper East Side, we quickly realized that everyday life was not going to be quite what we had expected. The Fifth Avenue parishioners took us to their hearts and involved us in activities and events beyond our wildest dreams. Almost immediately we arrived, we received an invitation to attend a gala black-tie charity ball at the American Museum of Natural History. Instead of the cutaway coat and striped trousers that my father had promised me for my ordination, I asked for—and got—a midnight blue tuxedo with all the trimmings. Ann's pregnancy was already showing, so I took her shopping at the Bonwit Teller department store right across Fifth Avenue from the church to buy her (of all the unexpected things!) a *maternity* evening gown, which she ended up wearing on many more occasions than we might have anticipated.

Perhaps the most significant invitation came near the end of the Advent season. Newlyweds Arthur Gray Jr. and Betty Johnson Gray gave an extravagant housewarming party to celebrate their new Park Avenue apartment. Betty was a two-hit pop singer who had appeared frequently on Don McNeill's *Breakfast Club* out of Chicago and then on Jack Paar's *Tonight Show* from New York. Arthur was a Wall Street powerhouse and one of a trio of entrepreneurs whose Citizens for Eisenhower effort had persuaded Ike to run (successfully) for the presidency of the United States.

Arthur and Betty took a shine to Ann and me and included us on their star-studded house-warming guest list. It fell on Sunday evening, December 20, 1964, the day before the due date of the arrival of our first child. Feeling better than she had through most of her pregnancy, Ann was determined to attend, which we did, enjoying the glimpses of celebrities and the attentions of bewigged and satin-breeched footmen bearing endless trays of canapes and flutes of champagne in which we freely indulged, not knowing (in those days) that the consumption of alcohol was a no-no, particularly in the advanced stages of pregnancy, when it could slow or stop the onset of labor. Who knew? Sarah Elizabeth did, apparently, for she eventually arrived exactly one week later, on December 27!

My mother flew to New York a few days before Christmas to be there to help us bring the baby home. Dad stayed in Windsor to spend Christmas morning with my brother Tom and then flew to LaGuardia to come and meet his first grandchild. Meanwhile, Ann had already been in and out of Doctors Hospital with false labor and was reclining on the sofa in our little apartment when Dad arrived. He, who I think I had never heard use profane language, took one look at Ann and blurted out: "What the hell are you doing *here?*"

On Boxing Day evening, Ann had had enough of being cooped up in our apartment with my disgruntled parents and insisted that we go out for a walk. We hadn't strolled but a block when we heard fire engine sirens; so, of course, we went looking for the fire, actually running down East End Avenue for a couple of blocks. We never found the fire, but by the time we got back to our apartment, Ann was suffering the first twinges of labor. I took her back to Doctors Hospital, stayed with her overnight, and in the morning learned from her wonderful obstetrician, Dr. Thomas Jefferson Parks, that she was not dilating very rapidly and that the actual delivery might still be several hours away. So, naturally, I went home, showered and dressed, and went down to church for morning worship and sort of lost track of the time in the rush and bustle that was typical of Sunday mornings at Fifth Avenue.

Eventually, during the post-service coffee hour, the church sexton came to tell me that the hospital had been calling for over an hour to tell me that my baby daughter had been born, and I was to get back up there ASAP! I was frantic: first, to get a cab, then to buy a bouquet of flowers (why, to this day, I am not quite sure), which was difficult in midtown Manhattan on the Sunday afternoon after Christmas. My cabbie and I finally found a florist open—I don't remember where—from whom I bought a big bouquet of lilacs—I don't remember why—and arrived at Doctors Hospital to meet my father leaving for the airport after having just seen and held his firstborn grandchild. For

as long as she lived and as often as she smelled the heady per-
fume of lilacs, Ann always reminded me of how I missed Sarah's
birth because I was at *church* and not where I *ought* to have
been!

There had not been a baby born to a minister of the Fifth
Avenue Church in many generations, and the ladies of the congregation were *in alt*. At her birth, Sarah received over 100
gifts—more than we had received at our wedding! And the gift-
ing continued, particularly as two *grande dames* of the congregation appointed themselves great-aunts and strove to outdo
one another in generosity to our baby daughter. Kay Dotterer
and Julia Rahr became an embarrassment of riches as toys,
clothes, and accessories piled up from FAO Schwartz, Bergdorf
Goodman, Bonwit Teller, Saks Fifth Avenue, and Blooming-
dale's. Years later, Ann would proudly recall that we hardly ever
bought our little girl *anything* during her first two years of life.

We chose our baby's names with great care: "Sarah" not
only because that was my beloved great-grandmother's name
but also because we believed (wrongly as it turned out) that she
would thereby never have to suffer a nickname; and "Elizabeth"
because it was Ann's first name and her mother's as well. At her
baptism, Dr. Kirkland insisted on administering the sacrament,
which was fine with me as I was afraid I might be so nervous as
to drop our baby daughter. Not so fine was the first question of
the first Southern parishioner to greet us after the service: "Are
you going to call her 'Sally,' like we do down South?"

One of my staff responsibilities at Fifth Avenue was loosely
referred to as "Children and Youth," of whom there were precious few when I first began my ministry there! In anticipation
of the arrival of our first child, the board of trustees had au-
thorized the renovation of a small inside room on the fourth
floor of the church house as a nursery for baby care during wor-

ship services and other appropriate events. Otherwise, the rooms used for what Sunday school classes were offered were dismal, dated, and, in most cases, dirty. Reflecting a very outdated concept in Christian education, each room also had a makeshift altar as the focus of a worship center, complete with a wooden cross and a pair of cheap candleholders with never-lit candles.

Over our first summer, Ann and I—with the help of a couple of eager young volunteers—cleaned, brightened, and equipped the various rooms with age-appropriate scripture resources, colorful Bible story pictures, and, in a few cases, new tables and chairs sized for the children we hoped would eventually use them. All of this was announced with some fanfare (which I wrote) in the monthly newsletters and weekly worship folders so that by the time mid-September rolled around, we actually had a few children registered for each class we offered.

Still dissatisfied with the overall program for children and youth, Ann determined and won session approval to start a Brownie Girl Scout troop if she could recruit enough little girls in the neighborhood of the church to make such a program worthwhile. Her efforts came to the attention of a reporter for the *New York Times*, who published a sort of tongue-in-cheek article about the very idea of a Brownie troop in midtown Manhattan. Of course, the publicity was wonderfully effective, and soon Ann had her hands full with more than a dozen little girls meeting every Tuesday afternoon in the third-floor auditorium of the church house.

Her Scouting skills were sorely tried on Tuesday, November 9, 1965, the day—or rather the night—of the Great Northeast Blackout. Just after 5:00 p.m. as the Brownies were putting on their coats and jackets to go home, New York City, along with 80,000 square miles of North America from the New York harbor to Hudson Bay, went totally and without warning BLACK! Without electricity, not only were there no lights but the church house elevators could not operate to bring the little girls down to the first floor where increasingly anxious parents and nannies awaited. Remembering all the unlit candles and cheap candle-holders we had removed from the Sunday school rooms, I was able to light the church house's spooky emergency stairwell with enough candles to get all the terrified little Brownies down to safety.

At the same time, the Presbytery of New York City was meeting in the church's main sanctuary and preparing to adjourn for a hot supper to be served in the dining room on the second floor of the church house. Although we as yet had no idea what had happened—an accident? sabotage? an atom bomb? the Apocalypse?—150 ministers and elders dutifully climbed the candlelit emergency stairwell to the dining room, where dinner by even more candlelight awaited. Not much more Presbytery business got done that night, but the camaraderie held until we began to get news of the blackout. Naturally, the total subway system was inoperable, taxis were at a minimum in dense traffic snarled by the lack of stoplights, and many prepared to spend the night camping uncomfortably somewhere in the church house.

Since there was a daybed in my office on which baby Sarah had been blissfully asleep for many hours, Ann and I hunkered down too, only to be wakened by a surge of light sometime between 4:00 and 5:00 a.m. With the baby awake and the adrenaline still pumping, we set off for home, hailing a cab the minute we hit Fifth Avenue. As the cabbie turned into East 88th Street, we could see lights flashing and fire trucks grouped at the far end. Terrified that our building was on fire, we held our breaths until we realized that the commotion ahead consisted of emergency generators set up to provide power to Doctors Hospital. What a relief! And what an adventure!

In truth, one never knew what might happen next in those heady days. At one of our weekly staff meetings in the fall of 1965, Dr. Kirkland casually informed his colleagues that he had been secretly negotiating with one of the Fifth Avenue Church's nearby neighbors, Duke Ellington, to present the New York premiere of the Duke's *Concert of Sacred Music* on Sunday evening, December 26. Almost immediately, the event was announced at a hastily-organized press conference, which produced a veritable deluge of mail-in ticket orders. Dr. Kirkland had made me responsible for setting up and running a box office of sorts, an appalling prospect given the curved pew seating of varying lengths throughout the sanctuary. Ken Jones and I set out to measure every seat space in every pew, backside to backside, and create a seating chart even before we began to open the bags of mail awaiting response.

As soon as we began to deal with the mail, we realized that the concert was already a sell-out, and the mail kept pouring in. Dr. Kirkland and Duke Ellington put their heads together to try to schedule a second performance, which eventually they did, at *midnight* on the same date! Another press conference, another deluge of mail, but no possibility of a third concert, so every mail-in ticket request had to be sorted by date on a first-come, first-served basis.

I remember nothing else about that autumn and its Advent season: the Duke Ellington concert became a total preoccupation for everyone on staff. In a nod to interfaith sensibilities, New York's senior senator, Jacob Javitz, was invited to be the concert's honorary patron and that brought in another deluge of mail. The vocal soloists were to be Brock Peters and Lena Horne, with additional choral contributions by the Herman

McCoy Swing Choir, which had sung with the orchestra at the Grace Cathedral, San Francisco, premiere of the concert the previous September. Born of African and West Indian ancestry, Brock Peters was well-known as an actor for his role of Tom Robinson in the 1962 film *To Kill a Mockingbird*. Brooklyn-born Lena Horne was a star of stage and screen who had notoriously been blacklisted by Hollywood and the House Un-American Activities Committee in the 1950s but had become an immensely popular television and nightclub performer as well as a civil rights activist.

The evening of December 26, 1965, remains one of the highlights of my life. I spent most of the evening in the Fifth Avenue Church's front vestibule, swathed in a floor-length wool felt cape and wearing my "dog collar" in hopes of gaining a little respect from the concertgoers entering a less-than-familiar venue. I got a brief mention in the *New York Times* review of the event for using a walkie-talkie to resolve seating problems with the associate pastor, Ken Jones, who was in his office on the sixth floor of the church house with files containing every piece of correspondence regarding the concert and our seating assignments!

Meanwhile, Ann was also in the church house, in my office, playing nursemaid to Lena Horne, who apparently was a hypochondriac and needed aspirin, throat lozenges, and lots of TLC before and after each of her concert appearances. But she was a true trouper, and, in my opinion at least, stole the show in a winter-white ensemble with a matching tight white turban.

Both performances were filmed by CBS-TV, which edited them for a two-hour television special. RCA Victor produced the official LP album from which the opening song of the concert, "In the Beginning God," won a Grammy award in 1967.

One of my ongoing pastoral responsibilities was FAYA—

Fifth Avenue Young Adults—that was a very popular draw for midtown Manhattan's single young adults. Meeting on Sunday evenings for a light supper and a program following, the group numbered as many as 100 members at any one time, with a weekly attendance of thirty-five to forty men and women. Aspiring (and often hungry) actors and actresses, singers, and dancers were a welcome part of the mix, especially some of the young women in the *corps de ballet* of the increasingly impressive New York City Ballet company under the artistic direction of George Balanchine. I remember particularly our mutual pride in the tremendous success of Suzanne Farrell, who had just been named a principal dancer and rocketed to stardom in Balanchine's productions of *Don Quixote* and *Jewels*.

Not surprisingly, my predecessor at Fifth Avenue, Philip Rodgers Magee, had been very theatrical, and the group had staged a series of amateur productions of which *The Pirates of Penzance* had already been scheduled for the winter following my appointment. I was really out of my depth, trying to organize a presentation rising to FAYA's expected standards, and the resulting performances were so substandard that we never tried to put on another show!

Instead, for the next year, we organized a black-tie dinner dance that was a huge success. We three clergy donned our tuxedos, and Mrs. Kirkland and Ann wore long gowns as did many of the FAYA ladies. A few artistic souls had made "Tiffany" lamps with hand painted plastic shades, which gave the second-floor dining room a genuine ballroom atmosphere. One of the church's elders, Jules Tihor, and his wife Natalie served as our honorary patrons and lent a very distinguished element to the event.

Afterward, Jules and Natalie took Ann and me for a late-night supper at a well-known (to them at least) Hungarian restaurant on the Upper East Side, not far from where we lived at the end of East 88th Street. Gypsy violins serenaded us, bottles of white wine appeared at the table without our even noticing, we ate and drank and laughed until finally we realized that the restaurant was empty save for us four, and the waitstaff were increasingly impatient for us to leave. For some reason, that seemed hilariously funny as we exited into the cold night air, whereupon my first breath made me realize that I was totally foxed and barely able to stand up straight. Seemingly unaffected, the Tihors loaded us into a cab and escorted us home. Even getting out of the cab and into our apartment struck me as equally hilarious, but my hangover the next morning was anything but funny!

While Dr. Kirkland was not prepared to let either Ken Jones, his long-suffering associate, or me preach on a Sunday *morning*, he regularly assigned us pulpit duty on Sunday *afternoons*, when a sparse congregation of 200–250 worshipers might seem almost lost in the 1,200-seat sanctuary. One of my infrequent opportunities fell during a midwinter snowstorm when the NYC transit system was on strike. As I waited for the right moment to enter the sanctuary, the church's redoubtable custodian, Arthur Liens, peeked through a spyhole in the big oak door by the pulpit and counted eighteen hardy souls in attendance. "Never mind, Mr. Russell," he assured me, "there wouldn't be many more here even if Mr. Jones or Dr. Kirkland were preaching!"

Many Manhattan celebrities attended those late Sunday afternoon services. My absolute favorite was the Metropolitan Opera's rising young soprano, Leontyne Price. Usually accompanied by her manager, she would slip unobtrusively into a pew just under the balcony above, sing the hymns softly, and slip out again during the benediction. On a few of the occasions when I was preaching, she would wait long enough to be one of the first attendees out the door where I was greeting after the service and always offered an understated but all-the-more-appreciated compliment on my message.

During most of 1964, 1965, and 1966, New York was all agog over the construction of the various venues at Lincoln Center. As the grand new Metropolitan Opera House was nearing completion, it was announced that the September 16, 1966, opening night opera would be the world premiere of Samuel Barber's *Antony and Cleopatra*, starring none other than Leontyne Price! To my amazement, shortly after that announcement, Miss Price lingered after one of the late-afternoon services at which I had preached and asked if she could speak to me in private.

Alone in the vestry, she confided that she had just learned that one of the costumes she was expected to wear in the opera was a metal breast-plate with cut-outs to expose her bare breasts. She was, by her own account, a good Southern Baptist girl, who did not feel that she could conscientiously wear this revealing costume. At the same time, she realized that her role on such an historic occasion would be a tremendous affirmation of African-American womanhood, and she did not want to betray the hopes and aspirations of black women who admired her with fervor. What should she do?

I was stunned—almost speechless! Thinking quickly, I asked her whether or not the proposed costume detail was historically authentic, which, she had been told, it was. "Are you going to be able to sing wearing it?" I inquired. "Yes," she thought she could. "Then, wear it," I challenged her, "and wow them!" Which she did, to great acclaim and immediate stardom as of one of American opera's most powerful and admired divas.

In 1966, Ann became pregnant again and again had lots of

difficulties with her pregnancy. In early December, two months before our second child was due, Ann had to undergo significant dental surgery to remove some, or even all, of her wisdom teeth as I remember. My mother offered to come to New York for a week or so to take care of Sarah and help with meals and housework. It was one of those well-meant but ultimately more-trouble-than-they-are-worth gestures.

The first time Mom took Sarah out in her stroller for a walk and to do some errands, she returned home amazed. "Everybody knows Sarah," she marveled, "the Chinese laundryman gave her a fortune cookie; the pharmacist gave her a lollipop; the butcher gave her a hot dog; and the greengrocer at Gristede's gave her a banana!"—all of which, of course, ended up in her crib as soon as she was put down for her nap!

"Aunt" Julia Rahr insisted on taking Mom to the Junior League clubhouse for lunch. "I haven't ever been there myself!" Ann complained. Then Gustav Eyssell, the president of Rockefeller Center and the chairman of the Fifth Avenue Church's Board of Trustees, invited us to attend the annual lighting of the Rockefeller Center Christmas Tree, but Ann didn't feel up to the outing; so Mom went with me in her place, while Ann stayed home and babysat. "Give me a break," Ann moaned, "I thought she came to give *me* a break!"

Ann's parents and her younger brother, Tom, came to spend Christmas with us that year. Tom was fourteen and determined to spend New Year's Eve in Times Square. As it happened, I was approached the day before New Year's Eve by a couple who had eloped from somewhere in the Midwest and were determined to be married in New York City on New Year's Day, one of the only days in the whole year when the church absolutely and totally shut down to give the entire staff a well-earned day off. I had been assigned to conduct the church's WatchNight service in the chapel, so I suggested that I would stay behind after the service in order to marry the couple in the early hours of what would by then actually be New Year's Day.

And that's what we did! I brought Tom downtown with me around 9:00 p.m., whereupon he set out on foot for Times Square, promising to return as soon as the ball dropped to ring in the New Year. I conducted the sparsely attended WatchNight service, our organist stayed behind to surprise the couple with a little wedding music, the church sexton tidied up and hung around to be the second necessary witness, Tom returned from Times Square just in time to be a congregation of one, and I performed the ceremony for one of the truly most starry-eyed couples ever.

Unfortunately, by the time the wedding and the registry signing and the locking up all took place, the New York subway system was beginning to close down. Tom and I walked from entranceway to entranceway, only to find each barred and locked. One IRT station remained open but was only accessible with subway tokens of which I had none, so we walked all the way home from Fifth and 55th to East 88th and East End Avenue, quite proud of ourselves and the unique New Year's Eve we had spent.

Of course, by the time we reached the apartment, Tom's parents were in a state: so worried, so angry, so determined to blame me—it quite took the enjoyment out of the occasion. Fortunately, the Trotters left the next morning to fly back to Windsor via Detroit, and I was spared any further tongue-lashing!

Ann was due to deliver our second-born child in the third week of January 1967. In the early hours of Friday, January 20, right on schedule, Ann's water broke, although she had no contractions to speak of. At about 8:00 a.m., I telephoned her obstetrician, still Dr. Thomas Jefferson Parks, to report. He replied to the effect that Ann's delivery would probably be very slow, and we should just relax until her contractions were about five minutes apart.

That winter, I had a fairly large confirmation class scheduled at the church for after school on Friday afternoons. As the time drew near for me to leave our apartment for the church, Ann's contractions were still minor and well-spaced. So I walked across the street to Doctors Hospital and preregistered her for a delivery that night. As I left for the church, she went to the apartment next door, rang the bell, and was warmly received by our neighbors who immediately (and loudly) agreed that it was DREADFUL for me to go off and leave her in such a delicate condition. To assuage her self-pity, they plied her with Bloody Marys until I returned about three hours later to find her quite comfortable with no labor pains at all.

Exactly two weeks later, the very same scenario began to play itself out again, but this time, before I left for my confirmation class appointment, I escorted Ann across the street to the hospital myself. When I returned to the hospital from midtown a few hours later, her labor pains were still infrequent, but Dr. Parks was on hand, and he encouraged me to go home and get some rest, which I did except I was intercepted getting off the elevator by those same nextdoor neighbors, who invited me in for a couple of Bloody Marys to help me cope with the waiting. When I finally returned to our apartment around 11:00 p.m., the phone was ringing off the hook: our son had been born about 8:00 p.m., and the hospital was frantically trying to locate me with the news. So, for the second time, I failed to be at the hospital when our baby was born, a failure Ann never quite let me forget.

My namesake for the next generation, William Kirk Russell, was a beautiful, big, blue-eyed, blond-haired baby boy: a delight in every respect save his frequent inclination to spit up his formula wherever and whenever possible. When Dr. Kirkland, who was sure that we had chosen Kirk's middle name to honor *him*, insisted that *he* was going to baptize *his* namesake, I reminded him of the potential peril. Sure enough, on the Sunday morning chosen for the sacrament, baby Kirk was fussy as usual; so Ann gave him a bottle (as usual) just before we entered the Fifth Avenue sanctuary; and as Dr. Kirkland named the child and invoked the Trinity, Kirk began to make an all-too-familiar face (as usual), whereupon Dr. Kirkland abruptly handed him back to me, and our just-baptized baby boy proceeded to spit up his milk, as usual, all down the black velvet front panels of my preaching robe. The usually staid Fifth Avenue congregation reacted with roars of laughter and even a bit of scattered applause.

1967 was probably our happiest year in New York City. Ann enjoyed good health, strengthened by almost daily walks from our apartment over to Carl Schurz Park across East End Avenue overlooking the East River on the south side of Gracie Mansion, the official residence of NYC mayors. She made friends with several other young mothers in the Yorkville neighborhood, and we enjoyed a burgeoning social life outside the congregational circles in which we normally moved.

A memory: at one point in the late summer, Ann determined that we should host a dinner party for some of her friends and their husbands. In preparation for this unwonted hospitality, I went to the wine store at the end of the block to buy a couple of bottles of cheap wine and a bottle each of gin and Scotch to stock my heretofore nonexistent bar. As each couple arrived, I proudly offered a drink; and, two by two, all of our guests asked for *bourbon*! They graciously settled for G&Ts, and, afterward, I eventually learned to drink Scotch when that was the only libation left—an acquired taste that I have indulged ever since!

By that fall, Kirk was old enough to begin enjoying the huge sandboxes in the park, where, eventually, he learned to toddle and then to walk. Some of my happiest memories of our life in Manhattan center around Sunday afternoon strolls through Carl Schurz Park and along the riverside promenade down to 1 East End Avenue, where Fred and Julia Rahr lived, and back again.

We became season ticketholders to the New York City Ballet at Lincoln Center and enjoyed taking the 72nd Street crosstown bus over to the New York State Theater on a regular basis. We were blessed by the willingness of Helen Stewart, a nurse at Doctors Hospital and a member of the Fifth Avenue Church, to babysit our children and sleep over in our apartment for a reasonable fee.

But with Sarah in the terrible twos and Kirk a tentative toddler, our little apartment on East 88th Street was beginning to seem woefully inadequate for the future needs of our growing family. So in the fall of 1967 as the Fifth Avenue Church's Trustees were gathering data to generate the next year's operating budget, I approached Dr. Kirkland about the possibility of being granted a larger housing allowance so that we could begin looking for a more adequate apartment. His response was disappointing, indeed. In effect, he reminded me that I was *only* an assistant to the minister—i.e., himself—*not* a called and installed associate pastor and that as such my services to the church were only worth so much, about as much as I was already earning. By now in the fourth year of what had turned out to be a very demanding position, I was totally frustrated and began to realize that the only way I would be able to provide more adequately for myself and my family would be to seek another ministry situation.

Ironically, Dr. Kirkland himself unknowingly provided the catalyst for that process to begin much sooner than either of us expected. That same fall, the Kirklands' youngest daughter had become engaged to one of Princeton Seminary's most recent graduates. In the Christmas season before the wedding, the Kirklands hosted a large party to honor the engaged couple and to introduce the groom's family to their relatives and friends, a gathering to which Ann and I were invited.

During the party, I made the acquaintance of the groom's father, who was the CEO of one of America's largest corporations. As we stood chatting about nothing in particular, Dr. Kirkland came over and spoke to him quite abruptly to the effect that he ought not try to steal me away from the Fifth Avenue Church! When Dr. Kirkland moved on, I asked my new acquaintance, "What was that all about?" Then he revealed that his home church in Millburn, New Jersey, was just about to lose its senior pastor, and since Dr. Kirkland had just sort of mentioned it, would I be interested in being a candidate?

In the week between Christmas and New Year's, Ann and I rented a car and drove out to New Jersey for an afternoon to check out Millburn and the Wyoming Presbyterian Church, a charming Sir Christopher Wren-style red brick Georgian Colonial edifice with a soaring white steeple. By the time of the Kirkland wedding in January, I was very interested indeed and told the groom's father so during the reception, and the rest, as they say, is history!

The candidature took place in deep secrecy through the winter and early spring. Finally, I was the pastoral nominating committee's sole nominee, and with the blessing of the Presbytery of Newark I was invited to preach my candidacy sermon on Palm Sunday, April 7, 1968. I planned a Palm Sunday service of hymns, readings, and a sermon and then on April 4, Martin

Luther King Jr. was assassinated! Realizing that despite the liturgical calendar and my own circumstances, the Wyoming congregation, like every other Christian congregation in America that morning, needed a pastoral message of compassion and calm, I scrapped everything I had prepared and wrote out a new sermon in longhand on foolscap paper and went out to Millburn to do my best on one of the worst Sundays in the nation's living memory.

I remember only three things about that Sunday. First, the actual desk area of the Wyoming Church's pulpit was very small and narrow—too small to hold two sheets of foolscap side by side—so as I read my manuscript during the earlier service that morning, I dropped page after page to the floor and proceeded to stomp on and smear them with my fresh shoe-polish as I moved around in the pulpit. Then I had quite a job smoothing and marking the pages sufficiently to make them readable again for the later service.

Second, I remember that at the end of each service I invited the congregation to rise and sing "O beautiful for spacious skies" instead of the closing hymn indicated in the worship folder. As soon as the first service was over, though, the chair of the pastor nominating committee came to me to correct my announcement of the hymn as "America," when, in fact, it was "America the Beautiful!" I figured then that I had already lost the job, so I could just relax and enjoy the rare privilege of leading in worship and preaching to a full house!

Third and most importantly, during the congregational meeting held after the second service, the congregation sustained the recommendation of the PNC that I be called and installed as the senior pastor of the then-1,100-member Wyoming Presbyterian Church and so I was, at the ripe old age of twenty-eight!

The Wyoming congregation wanted me installed as soon as possible and so a termination/starting date of May 1, 1968, was decided. Dr. Kirkland was furious! In fact, he never quite forgave me over the many years he remained at Fifth Avenue. He believed that my leaving him was too soon, too abrupt, and too significant for one as young as I.

Through the good offices of the man behind all this, we were able to order a new car through his corporation's fleet rental program. We shopped the various dealerships in midtown Manhattan and eventually settled on a stylish metallic chocolate brown two-door Buick Skylark hardtop coupe. Ann and I were convinced that we would have one of the smartest-looking cars in Millburn until we moved into our Sagamore Road manse and discovered that our next-door neighbors had exactly the same automobile except as a convertible!

I remember little of the month or so of farewells. The Sunday school that Ann and I had worked so hard to build up gave us a reception and a large engraved Revere silver bowl. Our FAYA friends hosted a dinner party in a private dining room at the Waldorf Astoria Hotel and presented us with a sterling silver serving spoon in the Gorham "Decor" pattern we had chosen for whatever parting gift the congregation might proffer.

But the most memorable gift was the remains of an old chapel pulpit chair I had discovered mouldering in the church basement. When I told Dr. Kirkland that *it* was what I wanted as my souvenir of my years at Fifth Avenue, he scoffed and said, "Well, then, have it!" with a scornful voice that clearly conveyed just how little he thought of my choice. Refinished by my own hand and reupholstered several times to match the changing decor of our several manses, that magnificent high-backed baroque-carved armchair remains a focal point in our home to this very day!

We moved out of our little East 88th Street apartment in the first few days of May. Our belongings were to be delivered to Sagamore Road in Millburn on Friday, May 3, but the moving van blew a tire on the way and did not reach us until late on Saturday afternoon. Our farewell reception at Fifth Avenue was to be held following morning worship the next day, so it was important that we awake early in our new home in order to make it into Manhattan in good time. The trouble was that our movers had packed up all our worldly goods in cartons clearly marked "___ & Misc," and it took us hours on Saturday night to find our only radio alarm clock as "Misc" in the very last carton we opened.

Ann and I were genuinely sad to leave the Fifth Avenue congregation: so many fine folk had been so good to us over the four years of my ministry there, and we would have been happy to stay longer had it not been for our cramped apartment and Dr. Kirkland's insistence that I wasn't worth any more than I was already being paid.

* * * * *

MY READY AVAILABILITY TO THE Wyoming congregation meant that there had been only a few months' vacancy since the departure of my predecessor, Henry B. Strock Jr. He was still fondly remembered and sorely missed by most of the congregation. Many of those who did not miss *him* still mourned the departure five years earlier of *his* predecessor, Donald M. Meisel, who had gone to be the senior pastor at the prestigious Nassau Presbyterian Church in Princeton. There had not been time or necessity for intentional interim ministry during either of the previous vacancies and so the congregation was really not quite ready to receive yet another new minister with any degree of warmth or enthusiasm.

To make matters worse (at least for me), the congregation's installed associate pastor had really wanted and had actually campaigned for the call I had received instead. With the connivance of the longtime church secretary, he spent about eighteen months trying to thwart every single thing I did to make the ministry there mine. Eventually, a group of elders appealed to the committee on ministry of the Presbytery of Newark, and he was persuaded to seek and accept a pastoral call elsewhere.

Symptomatic, I think, of the everyday tensions under which I was working was a little problem that eventually and quite unnecessarily became a big problem in my mind. A few months into my preaching ministry at the Wyoming Church, the chair of the pastor nominating committee suddenly appeared to be finding my sermons increasingly painful to sit through. Once I mounted the pulpit and began my message, he would begin to squirm in his pew and hold his hand to his forehead until the sermon was over. It bothered me more and more week after week until I could hardly bear to be with the man in church meetings, during which he seemed to be completely unfazed by the tortures my preaching was putting him through. Finally, I could stand it no longer and invited him to come to see me in my study at the church. When I asked him why he apparently found my sermons so unbearable, he was totally nonplussed until he figured out what I was talking about and why and began to laugh: "Bill," he chortled, "at this time of year, when you are in the pulpit, the morning sun shines down through the big window over your right shoulder and would blind me if I didn't cover my eyes! Okay?"

With the departure of the associate pastor, I confronted the church secretary with her complicity in his interference. She was astonished that I recognized her disloyalty and yet was willing to forgive it and try to establish a new working relationship. Tearfully, she agreed and served faithfully and well until almost the end of my five years in Millburn. Not long after that, the long-serving church organist and choirmaster resigned to take up a similar position at the big Roman Catholic church up the street. I was finally free to build a staff of my own and to get on with a ministry that until then had been both frustrating and disappointing.

I was invited by Princeton Seminary to become part of its teaching church fieldwork program, and I was thereby able to recruit a pair of extremely promising young men to assist with the congregation's various children's and youth ministries. I also happened upon a recently retired Methodist clergyman who was delighted to accept part-time employment as a minister of visitation.

And, ultimately, I found and hired a church musician and avid outdoorsman to become my full-time lay colleague as director of music and youth ministries. Ken Williams and his lyric-soprano-opera-soloist wife Lynette were veritable godsends, and things really took off for me and my ministry. The Wyoming congregation was, in many ways, a bellwether Presbyterian church. With its strategic proximity to both Princeton and Manhattan, it seemed always to be in the forefront of whatever was happening theologically and liturgically in the United Presbyterian Church (USA) and America's other mainstream Protestant denominations.

In the late 1960s, that meant liturgical adventurism, civil rights agitation, and Vietnam War activism, the three influences that shaped the remaining years of my ministry in Millburn/ Short Hills. With the imaginative support and involvement of Ken and Lynette Williams, we rose to what I like to remember as exceptionalism in chancel drama, liturgical dance, imaginative preaching, and outstanding music. I will never forget the thrill of Lynette's singing "I know that my Redeemer liveth" a cappella from the church balcony on Easter morning or the excitement of the costumed Tudor Christmas extravaganza or the mind-boggling chancel adaptation of a sermon's worth of the then-current bestseller *Oh, God!* dialogue or the absolute aptness of the Centennial Pageant's segment portraying my ministry with the opening words of the session's worship committee chair, "Well, I wonder where he's got the Communion table this week!"

A year or so before we moved to Millburn, there had been a frighteningly destructive race riot in nearby Newark. Out in the suburbs, many folk kept a loaded rifle or shotgun behind their bedroom door. In an attempt to bridge the racial divide between the affluence in Millburn and the poverty in Newark, the Wyoming congregation had twinned with Central Presbyterian Church downtown. We made weekly trips into the inner city for tutoring and mentoring programs, and we provided material aid in many and different ways. At one point, Central's manse burned to the ground, costing their African-American minister and his family everything they had. I warmly remember how Ann bundled up some beautiful table linens with the silver-plated flatware set we had been given as an engagement gift in Southampton a decade earlier for us to take down to the minister's wife and the tears of gratitude we all shed—ours for being able to give such a gift, theirs for being the ones to receive it.

The national ambivalence to the Vietnam War played out painfully in the congregation when one family's youngest son registered with the Selective Service Draft Board as a conscientious objector. With much misgiving, I agreed to be his advocate for his several appearances before the local draft board. As still a Canadian citizen and therefore unable to vote in the USA I had always strenuously avoided *any* political comment on *anything* from my pulpit, but espousing this young man's cause opened the can of worms and caused much dissention and debate in the congregation. The situation was, of course, exacerbated by a widespread American distaste for Canada as the haven of choice for American draft dodgers and so I was doubly tarred by the anti-war brush and dubiously supported by those whose sentiments lay with the beleaguered family during their time of trial.

My young man was eventually granted conscientious objector status and spent two years in alternative service as an orderly in a Veterans Administration hospital. Ironically, once his sentence was completed, he enrolled as a student for the ministry at Princeton Seminary, a career path option that would have automatically exempted him from the draft altogether had he invoked it two years earlier!

June 1961
University College, The University of Toronto
Bachelor of arts in Honours Philosophy

November 17, 1962
St. Andrew's Presbyterian Church, Windsor, Ontario
Ann's and my wedding day

June 1964
Princeton Theological Seminary
*Graduating with a master of divinity degree
with Ann, my father, and Grandma Russell*

The Presbytery of New York City
invites you to attend
the Ordination of
William Ray Russell
to the Gospel Ministry
in

The Fifth Avenue Presbyterian Church
New York City
Sunday afternoon, September 27, 1964

at 4:30 o'clock

September 27, 1964
The Fifth Avenue Presbyterian Church
The invitation to my ordination

THE PROTESTANT COUNCIL
OF THE CITY OF NEW YORK

AND

THE FIFTH AVENUE
PRESBYTERIAN CHURCH

PRESENT

a concert of

sacred music

BY

duke ellington

SUNDAY, DECEMBER 26, 1965
NEW YORK CITY
EIGHT O'CLOCK AND MIDNIGHT

December 26, 1965
The Fifth Avenue Presbyterian Church, New York City
"A Concert of Sacred Music" program
autographed by Duke Ellington and Lena Horne

THE
SEVENTIES

I N MANY WAYS, OUR LIFE IN Millburn at the turn of the decade was idyllic. We lived in a handsome two-story Tudor brick manse on a mountainside overlooking the New York skyline and the building of the Verrazano Bridge linking Brooklyn and Staten Island. Sarah, and later Kirk, went to kindergarten and elementary school in one of New Jersey's best school districts. Somewhere along the way, I acquired a little, old, bright red Fiat Spyder sportscar. A fine Lord & Taylor store stood at the foot of Wyoming Avenue, and the upscale Short Hills Mall was just on the edge of town. I had a complementary membership in the PGA championship Canoe Brook Country Club and an out-of-towner's free membership in the University Club in midtown Manhattan. New York City was close enough by train, bus, or car for us to continue to attend performances at Lincoln Center and for me to record radio messages for the Protestant Council of the City of New York.

Despite every word of caution during my Princeton Seminary's practicums on pastoral ministry, Ann and I became particularly close friends with a couple in the congregation, whose three daughters became babysitters and friends with our two—and, eventually, three—children. Bill and Bev Snyder, with their daughters Pam, Susie, and Nancy, became integral parts of our lives, a friendship that outlasted my Millburn ministry and continued into our time in Montreal. Other close friends were Frank and Jane Avery and their aspiring commercial artist daughter, Karen, whose mid-Manhattan studio apartment played a key role in the birth of our third child, Rebecca, which story is told a few pages later.

Perhaps the dearest friendship, though, was that that developed with Ruth Wooley Otis, the widow of elevator tycoon George W. "Bill" Otis, and a lifelong member of the Wyoming Church. Her compassionate concern for her pastor and his family led her to incredible acts of generosity. When Ann was newly pregnant and I was almost exhausted by the strain of dealing with my associate for a year and a half, Mrs. Otis insisted on sending us for ten days to her condo in Naples, Florida, whence began a long-term love affair with the Gulf Coast of Florida. A chauffeur met us at the airport in Miami and drove us across the Tamiami Trail to Naples and then left Mrs. Otis's Lincoln Town Car at our disposal for the remainder of our stay, reappearing only to drive us back to the airport again. This was but the first of several annual visits to Naples, some when Mrs. Otis was in residence, and others when she just made her condo available to us at times convenient to my ministry schedule.

The most memorable generosity came in the spring of 1971 as Ann was nearing the end of what became her last pregnancy. Ann's birth ordeal with Kirk had resulted in an Rh factor issue that came to the fore when she learned she was pregnant again. Since Manhattan was less than an hour away by car, train, or bus, it seemed wise to keep her in the experienced care of Dr. Parks. Again, Ann had a very difficult pregnancy, with such serious morning sickness that at one point, our local general practitioner rigged up an intravenous drip contraption in the manse and made twice-daily house calls to keep liquids flowing to the seriously dehydrated mother-to-be.

On the occasion of our last scheduled prenatal visit to Dr. Parks's office, Mrs. Otis became alarmed at the prospect of my driving Ann into the city for the appointment and back to the suburbs again, so she arranged for a car and driver to make the trip for us. We drove in style in a long black Cadillac limousine, and when the visit to the doctor's office was over and we were readying to head back to Millburn, the driver asked if there was anywhere else we would like to go while we were in the city. I would have declined, but Ann spoke up immediately and asked to be taken to look for stationery appropriate for the baby's birth announcements at the Georg Jensen shop on Madison Avenue. The driver willingly complied and even jumped out of the car to open the rear door for us when we pulled over to the curb at the store. One of the biggest kicks of our young lives was the stir of gawkers we created on the Madison Avenue sidewalk as we emerged from our limo and left them wondering "*Who* are *they*?"

Sarah had been born a week later than her due date, Kirk two weeks later, so we did not expect a prompt arrival of our third child. Since the baby was scheduled to be born at Doctors Hospital (as had been Sarah and Kirk), and the hospital was still about an hour away from Millburn, Frank and Jane Avery insisted that when Ann was in the middle of her third week late, we move into their daughter Karen's studio apartment to await the first birth pangs. We waited and waited until finally I went to see Dr. Parks on my own to explain that my week's paternity leave in Karen's apartment was almost at an end and to plead with him to do something to bring on the delivery. He agreed,

Ann was admitted to Doctors Hospital, labor was induced, Rebecca was safely delivered on May 5 and then in the middle of the night, Ann hemorrhaged and nearly died. Fortunately, I was only a few minutes away from the hospital and was able to rush by taxi to her bedside to sit with her and calm her while Dr. Parks worked to save her life. She survived, thanks to Dr. Parks, but no words could ever express to Karen and her parents our gratitude for that brief but unforgettable stay in her pied-à-terre!

Mrs. Otis's most ill-fated generosity occurred in the summer of 1972 as we Russells were preparing for our month-long summer vacation at the Little Pink Palace in Rondeau Park. Mrs. Otis dearly wanted us to visit her at her summer home on Cape Cod, but we were bringing along Pam Snyder as an au pair for the month, and we had just acquired a high-strung but beautiful Dalmatian rescued dog. "No problem!"

But there *was* a problem: while we went off sightseeing, Dale began to gnaw off the cedar shakes on the back corner of the garage where he had been tethered. Then, not satisfied with that much damage, he attacked and ripped apart one of two antique-looking wooden park benches in the garden. Though unfazed by the damage to the garage wall—"That can be fixed!" Mrs. Otis assured me—she was less sanguine about the ruined bench: "At least it wasn't the 18th century original," she remarked, "just the exact reproduction Bill made with his own hands!"

Every summer, we were excited to spend a month's vacation at the Little Pink Palace. And every fall as we returned to New Jersey from Canada, I felt it was finally time to take the big step of applying for United States citizenship. So every year, I began the burdensome process of acquiring the documentation and submitting the fingerprinted security clearance forms to become a full-fledged American citizen. And every year, just as I was doing so, some church in Canada would approach me about returning to my home and native land and denomination, and every year I would again take the possibility seriously and set aside my US citizenship quest. The suburban Toronto Leaside congregation, where Ann's mother's best friend was a member; the great historic St. Andrew's Church on King Street in downtown Toronto and then the almost 150-year-old St. Andrew's Church in Guelph, Ontario—each in turn nearly persuaded me to return to my roots.

As time went by, we began to realize that under the surface all was not as it seemed in Millburn/Short Hills. Illegal drugs were making their way into the high school and junior high schools of the district; shameless mate-swapping was going on among the members of the racquet club and elsewhere; sexual promiscuity was complicating even church-sponsored youth activities; and the overt political corruption that eventually became Watergate was also endemic in local, county, and state politics too.

The hardest problem of all for me to deal with as a working pastor was the almost total disconnect between the *suburban* life of the congregation and community in which I found myself and the *urban* workaday world in which those who commuted to New York or Newark earned their living. It was almost as if the commuters turned off the home-and-church switch as they turned on the work-in-the-city switch on the train to Newark or in the Holland Tunnel. With the leadership of a couple of CEOs, we started a monthly lunch gathering for our members who worked in Manhattan, which flourished for a season and then disintegrated under the weight of costly private dining rooms and too-long lunch hours away from the office!

Finally, in the fall of 1972 as Ann and I were wondering what special something we might do to mark our tenth wedding anniversary, I received a telephone call from my old Princeton

Seminary preaching professor, mentor, and friend, Donald Macleod. "Would you be interested in going to a Presbyterian church in Montreal?" he asked.

"Only if it were the Church of St. Andrew and St. Paul," I replied.

"I will find out and call you back!"

It was, and I was; and within an hour I heard from one William Stewart, the chair of an informal search committee looking for a successor to the cleric who for more than twenty-five years had been the senior minister of the "Cathedral Church of Canadian Presbyterians." In short order, we arranged for an exploratory visit to Montreal in mid-November, masquerading as a tenth wedding anniversary trip to one of the most romantic cities in North America.

The Church of St. Andrew and St. Paul boasts surely one of the most beautiful sanctuaries in Canada and certainly one of the most prestigious pulpits in the country, and I fell in love with it all at first glance. The retiring minister, Dr. R. J. "Rod" Berlis, a late-Victorian bachelor whose idiosyncrasies were both loved and laughable, was all charm as he greeted us until he belatedly realized that we were visiting not just as tourists but as his prospective successor and spouse. His bewilderment was evident, especially when his pastoral assistant, Stephen Hayes, whom I had known years before at Knox College, stopped by the vestry. As we were introduced, Stephen almost immediately comprehended that my visit probably meant that *he* was not going to be Dr. Berlis's successor. Eventually, I was made aware that *Dr. Berlis had already decided upon* his successor and was truly shocked and disappointed to be confronted with the fact that *anyone else* was even being considered.

Our brief visit to Montreal was, to say the least, uncomfortable, even more so when we met with the church's informal search committee and sensed that some on the committee were not pleased that I was (a) too young, (b) from America, and (c) not whom Dr. Berlis had already chosen. Before we left, however, we had a very frank and forthright conversation with three of the church's most senior and most influential elders: the informal committee's chair, Peter Stewart; the clerk of session, Lawrence McDougall; and the man who would eventually become the chair of the formal search committee, Walter Markham. They sought earnestly to assure Ann and me that any opposition to my candidacy would be dealt with in due course. We traveled back to Millburn with very mixed emotions, having completely neglected to celebrate our tenth wedding anniversary in any way at all!

The Advent/Christmas season of 1972 felt sort of surreal. We heard nothing from Montreal, but we spent many a sleepless night pondering "what if?" The Wyoming Church's new director of music and Christian education, Ken Williams, and his wife Lynette, produced, directed, and starred in a magnificent Tudor Christmas extravaganza in which Ann and I played the lord and lady of the manor, all the while wondering whether this might be our last holiday season in Millburn.

Early in the New Year, the three elders with whom I had met privately in November paid a weekend visit to Millburn to interview me again, hear me preach, and look over the church and congregation in which I was currently serving. They brought with them an invitation to participate in a mid-February continuing education seminar for Canadian clergy at Montreal's Presbyterian College on the campus of McGill University. It was, of course, the perfect cover for me to visit the Church of St. Andrew and St. Paul again, where I was also invited to be a guest preacher on the Sunday I was in Montreal.

The week was planned to its fullest by the newly-formed

pastor nominating committee, with whom I met this time very openly. I was taken to see the manse, a four-story Georgian red brick town house in an elegant mews a block away from the church; I met with the chair of the board of trustees to discuss salary and benefits and with the Presbytery of Montreal's nominee to be interim moderator of the session; and I had a long and liquid dinner with the church's director of music, Wayne Riddell, with whom I hit it off immediately and with whom I eventually worked with immense admiration and satisfaction.

Through it all, I began to realize that the Church of St. Andrew and St. Paul sat very loosely in its relationship to the Presbyterian Church in Canada and that very little (if anything) was being done according to the denomination's *Book of Forms*. When I came to the pulpit as guest preacher on that Sunday, the congregation would be blissfully ignorant that I was already the PNC's minister of choice; there would be no leet, a slate of candidates to preach in turn for the call before a vote was taken; Dr. Berlis would stay in active ministry right up until the time I would arrive; eventually, there would be a congregational meeting at which my name would be entered as the sole nominee for the call; but I would not be present, neither would I formally preach for the call, nor would my family and I be introduced to the congregation until the occasion of my induction.

As it happened, the Church of St. Andrew and St. Paul's congregational meeting was held on the Sunday after Easter, and I was, of course, in my Wyoming Church pulpit. Ann had invited the Snyder family to join us after services for lunch at the manse. While we were at table, the telephone rang, and Helen Stewart, that dear nurse and friend from the Fifth Avenue Church, began the conversation by shrieking, "Congratulations on your call to the A & P!"

I was so rattled, I asked, "How do you know?"

"My sister, Jessie, lives in Montreal and attends the United Church down the block from St. Andrew and St. Paul. When she heard that there was to be a congregational meeting to call a new minister, she went out of curiosity and was astonished to learn that it was to be *you*! So, naturally, she phoned me the minute she got home!"

Somehow, I managed to keep the conversation discreet enough that the Snyders had no idea what was going on, a feat I had to repeat a few minutes later when Lawrence McDougall called on behalf of the session to formally offer me the congregation's almost unanimous call to become the church's new minister. Apparently, there had been three determinedly dissenting votes, objecting that I was too young, to which Walter Markham had countered: "He will grow out of it!" I later learned that these dissents had been registered by a family of two spinsters and their bachelor brother, all of whom were convinced that if only Dr. Berlis had been allowed to stay on a little longer, he would have taken one of the spinsters as his bride!

While in Montreal in February, I had indicated that, should I be favored with the call, I would want to finish out the school year in Millburn and move to Montreal in time for Sarah and Kirk to begin their new school(s) in the fall. I was due my months' vacation from the Millburn congregation, and there were major renovations needed to make the four-story manse livable for a family of five and so began the transition.

One item of unfinished business in Millburn was an ambitious plan to open a weekday nursery school in the spacious church buildings on Wyoming Avenue. Time and again as we had moved through the planning process, our efforts were thwarted by various town and township regulatory authorities. I had become suspicious that *someone* in the chain of command was on the take but had been warned by the township clerk (a member of my congregation and its board of deacons) not to make a fuss. When so much evidence pointed at the township fire chief, and I knew that I would be leaving the community in mid-summer and be beyond anyone's retribution, I went to see the township clerk in his office, laid out my suspicions and my evidence, and told him that if the final license was not approved by the end of that week, I would make my suspicions known to the congregation on Sunday and to the local newspaper first thing Monday morning.

He shook his head and muttered, "That's a very dangerous thing to do, Bill." But on Friday afternoon, he hand delivered the final license approval in person, and I lived to tell the tale!

The thing I remember most about that summer's vacation at Rondeau was buying a pair of Aubusson-style oval Oriental carpets from a Windsor rug merchant and transporting them to Montreal in the back of the slightly-used Oldsmobile Custom Cruiser we had bought the previous spring. The carpets—one approximately 9' × 12', the other 10' × 14'—stuck out the rear clamshell window of the station wagon; the day was hot, the air conditioner did its best to keep the interior comfortable while the cool air was being sucked out the back until the compressor burned itself out somewhere between Kingston and the Quebec border, and it cost more than the carpets were worth to get it repaired in Montreal! However, those beautiful pastel ovals have graced my every home ever since until this very day!

While in Montreal on one of our previous trips, we made the ill-fated decision to have the second-floor manse kitchen and pantry and the third-floor master bathroom completely renovated before we moved in. *Not!* The rooms were gutted in early July; then the construction trades took a two-week holiday; then there was a rail strike that impounded our new appliances heaven knew where; then the warehouse in which all our new cabinets were being stored burned to the ground.

We were scheduled to finish up in Millburn and move to Montreal near the end of August, in time for Sarah and Kirk to begin school right after Labour Day. Through a mutual friend, we had engaged Florence "Flo" LeMarchand, the daughter of a large French family, to come to North America for a year as our au pair. By Labour Day, we had no kitchen and no master bathroom in the manse, the old stove and refrigerator were hooked up in the first-floor (basement) laundry room, and there was a large hole in the master bathroom floor through which a stacking washer and dryer combination was eventually to be hoisted to serve the family's laundry needs on the third and fourth floors. In other words, the house was uninhabitable.

To make things easier, we delayed our move from Millburn for a couple of weeks. Sarah and Kirk boarded with Eric and Jean Riordan and their two boys in Westmount so that they could start school on time. We actually moved our furniture and clothing into the manse just before my birthday; but we still could not live in the house, so the board of trustees put us up in a suite of rooms at the Holiday Inn about a mile away east along Sherbrooke Street.

I have three vivid memories from that dreadful period. The first memorable event took place at midsummer when I traveled to Montreal alone to camp out at the manse and try to deal with the impending renovation disaster. Dr. Berlis was still serving the Church of St. Andrew and St. Paul as minister when the aged widow of his predecessor, the Reverend Dr. George Donald, died. As was his wont, Dr. Berlis saw dramatic significance in just about everything that ever happened and so it was with Mrs. Donald's death and burial. It was a good omen, Dr. Berlis insisted, that he was still in place to link the past of his predecessor with the future of his successor; therefore, I must participate in the funeral of Mrs. Donald!

The problem was that I was in Montreal for only a few days of work at the manse, and I had only summer-weight casual work clothes with me. No problem: we borrowed black trousers and shoes from the short and stout church officer; we bunched up one of Rod Berlis's clerical shirts and collars; and we robed me in one of Dr. Donald's old pulpit gowns that still hung in the vestry closet. I shall never forget my very first pastoral act as minister-elect at the A & P, shuffling down the center aisle in pants that were too short, shoes that were too tight, a clerical collar that was too loose, and a gown that was too long, intoning, "I am the resurrection and the life."

The second vivid memory of that terrible time took place on my birthday. We were in the manse with all of our furniture just unpacked and not yet set to rights, when I lay down to rest on the bare mattress of our unmade bed. I was turning thirty-four that day, a year older than the traditional age of our Lord when he was crucified, and I began to meditate upon all that Jesus had accomplished in that brief lifetime and then upon the dreadful mess that seemed to be engulfing me and my little family with this move to Montreal. I began to weep and weep and weep inconsolably. In her gentle wisdom, Ann just let me cry myself to sleep, while she took baby Rebecca and au pair Flo to the Holiday Inn for supper and to check into the suite that was to be our home for the next couple of weeks.

Life for those two weeks was a constant uproar. I was supposed to be starting to work, the manse was uninhabitable, our two older children were boarding with a family a couple of miles away, there were no hotel amenities to help Ann, Rebecca, and Flo while away the days at the Holiday Inn until one memorable night—the third in this trio of rueful reminiscences—baby Becca crawled under our table in the Holiday Inn coffee shop and threw a tantrum to end all tantrums. While the other hotel patrons looked on aghast, I scooped up my overtired, overwrought, over-everything little girl, kicking and screaming hysterically, and carried her out of the coffee shop, barely registering Ann's announcement to the whole world, "That's it!"

* * * * *

THE NEXT DAY, WE MOVED INTO THE MANSE, where we lasted together about a month. Cooking in the laundry room, eating in what would eventually become Kirk's bedroom, carting laundry down and up three flights of stairs, coping with a husband who believed himself on call at all hours of the day and night, and comforting an au pair who did not find Montreal nearly as much like France as she had expected, Ann was soon worn to a frazzle. Sarah and Kirk came home to live, and parishioners were heartwarmingly generous with dinner invitations and potluck dishes. As a family, we survived my induction, the Canadian Presbyterian preferred word for "installation," my first Sunday service, my first celebration of the sacrament of Holy Communion, and our first Canadian Thanksgiving.

But with Halloween looming and costumes to be created and parties to be attended and goodies to be laid in and still no kitchen and no master bathroom, Ann reached the end of her rope. "I am going home to Mother, literally, with Becca and leaving you here with Sarah, Kirk, and Flo to manage as best you can. And you can tell the board of trustees that I will not be back until I have a kitchen and a bathroom—*period*!" And there was no dissuading her.

Well, we managed somehow, and the trustees got the message and then so did the renovations contractor, and suddenly everything moved ahead very rapidly, so much so that as the end of November approached and our dear Millburn friends, Bill and Bev Snyder, indicated that they and their three daughters would like to come to Montreal to visit us over the long American Thanksgiving weekend, Ann relented and returned home ... only to be swept up in the annual extravaganza of the St. Andrew's Society of Montreal's week of festivities leading up to their St. Andrew's Ball.

Learning of this looming highlight of Montreal's social calendar on the weekend nearest St. Andrew's Day, November 30, which almost always coincided both with American Thanksgiving and the first Sunday of Advent, the Snyders determined that they *would* come to visit, no matter the living conditions in the manse, and they *would* attend the ball with us, and they did!

Little did we know what was in store. The St. Andrew's Society traditionally imported a Scottish peer or clan chieftain for a week of wining, dining, dancing, and attending Sunday worship in the Church of St. Andrew and St. Paul of which so very many in the Society were members. That year's guests of honour were Viscount Melgund, heir to the Earl of Minto, and his charming viscountess, both of whom we met repeatedly at luncheons and dinners in advance of the Ball and again on the Sunday morning following the big event, when I began what came to be a new tradition for the week. I invited "Minnie," Viscountess Melgund—yes, as unlikely as it sounds in the retelling, by this time we were on a first-name basis with Gibby and Minnie—to light the first candle of the church's huge and handsome brass-based Advent wreath, which she did as did every succeeding lady guest of honour with varying degrees of aplomb.

The week also introduced us to the almost overwhelming role played in the festivities by the Black Watch (Royal Highland Regiment) of Canada, for which the Church of St. Andrew and St. Paul was the regimental church! The significance of the gorgeous *Christus Victor* memorial chancel window and the rows of royal and regimental colours laid up in the vaulted ceiling of the nave became abundantly clear as we were surrounded at every turn by pipers and drummers and officers in green regimental parade uniforms and red-and-gold formal mess dress. Little did Ann and I realize, during that first St. Andrew's Society whirlwind week, that by the next November, we would be totally immersed in the whole schedule of events and taking significant social, ecclesiastical, and even military leadership roles!

Truth be told, I remember very little of that first Advent and Christmas season in Montreal. The first snowfall of the season had fallen early in November; day by day, the weather was so bitterly cold that the local radio stations would broadcast morning warnings about how many seconds one's facial skin could be exposed before frostbite set in; so much snow fell on Christmas Eve that by the time the 11:00 p.m. carols by candlelight church service was over and the last parishioner's hand was shaken, Ann and I walked home to the manse down the middle of Sherbrooke Street before even the snowplows arrived to open one of the city's main thoroughfares to vehicular traffic.

In the week between Christmas and New Year's, we were invited to the *Lac Brulé* vacation home of Bill and Marjorie Stewart and their family to learn how to cross-country ski! Sarah had played Mary in the church's Sunday school Christmas pageant, and the Stewarts' son Peter had played Joseph, so there was some friendly joshing about what a cute couple they made! Sarah was not amused, but, much later in life, Peter became engaged and then married one of Sarah's dearest friends, Cynthia, and she and Peter resumed a friendship that truly became lifelong!

By the end of February, the renovations to the manse were pretty well finished, and Ann determined to host a Sunday evening buffet dinner party for all the couples in the congregation who had been so generous with hospitality while we were homeless. She chose the Sunday of Montreal's annual St. Patrick's Day parade and set about with Flo, our au pair, to make it a memorable social event.

Which it turned out to be, but not at all in the way Ann intended. After Sunday lunch, she sent me off with the children to stand on Ste. Catherine's Street and watch the parade pass by, which we did. About halfway through the parade, it began to snow: first a gentle drift of snowflakes, then a deluge of fat, fluffy wet stuff that felt like a blizzard. By the time the children and I had climbed up Rue de la Montagne and reached Place Richelieu, the manse phone was ringing off the hook as first one, then another and then yet another couple called to say that they were snowbound in the Laurentians or in the Eastern Townships or in Montreal West or in the Town of Mount Royal or eventually even in Westmount until *no one* was coming, except a couple of newcomers who had just moved into one of the townhouses up Redpath Street at the top of the hill! Ann was devastated, but Flo (bless her heart!) just cleared and reset the dining room table for four, opened a bottle of champagne, and served one of the most elegant dinner parties we ever held in Place Richelieu!

The snow that had fallen in early November was still on the ground in early May when Ann's brother, Tom Trotter, married Nancy Reeves in the Lady Meredith Chapel at the A & P. Nancy's father was a United Church of Canada minister and had served in so many different locations that he avoided offending any of his former congregations by coming to Montreal to assist me in the conduct of his daughter's wedding. It was a small wedding—about fifty guests in all—who just about filled the chapel. Sarah served as a junior bridesmaid and looked a delight in a bright green frilled pinafore dress.

The wedding reception was held in the sidewalk café of the Berkeley Hotel on Sherbrooke Street, the food and beverage manager of which was a member of our congregation and choir. Unfortunately, the hotel suffered a plumbing mishap on the morning of the wedding and had no running water for the day. In addition to the family members staying with us at the manse, Nancy and her whole wedding party trooped up to Richelieu Place to shower and dress, and Ann was just about beside herself keeping the bride and groom from seeing one another before the wedding.

Far more catastrophic, however, was the arrival of the custom-made wedding cake! On a previous visit to Montreal to make all their arrangements, Tom and Nancy had gone to our favorite patisserie to order what they described as a plain two-tiered yellow cake. Unfortunately, that's exactly what was delivered to the hotel: a two-tiered vanilla wedding cake with *yellow icing*! Nancy was at her wits' end: "Can't you do something, Bill?" she wailed. The bakeshop was closed by then, so I called our florist, who imaginatively came to our rescue with several stems of little yellow-and-white cymbidium orchids, which we pressed, one by one, into the yellow icing until the cake was covered in orchids, and the wedding guests raved that it was one of the most imaginatively beautiful wedding cake that they had ever seen!

I was still in my first year as minister of the regimental church of the Canadian Black Watch when rumours began to fly concerning a possible visit to Montreal by the Black Watch's colonel-in-chief, Her Majesty Queen Elizabeth the Queen Mother.

My eminent predecessor, Major (Ret'd) Rev. Dr. R. J. "Rod" Berlis, had served the Black Watch (RHR) of Canada as its chaplain with distinction during WWII and for decades afterward, eventually relinquishing the post to his then assistant minister, Captain (Ret'd) Stephen Hayes, whom I had known at Knox College and who left Montreal for ministry in Cobourg, Ontario, as part of the 1973 transition process at the A & P.

After Stephen's departure, the regimental chaplaincy remained unfilled for a while, largely, I suspect, because the Black Watch powers that be weren't quite sure of the fitness for the position of the new young minister on Sherbrooke Street. Though born and raised a Canadian, I had studied theology at Princeton Theological Seminary, had been ordained in New York City by the United Presbyterian Church in the United States of America, and had remained in the States for nine years of ministry before being called to the Church of St. Andrew and St. Paul, where I was regarded as an American upstart by some in the Presbyterian Church in Canada—and at least a few, probably, in my new congregation too!

The Queen Mother's impending visit changed all that. On a bitter winter's day early in 1974, I was summoned to the St. James's Club to lunch with the regiment's Honorary Colonel John G Bourne and one of his predecessors, Colonel James W. Knox, a dynamic duo if ever there was one! Apparently, terrified though I probably was, I passed muster because by the end of lunch, I was on my way to becoming the regiment's new padre.

It was a period in the history of the Canadian Forces when things were not made easy for the historic regiments, especially the kilted ones. One stumbling block after another was put in my way, including insistence from CF Quebec Command that I could not wear the uniforms of the regiment as an honorary chaplain but must be sworn in as a full-fledged Canadian

Forces officer and put on strength on the regiment's roster and payroll. I would have much preferred to remain honorary and unpaid: I always felt that my scant service to the unit was an unnecessary drain on its finances, and I strove through the years to return my pay to the regiment's resources in one way or another.

Colonel Bourne would have none of it, though. If I was to participate in the colour presentation—and, by God, I was—then I was to be properly kitted out. One of my first—and still most vivid—Black Watch memories is of the night I was taken to the quartermaster's stores in the bowels of the armoury and provided with the uniforms and accoutrements I would need to make a creditable appearance as a Black Watch officer. As a young soldier struggled to find me just the right kilt, jackets, sporrans, trews, and the like, I confessed *sotto voce*: "I'm new to all this. What *do* I wear under the kilt?" He blushed vividly, then looked me straight in the eye and replied: "Yer balls, sir!"

In the months leading up to the ceremony at CFB St. Hubert, I studied everything I could get my hands on from the previous colour presentation with HM Queen Elizabeth the Queen Mother at Molson Stadium on June 9, 1962, at which Dr. Berlis had served as regimental chaplain. During a Sunday after-church dinner party at Colonel Knox's home that spring, I mentioned jokingly that I thought Dr. Berlis had looked rather ridiculous wearing his black pulpit gown over his kilt. "Sort of like a flasher with diced hose," I am told I quipped.

Tootie Knox, bless her heart, took me seriously and undertook to discover an alternative clerical vestment for me to wear. Eventually, we settled on a tippet—a black preaching scarf we saw in a photo of a field chaplain during WWII. She paid for a pair of the beautiful regimental blazer crests then available; the Milne robemakers on Rue Ste. Catherine appliquéd them onto a custom-made black stole cut to just the right length to match the hem of my kilt; and *voilà*, I was ready to meet the Queen Mum!

When the day of the ceremony dawned, June 25, 1974, the first thing I remember is that the Canadian Forces' chaplains general came to Montreal to participate in the drumhead dedication of the new Colour. Colonel Bourne had (somehow!) secured me a staff car and driver for the day; but by the time the chaplains general arrived at Quebec Command, there was no military transport available for them, so I was immediately tasked with meeting them, taking them to lunch, and getting them to CFB St. Hubert. As they were vesting for the event in the men's locker room at the Badminton and Squash Club on Atwater Avenue and I was slipping my new stole around my neck, the chaplain general (Protestant) harrumphed: "Quite irregular!" To which the chaplain general (Catholic) rebutted, "But quite attractive, don't you think?"

The Colour presentation ceremony was, in a word, stupendous! The arrival of the regiment, the association, and the cadet corps sent up cheer upon cheer from the bleacher stands of spectators lining the parade grounds. The military band played "O Canada" for the Colours and "God Save the Queen" for the Queen Mother. After Her Majesty inspected the troops, the old Queen's Colour was marched off to the strains of "Auld Lang Syne." The new Queen's Colour was draped over the drums piled in the center of a hollow square. Her Majesty joined the chaplains general and me at the drumhead. We prayed; she presented the new Colour to Lt. Wm. Cotton and addressed the assemblage, then we gave her three resounding cheers. The regiment presented arms to the new Colour, Her Majesty took the salute as the Colours were paraded back and forth in slow and quick time, the whole parade advanced in review order for a royal salute, and the Queen Mother left the parade ground. The Regimental Colours were marched off to the massed bands playing "Highland Laddie," the troops marched off to the "Black Bear," and I began to learn to shout "Hoy!" at just the right moment.

Afterwards, there was a garden party on the grounds of the officers club at CFB St. Hubert. Ann and I had cards of invitation, of course. But when Colonel Bourne learned that my mother had come all the way from Windsor, Ontario, to attend the ceremony and take our children home afterward, he insisted that she must attend the garden party too. An invitation card was produced, a disappointed subaltern was ordered to take our children home to Richelieu Place in downtown Montreal in my staff car before returning to transport the chaplains general on their way, and in his own inimitable style Colonel Bourne contrived to present first me, then my wife and then my mother, to Her Majesty as she made her walkabout through the party.

When I was introduced to Her Majesty as the regiment's new padre and the new minister of the regimental church, she responded with a warm reminiscence of visiting the Church of St. Andrew and St. Paul for worship when she had been in Montreal on a previous royal visit. This gave me an opening to present greetings and good wishes from my predecessor, Dr. Berlis, one of the Queen Mum's most ardent admirers. She spoke of him so fondly that I was prompted to confide to Her Majesty that Dr. Berlis had *kept*—and I still *had*—the very bar of hand soap she was presumed to have used in the lavatory off the minister's study at the church on that memorable occasion. With a characteristic twinkle in her eye, the Queen Mother said, "I can assure you that I *did* wash my hands and so, I am sure, did Mrs. Campbell-Preston. About Sir Martin (Gilliat) I can't be so sure!" Thus was I introduced to Her Majesty's long-serving and much-appreciated lady-in-waiting and private secretary.

But our conversation was not over. When I presented my wife and my mother, Her Majesty made some appropriately vague comment about Ann's surely being proud of me, which I hope she was. To my mother, however, she asked the kind of question that made the Queen Mother beloved throughout the military, across the Commonwealth, and around the world: "Are they treating your boy well at the kirk?" My mother never forgot that moment, nor have I!

At the kirk the following autumn, on Sunday, October 6, 1974, I had the honour of conducting the impressive and nostalgic worship service held to lay up the "old" 1962 Queen's Colour. Among my favourite mementos of my decade of ministry at the Church of St. Andrew and St. Paul is a copy of the order of service for that occasion, along with the adjutant's lengthy cues and detailed instructions for laying the regimental colour and the *two* Queen's Colours on the Communion table in a particular pattern to honour what would be the last Black Watch Colour to be mounted in the vault of the nave of the regimental church for a very long time.

Before long, it was time (again!) for the St. Andrew's Society to kick into high gear for the week leading up to the St. Andrew's Ball. The guests of honour for that year were to be the Duke and Duchess of Argyll, Ian and Iona Campbell. His Grace had been a student at McGill University not many years previously and was well-known and much-beloved in Montreal's Scottish community.

To Ann's and my utter amazement, the powers that be in the St. Andrew's Society approached us with the express concern that the duke and duchess were so very young, and they were all a bunch of old fogeys! Would we, they asked, consider entertaining Their Graces for lunch following the command performance in the Church of St. Andrew and St. Paul and perhaps invite a few other young couples of the congregation to join in entertaining them on that occasion?

We would, and we did! First, though, we were thrown together with Ian and Iona at almost every social function scheduled for that momentous week so that by the time we got to the ball and the Royal Montreal Curling Club's Saturday luncheon and Sunday morning's worship service at the kirk, we were certainly and comfortably on a first-name basis with one of Scotland's premier dukes and his delightful duchess!

As they did the year before, Bev and Bill Snyder and their three daughters traveled to Montreal to spend what was, for them, their Thanksgiving holiday weekend. I remember that they were so agog about spending time in the company of a duke and duchess that Bill rented a white tie and tails outfit to wear to the ball, only to be completely outshone by the Black Watch regimental padre in his dress kilt ensemble with its red-and-gold formal mess jacket and white horsehair sporran!

After considering—and rejecting—a dizzying array of menu options fit for entertaining the duke and duchess, Ann wisely settled on her tried-and-true chicken and wild rice casserole. One of my most vivid and lasting memories of the weekend is of Bev Snyder elbow-deep in cut-up chicken pieces muttering "This is not as glamorous as it sounds!"

Another vivid memory involves Iona, whom I had invited to light the first candle on the church's Advent wreath just before Ian was to read the gospel lesson in the Sunday morning service. As I had done the year before with Viscountess Melgund, I lit a delicate taper from one of the candles on the Communion table and handed it to Iona to light the first Advent candle, but she was so nervous that her hand shook sufficiently violently as to extinguish the taper, and I had to go back to the

Communion table to relight it!

The third indelible memory was provided by Ian, who, during lunch at the manse with a roomful of the young elite of the congregation, several of whom were already ordained elders, began to comment on the details, liturgical and otherwise, of the very solemn and traditional high church celebration of the sacrament of Holy Communion, always held on the first Sunday in Advent. "I have to tell you, Bill—and you young elders in your striped trousers and cutaway coats—that you do it better than they do it in the high kirk in Edinburgh!"

The New Year of 1975 marked the centennial of the formal denominational beginning of the Presbyterian Church in Canada (PCC). Although there had been Presbyterian congregations in Montreal since at least 1803, they had each and all begun as Canadian offshoots of the various branches of Reformed and Presbyterian bodies in Scotland and America. The first General Assembly of the new denomination was held in 1875 in Montreal, so it seemed perfectly clear to the powers that be in the church offices in Toronto that the centennial celebrations should take place in Montreal too.

The problem was that there was no realistically viable place to hold the festivities. Place des Artes was discussed then dropped when the costs became prohibitive. The First Presbyterian Church (the actual historic link to the Saint Gabriel Street congregation where it had all begun) had fallen on hard times with a dwindling congregation, a dilapidated building, and a vacant pulpit. To many, the big, beautiful, impressive Church of St. Andrew and St. Paul seemed the obvious choice, *but* the original St. Andrew's portion of the congregation had refused to enter the new denomination in 1875 and had remained in correspondence with the Church of Scotland and that made it totally unacceptable to one of the PCC's self-appointed historians.

The battle between him and the rest of us waxed and waned for months until finally a compromise was reached. The opening sederunt (session) of the 100th General Assembly would be held in the shabby sanctuary of First Presbyterian Church; the workaday sederunts would be housed in the Presbyterian College on the campus of McGill University; the big celebratory banquet would be hosted in the grand ballroom of the Windsor Hotel by the congregations of First Church, Knox-Crescent-Kensington Church in Notre Dame de Grace, and the downtown Church of St. Andrew and St. Paul. But the actual centennial worship service, to be broadcast live across Canada by the CTV network on Sunday morning, June 15, 1975, would be held in the sanctuary of the A & P.

My distinguished friend, mentor, and Knox College Professor of Homiletics and Liturgics, Dr. David Hay, was elected moderator of the Centennial General Assembly, and it was agreed that he would conduct the first part of the televised service and preach the sermon, resplendent in his royal blue robes and moderator's laces and ruffles. Between ourselves, Dr. Hay insisted that I, as the installed minister of the Church of St. Andrew and St. Paul, should preside over the Lord's table and the centennial celebration of the sacrament of Holy Communion. He also acquiesced, after some fairly heated discussion, to *my* insistence that, whereas he was robed in moderatorial splendour, I would dress in absolute simplicity, wearing only my black cassock, white stole, and preaching tabs. Visually, the contrast was so striking—and was interpreted so liturgically—that it became one of the most memorable elements of the centennial service.

The centennial banquet at the Windsor Hotel was memorable in quite a different way. First, a General Assembly banquet had never been held (at least not in living memory) in a setting as glittering as the grand ballroom of the Windsor Hotel—where, by the way, the St. Andrew's Society balls were held. As co-host, the Reverend Dr. Clifton J. MacKay waxed eloquently in welcoming the General Assembly's delegates, staff, and friends. I was honored to present the evening's entertainment, my dear friend and one of Quebec's most popular pop singers at that time, André Roc, whom Ann and I had met and befriended on a winter's cruise to the Caribbean earlier in the year.

But for me personally, the most moving and memorable moment in the whole week of events came during the closing sederunt, when Dr. Hay as moderator nominated me to accompany him to Edinburgh the next year to represent the Presbyterian Church in Canada at the General Assembly of the Church of Scotland of which more later.

As 1976 arrived, all thoughts in Montreal (or at least *most* of them) revolved around the Games of the XXI Olympiad, scheduled to be held in our city that summer. Looking ahead, the kirk session, at its January meeting, requested that I plan to be in the St. Andrew and St. Paul pulpit throughout the six weeks or so before, during, and after the Olympic Games. It was suggested that the elders would support my accepting the invitation of the moderator of the General Assembly to accompany him to the General Assembly of the Church of Scotland in mid-May that year and then combining the trip with a vacation visit to Scotland's places of particular interest to a young Canadian preacher.

The so-called "Quiet Revolution" of French separatists in Quebec had taken hold in *la belle province* during the 1960s but had become much noisier with the election of René Levesque as head of the *Parti Québécois* leading up to a provincial election to be held in the fall of 1976. Even before the election was called, things grew increasingly difficult, even dangerous, for English-speaking Quebeckers (anglophones), most of whom lived in and around Montreal. Fearful for the future, many anglophones fled the province, relocating to Kingston, Ottawa, Toronto, and points west, all the way to Calgary and Vancouver.

Nevertheless, with the encouragement of the kirk session and some of the leading Scottish-Canadian members of the congregation, we began to make plans to travel to the United Kingdom for the opening of the General Assembly of the Church of Scotland in mid-May and then on to England for a week or so, ending up in Paris for Ann's birthday on June 2. As we began to shape our plans, several truly astonishing things happened. First, the Duke of Argyll, Ian Campbell, invited us to visit Inverary Castle and arranged also for us to stay overnight on the Isle of Iona as guests of the parish minister. Then Viscount Melgund, newly come into the Earldom of Minto, invited us to visit him and Minnie in the Scottish border country. Alan McPherson, a dear friend from our year together at Princeton Seminary and now ministering in a parish church between Edinburgh and Glasgow, insisted that he would meet us at Prestwick Airport and take us home to rest up after our transatlantic flight.

Before long (and I don't remember the how's and whys) I also had an invitation to preach at vespers in a Norman-vintage church adjacent to the Cathedral of Warwick in the Cotswolds and another to preach the Sunday morning service in the Crown Court Church of Scotland in London's Covent Garden. Most astonishing of all, we received an invitation from Sir Martin Gilliat to have lunch with Her Majesty Queen Elizabeth the Queen Mother at Clarence House while we would be in London!

In no time at all, it seemed, we were winging our way across the Atlantic. As promised, Alan McPherson met us at Prestwick Airport, and I immediately stepped off the plane on the wrong foot. For the trip, I had decided to wear my black suit and clerical collar in hope, perhaps, of an upgrade to first class, which did not happen. As soon as Alan saw me—for the first time in twelve years—his face fell, and he muttered: "Why are you dressed like a Catholic priest?"

What Alan objected to, it turned out, were the steps I wore surrounding all but about two inches of my clerical collar. Presbyterian clergy in Scotland did *not* wear steps, and Alan suggested as diplomatically as possible that I divest myself of them, which, of course, I could not do, since they were attached to the rabat vest I wore with my collarless white clerical shirts.

But that turned out *not* to be the worst of my fashion faux pas! For informal travel and touring, Ann and I had equipped ourselves with matching patchwork denim jackets and jeans, complete with orange-threaded seams and huge bell-bottom cuffs. Alan and Maureen couldn't help laughing at our ridiculous mid-seventies attire. They were also surprised and clearly disappointed on learning of our plans to set off the next morning to rent a Morris Mini and begin our touring of Scotland. In anticipation of our visit, they had redecorated their guest room and hoped that we would occupy it for many more days. So we contented ourselves with a visit to Stirling Castle and Glasgow's St. Mungo's Cathedral and another long afternoon's nap, which in retrospect was just what we needed to overcome our jetlag.

On the following day, we undertook to track down Grandma Russell's family living in Coatbridge, a suburb of sorts between Glasgow and Edinburgh. Alan helped us find a telephone number; we called to make sure it would be convenient to visit later that same day; so when we pulled into the driveway of the Aunties' address, there they were, sitting on the front stoop, awaiting our arrival. As I unfolded myself from our Morris Mini and approached the front door, these two dear little old ladies burst into tears. "You are the spitting image of our father!" they exclaimed.

Once inside their very handsome townhouse on a very attractive tree-lined street, Ann and I were introduced properly to Uncle Matthew Murdoch, his wife Aunt Crawford, and her sister Aunt Annie Brown. In anticipation of our visit, they had prepared a sumptuous tea, and we had a long and lovely visit. I was particularly anxious to learn more about the distaff side of the Russell family in Scotland, especially the Browns, the Blairs, and the Clows. It turned out that Uncle Matthew, now retired, had long been the general manager of the Airdrie Dry Goods Store, somewhat akin to a department store in North America and was clearly a distinguished and prosperous retailer. All this information certainly put the lie to Grampa Russell's inferences that our Scots forebears were all poor, ignorant Kirkentilloch coal-miners and such! Over the succeeding years, it was my privilege to visit Uncle Matthew and the "Aunties" several times in the course of my Bible Society travels.

Early the next morning, we finally set off for Argyllshire and Inveraray Castle, which, unbeknownst to us, had suffered a devastating fire a few months before. On arrival, we found the castle in utter disrepair, the Duke of Argyll off in the United States raising funds for its restoration, and the duchess and her two children living in a wee croft on the estate, while sufficient repairs were being made to the castle to allow them to return there. Iona Campbell was graciousness itself, offering us tea and then a bed for the night.

After Ann did a quick tour of the croft, she realized that there was only one bedroom and that if we stayed the night, the duchess would have to sleep on the sofa in the main room. Since we already had a reservation for a bed and breakfast in Oban and an early start for our tour of the Isle of Mull and thence to the Isle of Iona, we firmly declined the offer of overnight hospitality.

But Iona wasn't finished with us yet. Earlier in the day, she had promised their son Torquhil, Marquess of Lorne, an afternoon's trip up into the highlands on the estate to a small loch where he wanted to go gull egg hunting. "Would I like to go with him?"

Of course, I would! So off we went, Iona and Ann in the front seats, Torquhil and I in the back of a dilapidated Range Rover, climbing higher and higher into ever more rugged and breathtaking terrain until we reached the loch in the middle of which sat a small island aswirl with white seagulls. We unpacked and inflated a small rubber dinghy and with one paddle Torquhil and I made our way over to the island to the squawking objection of all the gulls. The island was literally covered with small round nests in most of which two or three eggs were visible. With serious mien, Torquhil explained to me that we had to leave at least one egg in each nest to encourage the mother hen to lay at least another and then to remain on the nest until her eggs hatched. Within moments, the little plastic basket Torquhil had carried over to the island was full, but he wanted to collect more, since they were there in such abundance.

By then, it had started to rain—a soft gentle Highland rain—and we were getting very damp very quickly. To encourage Torquhil to finish up this adventure, I offered him my trilby rainhat, which he enthusiastically filled with still more eggs before calling it quits. By this time, the dinghy had an inch or so of rainwater in its bottom in which we both sat as I paddled us back to shore and thence back to the croft.

Nothing would do but that we must remain at least for more tea, which Iona began to bustle about preparing. Torquhil went upstairs to change out of his wet clothing, and Iona had the bright idea that I should take off my patchwork jeans and jacket to dry by the fire while we had tea. She gave me a blanket to wrap myself in and so there I sat in my damp underwear, being entertained by Her Grace, the Duchess of Argyll!

As a sort of footnote, let me add that my denim outfit did not dry by the fire, neither over the next couple of days on the Isle of Iona, and not until we reached Perth and the home of the parents of an A & P elder, Susan Stevenson, where central heating finally dispelled the Scotch mist of Inveraray.

While preparing tea, Iona had also hardboiled a half-dozen of the gull eggs Torquhil and I had collected and insisted that we take them with us as we left for Oban. Glad we were to have them, when we eventually made it to the manse of the Church of Scotland parish minister to spend the night on the Isle of Iona. His sister and housekeeper was *in alt* when we told her about the eggs: they are apparently considered a great delicacy in Scotland and doubly so to have been collected and cooked by the Marquess of Lorne and the Duchess of Argyll!

Our day at the Iona Abbey was memorable on many counts. Iona is actually a small fishing village on the edge of which sits the renowned Abbey, begun as a monastery in AD 563, where St. Columba first brought Christianity to Scotland. The abbey is not only a revered pilgrimage destination, but it houses a con-temporary worldwide fellowship of Benedictine-like monks with a monastic rule and almost-mystic liturgical tradition.

The island is very bleak. Harsh and bitter winds blow con-stantly, unimpeded on their transatlantic course from Canada's arctic clime. In fact, at times the wind blew so hard we could not walk forward and had to cling to fence posts to keep from being blown backward.

The night we were there was the occasion for the weekly candlelit 10:00 p.m. service of healing. The liturgy was intensely moving in its simplicity, and Ann and I were inspired to petition healing for a young woman of our congregation back in Montreal who had told me of her diagnosis of terminal cancer just before we had departed for Scotland.

Here, another sort of footnote: When we returned to Montreal after being away almost a month, one of the first calls we received was from this young woman, whose tumor had miraculously shrunk to an operable size and whose life was no longer in immediate danger of death. She, Ann, and I all wept as we related to her our prayers on her behalf at Iona Abbey just days before she had received the wondrous news of her remission!

From Iona, we recrossed the Isle of Mull, stopping briefly in Bunessen, to whose Scottish Gaelic hymn tune English poetess Eleanor Farjeon set the words to her 1931 song "Morning Has Broken." Once on the mainland, we drove up Scotland's west coast before turning inland across the top of the Duke of Argyll's massive estates on our way to Perth, the location of the historical museum of the Black Watch (Royal Highland Regiment) and the home of the aforementioned parents of Elder Susan Stevenson, where we finally dried out!

Saturday morning, we set out for Edinburgh by way of St. Andrew's, where we stopped briefly to pay our respects to the ancient University of St. Andrew's and golf's St. Andrew's Old Course. Heavy rain dampened our enthusiasm and urged us on to Edinburgh, where we had several days' reservations at a bed and breakfast establishment somewhere in the New Town's Royal Crescent.

Despite the grandeur of the address, the townhouse itself

proved to be dreadful: small, cramped, smelly, totally unacceptable as a place for us to stay for almost a week during the General Assembly of the Church of Scotland, which was due to
open on Monday. As we had made our way through Edinburgh
in the rain, we had recognized the venerable Roxburghe Hotel
on Charlotte Square, one of the hotels to which I had written
originally enquiring about room rates, availability, etc., before
realizing that it was really out of our price range.

However, by then we had actually spent very little on overnight accommodation, so we hauled our luggage out into the
little red Mini Minor and drove back to Charlotte Square and
threw ourselves on the mercy of the Roxburghe front desk. Be-
draggled and distraught as we were, we engaged the sympathy
of the desk clerk, who managed to find us a room for three
nights, a room that turned out to be the oval premier first-floor
center Adams Suite. We were thrilled! As soon as we had unpacked, I got on the telephone and contacted all those who were
expecting to be in touch with us in Edinburgh to explain that
we were *not* in Royal Crescent but in Charlotte Square. Then
we went out for dinner.

By the time we returned from dinner, the warm and gracious
hospitality that had marked our arrival had turned mysteriously
chilly! We had several messages: from the Duchess of Argyll;
the Countess of Minto; Lady George MacLeod, wife of the recently ennobled Baron MacLeod of Fuinary; and Sir Thomas
Waterlow, chairman of the board of the Royal Bank of Scotland.

Following Sunday morning worship at St. Giles High Kirk,
we were invited to the seaside home of Sir Thomas, who proved
to be a longtime friend of Ross and Betty McMaster, prominent
members of the A & P. After lunch, he arranged to take us down
the road a bit to have tea with the Earl and Countess of Weymss

and March. Gosford House, in East Lothian, was the earl's
family seat, which had been much damaged by fire while occupied by ailing veterans during World War II. The earl had represented Queen Elizabeth twice as Lord High Commissioner to
the General Assembly of the Church Scotland and would, in
fact, serve Her Majesty in that capacity again the following year.
He and his countess were certainly among the most interesting
members of the Scottish peerage we met during the whole trip!

We returned to Edinburgh just in time to attend the Sunday
evening service at the Greyfriars Kirk, after which we had
supper in a raucous pub as unexpected guests of a punter who
had just won the "pools!" Back at the Roxburghe, there were
more messages from the Duchess of Argyll and the Countess of
Minto; but it was too late to return them, so we just went to
bed.

The next morning, the atmosphere in the breakfast room at
the hotel had chilled from frosty to downright rude. We were
bewildered but had no idea what had gone wrong. Lady Mac-
Leod had kindly arranged a soup-and-sandwich luncheon in our
honour before the formal opening of the General Assembly.
That, she explained to her bemused guests, was what she
thought two young people from Canada would enjoy!

Another footnote: Lord and Lady MacLeod were occasional
visitors to the Church of St. Andrew and St. Paul whenever they
were in Canada, so Ann and I had already made their acquaintance and were charmed to be included in a party of Church of
Scotland dignitaries and, of course, Canadian moderator, Dr.
David Hay.

During lunch, after someone teased her Ladyship about the
humble fare by Edinburgh standards, she shared the following
riddle with much hilarity:

What is the difference between a Glaswegian and an Edinburgher?

When you visit a home in Glasgow, the host or hostess will say, "You'll have something to eat, won't you?"

But in Edinburgh, the question will be worded, "You'll have eaten, haven't you?"

Monday evening marked the formal opening of the General Assembly. Lord MacLeod was much in evidence, as was the Duke of Argyll, in his dual capacity as Hereditary Master of the Royal Household in Scotland and Keeper of the Great Seal of Scotland. David Hay and I were introduced and seated as representing the Presbyterian Church in Canada and then promptly but not completely forgotten.

Earlier in the afternoon, I had made contact by phone with Minnie, Countess of Minto, who, to my utter amazement, pleaded with me to check out of the Roxburghe Hotel and come to stay with them for a few days in the border county of Roxburghshire. She promised she would explain when we arrived. By then, the situation in Charlotte Square had gone from bad to worse—we were actually alarmed by the overt hostility of the hotel staff. It was clear that, once we had made an appearance at the opening of the General Assembly, there was actually nothing else for David Hay or me to do, so we made the difficult decision to check out of the Roxburghe in the morning and travel down to the Borders to stay with the Mintos.

Unfortunately, it did not occur to us to let anyone at the General Assembly know that we were leaving town. Unbeknownst to us, Her Majesty Queen Elizabeth the Queen Mother was currently in residence at Balmoral Castle and had instructed Sir Martin Gilliat to reach out to us at the assembly to invite us to have lunch with her there rather than the next week at Clarence House in London. So urgent announcements of a royal telephone call echoed through the assembly hall, where no one, including David Hay, knew where we had gone!

Gibby and Minnie lived in an apartment above what had originally been the Minto estate stables. The manor house had burned to the ground a generation or more before, and the makeshift home was all they truly could afford. During a walk on the grounds, Gibby explained how devastating death duties were for the landed gentry as were the annual ad valorem taxes on mature trees: the Mintos were actually cutting down at least one huge old tree a year simply to reduce their land taxes!

Over drinks before dinner, Minnie explained why she had been so insistent that we leave the Roxburghe Hotel to come and stay with them. She was a cancer survivor; but while she was undergoing treatments in Edinburgh, she had stayed at the Roxburghe, only to be treated as rudely as we were. She explained that the hotel was notorious for being anti-aristocracy; she had been consigned to a broomcloset-sized room over an airshaft above the kitchens, and she was fearful of how the hotel staff would treat us once we began to receive the very messages that had apparently turned everyone at the Roxburghe against us!

Staying with the Mintos was a real eye-opener for Ann and me. They were living just above the poverty line; Minnie confessed that she was always glad to have houseguests as that was the only time Gibby would allow her to turn on the hot water heater! Yet they were expected to dress and act and entertain as befits the public's image of an earl and countess.

A case in point was the so-styled world premiere of a documentary film about a "famous" local poet, William Knox, which the Mintos were inveigled into hosting for a group of Edinburgh literati one of the evenings we were there. We helped set up folding chairs, passed canapés, served drinks, and generally made ourselves useful to the Mintos, who had not arranged any extra servers for the evening. To our astonishment, once the film had been shown and discussed, the entire group got up and left without a word of thanks or "can we help?" In fact, one of the Edinburgh grande dames said to the Countess of Minto as she was departing: "You must be so pleased to have hosted the world premiere of such an important documentary film!"

With the weekend drawing near and my appointment to preach in Warwick looming large on my mind, we bid the Mintos a fond farewell and set off for York, just over the Scottish border in England. As we drove, we thought it might be wise to get in touch with Sir Martin Gilliat at Clarence House to make sure our lunch date with the Queen Mother was still on. Having been taught by Alan McPherson how to use tuppence coins in the public pay telephones, we stopped at a kiosk by the roadside, and I put in a call to London.

As Sir Martin answered the phone, the characteristic "beep-beep-beeps" of the pay phone system kept interrupting us until in exasperation he yelled at me: "For God's sake, man, put in a 10p coin!" Of course, Alan, thrifty Scot that he was, had never thought to teach me that a British ten-pence coin was the same size, shape and weight as a tuppence and bought more than *ten times* the length of phone conversation between the infernal "beep-beep-beep" interruptions! Fortunately, I had a couple of ten-p's in my pocket, and we were able to confirm our lunch date with the Queen Mother for the following Thursday.

Visiting Yorkminster Cathedral for the first time was an incredible experience. There is a narrow spiral stone staircase up one corner of one of the two huge stone towers that front the cathedral, then a narrow catwalk across the eave of the roof to the opposite side where an identical well-worn narrow stone spiral staircase leads one back down again, which we climbed, traversed, and descended with heart-in-mouth trepidation and heart-felt thanksgiving when finally we were once again on terra firma!

York is very near the archeological site of the remainder of Hadrian's Wall—a defensive fortification in the Roman province of Britannia, begun in AD 122 in the reign of the Emperor Hadrian—which we visited in honour of our fondly remembered high school Latin teachers. We found the city of York charming, especially the narrow streets of half-timbered houses leaning out over the sidewalks. Our bed and breakfast accommodation was a rambling old inn with uneven floors, sloping ceilings, and lumpy beds: all part of the Yorkshire tourist experience.

Our next destination was the industrial city of Coventry, where the historic old cathedral had been all but destroyed by German bombs during World War II. The newly rebuilt cathedral featured striking stained-glass windows on which Lawrence Lee, the artisan responsible for the ten gigantic clerestory windows in the Church of St. Andrew and St. Paul, had worked under the supervision of the renowned stained-glass designer John Piper.

Unfortunately, we reached Coventry at the height of a Friday rush hour. As we followed a very congested ring road into the heart of the city, we could see the cathedral spire ahead on the right, but driving on the wrong side of the road as I was, I could not find a way off the ring road until suddenly the cathedral spire was in my rearview mirror. We made the circuit three times, never finding an appropriate exit until we gave up and retraced our travels out to the suburbs, where we found our reserved bed and breakfast accommodation.

The next morning, we set off again and found our way easily into the city on regular streets. As we drove, we discussed our day. We wanted to see the Lawrence Lee windows, true; but we were by now so close to Stratford-upon-Avon that we thought it would be fun to try to see a matinee performance of a Shakespearean play if one were offered that day. Given that we had been on the road for over a week by now, Ann was anxious to do some laundry. Seeing a laundromat with a parking place in front of it, we stopped and offloaded the suitcase full of dirty clothes for Ann to wash, while I set off on foot to find a post office and a store where I could buy the makings of a picnic lunch when we reached Stratford-Upon-Avon.

At a convenience store next to the laundromat, Ann bought a small box of detergent and proceeded to do a load of wash-and-wear. I found the post office, mailed a batch of postcards back to Canada, then found a delicatessen where I bought a couple of sandwiches, a bag of crisps, and a couple of chocolate chip cookies for lunch, all of which I packed in the boot of our little red Mini. By the time I returned to the laundromat, Ann had finished her work and had packed everything freshly laundered into the suitcase in which she had brought them. When I told her that I had done my errands and had packed a picnic lunch in the boot, she immediately asked, "Did you get us something to drink?"

Whoops! No, I had not, whereupon she suggested that I duck into the convenience store where she had bought her detergent because she had noticed that they also had some beer for sale, which I did. The place smelled very odd, and I almost left, when a very polite Pakistani store-keeper offered to fetch me a four-pack of a popular brand of beer. I agreed, hastily paid, and breathed a sigh of relief when I got back to the car and squeezed the beer in its cardboard carrying case into the boot.

Then we were off: a quick visit to the cathedral to see the Lawrence Lee windows (magnificent!), then a mad dash to Stratford-upon-Avon where, mirabile dictu, there were tickets available for the afternoon performance of *As You Like It*.

We found a charming picnic spot on the banks of the Avon River, but when I raised the boot cover to get out our lunch makings, out wafted instead the reek of the convenience store! Horrified that I had fouled the air with the cardboard beer carton, I quickly threw it away! We managed to eat our lunch despite the foul odor emanating from everything we took out of the boot, saw the play (eminently forgettable!), and drove on to Chipping Campden, where we had a two-night reservation at the Noël Arms Inn, one of the oldest hostelries in the Cotswolds.

Unpacking our luggage, we were dismayed to realize that everything smelled even worse than it had at lunchtime. Since I was scheduled to preach in Warwick the next day, Ann decided to forego dinner in the very fine restaurant attached to the inn in favor of finding a laundromat and rewashing at least our underwear and a clean white shirt for me, which we did.

Rewashing made absolutely no difference, so off we went to Warwick the next day, reeking like what I was now calling "the beer store!" To our amazement, we learned that I was actually to preach in the Beauchamp Chapel of the Collegiate Church of St. Mary, founded in 1123 and rebuilt in 1704 after a disastrous fire in 1694. It turned out that Warwick does not have a cathedral exactly but rather a collegiate church equivalent to a cathedral but with a college of secular canons instead of a bishop. One of the oldest extant houses of worship in Britain, it was breathtakingly beautiful in architecture as well as in music, and I would have enjoyed myself immensely had I not smelled like a beer-storekeeper!

On Monday morning, we set off on the short drive to Bath, where we intended to spend the day enjoying the many tourist attractions made famous in the Regency novels of Georgette Heyer. First, we toured the Abbey Church of Saint Peter and Saint Paul, commonly known as Bath Abbey. Founded in the seventh century, Bath Abbey was reorganised in the tenth century and rebuilt in the twelfth and sixteenth centuries and is one of the largest examples of Perpendicular Gothic architecture in the West Country. Spectacular in every respect, this was probably the ecclesiastical high point of our entire trip.

By the time we were finished in the abbey, Ann was beginning to feel unwell. We had luncheon reservations in the actual pump room of the Roman Bath, but Ann had lost her appetite, so we sat on a park bench, shared some ice cream, after which Ann pleaded with me to fetch the car and drive her to the bed and breakfast at which we had a night's reservation halfway between Bath and Wells.

Leaving Bath by car was a nightmare of one-way streets and inadequate signage. Ann tried to help navigate, but she was so nauseous it took all her energy and concentration to keep from throwing up all over the interior of our little red Mini. Eventually, we made it out of the city and were nearing the bed and breakfast locale, when Ann began to feel better. By the time we reached the driveway into the charming rural farmhouse that was to be our home for the night, Ann confessed that she was "feeling fine, didn't want to stop; maybe we could make it to Wells?" which we did.

Wells Cathedral is set in the medieval heart of England's smallest city and is the earliest English cathedral to be built in the Gothic style. The current building was erected between the twelfth and fifteenth centuries and is a significant landmark in Somerset and the South West. The cathedral boasts the famous

Wells Clock, which is considered to be the second oldest clock mechanism in Great Britain; the fascinating octagonal Chapter House; the Jesse Window, which is considered to be one of the finest examples of medieval stained glass in Europe; one of only four chained libraries in the UK; and the medieval Vicars' Close, believed to be the most complete example of a medieval Close in the United Kingdom.

Not having expected to spend much time in Wells, we were charmed! After enjoying the cathedral, we went to a delightful little tea shop for some refreshments, having missed lunch altogether. Ann began to tell our waitress how she had felt so badly earlier in the day and now felt just fine. Our waitress explained that she had heard the same story over and over. Many people prove to be violently allergic to Bath's sulfurous vapors from the Roman baths but recover as soon as they leave the area. "Tomorrow," she warned, "don't be surprised if your poop comes out bright yellow!" which, in fact, it did!

Refreshed — and the day still young — we set off for Salisbury, hoping to find a bed and breakfast along the way. What we found instead was Longleat House, the ancestral home of the Marquesses of Bath and the setting for the BBC's immensely popular televised adaptation of Anthony Trollope's chronicles of the Pallisers, which had begun being shown on American and Canadian television just the year prior to our visit. Our little guidebook informed us that Longleat House currently housed the complete collection of Victorian era costumes from the television series, and I decided that we *had* to stop. It was nearing the end of the day, and we had the house nearly to ourselves, along with a very patient curator who was delighted to meet Canadian fans of the series and who escorted us through the magnificent state rooms of what many historians describe as one of the finest examples of Elizabethan architecture in Britain.

The original house caught fire and burnt down in April 1567, and a replacement house was effectively completed by 1580, eventually to be surrounded by a 9,800-acre park including gardens designed by Capability Brown and the world's longest hedge maze with 1.69 miles of pathways.

On the recommendation of that curator, we drove on into Salisbury and found an amusingly historic little bed and breakfast, where we spent the night, very tired and very happy.

The next morning, our first stop was Salisbury Cathedral, formally known as the Cathedral Church of the Blessed Virgin Mary, an Anglican cathedral and one of the leading examples of Early English architecture. The main body of the cathedral was completed in only thirty-eight years, from 1220 to 1258. Since 1549, the cathedral has had the tallest church spire in the United Kingdom at 404 feet, plus the largest cloister and the largest cathedral close in Britain at eighty acres. It contains a clock that is among the oldest working clocks in the world and has the best surviving example of the four original copies of Magna Carta.

Only eight miles north of Salisbury is Stonehenge, England's most iconic prehistoric ruin, built in several stages, with the earliest constructed an estimated 5,000 or more years ago. It is an eerie place, despite the throngs of visitors; but the day was fine, and we spent an enjoyable hour or so absorbing the aura of a place of worship archeologists believe may have served humans for that purpose as many as 10,000 years ago.

By now, we were about eighty miles southwest of London and were beginning to think about the enormous consequence of the first item on our itinerary there: lunch with Her Majesty Queen Elizabeth The Queen Mother at Clarence House on Thursday. Despite several laundromat efforts as opportunities arose, Ann had thus far been unable to eradicate the beer store smell from our underwear, socks, and shirts and wanted one more chance to wash away the foul odor. Besides, we had pretty well seen and done all that we had hoped to do on our brief tour of rural England, so we decided to spend another night in our Salisbury bed and breakfast, do the laundry, and go to bed early. Using a telephone at our b. & b., I contacted a Holiday Inn in London's Holland Park neighborhood, recommended by some friends in Montreal as a more economical part of the city in which to stay, and succeeded in getting a reservation for one night, the night before we were to visit the Queen Mother at noon.

On Thursday morning, we ate a light breakfast, packed the car for our eventual departure, and figured out how to get relatively close to Clarence House on the Tube. We arrived just before 11:00 a.m., in time to see the actual daily Changing of the Guard, which included an impressive display of soldiers marching to and fro, replacing one another, including several posted at the front and back entrances to Clarence House. We had been instructed to appear at the back door, facing the surprisingly stark approach to St. James's Palace next door, the most senior royal palace in the United Kingdom and the formal base for the Royal Court, which makes it the actual diplomatic heart of the United Kingdom.

Assuring the busbied soldier standing guard right beside the door that we were, indeed, expected by the Queen Mother, we knocked and were admitted by William, Her Majesty's long-serving butler and general factotum. He led us through a warren of working offices to a sort of waiting area adjacent to Sir Martin Gilliat's office, where we were invited to wait until Her Majesty would be free to receive us.

And wait we did. In due course, we were welcomed by Sir Martin as well as HM's Comptroller (whose name and title we never did learn) and her faithful and familiar lady-in-waiting, Mrs. Frances Campbell-Preston, whom we had previously met in Canada. Each and all apologized for the delay in joining the Queen Mother for lunch, explaining that she was minding the store while the Queen and Prince Philip were abroad somewhere. Apparently, there was that very day a run on the Bank of England's stash of pounds sterling, and the Queen Mother was being kept busy by the Chancellor of the Exchequer, who was running back and forth between Clarence House and St. James's Palace to obtain royal assent for an ongoing crisis management effort to prop up the British economy.

After a couple of hours of this fascinating ado, we realized that we had to get back to the Holiday Inn to check out, return our rental car, and check into the bed-and-breakfast establishment in Ebury Street where we had a reservation for a week's stay. We kept offering to leave, Sir Martin kept insisting we stay until we explained that we simply *had* to leave, which we prepared to do. At the back door, we were intercepted by William, profusely apologizing on the Queen Mother's behalf and insisting that we return at four o'clock at least to have tea with Her Majesty before she left Clarence House to preside over some ceremony at the University of London of which she was chancellor. Naturally, we agreed.

I still break into a sweat when I remember our frantic trip out to Holland Park and then our drive back into the city to find our Ebury Street b. & b., literally a stone's throw from the Royal Mews and a couple of blocks from Pall Mall with Buckingham Palace at one end and Westminster Abbey and the Houses of Parliament at the other. We roared into the b. & b., dropped off our luggage with a hurried explanation that we were late for tea with the Queen Mother, rushed to return our rental car at a kiosk nearby, and hailed a taxi to Clarence

House, leaving behind a series of bemused and skeptical folk who (in our imagination, at least) couldn't quite believe that two tourists who smelled like we did could *possibly* have an urgent appointment with *royalty*!

But we did, and the minute we arrived again at the back door to Clarence House, we were met by William and whisked into the front part (actually the Clarence House part) of the residence to join Sir Martin and Mrs. Campbell-Preston in the Queen Mother's private parlour. There was no time for instructions or explanations: the arrival of a bouncy pair of Welsh corgis announced the entrance of Her Majesty Queen Elizabeth The Queen Mother! Ann and I rose as one; I bowed and murmured, "Your Majesty"; Ann curtsied and said nothing because Her Majesty was already smiling and saying, "How kind of you to come back after the way we treated you this morning, and how nice to see you both again!"

And that's how the rest of the visit went. After a few moments' chitchat, Her Majesty invited us to come into her private dining room for tea. A small round table was set for four with fine china cups and saucers, gleaming sterling silver, crisp white linens, a nosegay of fresh flowers, and a mind-boggling array of tea sandwiches, petits fours, chocolates, and mints. As we were about to sit down, the Queen Mother remarked that there were only four places set, but there were five of us, including Sir Martin and Mrs. Campbell-Preston. "Never mind," Her Majesty said, "we'll just squeeze the chairs a little closer and make room for Martin!"

Her Majesty presided over her tea table; in fact, other than William, we never saw another servant during our entire visit. As she poured out the tea, she managed to dribble a spot on the beautiful white linen table cloth. She glanced at me, seated at her left, checking to see if I had noticed, which, of course, I had.

As soon as she had poured out her own cup of tea and invited us to help ourselves, I immediately offered her a plate of cucumber sandwiches, which she graciously declined, so I set the plate down right over the tea stain, at which she glanced at me and gave me a wink!

Amid rambling general conversation, the Queen Mother suddenly turned to me and asked, "Will our daughter be safe in your city during the Olympics?" I was stunned not only at the intimacy of her question but even more at her awareness of the dangers of the francophone sovereignty issues already roiling the political and social landscape in Quebec. I realized that hers was not a polite topic-of-conversation question, but rather an expression of her deep personal concern for the Queen's safety as she traveled to Canada to preside over the opening and closing ceremonies of the Olympic Games as the sovereign head of the host country.

Eventually, I replied, to this effect: "Ma'am, I believe that the Queen will be safe in Montreal. Like most English Canadians, the French Canadians by and large love and admire the Queen and the Royal Family. Their argument is not with our constitutional monarchy but with the two-hundred-plus years of history during which the French fact in Canada has largely been suppressed in favor of the overwhelmingly English majority in every province save Quebec.

"The very most helpful thing the Queen could do to further Canadian unity would be to go to the games' opening and closing ceremonies fearlessly, visit the various venues as often as possible, entertain frequently on board the Royal Yacht, and maybe hold some kind of heads of state dinner in one of the historic old downtown hotels like the Ritz Carlton," whereupon I sort of ran out of steam.

"You have given us a lot to think about," responded Her

Majesty, "but we shall share your suggestions with the Queen." And, lo and behold, when the games of the XXI Olympiad began in Montreal's Big O on July 17, 1976, that is exactly what the Queen did!

It turned out that the Queen Mother was already dressed and ready to leave for the University of London to preside (as I have already mentioned) over some ceremony as chancellor. When it was time for her to leave, she was all apologies for cutting our visit so short. Then she explained that there was a custom at Clarence House that whoever was in the house when Her Majesty departed for some royal event would gather on the front steps and wave the Queen Mother off. Would we like to do that? Would we! "Well," Her Majesty asked, "where is your camera?"

"We didn't presume to bring one to such a private occasion," I replied.

"Good for you! Then," she said, turning to her butler, William, "once we are gone, show the Russells around. Surely they would enjoy seeing some of the things we would have shown them had there been more time." Her Daimler was waiting at the door. Sir Martin and Mrs. Campbell-Preston climbed in, then so did she, and they were off, leaving William, Ann, and me waving serenely as though this were an everyday occurrence.

"Her Majesty must think a lot of you," William confessed once they were out of sight. "She doesn't often instruct me to show people around," which he did for about an hour, casually handing us precious mementos of her travels and taking us into her formal reception room, where we saw the incredible collection of the framed line drawings of Windsor Castle by artist Augustus Johns, commissioned by King George VI at the outbreak of World War II when he feared that Hitler would perversely try to destroy the famed castle from which the Royal House of

Windsor drew its name.

Eventually, we made our way back to Ebury Street, where the owner of our b. & b. was waiting to ask us: "Who *are* you?" and, "Did you *really* just have tea with the Queen Mother?" It turned out that, in our brief absence, a bouquet of flowers, a bottle of champagne, and a cluster of telephone messages from various distinguished and titled personages had all been received at Haggis House (as we learned to call our London residence), whose owner was quite unaccustomed to such ado over arriving guests. So we explained who we were and why we were in London, and, yes, we had just returned from Clarence House where we had indeed had tea with Her Majesty.

But our most important question for "Lord Haggis," as we began to refer to our host between ourselves, was, "Is there a *laundromat* nearby?" There was, and with instructions as to how to find it, her suitcase full of smelly clothing and her half-empty box of laundry detergent, Ann set off to try again to rid our belongings of that beer store smell! Once she found the laundromat, Ann emptied the suitcase into a washing machine, took out her detergent, and prepared to add it to the load, whereupon several of the other ladies doing their laundry began to shriek: "You can't use that stuff here! You'll have us all smelling like '*Pakis*!'"

At last, the mystery was solved: the foul odor culprit had all along been the Pakistani-preferred laundry detergent, and instead of improving the smell of our underwear, socks, and shirts, it had been worsening that acrid aroma with every washer load that Ann had done using that particular product!

Back at Haggis House, we had become instant celebrities, with Lord Haggis telling each and every tourist staying there that we were on intimate terms with the Royal Family and had just had tea with the Queen Mother. His sycophantic admiration only expanded when, as arranged by Sir Martin, we went to the Tower of London for the Ceremony of the Keys, during which the Yeomen Warders of the Tower lock themselves and their nightly handful of special guests in, gate by gate by gate until we all stood in the central courtyard and they lowered the Union Jack to the strains of "God Save the Queen."

To Lord Haggis's delight, we also attended a West End theatrical performance of which Sir Martin was one of the investing angels, followed by supper at one of London's most exclusive after-theatre restaurants. Another night, Angus Murray, an elder at the Church of St. Andrew and St. Paul who happened to be in London at the same time as us, arrived at Haggis House in a black limousine to escort us to a dinner at one of his clubs.

By Sunday, it almost felt anticlimactic to find our way to Covent Garden, where I was to preach in the Crown Court Church of Scotland, the actual Protestant place of worship founded by King James I when as King James VI of Scotland he had come to London in 1603 to succeed his aunt, Queen Elizabeth I, on the throne as King of Great Britain. By comparison with the spectacular Anglican churches, abbeys, and cathedrals we had been seeing, the Crown Court Church was puritan-plain, a simple sanctuary dominated by a huge hand-carved representation of the royal coat of arms of James I.

The most memorable part of that event turned out to be the appearance of my uncle, Henry Russell, and his wife Josie in the congregation. One of my father's three younger brothers, Hank had served in the Royal Canadian Navy during World War II and had returned to a promising career with the Ford Motor Company of Canada, which at that time was headquartered in Windsor, Ontario. He was presently working for Ford as an executive with a NATO project and living in Brussels.

Learning from my father of our visit to London, he and Aunt Josie decided to travel over to England for the weekend and surprise us at the Crown Court Church, which indeed they did.

The Monday following all this excitement, we took time to do some souvenir shopping in London. In particular, we bought *something* (I can't remember what, maybe a tea towel?) at Harrod's in order to obtain one of their iconic shopping bags. But our main purchase was at Selfridge's, where we fell in love with a charming Goebel porcelain nativity set comprised entirely of precious little Hummel figurines of children complete with a rustic crèche, all of which we were able to have shipped directly home to Montreal rather than carrying it around for the rest of our trip. Ann and I displayed it fondly in our several homes for the rest of our lives together, and eventually I was pleased to send it to the Klopp family as one of their first heritage gifts after Sherri and I moved from Destin to Ponte Vedra Beach.

I also had the temerity to deliver to Clarence House one of the little jugs of pure Canadian maple syrup we had obtained before we left Montreal as bread-and-butter gifts for our various hostesses of which, I figured, the Queen Mother had certainly become one. Sir Martin sent us a sweet little handwritten thank-you note on behalf of Her Majesty, which I believe I still have somewhere among my memorabilia.

In truth, Ann had originally not wanted to make this trip with me, thinking it would be heavily laden with ecclesiastical appearances and obligations. To sweeten the deal, I had promised to take her to Paris for her birthday on June 2. So on Tuesday morning, we packed up and left Haggis House, taking the boat train all the way to Paris, where we had a reservation at a small, out-of-the-way *boite* near the Champs Elysées and the Arc de Triomphe. Fortunately, the English Channel was calm for our crossing, and we fell asleep in our deck chairs.

Our hotel room was small but charmingly Parisian, with floor-to-ceiling French window doors opening onto a tiny balcony where the sun shone every late afternoon. Our first full day in Paris we spent walking, walking, and walking until we were exhausted. That evening, I had arranged as a birthday treat tickets for the famed Folies-Bergère, which we didn't find nearly as risqué as we had expected. No matter: we could hardly keep our eyes open and left at the intermission to go back to our hotel and to bed.

The next day, after a continental breakfast of incredible coffee and mouthwatering croissants, we had our sights set on the Notre Dame cathedral church on the Île de France and then the Louvre museum. We made it to Notre Dame and climbed the winding stone staircase to one of the towers, which nearly did us in. Determinedly, we trudged across the Seine to the Louvre, took one look at the line of tourists waiting patiently to be admitted, and went back to our hotel for a long nap. *Bifteck et frites* at a little restaurant near the hotel rounded out our day of Paris sightseeing.

After another scrumptious continental breakfast, we gathered our belongings and headed for the relatively new Charles de Gaulle airport for our nonstop flight back to Montreal. The airport's Terminal I was already famous for its contemporary circular design of tubular glass-enclosed escalators and walkways leading up and over and out to the radiating satellite buildings. But the thing that most sticks in my memory was my first experience of wide-open restrooms with female attendants to hand us men linen towelettes *after* we washed our hands!

The two weeks of the Olympic Games were, in fact, a bit of a letdown for me. Even though we had volunteer docents on duty in our open sanctuary every day, very few visitors actually came in. Likewise, the anticipated influx of Sunday worshipers turned out to be about what any summer Sunday might bring. The big thrill for me was the presence of Queen Elizabeth II and Prince Philip not only opening and closing the games but attending one or more venues every day and entertaining nightly on the Royal Yacht *Britannia* and actually hosting a semi-state banquet for visiting heads of state one evening at the Ritz Carlton Hotel, a block from Richelieu Place—exactly what I had suggested to the Queen Mother during that fateful May tea party.

That autumn, I confess, is entirely missing from my memory bank now, some forty years later! What I do remember, for reasons that will be apparent as I record it, is how the St. Andrew's Society was in full flight with its distinguished guests of honour for that year, Angus, the newly elevated 15th Duke of Hamilton and 12th Duke of Brandon and his duchess, Sarah. As Hereditary Keeper of the Palace of Holyrood House in Edinburgh and Hereditary Bearer of the Crown of Scotland, he was the premier Scots peer, save for the Prince of Wales, who bears the preeminent hereditary title of Duke of Rothesay when in Scotland. His Grace was reputedly, as our Scottish-Canadian friends used to say, very high in the instep. The powers-that-be of the St. Andrew's Society stood in such awe of him as compared with the previous years' peers that Sunday-after-church brunch at the manse was out of the question. According to Ann, this was a mixed blessing. On the one hand, it was a blessed relief not to have to plan and prepare for another ducal entertainment; but on the other hand, it was, in her opinion, a genuine insult for us not to be considered *worthy* of doing so!

As it turned out, Angus and Sarah did attend worship in the kirk that year: she lit the first candle on the Advent wreath and he read the gospel lesson. After the service as we were saying our goodbyes, His Grace took me aside and queried: "Two years ago, you had Ian and Iona Campbell for Sunday brunch after church. Why didn't we rate such an invitation this year?"

"Oh, Your Grace," I replied, "you and your duchess were considered to be much too important to be offered such humble fare as ours!"

"Too bad!" he replied. "Iona Campbell told Sarah that they had had such a wonderful time with you that we were really looking forward to it!"

And so began and ended the tradition of our entertaining the St. Andrew's Society's annual titled guests of honour at the manse. The only exception was in 1981, in our final month in Montreal, when we happily provided Sunday lunch *en famille* for the Earl and Countess of Strathmore and Kinghorne, cousins of HM the Queen Mother, whose deft hand—or perhaps Sir Martin's—made it happen.

In the dead of winter (pun intended), one of the most distinguished members of the congregation, Richard B. Angus, died after a brief illness, and I was asked to conduct his funeral in the Church of St. Andrew and St. Paul and later the same day his interment in a private family cemetery on the family's historic estate near Senneville in the Eastern Townships. Mr. Angus was a scion of the Angus family, which had figured so prominently in the development of the Canadian Pacific Railway in the nineteenth and early twentieth centuries of Canadian history. The turnout for his funeral was huge! Up to that point, I had never seen the sanctuary quite so full for such an occasion, but what I remember most was his interment later in the day.

Even before the start of the funeral in Montreal, it had begun snowing, and by the time his cortège set off for the Eastern Townships we were creeping along under near-blizzard conditions. It took us hours to reach the Angus property and the charming little local chapel Richard had had demolished, moved, and rebuilt in a remote corner of the estate. He had even registered the parcel of land as a cemetery so that his remains could be buried there.

As the hearse and my limousine pulled up at the chapel doors, I wrapped myself in my wonderfully warm full-length wool felt clergy cape, stepped out of the limo at the back of the hearse, and escorted the casket—as was my wont—into the chapel. Once inside, I slipped off my cape—again as was my wont and an action familiar to the undertaker—and led the procession down the chapel's short aisle, realising as I walked that the sanctuary was jam-packed with local residents, family retainers, and representatives of the local municipality, all of whom had been waiting for hours in an unheated building and were all chilled to the bone.

I was almost as cold, for, having doffed my cape, I was in my shirtsleeves under my lightweight cassock, so I made the second funeral of the day mercifully short and quickly led the casket and pallbearers back up the aisle, where the undertaker was waiting with my cape in his arms. Once outside, where it was snowing and blowing ominously, I was led around the corner of the chapel to a raw grave, freshly dug, with a mound of earth to one side and flimsy straps laid across the hole on which the casket was placed for my words of committal.

"I am the resurrection and the life . . ." I began, when a sudden gust of wind swirled around the corner of the chapel, caught my cape like a sail, lifted me off my feet, and slipped me down into the grave between the casket and the edge of the hole. I paused, not knowing quite what to do next, when the undertaker and Mr. Angus's son, Freddie, reached down, grabbed my arms at my elbows, and neatly lifted me up out of the grave, set me firmly on my feet, and I continued: "He that believeth in me, though he were dead, yet shall he live" (Jn 11:25)!

Unfortunately, neither the success of the XXI Olympiad nor the valiant efforts of Queen Elizabeth II during the two weeks of the Games the previous summer had dampened the rising tide of French-Canadian nationalism and enthusiasm for Quebec sovereignty if not complete separation from the rest of Canada. As far back as 1968, with the founding of a new pro-independence political party, le Parti Québécois, agitation in favor of separation had been ominously growing and troubling *la belle province* politically, economically, socially, and ecclesiastically. Unbeknownst to most of the rest of the world, pro-independence factions within the province had terrorized the anglophone population with bombings, kidnappings, assassinations, and threats of even more violence. So dangerous had everyday life become that Ann and I decided upon a code word that if spoken over the telephone in an otherwise innocent-sounding conversation would prompt her to get in the car; drive to each of our children's three schools; gather Sarah, Kirk, and Rebecca together; and flee the province as quickly as she could!

After enjoying but modest success on the political scene at first, on November 15, 1976, the Parti Québécois won a Quebec general election under the leadership of the charismatic René Lévesque with his insistent promises of a referendum on what he termed "sovereignty-association" during its first term in government.

True to its word, on April Fool's Day, April 1, 1977, the Parti Québécois cynically published its long-awaited White Paper on Language Policy, which eventually became known as "Bill 101."

The consternation in anglophone Quebec was palpable, so much so that it overwhelmed any other conversation or consideration in the congregation and community represented by the Church of St. Andrew and St. Paul. It was, ironically, the week before Holy Week, and I was scheduled to complete a Lenten sermon series on "Revelation's Seven Cities" with a Palm Sunday message referencing the apocalyptic promise in St. John's letter to the church at Philadelphia:

> Because you have kept my word of patient endurance,
> I will keep you from the hour of trial that is coming on the
> whole world to test the inhabitants of the earth (Rev 3:10).

As tempting as was this particular text, I instead announced to my congregation that during the past forty-eight hours I had become convinced that the completion of a sermon series was not as compelling a concern in the minds and hearts of my parishioners today as was the consternation caused by the provincial government's publication on Friday of its White Paper on Language Policy. "Oblique, if not direct, political comment has been an important part of this winter's sermon series, drawn from the apocalyptic books of the Bible," I admitted. "Perhaps the time has come for a frank and forthright application of what I have been preaching to the developing political and cultural crisis in Quebec."

At the conclusion of the sermon (see Appendix I), I informed the congregation that I had prepared a letter protesting several aspects of the proposed language legislation and addressed it to Dr. Camille Laurin, the Minister of State for Cultural Development in the Parti Québécois government. Indicating that it had been an intensely personal and uniquely difficult exercise and that I had consulted neither the kirk session nor the board of trustees, I admitted that I realized that, like it or not, my writing to the provincial government as I had done would reflect upon this church and its congregation. Thinking that it might be well to provide an opportunity for a few of those in attendance to associate themselves with me and my letter in a supportive way, I left some blank sheets of church stationery on the tables in the narthex, which if there should happen to be any signatures on any of them after the service, I would attach them to my letter before mailing it.

Any signatures? There were more than *a hundred*! My open letter to Camille Laurin became an immediate cause célèbre, and I was suddenly the unofficial spokesperson for the English-speaking minority of Quebeckers, at least in and around Montreal. Someone provided a copy to the *Montreal Gazette*, and by Tuesday the entire text headlined the op-ed page of the newspaper. On Wednesday, the paper published a very laudatory article written by its religion editor, complete with a large photograph of me with the A & P's distinctive tower in the background, praising me for championing the anglophone cause!

Then all hell broke loose! I was summoned to Dr. Laurin's office in Montreal, where he demanded an opportunity to address the St. Andrew and St. Paul congregation in rebuttal to my letter. I responded that he would be welcome to attend an informal congregational gathering in the church's Kildonan Hall following the morning worship service on any Sunday at his convenience. Not Easter Sunday (thank goodness!) but a Sunday six weeks hence was his choice.

On the day appointed, Kildonan Hall filled rapidly and completely in anticipation of Dr. Laurin's remarks. I introduced him graciously and then joined Ann, sitting amid my congregation. Dr. Laurin, who spoke beautiful English, immediately launched into an excoriating ad hominem attack on me personally, during which and totally spontaneously various members of the congregation began to hiss, softly at first and then with increasing volume until Dr. Laurin stopped in mid-sentence and said in effect, "I've gotten off on the wrong foot, haven't I? You obviously think very highly of your minister, so I think I had better begin again on a different tack."

The congregation sat respectfully through the rest of his lengthy remarks, completely unmoved and unimpressed. At the end, Dr. Laurin offered to respond to questions of which there were few and then the congregation rose in one body and silently left the room. Dr. Laurin was at once both chastised and furious. "We will speak of this again," he muttered to me and left, his entourage following in the same sort of silent standoff.

From that day on, I was the go-to guy for the local media whenever a new development in the French-language legislation process became public. Radio, television, and newspaper reporters were calling me time and again and recording and reporting with varying degrees of accuracy what I had to say about whatever was on people's minds that day or week. More rapidly than anyone expected, the Charter of the French Language was passed by the Parti Québécois in the provincial Legislature on August 26, 1977.

In the aftermath of my initial confrontation with Dr. Camille Laurin and leading up to the June 1977 General Assembly of the Presbyterian Church in Canada, I had been approached about heading up a special committee on national unity about which I felt honored and with the support of the kirk session I agreed to do. The General Assembly approved the idea, and the committee was formed to meet at the call of the convener and to report back to the 1978 assembly.

The deliberations of the special committee on aational unity were held alternately in Toronto and Montreal. From the outset, it became clear that the committee members from parts of Canada other than Quebec had little knowledge of and even less interest in the rise of Québécois nationalism and its impact on the everyday lives of the anglophone and ethnic minority communities in and around Montreal. Over the year, we drafted a statement that praised Canadian unity, acknowledged the French fact in the British North America Act that functioned as Canada's constitutional document, and pleaded with all sides to conduct the necessary bilingual conversations and debates in an orderly and law-abiding manner.

Sadly, my retained files do not contain any of the materials generated during the meetings of the special committee. However, on the Sunday after Easter, exactly one year after my initial contretemps with Dr. Camille Laurin, my sermon offered an intriguing perspective on "One Year Later . . ." and is included in this volume as Appendix II.

Following upon the June 1977 General Assembly of the Presbyterian Church in Canada, there came a chain of events that had been the subject of scuttlebutt controversy behind the scenes throughout the Assembly. During that period in the history of the Presbyterian Church in Canada, every graduating theologue from either Knox College or Presbyterian College was required to accept a minimum two-year appointment by the denomination's Board of Home Missions in order to staff small and non-self-supporting pastoral charges in various (usually) remote parts of Canada. Graduating from Presbyterian College that year was a middle-aged woman with a successful husband and several children. Somewhat brittle and certainly self-willed, she had refused any and all possible mission appointments in order to remain in the Montreal area with her husband and family.

Eventually, she, the Board of Home Missions, and the Church of St. Andrew and St. Paul agreed to her two-year appointment as assistant to the minister of the A & P. It appeared to be a win-win, although decidedly irregular, situation: she was eligible for ordination, thereby; I was certainly in need of pastoral assistance; and the arrangement would end in two years, when she would presumably have secured a satisfactory and regular call to a self-supporting pastoral charge.

She came to work in June, fresh from her studies at the Presbyterian College on the campus of McGill University. I was gratefully able to take a much-needed whole month's vacation before the start of the new school year. At the Little Pink Palace, we were joined by Bill and Bev Snyder and their three daughters. Hilarity was the order of the day as we coped with eating, sleeping, and bathroom-ing with ten people in that tiny, two-bedroom cottage.

While at Rondeau, we visited Ann's Aunt Norma and Uncle Bill Williamson in Kitchener and learned of the impending autumn wedding of Ann's favorite cousin, Janice. We agreed that Ann should return by train with Sarah to Southwestern Ontario at the end of September to participate in the events surrounding Janice's wedding, which she did. The edge was somewhat taken off the festivities when Janice's younger brothers both took ill with an undiagnosed ailment just before the wedding.

Shortly after Labour Day, I was again summoned to a meeting of various anglophone leaders in the Montreal office of Dr. Camille Laurin. The meeting itself was inconsequential, but what happened immediately afterwards was not. One of Dr. Laurin's English-speaking aides took me aside, ostensibly to chat me up about the Church of St. Andrew and St. Paul and my ministry there.

"Do you have a lot of older people in your congregation?" I admitted that we did.

"Then you probably have to conduct a lot of funerals every year?" I conceded that I did.

"It's a beautiful church. Do you do a lot of weddings there?' I agreed that we did.

"Then, perhaps, you have a lot of babies born to your congregation and a lot of baptisms?" Again, I agreed that we did.

"Then," he concluded, "how long would your ministry last if you had no registers of civil status in which to record all those births, marriages, and deaths?"

There it was! There was the threat I had felt hanging over my head ever since Dr. Laurin visited the Church of St. Andrew and St. Paul back in April. Every church in the Province of Quebec had two registers of civil status: one a cumulative register that recorded every baptism, every wedding, and every funeral in sequential order on numbered pages, and another one granted by the provincial government for the same details to be registered and filed with the government at the end of each calendar year. These were the *official* records by which the province recognized births, marriages, and deaths and the *only* records from which the government could issue certificates of these rites of passage and the changes in one's civil status that they registered.

In other words as I explained when I reported this conversation to the kirk session at our next meeting, if the Province of Quebec were to withhold our annual registers of civil status, no one in our congregation would be officially *born*, *married*, or *dead* if their baptism, wedding, or funeral had been held in the Church of St. Andrew and St. Paul. "How long would my ministry last?" Not very long!

The elders were aghast, not only at the threat to me personally but at the death knell that the Province of Quebec had the power to ring out over any church without any discussion or defense! Their collective wisdom congealed around the idea that I needed to shut up! I was to assume a very low profile in the pulpit and in the media and allow the situation to unfold without comment or criticism from me. This I agreed to do.

Far more serious at that moment, however, was a rift in the Russell family that I regret to this day. Living as we were in a narrow four-story townhouse in the tightly-packed mews that was Richelieu Place in the heart of downtown Montreal, Ann and I had been feeling more and more restless and had begun to talk about finding a second home somewhere outside the Province of Quebec, with its increasingly troublous resurgence of separatist politics and politicians. In September, we made a couple of daytrip forays across the St. Lawrence River into up-state New York, where, amazingly, we happened upon an almost derelict old stone cottage for sale just outside a charming little town with a charming little yacht basin. Dreaming of a vacation home with a harbour for the *Cuddy Sark* less than two hours away from the city, we began to make inquiries about an American-dollar purchase and mortgage.

I still remember the dismay and anger and out-of-proportion sense of betrayal I felt when I learned from a casual mention in a letter from my mother confirming my parents' plans to travel to Montreal by train to spend the Canadian Thanksgiving weekend with us, that my father (totally unbeknownst to us) had sold the *Cuddy Sark* to his Rondeau next-door neighbour. Although it had always been my *father's* boat, my family and I were the ones who had cared for it and sailed it and enjoyed it for many summers past, and somehow it felt like *mine*, at least enough that my father might have offered it to me if he was of a mind to sell it.

After an angry telephone exchange with Dad, who was totally blindsided by my reaction to his sale of *his* boat, I suggested that it might be best if they did *not* come to Montreal for Thanksgiving as I would be in no mood to be thankful! And there we left it, never to be mentioned again.

By the time Ann and Sarah returned to Montreal from Janice's wedding, it had been established that the Williamson cousins both had the mumps and, by then, so did Ann. Soon after she arrived back in Montreal, she was so ill one day that she fainted on the manse stairs between the first and second floors, prompting our family physician and great friend, Dr. Ian Hutchison, to insist that we either get some household help or he would put Ann in the hospital. Swallowing my pride after the *Cuddy Sark* episode, I telephoned my mother in Windsor, who dropped everything, of course, and came by train to Montreal to nurse Ann and keep house for us.

Within days of her arrival, I fell ill—even worse than Ann— with painfully swollen glands in my neck and groin and then a virulent attack of pancreatitis. To make a long story short, I was ill and away from my work at the church for almost two months. Eventually, Ann recovered enough that we thought that we could send my mother, now worn down to the point of exhaustion, home for the Christmas season.

Having grown a full black, bushy beard during the orchitis stage of my mumps, I returned to my pulpit for worship during the second half of December, although I remember almost nothing of it. We had completely missed the St. Andrew's Society's end-of-November extravaganza and their special guests, the Viscount and Viscountess Thurso. I was too worn down even to ask if Lady Thurso had lit the first candle of the Advent wreath!

My prolonged illness offered my new assistant minister many opportunities to exercise a much broader range of pastoral responsibilities than had been envisioned at the time of her appointment. In my almost two-month absence, she filled in admirably as de facto minister at the kirk. Unfortunately, the hiatus allowed her to undertake (among other things) totally rewriting and recasting the long-celebrated Sunday school Christmas pageant. I was too ill to object or even be involved in that year's pageant, other than to have a few walk-on lines at the end of the program. Sad to say, the new Christmas pageant was such a disaster that a delegation of Sunday school teachers and parents came to see me to demand that for the next year we would revert to the old tried-and-true pageant production that everyone knew and loved. With some foreboding, I agreed—

For which my assistant never quite forgave me. Confined to a lesser pastoral role since my return from the mumps, she concentrated her efforts on the Sunday school, the youth program and the women's association. Throughout 1978, she subtly gathered a congregation within the congregation, comprised largely of single women with increasingly strident views on gender equality and women's liberation from presumed male dominance.

1978 marked the 175th anniversary of the founding of the little Scots Presbyterian congregation in Old Montreal that eventually became the Church of St. Andrew and St. Paul. I remember it as a bittersweet celebration. On the first anniversary of my famous "open letter" to Camille Laurin, I spoke of how the spectre of change overhung—and overwhelmed—any joy in remembering, let alone reveling in, the distinguished past of the congregation and its members. That sermon is reprinted in full as Appendix III. Here, I quote one of the key paragraphs:

> But, Christian friends, continuing change—perhaps even accelerated change—is inevitable, separation or no, for our country and our province and our city and our people. Things will never again be the way they were. The future belongs to those who will prove themselves willing to adapt and advance, rather than resent and retreat. Our 175th anniversary motto is "to

be continued." The cost of continuing, I insist, is going to be a fearless and faithful acceptance of the future, far exceeding our proud and grateful appreciation of the past.

Nevertheless, in a determined attempt to make the occasion somewhat memorable, a special committee of the congregation planned a gala weekend near the end of April. Festivities began with a black-tie dinner dance held at the Royal Montreal Golf Club—the oldest golf club in North America—on Friday evening, April 21, an event that warranted a half-page of coverage in the "people" section of the next Monday's *Gazette*. The guest of honour was my dear and revered predecessor, Rod Berlis, who preached the sermon at the Sunday morning service celebrating our "Roots of 1803." The Saturday morning brunch in the church's Kildonan Hall drew the newspaper's special attention, since it featured the cuisine of the congregation's own Albert Schnell, then the executive chef for the Hilton International hotel chain. Breathlessly, the paper described the menu as "eggs Benedict, crêpes, ham and sausages, croissants, and the Queeen Elizabeth Hotel's famed banana bread."

With so much going on in Quebec around the burgeoning issue of francophone "sovereignty," I confess that I had hardly taken notice of what my female colleague was up to. Frankly, most days passed in a blur as I kept silence on matters political, both from my pulpit and in my personal life—

That is, until one fateful day in November, when my clerk of session, who was the deputy chief of security for the Canadian Pacific Railway system, came to see me in my study at the church. In his professional role, he was privy to reports from the Royal Canadian Mounted Police (RCMP) pertaining to the security of the national railroads. He had learned that the

RCMP had infiltrated a cell of *le Front du Liberation de Québec* (FLQ), one of the most violent of the secessionist gangs of Francophone thugs in Quebec, and had seen a report of a bomb target list of Montreal structures the FLQ was determined to blow up if the eventual referendum on "Sovereignty Association" failed to win the popular vote whenever it came to pass.

First on the list was the venerable Sun Life Assurance Building in the very heart of downtown Montreal. Second was the Windsor Station, since 1889 the statuesque terminal headquarters of the Canadian Pacific Railway. The third target was to be the Church of St. Andrew and St. Paul! It was devastating news not only for me and my family, whose vulnerability we had pretty much downplayed until then, but also for the elders, trustees, staff, and members of the congregation, any and all of whom seemed suddenly very much at risk at the hands of the FLQ's undisciplined thugs.

I remember that being a particularly joyless Advent and Christmas at home and at church. Already, many of the younger couples in the congregation, along with, in some cases, their parents and their children, had already fled the province for the presumed safety of Ottawa, Kingston, Toronto, and all points west. Though Ann and I tried to shield our own three children from the most frightening aspects of this latest development, there was no denying that our everyday lives were under everyday threat. Ann began driving the children to their three different schools every morning and picking them up every afternoon. When we were at home, police cruisers regularly made their way through Place Richelieu between Rue de la Montagne and Avenue du Musée, much to the understandable consternation of our neighbors. When I was at the church whether for work or worship, the same cruisers patrolled the corner of Sherbrooke and Redpath Streets in plain view almost constantly.

As the date for the annual Sunday school Christmas pageant drew closer, I grew more and more irritated as my assistant became more and more petulant in her unsuccessful attempts to revive her own version of the event, even in the face of my disapproval and the complaints of so many Sunday school parents and teachers.

Ironically, attendance at Sunday worship actually picked up as word got around about the FLQ threat: it was as though many anglophones—and certainly some francophones—wanted to demonstrate to the FLQ extremists that Montrealers would not be intimidated! Fortunately, there was no violence throughout the holiday season. But in the New Year, every so often a large visible and threatening note would be slipped between the front doors of the church, reminding me and the whole church that the FLQ had us in its sights.

In the spring of 1979 as the end of my assistant's two-year mission appointment drew nearer and nearer, the full extent of her duplicity became apparent as she presented to the kirk session her demand that instead of her leaving at the end of June as expected, she be called and installed as the Church of St. Andrew and St. Paul's *co*pastor! A handful of prominent women in the congregation attended the kirk session meeting to support her demand; but as the whole unprecedented idea had come as a complete surprise not only to the moderator and clerk of session but also to the personnel committee, one of the elders wisely moved that the matter be referred to the personnel committee, and so it was.

What a furore ensued! It soon became clear that the lady had very much overestimated her popularity in the congregation and the presumed indispensability of her pastoral services. Neither I as the moderator, nor the clerk of session, nor any member of the personnel committee supported the notion. Sensing my displeasure, the chair of the personnel committee asked me directly what I would do if such a call were to be issued and she were to be installed as my copastor. "I would begin immediately to look for a call to another ministry!" was my prompt and final reply.

As the date for the May kirk session meeting approached, a consensus emerged in the personnel committee that the matter needed to be dealt with decisively once and for all! A motion was drafted to the effect that the assistant to the minister, the congregation, the Presbytery of Montreal, and the Board of Home Missions of the Presbyterian Church in Canada should all be informed that her two-year appointment would expire at the end of June 1979, and her employment as assistant to the minister would come to an end on that date.

When she was informed by the clerk of session and the chair of the personnel committee (as I remember), she came, unannounced and unexpected, to the manse, tearfully and unashamedly begging me to forgive her impertinence and to allow her to continue indefinitely in her employment while she actively sought another pastoral position. I was shocked and unmoved. I told her that I could and would forgive her impertinence, since I should have recognized it for what it was and put a squelch to it long before I did. "But," I continued firmly, "I cannot and will not work with you now or ever. You have proven yourself to be a dangerous and disloyal colleague, and I want nothing more to do with you!"

Amid all this ado, it was announced that Her Majesty Queen Elizabeth the Queen Mother would make what became a sort of "state visit" to the Province of Ontario, primarily in Toronto, in the coming month. Her trip was, I realize in retrospect, a blessing in disguise, for it distracted me and a lot of members of the Church of St. Andrew and St Paul not only from my colleague's painful departure but even more from the almost unbearable stresses and strains of the growing "Sovereignty Association" political crisis brewing in the Province of Quebec.

Whenever Her Majesty came to Canada, which she did almost every other year during this period, the Canadian Black Watch had a significant part to play as one of the two regiments of which she was colonel-in-chief. With a rivalry that was both healthy and, at times, alarming, we alternated in providing honour guards, equerries and, of course, chaplains as Her Majesty's itineraries required. The other regiment was the Toronto Scottish, whose honorary lieutenant colonel was MacKenzie Robinson, an elder in Alan McPherson's Central Presbyterian Church in Hamilton and the father of young Ian Robinson, who with his family were at that time members of the Church of St. Andrew and St. Paul.

During Her Majesty's significant visit to Ontario in June 1979, the province hosted a state banquet in the ballroom of the Royal York Hotel in downtown Toronto. I was honored to be invited to offer the prayer of invocation at the start of the banquet and even more delighted to be identified in the printed program as the "Padre of the Black Watch" because "padre" was what Her Majesty always called me!

An aside: a longstanding tradition of the Black Watch was that the padre, when present wherever, assumed the rank of the highest-ranking officer present: this so that all felt equal to the chaplain and the chaplain was able to feel at ease with all ranks. This tradition pleased Her Majesty immensely. "You know, padre," she once confided to me, "you're the only person in the room I can talk to as an equal!"

Following the banquet at the Royal York, the lieutenant governor of the Province of Ontario, the premier of Ontario, and I escorted Her Majesty to a special elevator from the mezzanine down to the main lobby of the hotel. As we made our way through the crowd of well-wishers toward the doors beyond which Her Majesty's limousine was waiting, my wife, Ann, otherwise left behind, began to descend the majestic curving staircase that was an iconic feature of the Royal York lobby. She was wearing one of her favorite evening gowns, a pastel rosy pink silk crepe slip beneath a hand-painted chiffon poncho-like over-dress. As she came down the stairs, the back panel of her chiffon "poncho" floated out on the steps behind her. The Queen Mother glanced up, saw Ann, and muttered, "You know, padre, I wish I could wear something like *that*!"

Her Majesty's visit included an appearance at Toronto's Woodbine Racetrack for the 120th Running of the Queen's Plate, Canada's horse-racing equivalent to the Kentucky Derby in the United States. As a courtesy, the senior officers of the Black Watch and I as the Queen Mum's "padre" were invited to attend the event, where we greeted Her Majesty in the paddock before the race and had a wonderful visit with Sir Martin Gilliat, her personal secretary, and Frances Campbell-Preston, her ubiquitous lady-in-waiting.

On Sunday after church, there was to be a parade of the Queen Mother's regiments down University Avenue in Toronto. The reviewing stand was in front of the Royal Canadian Military Institute, and the honorary colonel of the Canadian Black Watch at that time, John G. Bourne, had arranged for the entire Russell family to be seated behind the Queen Mother at the reviewing stand.

For the weekend, we were staying not at the pricey Royal York Hotel but at the much more modest Holiday Inn just a few blocks from the RCMI. I was to be in parade dress for the event; but somehow in the cramped confusion of the hotel suite, I forgot to buckle on my sporran, which lapse I only discovered when I got to the RCMI ahead of the family and saw myself in a mirror! A quick phone call to the hotel caught Kirk in time for him to gather up the sporran and belt and run with it to the institute, where until he arrived I hid out in the men's room, fearful of being caught by Col. Bourne without proper kit!

There was no time for introductions or conversations with the Queen Mother on the reviewing stand. She arrived by limousine just before the parade approached and was whisked away as soon as the parade had passed by. I felt badly that Sarah, Kirk, and Rebecca had not been presented to Her Majesty.

But never mind! There was still a garden party and walkabout scheduled for later in the afternoon at Toronto's Old Fort York at which I was to be present again, still in my parade dress uniform. So, off I went to hurry up and wait for Her Majesty to appear and be photographed, seated with the officers and NCOs of her beloved Black Watch and have a precious moment for her to meet and greet Ann and Sarah and Kirk and Rebecca! In anticipation of such a thing happening, our girls had been practising their curtsies and did us proud!

Back in Montreal at the end of the summer, there was no escaping the anxiety and distress being felt by many francophones and almost all anglophones as the political climate rapidly and unexpectedly deteriorated. On May 22, 1979, in a federal election, the liberal prime minister, Pierre Elliott Trudeau, the most popular politician in Quebec, was defeated by the progressive conservative leader, Joe Clark, who became the head of a minority government with little influence in Quebec. Premier René Lévesque immediately realized that circumstances had never been more favorable for a referendum vote on Quebec's separation from the rest of Canada.

For almost two years, I had kept silent about anything having to do with Quebec's linguistic and political struggles, and I continued to do so even when René Lévesque announced on June 21, 1979, that the promised referendum on Sovereignty Association would be held in the spring of 1980 with the question to be announced before Christmas. In November, the Parti Québécois published its White Paper on Sovereignty Association—*la nouvelle entente Québec-Canada*—asserting that sovereignty is indissociable from association.

As if I did not have enough on my plate, in September I was elected moderator of the Presbytery of Montreal, a position in the church political that I neither wanted nor sought. However, it was deemed by some of the elders in the presbytery that it was my turn, and so it was. Unfortunately, hard feelings lurked in the hearts of many of my fellow clergy over my treatment of my former assistant minister. From the start, every monthly meeting was fraught with tension, usually expressed in a frivolous or nitpicking challenge to the chair for some procedural decision I made. After three months of this, I confronted the court with an ultimatum: either the challenges would cease, or at the next occurrence I would step down as moderator on the spot! That did it: for the rest of my term, I "ruled" the court without a single challenge.

Needless to say, the Earl and Countess of Cathcart got short shrift during the end of November week of St. Andrew's Society festivities. I do not remember that Ann and I even attended the St. Andrew's Ball that year as festivity seemed almost inappropriate in the face of the fear and foreboding felt throughout the anglophone and ethnic communities in Montreal.

At the Church of St. Andrew and St. Paul, the Advent Sunday services continued to be well attended, but there was an edge of anxiety to every traditional aspect of the season. The choir's annual Carols by Candlelight service packed the sanctuary as always, but there were tears in many eyes as we processed to the chancel, singing "Once in Royal David's City" and pondered the uncertain future of Quebec's largest city. The icing on the cake was the announcement on December 20th that the referendum question would be a "Yes" or "No" referendum on giving the government of Quebec the mandate to negotiate a new agreement with the rest of Canada, based on the equality of nations.

On Christmas Day, it started to snow, and by Boxing Day the city was at a snowbound standstill. Our good friends, Eric and Jean Riordon, always held a magnificent black-tie open house on the evening of Boxing Day, but we figured that no one would be able to attend that night. Remembering our own disastrous St. Patrick's Day open house a few years earlier, Ann and I determined that we would get to Westmount, come hell or deep snow. We packed my tuxedo and her evening gown, plus shoes and other accoutrements, in two of the children's school backpacks, got out our crosscountry skis, and glided down Rue de la Montagne and westward on a totally trafficless Sherbrooke Street to the Riordons' party. It turned out that another couple had had the same idea, so the six of us made very merry, despite the snowstorm outside and the political storm brewing for the New Year and eventually skied home about 3:00 a.m. having forgotten, at least for a few hours, all the world's woes!

December 12, 1971
The Wyoming Presbyterian Church, Millburn, New Jersey
Lord of the Manor for "A Tudor Christmas"

July 28, 1972
On Lake Erie near Rondeau
At the helm of the "Cuddy Sark"

September 23, 1973
The Church of St. Andrew and St. Paul, Montreal, Quebec
With my family at my induction

St. Andrew and St. Paul

New pastor finds city vibrant, perfectly safe'

By BOB HAYES
of The Gazette

Rev. William R. Russell, the new minister of the Church of St. Andrew and St. Paul, thought he was coming to "a quiet church."

"Not that I wanted a quiet church, but from outside appearances it would look that way. I'm just amazed because it's a tremendously busy place," he said this week.

Russell, who came to Montreal from Wyoming Presbyterian Church, Millburn, N.J., was inducted as the fourth minister of St. Andrew's and St. Paul's last night.

He succeeds Dr. Rudolph J. Berlis, who had served the downtown church since 1946 and will take over as minister of visitation at Knox Presbyterian Church in Guelph, Ont., Nov. 1.

NOT NEW

A church in the central core of a big city is nothing new to the 34-year-old University of Toronto graduate, former assistant minister of the historic Fifth Ave. Presbyterian Church in New York City from 1964 to 1968. At that time he was installed as senior minister of the Presbyterian Church in Millburn, where he served until last month.

"But from what I have seen in the last few weeks, there's just no comparison between New York City and Montreal.

"There is a certain desperation about life in New York that I haven't seen in Montreal. Here, I have felt a certain joie de vivre, although I am sure behind it there are a lot of troubled people with serious prob-

REV. WILLIAM R. RUSSELL

(Gazette. Todd Church)

September 24, 1973
Outside the Church of St. Andrew and St. Paul
A clipping and photo from the Montreal Gazette

The first Sunday in Advent, December 2, 1973
Montreal, Quebec
In the pulpit of the Church of St. Andrew and St. Paul

Montreal honors Queen Mother

MONTREAL (CP) — A thunderous 21-gun salute from the Canadian Forces base at nearby St. Hubert marked the close of a fast-moving one-day visit Thursday by Queen Elizabeth, the Queen Mother, highlighted by the presentation of the new Queen's Color to the Black Watch Royal Highland Regiment of Canada.

The Queen Mother, colonel-in-chief of the regiment, arrived a few minutes behind schedule at the base for the presentation after a private luncheon with dignitaries at the Queen Elizabeth Hotel downtown.

Awaiting her was a colorful display of military pageantry, with the Black Watch regimental pipe and brass band and more than 200 soldiers, veterans and cadets in impressive formation.

The Queen Mother, 73, more a floral orange dress and orange hat throughout the day and looked radiant as she stepped onto the presentation platform, waving at more than 2,500 military personnel and their wives and children who gathered to watch the ceremony.

The band played the British and Canadian national anthems and several military marches as the soldiers went through a well-rehearsed drill before the new Queen's Color was unfurled.

The new flag, a maple leaf with a bold crown and the regiment's name inscribed at the centre, was blessed by Rev. W.R. Russell, the regimental chaplain, and Brig.-Gen. Rev. R. G. C. Cunningham and Brig.-Gen. J. A. McLean, the chaplains-general, before the Queen Mother made the formal presentation to the Black Watch.

"I am so proud to present on behalf of her Majesty the Queen the new Queen's Color to this regiment," she said.

Congratulating the soldiers on "an excellent display" of drill, the Queen Mother said the Black Watch stands for "the highest tradition of military service."

"This regiment stands for loyalty, trust and pride and belongs to something very special," Her Royal Highness said. "Its role is of the greatest importance."

The Queen Mother presented the Black Watch of Canada with the regiment's original Queen's Color in 1962.

The hour-long ceremony closed with the traditional three cheers for the Queen Mother who was escorted to the officers' mess to mingle with members of the regiment, their wives and guests during an informal garden party.

Thursday, June 27, 1974
CFB Montreal, St. Hubert Garrison, Quebec
A clipping from the Montreal Gazette

November 1977
Richelieu Place, Montreal, Quebec
With Sarah, Kirk, and Rebecca in kilts
on Saint Andrew's Sunday in the Manse

Saturday, April 22, 1978
The Church of St. Andrew and St. Paul, Montreal, Quebec
"A young, handsome, bearded prophet"
according to the Montreal Star

Pentecost Sunday, May 14, 1978
The Church of St. Andrew and St. Paul
Releasing helium-filled message balloons,
celebrating the 175th anniversary of the church

September 28, 1978
At the door of the Church of St. Andrew and St. Paul
With Col. J. G. Bourne, awaiting the arrival of the annual
Black Watch regimental church parade

September 28, 1978
On Sherbrooke Street, Montreal, Quebec
Another Black Watch church parade

June 29, 1979
The Royal York Hotel, Toronto, Ontario
*I am in Black Watch formal mess kit for the state banquet,
Ann is in the gown the Queen Mother envied*

July 1, 1979
The Royal Canadian Military Institute, Toronto, Ontario
*Saluting the Queen Mother as she arrives
at the parade reviewing stand*

July 1, 1979
Old Fort York, Toronto, Ontario
The Queen Mother greets Rebecca at a Royal Garden Party

July 1, 1979
Old Fort York, Toronto, Ontario
Black Watch officers' "photo op"

CLARENCE HOUSE
S.W 1

30th July 1979

Dear Bill.

It was good to get your excellent letter
of 12th July for which thank you very much.

Our Toronto meeting was most exciting and
I was especially delighted to have the good fortune
to be with you and Ann again and to find you both
in such good form.

It was lovely, too, that Kirk, Sarah and
Rebecca were all at that splendid Sunday afternoon
gathering.

Queen Elizabeth The Queen Mother and those
of us who were lucky enough to be with Her Majesty
will always have the happiest memories of the latest
Canadian odessy and I only hope it will not be too
long before we all meet up again.

Yours ever,
Martin.

The Reverend William R. Russell.

July 30, 1979
Clarence House, London S.W.1, England
A typical letter from Clarence House

THE EIGHTIES

THE NEW DECADE DAWNED WITH ALL OF THE issues of the previous one still in place, plus a new one to complicate the situation further. In early December 1979, the minority government of Joe Clark was ignominiously defeated in a vote of no confidence on its first budget and was forced to call another federal election for February 18, 1980. This time, Pierre Trudeau and his Liberal Party won—taking seventy-four of Quebec's seventy-five ridings and forming a strong majority government.

Prime Minister Trudeau lost no time in assuring Canada—and Quebec in particular—that his government would reform Canadian federalism so that a "No" vote in the upcoming referendum would not be a vote just for the status quo. Heartened somewhat by these developments, many anglophones in Montreal, and particularly in the congregation of the Church of St. Andrew and St. Paul, began to politick against the prospect of "Sovereignty Association."

Among them was my own wife, Ann. Despite the gag rule imposed on me by the kirk session in response to the implied threat of Camille Laurin to take away the church's registers of civil status, Ann began to go house to house, door to door, in our neighborhood, encouraging folks not to be downhearted but to plan to get out and vote "No" on the day scheduled for the referendum, Tuesday, May 20, 1980. Meanwhile, I studiously maintained my silence, demurring to discuss any aspect of "Sovereignty Association" with anyone outside of the kirk session.

Despite the assurances of Prime Minister Trudeau, morale remained low within the anglophone and ethnic communities, as one opinion poll after another heralded the invincibility of the Parti Québécois and its underlying intention eventually to separate Quebec from the rest of Canada. Week by week, friends and neighbors just "disappeared," moving westward without notice to new jobs, new homes, and new lives away from the constant antagonism toward English business, English institutions, English churches, English ways of life. The truth about the suppression of those very same entities by the English-speaking minority in Montreal over the past two centuries found a growing acceptance in many anglophone hearts and a grudging agreement that some things *had* to change, whatever the future held for Canada as a whole and the Province of Quebec in particular.

At the kirk session meeting in early May, I confessed to the assembled elders how hard it had been for me to remain silent at their insistence for almost two years as the controversies over Sovereignty Association had raged all around me. There had, in fact, been no violence against me personally or my family or the church, for which we were all eternally grateful; and I fervently prayed that that would continue to be the case throughout the days leading up to the referendum as well as following upon it, no matter the outcome!

But I also gave notice that my pastor's heart could not remain absolutely silent while my people struggled with their own fears and feelings as the day appointed for the voting came nearer and nearer. I did not know what I would say from my pulpit—*their* pulpit!—on the Sunday before the referendum, but I would have to say *something*, and I would have to trust the Holy Spirit to lead me to say something *positive* in the face of so much relentless negativity.

The result of that inspiration (such as it was!) was a sermon titled "Positively 'No,'" which title I routinely provided for the church officer to post in capital letters on the large bulletin board on the church lawn facing Sherbrooke Street and then went to work on a message that would try to say just that.

On Saturday mornings at that point in our family's lifestyle, Ann and I usually enjoyed breakfast in bed with the *Gazette*'s weekend version of a Sunday paper. I was busy in the kitchen, preparing our breakfast tray when from the master bedroom, Ann shrieked: "Oh, Bill, what have you done?"

What I had done without realizing it was to provide a photo op for a *Gazette* news photographer to snap a picture of the church's outdoor signboard with my sermon title prominently displayed and then to publish it writ large on the third page of the newspaper with a somewhat sarcastic editorial caption that at least one of Montreal's preachers would apparently be having the courage to address the referendum issue from his pulpit the next day!

I had barely scanned the article when the phone rang. It was Herb Luft, the chief news anchorman for Montreal's English-language television outlet, CFCF-TV. He wanted permission to broadcast something from the sermon for CFCF's nightly news on Sunday before the traditional twenty-four-hour blackout on election coverage took effect in advance of Tuesday's referendum vote.

I was stunned! Buying time, I replied that I would have to consult the church's clerk of session, which I did immediately. He wisely counseled that it was always better to accommodate rather than antagonize the press but that I should set down some very definite conditions to apply to whatever coverage CFCF might choose to air. So I gave Herb Luft full permission to film and eventually broadcast *whatever* he chose on the condition that he could not air *even one word* of my sermon message without broadcasting the *entire paragraph* from the sermon manuscript in which it appeared. To my amazement, Herb agreed and thence set in motion what in retrospect became the most significant single day in my whole ministry.

As I arrived early for church the next morning, Sunday, May 18, 1980, I was shocked to see people waiting below the church's front steps and lined up along Sherbrooke Street and around the corner up Redpath Street as far as my eye could see. Inside the sanctuary, the CFCF-TV crews had set up a fixed camera position and huge floodlights in the balcony and a roving camera with its own light-pack in one of the main floor side aisles. My redoubtable clerk of session had somehow recruited some burly CPR railroad security officers to control the crowd waiting to be allowed in and to maintain order thereafter. Although I had forewarned Wayne Riddell, our director of music, about what might be going on, the chancel choir was all agog at the turmoil as they held a suddenly much-more-important-than-usual anthem rehearsal in the choir stalls.

With grim determination, I slipped my sermon manuscript (over which I had labored even longer than usual the night before) onto the pulpit desk as the nave and balcony began to fill with people. Nevertheless, it was actually breathtaking to enter the brilliantly lit and jam-packed sanctuary singing the processional hymn,

O God of Bethel, by Whose hand
Thy people still are fed,
Who through this weary pilgrimage
hast all our fathers led;

Our vows, our prayers, we now present
before Thy throne of grace;
God of our fathers, be the God
of their succeeding race.

It had become my custom to invite the children present in worship to gather with me at the chancel steps, which I did and then sat down with them, my black robes spreading around me on the gold and green marble steps. I spoke to the boys and girls about the tense times we were all going through and how what they might see and hear and feel—and not understand—at home and at school was not their fault or their doing. Then I went on to plead with them to be "extra good and obedient and loving" toward all the adults in their lives who really needed their care and their help to get through the next few difficult days in all our lives.

After the offertory, the sermon hymn was actually an old Scottish Psalter paraphrase of Psalm 46:

God is our refuge and our strength, in straits a present aid,
and, therefore, though the earth be moved, we will not be
afraid.

The sermon, "Positively 'No'" is reprinted in its entirety as Appendix III, there for those who might wish to read it. Its thrust was that my "No" vote on the following Tuesday would be a *positive* "No" for

it says "Yes" to Canada, my country; "Yes" to a federal

political system which, though perpetually in need of renewal, is still more appealing to me than any other option presented thus far; "Yes" to a way of life that I find abundant, prosperous, optimistic and diverse, especially in terms of a bilingualism and biculturalism that is uniquely to be encouraged and enjoyed.

I concluded with words of assurance from my heart:

> Positively know that God has a hand in all this—though what his purposes are may not be clear to us or to anyone else and may, in fact, be thwarted for a time by the ill-will and disobedience of those who love him not. God is still sovereign, still strength and refuge to those who trust in him, still "in straits a present aid!
>
> "Therefore, though the earth be moved, we will not be afraid!"

Then, instead of a prayer with which to close, I asked Wayne Riddell to play Canada's then-not-yet-official national anthem, "O Canada." And I asked the congregation to sing it and the hymn to follow immediately, not as a national anthem and a hymn but as a tribute and a prayer and an affirmation of faith:

> *From ocean unto ocean our land shall name you Lord*
> *and, filled with true devotion, obey your sovereign word.*

Truly, there was not a dry eye in the house during the singing of *O Canada*. Somehow, I maintained my own composure, standing alone at the chancel steps until I looked down and saw Sarah, our beautiful teenaged daughter, standing at the center aisle end of the first pew in the congregation, tears streaming down her cheeks as she sang her heart out:

> *O Canada! Our home and native land!*
> *True patriot love thou dost in us command . . .*

God keep our land glorious and free!
O Canada, we stand on guard for thee.

The CFCF-TV coverage at 6:00 p.m. was brief and focused mostly on the crowd of people standing in line to get into the St Andrew and St. Paul service—a bit disappointing after so tense and emotional a buildup. Then I received a telephone call from Herb Luft himself, informing me that the national CTV network had picked up his entire feed and would be using some of it at 11:00 p.m.

As I have already explained, in Canada (at least in those days) there was, in effect, a twenty-four-hour embargo on all media coverage leading up to any election day. The referendum voting scheduled for Tuesday, May 20, meant that all press coverage had to cease at midnight on Sunday, May 18. At 11:00 p.m., CTV began airing a nationwide special program on the referendum. First came a statement from the Prime Minister of Canada, Pierre Trudeau, followed by a statement from the Premier of Quebec, René Lévesque, paired with a similar statement from the Liberal Opposition Leader, Claude Ryan, then another from the Mayor of Montreal and yet another from the editor of the French-language newspaper *Le Devoir.* Then, following a brief station break at 11:30, came an announcement that the remainder of the hour would attempt to share with the rest of Canada what it was like to be an English-speaking Canadian in Montreal as the referendum was about to take place.

First, Herb Luft repeated his coverage of the crowd in line along Sherbrooke Street waiting patiently to enter the Church of St. Andrew and St. Paul, where the sign outside on the church lawn promised a sermon titled "Positively 'No.'" Then a voice-over I recognized as Lloyd Robertson's took us inside the sanctuary for the whole of my children's sermonette from the chancel steps. After a brief snatch of the chancel choir's offertory anthem, the stirring John Redford piece, "Rejoice in the Lord," the fixed camera in the balcony focused on the imposing stone pulpit and broadcast for posterity *every word* of my sermon!

Without a break, the coverage ended with the congregation singing "O Canada." As midnight approached, the roving camera moved in for a close-up of a beautiful young teenager standing in the front pew wearing a Canadian-flag-red silk blouse, tears streaming down her cheeks as she affirmed "O Canada, we stand on guard for thee!"

Needless to say, we Russells were literally stunned. As thrilled as we were with the excellence and completeness of the TV coverage, we all felt somehow that the whole sovereignty association conflict of the past three years and more had been distilled down to our family's—and in particular my personal—passionate stance for Canada as over against Quebec. And we realized that more than ever before in this long drawn-out political, social, financial, and spiritual struggle, we were afraid, well and truly *afraid*.

Despite the lateness of the hour, the phone started ringing almost as soon as the program ended. Elders, trustees, parishioners, friends, and neighbours in Montreal and across Canada, and, worst of all, our parents back in Windsor, all seemed to have the same two questions: Had I *known* that the coverage would be so extensive and so nationwide? And, *now what*? The answer to the first question was an honest if almost unbelievable, "No." There was as yet no answer to the second question, nor would there be, at least not until the referendum was held on Tuesday and the vote counted and the aftermath endured.

Looking back from the vantage point of almost four decades, I see clearly *now* that that half hour of national television exposure across Canada was, for good and for ill, the defining hour of my life, both personally and professionally. Nothing was ever quite the same again, and I can readily confess that most of the major decisions I have made through the rest of my life have been influenced in some way by that experience and all that came tumbling down afterward.

On the morning after the night before, I tried to take my regular day off as usual, but nothing seemed usual. The phone rang incessantly until we gave up answering it and forwarded every call to voicemail for screening before responding. The church secretary was determined to keep her office open, but she and her assistant as well as the church officer were so nervous that I consulted the clerk of session, and we decided for safety's sake to send the staff home and keep the office wing as well as the sanctuary closed up tight through Tuesday or whenever, depending on the outcome of the referendum vote.

On Tuesday morning, Ann and I slipped out of Richelieu Place unnoticed, made our way to the polling station nearby, and cast our votes without incident. By the time we returned to the manse, our devoted clerk of session had seconded a couple of CPR security guards to monitor the front and back entrances to our townhouse. All of the city schools were closed, so our three children were at home safe and sound with us in what increasingly through the day felt like a prison more than a home.

It did not take long into the evening for the vote tallies to begin to trickle into the "Yes" and "No" headquarters and thence to the local broadcast media, which almost from the beginning began to project a narrow defeat for the "Yes" faction. What should have felt like good news felt fearsome instead, and we really had no appetite for the quick supper Ann prepared.

As the evening wore on, the voting results trended more and more clearly to a defeat for the Parti Québécois' effort to secure a mandate from the people of Quebec to "negotiate a new constitutional agreement with the rest of Canada based on the equality of nations." By morning, we wakened to the almost unbelievable news that nearly sixty percent of all Quebeckers and a clear majority of francophones had rejected the option of sovereignty association! More significant still, the news media reported breathlessly, the night had passed virtually without significant violence. The referendum had obviously been defeated in the French-speaking constituencies of Quebec as well as in the anglophone and ethnic communities and the suppressed rage of the FLQ fizzled without a fight.

I confess that for us Russells the defeat of the referendum felt more like a dull thud than a thrilling victory. Relief turned to exhaustion for Ann and me, and returning to classes meant only back to normal for our three children, who had been and had felt like the primary focus of our concern, especially for the past few days. After I managed to rebuff the first wave of telephone calls from reporters wanting my direct quotes on the result of the referendum, even the telephone stopped ringing off the hook as people got back to the pursuit of their everyday lives.

By the following Sunday, my sermon title—simply "*Merci*"—elicited no media interest whatsoever. I commented,

> The referendum seems for many like a bad dream to be quickly forgotten in the thrill of victory and the relaxation of anxiety too long lived with. [Yet] for others, the focus of concern has already shifted to the rush for constitutional reform at the federal level and the fear that too little eventually too late may put us right back in the separatist situation from which we have but so recently escaped [see Appendix IV for the full text of that sermon].

For me personally as well as professionally, any sense of respite was short-lived. The General Assembly of the Presbyterian Church in Canada was, ironically, scheduled to meet in my hometown of Windsor, Ontario, concurrent with the meeting of the General Assembly of the United Presbyterian Church of the United States of America (UPUSA), scheduled to be held in Detroit, Michigan. Some months before, the minister of Knox Presbyterian Church in Windsor, Ontario, my paternal grandparents' home church, had invited me to be the guest preacher on the Sunday morning that was to be the date for the evening opening of the concurrent Assemblies.

My sermon was titled, "The 'No' That's a 'Yes,'" and re-reading it almost four decades later, I have found it eerily prescient and surprisingly bold, which is why I have included it to be my last word on the Quebec Referendum of 1980 as Appendix V. Here is a sample that, as things turned out, says it all:

> Even more than fear, it was fatigue and frustration that kept Montrealers—French and English—from feeling too exuberant about the referendum results. We have already lost so much because of Quebec separatism, and many of us suspect that there may be still more losses ahead. We have lost relatives and friends who have moved away to other parts of Canada; we have lost jobs and income and future prospects as companies large and small have fled the economic and political uncertainties of our province; we have lost the excellence we can no longer maintain in our depleted and demoralized schools and hospitals and churches and clubs; we have lost the faith that the rest of Canada ever really cared about us as individuals and families and congregations and communities caught in the separatist storm. We remember, and we grieve that until a few short months ago, many, many Canadians outside Quebec virtually abandoned us loyal Canadian Quebeckers—Eng-

lish as well as French—with a contemptuous "Let them go." At such high cost, there is little joy in winning, only profound relief that the worst may be over.

As if I didn't have enough on my mind, it had, for some reason I never quite fathomed, been agreed that the UPUSA General Assembly and our own would hold a joint opening sederunt in Detroit's Cobo Hall. All of the traditions of both denominations were to be observed in this uniquely ceremonial gathering. For us Canadians, that meant, among other things, the traditional General Assembly Loyal Addresses to the Queen, the prime minister of Canada's Parliament, and the premier of the government of Ontario. Our American brothers and sisters knew of no such tradition but were charmed by the idea and insisted that they would draft a loyal address to the president of the United States if we would present all of our own loyal addresses both in English and in French as they were always done.

Since I was already prepared to present the final report of my special committee on Canadian unity in both languages, it somehow fell to me to deliver the joint assemblies' loyal addresses as well. So there I was, some twelve days after the defeat of the referendum, far from my Montreal home and family, yet a mile across the Detroit River from my hometown and anxiety-ridden parents in Windsor and still under orders from my kirk session not to say anything more in public or to the media about the political situation in Quebec! We suppressed every mention of my involvement in every press release and everybody else's radio and television interviews leading up to the opening night. With very mixed emotions, I made my international ecclesiastical debut in such an understated way that none of the Canadian reporters picked up on my identity, and everybody else found the whole rigmarole so boring as not to warrant mention on either side of the border!

Returning to Montreal after the Assembly, I found it almost impossible to ignore and be ignored by the news media altogether. I was once again the go-to guy for comments on anything and everything deemed newsworthy and relating to the anglophone and ethnic communities. To thwart any public misapprehension that I had become aloof or smug in my post-referendum notoriety or that the Church of St. Andrew and St. Paul was a closed and arrogant anglophone institution, my savvy friend Eric Riordon, an advertising executive and one of the A & P's most influential young elders, proposed that we do some radio broadcasting efforts to project me as humble and winsome and the Church of St. Andrew and St. Paul as open and inviting.

The unexpected result was an earnest invitation from the national radio network of the Canadian Broadcasting Corporation to record a special version of the chancel choir's annual carols by candlelight concert-service to be broadcast nationwide at Christmas in 1980. As the plan developed, I would conduct the service and be featured doing a distinctly Canadian Christmas reading; the chancel choir would sing several distinctively Canadian carols in French and English and lead the congregation in several familiar sing-along carols; and the starring special guests would be none other than the newly-organized and already fantastically popular Canadian Brass.

The CBC's "Sing-along Christmas" was advertised heavily as a free gift from the church and the corporation to the people of Montreal—and eventually the rest of Canada—and it drew a standing room only audience on a cold and snowy Sunday afternoon in mid-December. I was tickled pink to be required to become a member of ACTRA—the Alliance of Canadian Cinema, Television, and Radio Artists; Wayne Riddell was overjoyed to be presented to a nationwide audience as one of Canada's foremost choral conductors; the Canadian Brass was impressed to be performing in what one of them later recalled as probably the most beautiful church sanctuary in Canada; and I had the unexpected fun of chancing to hear a portion of a repeat broadcast of the event in the Windsor living room of my lifelong friends, Lex and Ann McCrindle, sometime in the week between Christmas and New Year's. As I write this paragraph in 2018, I am pleased and proud to note that the CBC is still recording and broadcasting its annual sing-along from the Church of St. Andrew and St. Paul!

The other aspect of our media-messaging had similarly surprising results. Throughout the month of December 1980, the Church of St. Andrew and St. Paul had been airing sixty-second spot announcements on Montreal's then pop music radio station CJAD. Against the recorded background of the church choir singing a carol, my gently-modulated voice invited listeners to come to the 11:00 p.m. Christmas Eve service, ending with me saying, "I would love to wish you a merry Christmas in person!"

A squad carload of Montreal Police officers was called to maintain order and security when over 1,000 people turned up to do *just that*! Even with another team of wonderfully unobtrusive CPR armed guards in the narthex, security was slim at best, while I stood and greeted insistently waiting worshipers with "Merry Christmas" *in person* for over an hour and a half into Christmas morning!

By the time of the traditional post-holiday lull in church attendance and church activities in January 1981, every Protestant congregation in Montreal was beginning to face up to all the various and sundry losses that we had suffered in the years leading up to the referendum. The Church of St. Andrew and St.

Paul was not alone except for the fact that our resistance to the sovereignty association premise had been writ large on the collective mind of the city for both the *Oui*'s and the *Non*'s, and the admiration we had enjoyed before the vote seemed too easily to warp into unfair assumptions that we were a rich, powerful, well-connected bastion of the anglophone issues. By my own informal count, we had lost one way or another more than twenty of the twenty-five promising young couples we had met at a house party soon after arriving in the city and that translated into a whole generation of rising lay leadership gone. Even more gone was much of the older, wealthier, socially, and politically significant leadership that had always been characteristic of the A & P.

The impact of the language legislation inherent in Bill 101 was effectively discouraging younger business executives with school-aged children from accepting transfers to head offices in Montreal. Many of those head offices were actually gone—in truth if not in fact—with executive functions gone to Toronto or Western Canada and the corporate secretary with his/her symbolic seal left behind to maintain a façade of business as usual, where there was really none.

For me personally, my media exposure before the referendum had become a two-edged sword. On the one hand, it was flattering to be that "go-to guy" everyone in the English-speaking media (and increasingly in the francophone media too) turned to for a comment or an opinion on all things cultural and religious. But on the proverbial other hand, I had become so politicized—such a celebrity of sorts—that many in my own congregation were beginning to feel distanced from me as their pastor. To make matters worse, congregations in both Canada and the United States, Presbyterian and otherwise, began sounding me out about a possible call to a new and different ministry elsewhere.

Although flattering in a way, these overtures were actually both troubling and demoralizing. I caught myself wondering what it would be like just to be *me* again, not this celebrity preacher I had no desire to be, and each temptation made me feel more torn and disloyal and conflicted within myself. I actually took one of these opportunities seriously enough to arrange an interview, camouflaged by a trip back to New Jersey to officiate at the wedding of Bill and Bev Snyder's middle daughter, Susie.

The interview did not go well. After driving south on what eventually became I-87 and spending the night in Bronxville, New York, I forgot to disconnect the little cooler plugged into our station wagon's electrical system and drained the battery dead! It was not an auspicious start to an interview for what was actually a Reformed Church in America (RCA) congregation that had traditionally been pastored by Presbyterian graduates of Princeton Seminary. When I asked why Presbyterian rather than Reformed clergy were serving the church, the search committee was at a loss. But they took my question to heart and eventually called an RCA military chaplain as their new pastor.

Unfortunately, and I never quite knew how, the camouflaged purpose of our family trip to New Jersey became known to at least one of the elders at the A & P. At the next session meeting, he confronted me with the angry question, "Are you considering a call to another church?"

I remember his question clearly because I was so relieved to be able to answer honestly, "No, I am not! Why do you ask?"

"Because I have heard a rumour to that effect."

"Well," I responded, "you will. At least a half dozen churches in Canada and the United States have approached me since the resolution of the referendum question, inquiring whether or not I might be open to the possibility of moving elsewhere. I am not presently considering any of them."

Even our relationships with the Black Watch and the Queen Mother felt diminished somehow. By the early eighties, the rivalry between the Black Watch and the Toronto Scottish had become unpleasant. In the summer of 1981 at the end of the last royal visit during which I attended upon Her Majesty as padre, the camaraderie between the two regiments had descended to a level of nastiness that bordered on childishness.

The Queen Mother's brief visit to Canada in 1981 focused primarily on Toronto and Halifax; but, of course, the Black Watch, as one of Her Majesty's Canadian regiments, had to be included in honour guards and state occasions. There was another banquet at the Royal York Hotel, hosted this time by the premier of Ontario, Bill Davis. The Anglican dean of Toronto offered grace.

The next day was another running of the Queen's Plate at the Woodbine Racetrack in suburban Toronto. One of our Montreal friends and neighbors, Jean-Louis Levesque, was a financier and philanthropist, who several years before had been instrumental in creating the Jockey Club of Canada. Knowing that the Queen Mother would be present at the race and that we Russells had a special relationship with Her Majesty, he invited Ann and me to attend the event with him and his shy and retiring wife, Jeanne. As an afterthought, he included our elder daughter, Sarah, in the invitation to sit with them in the Jockey Club's trustees' box where Her Majesty would also be seated. Thrilled to be included and deciding to wear the beautiful white dress we had bought her for her graduation that same month from the Trafalgar School for Girls, Sarah went down to Ogilvy's Department Store on her own, bought a perky white straw hat and a nosegay of pink silk flowers and put together an outfit appropriate for the running of Canada's equivalent of the Kentucky Derby.

Although Jean-Louis had three horses competing in the Queen's Plate that year, he was also running one of his best racers in a preliminary event that afternoon. As is the custom at Woodbine, we all went down to the paddock before that race to check out Jean-Louis' horse and her competition. Milling around in the crowd, we were surprised to see the Queen Mother come striding into the paddock with her lady-in-waiting, her private secretary, and several prominent members of the Jockey Club who were hosting her for her weekend's visit.

Glancing around for someone familiar to greet, Her Majesty spotted Ann and me and made a beeline for us. We were thrilled to be acknowledged in this way and proud once again to present our elder daughter to the Queen Mum. Sarah dropped into a full-court curtsy, the flounced hem of her dress drooping into the muddy turf, while every news photographer's flashbulb popped a blinding burst of light.

As we stood chatting with Her Majesty, we all noticed that she was exhibiting what appeared to be almost a tic, something quite uncharacteristic of the Queen Mother, who was usually the paragon of self-controlled decorum. Every few seconds, her hand would brush across her face as though she were trying somehow to clear her line of sight. Suddenly, without a word to Ann and me, Sarah stepped forward, spoke softly to Her Majesty, and began to fiddle with the characteristic veil on the Queen Mother's hat.

My heart just about stopped beating: one does *not* suddenly approach royalty, let alone fiddle with their clothing! Then Her Majesty put my mind at ease, smiling at Sarah and saying, "Thank you, Sarah; you were the only one with sense enough to help me!" It turned out that there had been a small dried willow leaf caught in the royal veil. Sarah noticed it and fished it out, for which the Queen Mother never forgot Sarah and asked after her whenever we corresponded with Clarence House.

In the ensuing race, Jean-Louis's mount won, which was exciting enough! But Her Majesty, having known and admired Jean-Louis for many years, declared that she would like to go down to the winner's circle to present M. Levesque with his prize. Jean-Louis was startled, to say the least, as was his wife Jeanne, who at first declared that she was much too timid to accompany her husband to such a public presentation.

"Would *you* like to come with us, Sarah?" Jean Louis asked with a twinkle in his eye. For if Sarah would, then surely Jeanne could; and so the three of them did, and Sarah got to meet the Queen Mother for the second time that afternoon. Later, we obtained one of the newspaper photographers' pictures of the presentation with the Queen Mum, Jean-Louis, Jeanne, and Sarah together, which photo is to this day prominently displayed on Sarah and Kevin's fireplace mantel in Calgary, Alberta!

Later that same afternoon, there was yet another Royal Garden Party and Walkabout at Toronto's Old Fort York. The Black Watch Pipes and Drums as well as the officers, veterans, and honour guard participants were included on the guest list. The Queen Mother's "walkabout" provided us yet another moment of conversation. When she spoke appreciatively about our pipes and drums, I had the honour of presenting to Her Majesty my own personal piper, Andy Kerr. This introduction caught the Queen Mum's fancy, and she enquired how it was that I had my own personal piper. I recounted one of my favorite things about being the Watch's chaplain: wherever I went when I was in the Black Watch Armoury on Bleury Street in Old Montreal, I was always preceded by my own personal piper, playing one or another of my favorite tunes.

Her Majesty smiled—a bit oddly, I thought—and walked on. Then the regimental sergeant major, who had overheard this exchange, took me aside and explained: "Padre, maybe it's time we told you *why* you have your own personal piper wherever you go in the armoury. It's so *we know you're coming*!"

When the Queen Mum departed Canada from Toronto, the Black Watch provided the final honour guard. The highest-ranking officers of the Toronto Scottish escorted Her Majesty right up to the stairway of her plane, while the various brass of the Black Watch were relegated to a vantage point behind a velvet rope over one hundred feet from the action. Just before she came to the stairway, the Queen Mother glanced around, obviously—very obviously, I realized later—as though looking for someone. Out of the corner of her eye, she spotted us, confined behind our velvet rope, stopped, turned left, and marched over to greet the colonels and me before she departed. Later, I learned to my satisfaction that she had sized up the situation pretty insightfully and had said in a very loud voice, "We cannot leave without saying 'goodbye' to our dear Black Watch officers!" It was the last time I attended her as padre, although we remained in occasional communication through Sir Martin Gilliat throughout the remainder of Her Majesty's long life.

Lest any of my readers have the impression that the Black Watch (Royal Highland Regiment) of Canada had to do only with garden parties, balls, and parades, let me set the record straight. In the seventies and eighties, the Canadian military establishment was undergoing many changes and challenges. On strength, the Black Watch Regiment comprised three battalions. However, through the unification of the Canadian Armed Forces, the first and second battalions were stationed at CFB Gagetown in southwestern New Brunswick and were gradually being assimilated into the mean green machine that was training for and distinguishing itself largely in peacekeeping deployments for the United Nations.

The Third Battalion, now under the Quebec Command and stationed in Montreal, carried on the historic traditions of the oldest highland regiment in Canada, dating back to 1862. Originally raised as a militia company to protect the Canadian border during the American Civil War, units of the Black Watch fought in the Boer War, WWI, WWII, and the Korean War. In my time, the Watch trained strenuously and constantly as a militia to be prepared to assist and defend in natural disasters and civil unrest locally as well as in peacekeeping assignments in the Middle East, Eastern Europe, and the Caribbean. Wearing the Black Watch kilt on every possible occasion, the Third Battalion supported—and still maintains—the regiment's pipes and drums, several cadet corps, and veterans' associations across Canada.

I often found myself in the armoury on Wednesday evenings, sometimes sharing in a training exercise with the men—and eventually women—or consulting with the commanding officer about issues of morale, discipline, and, occasionally, the death of one of our soldiers. Given the degree of civil unrest percolating through all levels of Quebec society at that time, the Watch was on high alert and steadily reviewing the levels of military intervention that might require deployment around the time of the referendum and its aftermath. I worked particularly closely with Lt. Col. G. Douglas Robertson, who was also a young elder in the Church of St. Andrew and St. Paul. With his encouragement, when the time came for me to be eligible to apply for promotion to field-grade rank, I did so and began a rigorous program of self-preparation to attain the rank of major.

That summer, there came an unexpected opportunity for me

to go to Gagetown for two weeks' training, participating in a huge division-level military exercise. I was designated a "padre at large" and assigned to bunk with *le 12e Régiment blindé du Canada,* a French-speaking tank battalion from Valcartier, Quebec. In order to conduct nondenominational worship services at the multiple encampments spread through the 1,100-square-kilometre base, I had the use of a jeep and driver and, on Sundays, a helicopter and pilot.

At the end of the exercise, there were three days of war games. The *Douzieme* commanding officer invited me to tag along for extra training credit. I had a ball! Each night we slept in squads of three under our tanks. Every day we practised manouevres to be demonstrated in the warfare to follow. On the third day, I was installed in one of the umpire tanks and instructed to throw out noisy and smoky cherry bombs when and where commanded!

At the conclusion of the games, I was given the great honour of commanding the retreat back to our quarters in the lead tank. I shall never forget the thrill of standing in the turret of that huge and menacing Leopard, leading a column of vehicles and weaponry as far behind me as the eye could see. During an informal mustering out, the CO spoke warmly of the role I had played in the activities of his regiment over the past two weeks and concluded, shaking his head as if in regret: "Just one complaint, Captain Russell, you're much too *warlike* to be a padre!"

Back in Montreal, after a brief holiday sojourn at the Little Pink Palace and unbeknownst to the A & P elders or the trustees for that matter, I was feeling unexpected pressure from a source totally unrelated to all we had been through over the sovereignty association question in Quebec. Down in the United States, several big-name Christian pastors and televangelists had been exposed for scandalous and unscrupulous behavior, including extravagant lifestyles that belied their commitment to the gospel of Jesus Christ. At this time, I was becoming more and more keenly aware of the deepening ambivalence with which I believed some people were viewing me and my leadership roles in Montreal and in the Presbyterian Church in particular. I was also becoming increasingly uncomfortable about some of the perks that defined our family's lifestyle. Living in the manse in Richelieu Place—a then $800,000+ four-story Georgian brick townhouse at the top of one of the most desirable residential addresses in the heart of downtown Montreal—topped the list. I could just imagine the headlines, to say nothing of the twisted truths, about our expensive address, about our three children each in a different (and very expensive) private school, about my wife Ann's involvement in the snooty Junior League of Montreal (of which she had just become president-elect), and about my memberships in the Royal Montreal Curling Club and the Montreal Badminton and Squash Club, and on and on.

It occurred to me that this period in which some of the church leaders were concerned about the possibility of my leaving Montreal might be the ideal time to raise a possibility that had lurked in the back of Ann's and my minds for over a year already: that the church might help us buy a modest home, probably in Westmount, from which our children could attend the excellent public schools available for residents of that community and for which, over the remaining years of my ministry, I might manage to pay down a mortgage and actually own a home by the time I retired.

I took into my confidence the clerk of session, the chairman of the board of trustees, and the chair of the session's personnel committee, who agreed to form a small task force to consider the possibility of doing as we were asking. For six months, we bided our time, read the real estate section of the *Gazette* weekly, and dreamed of the joy and relief that would be ours if the powers that be agreed.

But they did not. Although they all could see the merits in our proposal, they pooh-poohed the idea that I was sufficiently newsworthy for a reporter to dig into my personal life enough to create a scandal over our living in Richelieu Place. Beside which, the manse had been gifted to the church for use as a manse by a Mrs. Mabel Cottingham, who remained one of the wealthiest and most generous benefactors of the church and who might be offended if the minister and his family were allowed—and, God forbid, supported—to move and live elsewhere!

I was deeply disappointed and grievously hurt. Ann was furious and never really got over her anger and disgust. With Rebecca now in kindergarten and our empty nest an unhappy home, Ann accepted an offer of employment by the Montreal district secretary of the Canadian Bible Society and went to work full-time as the district's financial secretary. She virtually withdrew from the activities of the women's association, although she attended worship faithfully (as a good minister's wife should) and participated in some of the social events of the St. Andrew's Society. At the end of November, as mentioned previously in passing, we quietly entertained the Earl and Countess of Strathmore and Kinghorne, cousins of Her Majesty Queen Elizabeth the Queen Mother, not realizing that this would be our last brush with the Scottish aristocracy we had come to admire and enjoy so much.

The CBC had been so pleased with the success of their sing-along event for the previous Christmas that they approached us early in the summer about doing it again, to which we agreed. In the same way, our sixty-second advertising spots on CJAD

radio had sparked such interest (and attendance) that it was resolved that we should actually enlarge the scope of the effort
and prepare a month's worth of messages, each highlighting a
worship and music event for each of the Sundays in Advent and
then, of course, for Christmas Eve. The excitement and challenge of preparing for all of these events proved a healthy anti-
dote to the malaise of spirit I had been feeling earlier in the year,
and I put all tempting thoughts of moving *anywhere* out of my
mind. To seal the deal, at least for myself, I recruited and em-
ployed a retired United Church of Canada minister, Donald
Burns, as a minister of visitation and Norma Goldsmith, the
deaconess wife of a fellow clergyman in the presbytery, as the
church's director of Christian education.

Other than the two unforgettable weeks I spent at CFB
Gagetown, I remember little else about that second half of
1981, save that eventually Montreal's winter weather played
havoc with each and all of our planned special Advent and
Christmas events. Although the children's Christmas pageant,
the CBC Christmas sing-along and carols by candlelight all went
off without a hitch, attendances were disappointing, despite the
intensive and costly radio advertising, and my spirits sank
further and further with each new disappointment.

A week before leaving for Rondeau and a much-needed
post-Christmas vacation, I had relented and given a lengthy telephone interview to Claude Arpin, one of the most distinguished
journalists, whose byline regularly appeared in the *Gazette*. Ostensibly, we were to talk about the CJAD radio advertising cam-
paign, but M. Arpin kept introducing the subjects of evangelical
megachurches and their purported "sheep stealing." I learned
a bitter lesson when I returned to Montreal after New Year's to
realize that his account of our interview had been twisted almost
out of shape to support his preconceived idea that traditional

churches were fighting for their lives in competition with the nondenominational megachurches springing up in both Canada and the United States.

In the interview, I had explained that what we are really trying to do is not necessarily promote the Church of St. Andrew and St. Paul as much as to suggest that churchgoing is an attractive option or experience and that the mainline churches are every bit as welcoming and every bit as full of spirit as the more extreme churches. Later, I added,

> Another thing we're trying to do with this campaign is to revitalize the morale of English Montreal with the realization that one of its very old, very traditional, and very threatened institutions is alive and well.

To which M. Arpin commented in print: "The situation has to be drastic indeed for this conservative church, above all others, to use such a secular tactic."

The church's parishioners were angered! The elders were enraged! The trustees were apoplectic! And I was all to blame. At the next session meeting, the elders reinvoked their quasi-gag-rule against my speaking to or in the media—*any* media, on *any* subject—for the foreseeable future. Needless to say, I was heartsick and hurt and bewildered.

Ironically, it was exactly at this point in mid-January of 1982 that our Richelieu Place neighbours, Herb and Lois McLean, invited me down to their townhouse to meet their son-in-law, a Toronto lawyer and elder at St. Andrew's Presbyterian Church, King Street. To my amazement, he confided to me that his church was about to lose its minister, and he wanted to discuss the possibility that I might be open to a call to ministry in Toronto's most prestigious downtown Presbyterian Church. I say "amazement," indeed, since twice before during my years in ministry, St. Andrew's King Street had tried to call me to their ministry, and I had twice rebuffed their advances!

I was feeling so vulnerable, though, that this time I agreed to consider the possibility. Truth be told, St. Andrew's King Street was probably the only Presbyterian congregation in Canada to which I could have moved at that point in my career without taking a tremendous step backward ecclesiastically as well as financially. So we made arrangements for me to create some excuse to have to travel to Toronto for a couple of days, during which I would very quietly and confidentially take another look at St. Andrew's.

I was not impressed. In fact, I was terribly distressed to recognize how far St. Andrew's had fallen since I had last looked it over a decade before. The historic building was in a shambles of disrepair; the average Sunday morning attendance was below one hundred; a proposal to sell off the church's center-city-Toronto air rights (as the Fifth Avenue Church in New York City had just done successfully) was stalled in uncertainty. Nevertheless, my host and a couple of trustees painted an optimistic picture of the effect that my energetic and visionary pastoral leadership could have in restoring this once-great congregation to at least an echo of its former self.

Back in Montreal, the Canadian Bible Society was gearing up for its district annual meeting, and the district secretary was determined to have me accompany Ann to the dinner and to take some part in the program. The guest speaker was to be the Reverend Dr. Kenneth G. MacMillan, a former moderator of the Presbyterian Church's General Assembly, with whom I had worked closely as chair of the Special Committee on National Unity as well as the Assembly's Nominating Committee during the year of his moderatorship.

To everyone's evident surprise, Dr. MacMillan took the opportunity of the district annual meeting to announce his plans to retire at the end of 1982. In the general conversation following the dinner, the current president of the Montreal District Board of Trustees, an ecumenically-minded Roman Catholic nun, took me aside and indicated that she wished to nominate me to be Dr. MacMillan's successor! Even Ann had no idea this was coming!

With two very different, equally intriguing and equally unexpected opportunities to leave Montreal and start a new life and work in Toronto, I was deeply torn but unexpectedly convinced that this was God's providence at work for good in not only my life but in Ann's and in our three children's lives as well. Ann was equally torn. She loved her Bible Society work and her involvement in mission endeavours that spanned the globe through the worldwide undertakings of the United Bible Societies. But she was the president-elect of the Montreal Junior League, an organization to which she had belonged first in New Jersey and ever since we came to Montreal and had just attended the League's international convention in San Francisco a couple of months before.

February and March were painfully conflicted for us both. Keeping all this secret from our family, friends, coworkers, and parishioners was a terrible strain. Unbeknownst to either party, both St. Andrew's Church and the Canadian Bible Society kept trying to sell us on their job offers. It all came to a head in mid-April, when I went to Toronto to meet with both parties. I spent the first two days of the week at the Bible Society headquarters, where Dr. MacMillan was more than a little surprised to learn that I might be the candidate to succeed him, a possibility about which I was still less than sure.

On Wednesday evening, I met with the pastor nominating committee of St. Andrew's Church at a beautiful home in Rosedale. I could not believe how the conversation left me cold. There was about these congregational leaders a smug self-satisfaction that I found chilling, and their blithe confidence that I, personally, was the answer to all their church's problems felt like ice water poured over every expectation that I had found intriguing. By the end of the evening, I left, knowing in my heart that whatever the next couple of days brought, they would not be bringing me to St. Andrew's King Street!

On Thursday morning, I met with the Bible Society's national board of directors' executive committee. We had a very frank discussion about the leadership needs and challenges the Bible Society faced, not only in Canada but worldwide. Direct mail fundraising had been introduced in Bible Societies in the United States and Europe and was challenging the appropriateness of the district secretary and board pattern of operation that had prevailed ever since the founding of the British and Foreign Bible Society in the early 1800s. They offered a generous salary package, the assurance of a role for Ann to play at the national level, the prospect of a low-interest mortgage loan to enable us to buy at least a vacation home of our own while we lived in the handsome manse in Toronto's very desirable Lawrence Park neighbourhood, and the freedom and flexibility to carve out a new general secretary leadership role both nationally and internationally, differing from the benevolent dictatorship that had prevailed during Dr. MacMillan's tenure.

As noncommittal as I thought I was being as we parted for lunch and I went back to my hotel to telephone the chair of their PNC to say that St. Andrew's was not the call for me, I was astonished to learn that in the afternoon meeting of the whole Bible Society national board, district secretaries, and representatives as well as senior staff at the national headquarters, it had been announced that I was the candidate of choice and that I would be introduced the next morning before being voted into office!

Which I was with evident and welcoming enthusiasm from everyone I met, save Dr. MacMillan. By the time I flew back to Montreal that afternoon, the sun was already beginning to set on my ministry in the Church of St. Andrew and St. Paul, and I felt unexpectedly wistful. Ann was astonished to hear about all that had happened and confessed that she, too, felt uncharacteristically uncertain about this abrupt swerve in our mutual career paths and that she would particularly regret turning her back on the Junior League to which she had devoted so much time and attention.

Within days, uncertainty turned to unhappiness at seemingly every turn. As we explained to our children that we would be leaving Montreal at year's end, Rebecca burst into tears, and Kirk vowed that he would not go. Sarah, who was living at home, recovering from a nasty bout of mononucleosis acquired during her first semester at the University of Windsor, was unusually quiet about it all, but I could see that the wheels were already turning in her mind.

We got through the weekend without anyone in Montreal learning of our momentous decision, but the hiatus did not last long. Monday evening was to be the regularly scheduled monthly meeting of the kirk session, and I knew that I had to break the news to them before any of the elders learned of it elsewhere. The elders' reactions were far worse than I had expected. John Durnford asked whether I would change my mind if the board of trustees would agree to help us buy a home in Westmount. Lawrence McDougall sneered that the Bible Society was about as relevant as the IODE! But Bruce Gill evidently spoke for them all when he confessed tearfully, "I feel betrayed!"

It felt as though my ministry came to an end that night. Everything I did from that moment on was tinged with recrimination, rejection, and regret. The personnel committee objected to my staying on until the end of the year, preferring that I resign by the end of the summer. An informal search committee was formed without my knowledge or advice and set to work as had been done in the past, only to have the whole effort overturned when the Presbytery of Montreal stepped in and appointed an interim moderator.

I made the mistake of appealing to the chairman of the Bible Society's executive committee to see whether Dr. MacMillan might change his retirement and departure dates to allow the Russells to move in September rather than at the end of the year. Dr. MacMillan was infuriated by the suggestion and angrily refused to budge. Our once-friendly relationship was shattered at that point, never to be retrieved.

Sarah surprised us—pleasantly—with a decision to transfer from the University of Windsor to the University of Toronto, beginning after the first of the new year of 1983. Upon reflection, Kirk announced that he would only move to Toronto and Upper Canada College either before the new school year began in September 1982 or after it ended in June of the next year. Rebecca remained heartbroken and tearful on every possible occasion. She hated the idea of transferring from Collège Marie de France to the Trafalgar School for Girls for a half-year of English-language education and made our lives miserable on pretty much a daily basis.

Nor was Ann spared the general unhappiness. Although her colleagues at the Montreal district offices of the Canadian Bible Society were thrilled at the prospect of her becoming a national staffer, her Junior League friends abandoned her and her leadership role forthwith. So bitter were the feelings of so many

Montrealers that some of them never spoke to her again.

One *happy* cluster of memories from that fateful year bears recording here. While serving as the minister of the Church of St. Andrew and St. Paul, I had become friends with the Roman Catholic archbishop of Montreal, Msgr. Paul Grégoire. In January 1982, he accepted my invitation to preach in the A & P on the Sunday of the Week of Prayer for Christian Unity, the first time he had ever worshiped in a Protestant church.

The service amazed His Excellency: the long choral processional, the prayerful elements of the liturgy he recognized as being very similar to his own, even the neo-Gothic architecture with its vaulted ceiling, soaring stained glass clerestory windows, and alabaster Communion table he quite rightly thought was an *altar*! As we were processing up the center aisle at the end of the service, Grégoire turned to me and whispered: "Ah, Reverend Russell, I confess that I am a sinner: I *envy* you your cathedral!"

Afterward, Ann invited His Excellency to return with us to the manse for Sunday dinner, which he was delighted to do. It was a simple meal, as I remember it, but Ann presented it in the dining room of our Richelieu Place townhouse with grace and flair. As he was leaving to return to his own residence downtown, Grégoire said with a twinkle in his eye: "Ah, Reverend Russell, I confess that I am now *doubly* a sinner: I envy you your *wife* too!"

Later that year, on October 31st in fact, Pope John Paul II canonized the first Canadian woman saint and the first Canadian person to be canonized since the elevation of the eight so-called "Canadian martyrs" in 1930! The canonization of Ste. Marguerite Bourgeoys, founder of *la Congregation de Notre Dame* (ca. AD 1700), was an occasion of immense historical and ecclesiastical significance in Montreal, where it was celebrated by a mass conducted by Msgr. Grégoire in the Cathedral Basilica of Mary, Queen of the World on Dorchester Street, where I was invited as the archbishop's special guest.

When I arrived at the basilica, robed in my fullest clericals, I was escorted to an elevated seat in the apse and was told, more or less, to sit, stand, and kneel when the other clergy did but otherwise to stay out of the way until the mass was over. Later I learned that I had been seated in the archbishop's own *cathedra,* which he would not need that afternoon because he would be on his feet the whole time.

After the Mass, there was a brief reception, then a very formal dinner, in Grégoire's official residence. I was seated at a table of French-speaking nuns, all of whom were amazingly respectful and excited to be seated with me. During the course of conversation, I mentioned *"ma femme"* (my wife), which startled the nuns, one of whom blurted out in shock, *"Votre femme!?"*

As best I could, I explained, in French, that I was *un pasteur presbyterien* and that I was allowed to have a wife. To which my bewildered questioner responded, *"Alors, pourquoi la bague?"* (Well then, why the ring?) To my amazement and their amusement, I realized that they had been thinking that I was at least a *bishop,* probably even an *archbishop* because of where I had been seated in the chancel of the cathedral and that my amethyst ring was a sign of my *episcopacy*!

Otherwise, the rest of the year ground on inexorably toward our eventual departure for Toronto. Providentially, one of the young families of the congregation—the aforementioned Ian Robinsons—moved back to Toronto at the end of the summer and took Kirk with them as a boarder for the fall term at Upper Canada College to which he had been admitted as a transfer student from Selwyn House without question. It proved to be an unexpectedly difficult time for Kirk; but he had insisted on such an arrangement, and he bore it manfully.

Sarah kept a low profile, gaining strength as she recovered from her bout of mononucleosis and managing the paperwork flow that resulted from her application to move her Assumption University credits to a bachelor of commerce degree program at the University of Toronto.

Rebecca was enrolled, much against her wishes, as a one-term student at the Trafalgar School for Girls, which had a long and historic association with the Church of St. Andrew and St. Paul. One of the perks of that relationship was that I served as vice chair of the board of governors. Becca was in rebellion from day one, all of which came to a head on the occasion of the annual Trafalgar-Ross lectureship to perpetuate the memory and intention of the school's benefactor and founder, Donald Ross,

> to bring before a large audience of students, old girls, parents, staff and friends of the school, a speaker of prominence and personal distinction, whose address will prove of lasting influence and inspiration for our students.

The Trafalgar-Ross lectureship had been my brainchild in the year before, and I thought I had been fortunate to secure as the second lecturer Mme. Marie-Josée Drouin, an eminent Canadian economist and the wife of Charles Dutoit, the conductor of the Montreal Symphony Orchestra. As it happened, I needed to be in Toronto for some reason on the day of the lecture, so I missed experiencing in person Becca's crowning achievement at "Traf!" Bored to tears—so were most of the girls as it turned out—Becca and a classmate, seated on folding chairs in the second row of the auditorium, began quietly untying the distinctive uniform sashes of the girls seated in the front row and then just as surreptitiously retying them around the backs of their folding chairs. At the end of the lecture, the requisite standing ovation for the guest speaker exploded in a hilarious clash and clatter as the front row girls stood up tied to their chairs!

On returning to Montreal from Toronto, I was livid upon learning what Becca had done to "my" lectureship! I dragged her over to the school for an appointment with the principal, Mrs. Janette Doupe, who earnestly tried to discipline Rebecca for my benefit while barely containing her admiring laughter. Ironically, a year later, on our first Halloween in the Bible Society manse on St. Leonard's Avenue in Toronto's Lawrence Park, a cluster of youthful trick-or-treaters from Branksome Hall regaled Becca with a story told by their new principal, Mrs. Doupe, which, of course, was all about Becca!

I have no recollection of meeting, let alone entertaining the Earl and Countess of Mansfield at the end of November, so perhaps Ann and I did not even attend the St. Andrew's Ball during our last month in Montreal. The traditional Advent special services unfolded as they should, I imagine. Again, I have no recollection of our last events—the Sunday school Christmas pageant, the CBC's Christmas sing-along, the chancel choir's carols by candlelight—my heart was just not in them! Our congregational farewell was held in Kildonan Hall, following morning worship on the fourth Sunday in Advent; I was to be spared the emotional upheaval of conducting the Christmas Eve service, where we were presented with silly little gifts for the children and a magnificent painting of *Baie St. Paul* by Marius Mauro, which now takes pride of place in Kirk's family home.

Our worldly goods had been packed and shipped at the end of the week preceding our farewell, and we stayed as a family with Dorothy Stairs through the weekend before setting out for Toronto and our new life with the Canadian Bible Society. The

MacMillans had finally—and grudgingly—vacated the manse on St. Leonard's Avenue, and some modest renovations had already begun there; so we stayed overnight in a motel nearby, unpacked what needed to be left in Toronto, and set off for Windsor to visit the Russell and Trotter grandparents and thence overnight to Saint Petersburg, Florida, for a ten-day respite at Nana's Place.

* * * * *

EARLY IN THE NEW YEAR OF 1983, we returned to Toronto in time for Kirk to resume classes at Upper Canada College and Rebecca to begin her education at a local Toronto public elementary school. Disappointingly, not much progress had been made on the renovations to the St. Leonard's house during the holidays, so we coped with much ado about nothing for a while.

Before we left Montreal, Ann had ordered half a butchered lamb that we carried from Montreal to Toronto, frozen, on the roof of our station wagon and then carefully placed in our freezer chest left sitting in the middle of the about-to-be-renovated kitchen. Unfortunately, some thoughtless workman unplugged the freezer to move it and forgot to plug it back in. By the time we discovered it, the stench of rotting meat had pervaded the chest and filled the downstairs of the house the minute we opened the lid. The lamb was a dead loss—pun intended—as was the ruined freezer chest, and the odour lingered for many months as a reminder of all the mixed emotions with which we had moved from Montreal to Toronto.

As Ann and I began work at the Canadian Bible Society national headquarters on Carnforth Road in East Toronto, we were surprised to learn that Dr. MacMillan had decided that I should undertake a tour of the nineteen Bible Society districts as the guest speaker at their various annual meetings held during the month of February. Ann was not to accompany me, as she had been assigned a desk in the financial offices under the supervision of the society's chief financial officer, Dr. Russell T. Hall, who became a wonderful friend and pillar of strength for both of us during all of our Bible Society years.

We quickly learned that both the national offices and the Central Ontario District office and bookstore had only recently been moved from their original and historic location in downtown Toronto to spacious commercial premises off Lawrence Avenue in the city's eastern suburbs. The building, which featured a warren of small cut-up office suites fronting a huge warehouse, had been taken as is and moved into without any renovations or even any significant forethought as to the best uses for the existing spaces. The prime space at the main entrance had been given over to the Central Ontario District, whose district secretary, Andrew Brndjar, was a great favourite of Dr. MacMillan. The general secretary's office was tucked into the farthest back corner of the administrative area—virtually invisible and certainly hard to find—which apparently suited Dr. MacMillan's administrative style but would hardly do for mine.

I also learned that as I visited each district location and spoke at the annual meeting thereof, I would be expected to illustrate my speech with slides depicting Bible Society work. Having none, I bought a good camera, took a lot of photos depicting the new Toronto offices and warehousing and the people who worked there and developed a set speech titled "First Impressions." As I began to tour the districts, I took photos in each location and added them to the set speech. To my surprise and relief, the speech was enthusiastically received across the country. Most Bible Society supporters had never visited the new Toronto facility or had any idea of the vastness and incongruity of the eighteen other district offices and personnel beyond their own.

Other aspects of the trip were not so satisfactory. Cross-Canada travel in the depths of winter was neither easy nor comfortable. Apparently, Dr. MacMillan had always insisted on staying in the homes of the district secretaries or officers of the district boards wherever he went. I found this an intolerable imposition, not only upon my district staff colleagues but even more so upon the few hapless district board presidents who were expected to provide room and board for as many as the three or four days of my stay in each locale. Particularly egregious, I still remember, was the situation in Saskatoon, Saskatchewan, where the district board president was compelled by the district secretary to house and feed me even though his wife had been called away to tend to a family medical emergency elsewhere, leaving an empty refrigerator and an unmade guest bed for her poor husband to cope with.

As graciously as possible, I expressed sincere gratitude for whatever hospitality I received wherever I went, but I also made it clear to each district secretary that I would henceforth prefer to be put up in a local hotel, where I could have some peace and privacy as I prepared for and undertook whatever duties future visits might entail.

One of the unexpected delights of several of these initial visits was meeting and getting to know the provincial lieutenant governors who were "patrons" of the various district societies. As titular representatives of Her Majesty Queen Elizabeth II, they were gracious, charming, and hospitable supporters of the Bible cause, and in several provincial capitals extended sincere invitations to me and my wife to stay in their respective "government houses" on future visits to the districts.

I shall never forget my first encounter with the lieutenant governor of British Columbia at a church supper preceding the annual meeting of the Bible Society in Victoria, BC. Arriving at the church and clambering out of the back seat of a small sedan driven by the district secretary, I caught my trousers on a seat-belt anchor and ripped open the backside seam of my suit pants from waistband to crotch! Mortified, I spent an hour and a half with my back to whatever wall I could find, while chit-chatting with the very regal vice-regal "patron" of the district society. To my horror as the formal meeting began in the church sanctuary, a large choir unexpectedly filed into a spacious choir loft immediately behind the podium. Realizing that I could never keep my secret and maintain my dignity while standing in front of them to deliver my speech, I decided to be proactive about my plight and throw myself on the merciful understanding of the lieutenant governor and the whole assembled audience.

Following my address, which, unfortunately, was punctuated by peals of laughter when one after another of my prepared remarks disclosed another unintended but hilarious double entendre, the lieutenant governor began his formal "thank you" speech with the words, "I never expected the new general secretary of the Canadian Bible Society to be such an *open* young man!" Amidst the uproar of laughter, we became fast friends from that very moment!

To my surprise and dismay, I also learned several things that disturbed me very much. First, I came to realize that however much he was admired for the decades of work he had put into making the Canadian Bible Society what it had become, Dr. MacMillan had become personally disliked by many Bible Society supporters and was regarded by most of the district secretaries as having been a benevolent dictator, who had been unpleasant to work for and hard to please. Second, I was told a number of times as I traveled across the country that many in the Bible Society had been surprised and not necessarily pleased that another *Presbyterian clergyman* had been chosen to succeed Dr. MacMillan when the society was emphasizing its interdenominational character and lay leadership. Third, it was finally put to me by a group of disgruntled board members in Newfoundland that the long-time head of Bible production and distribution for the national society had been their preference to become general secretary, and they would find it hard to give their loyalty to my leadership. By the time my "First Impressions" national tour came to an end, my unspoken first impressions were bleak indeed!

Meanwhile, back in Toronto, one of my few stalwart supporters on the national executive committee had engaged a young Presbyterian architect to conduct a feasibility study with regard to a more thoughtful use of the newly-acquired facilities on Carnforth Road. The architect turned out to be one Murray Ross, with whom I had traveled across Canada many years previously on that summer of 1960's NFCUS train tour for a band of university students chosen for their potential leadership qualities for Canada's future. Murray and I had hit it off way back then and had kept in sporadic touch over the years since. We hit it off again as we shared our various insights and ideas for a better use of the spacious resources at our command in the national headquarters of Canada's "Bible House."

My main concern was that my personal office space should be as close as possible—and as accessible as possible—to the front entrance of the building. In Murray's eventual plan, that involved moving the whole Central Ontario District operation out of the prime space they then occupied. Logistically, it was the right thing to do; emotionally, it created such resentment in the Central Ontario District secretary and his secretary/wife that eventually they left the Bible Society's employ in a manner that caused reverberations across Canada. It mattered not a whit to them that the new design placed their district office and Bible bookstore in an equally prime space immediately inside the front entrance, just to the left rather than to the right of where they had previously been located.

The other design features received a more welcoming response from the national staff. The chief financial officer and his staff were relocated to the peace and quiet of the far back corner where my office had been. A bright and airy staff lunchroom was carved out of excess warehouse space as was a spacious conference room large enough to hold the full complement of district secretaries and representatives who traveled to Toronto every year for the national society's annual meeting, thus saving us the expense of hiring a meeting space in one of the nearby hotels where the delegates were housed. Handsome modern furniture was purchased for the offices of all the management personnel, and the main entrance was equipped with a stunning reception area that made a tremendously positive first impression on visitors.

One of the very first distinguished visitors to see the renovated facilities was Dr. Ulrich Fick, the general secretary of the United Bible Societies, who detoured from his constant world travels to come to Toronto to meet the new Canadian general secretary. Uli and I felt an instant rapport, and he suggested that at the earliest possible opportunity I should make a trip to Europe to visit the British and Foreign Bible Society in London, the national Bible Societies in Germany, France, and the Netherlands as well as the UBS global offices in Stuttgart. That conversation set in motion a truly memorable tour for both Ann and me that included an unexpected foray behind the Iron Curtain to do some work with four of the national Bible Societies operating in Communist-controlled countries in Eastern Europe.

But first, accompanied with icy determination by my aforementioned Bible production and distribution colleague, I traveled via Miami to Panama City and my first annual meeting of the heads of the national Bible Societies in North, Central, and South America. In hasty preparation for the trip, I purchased the Peter Pimsleur Harvard University cassette tapes offering a crash course in learning Latin American Spanish. As we drove back and forth to work each day, Ann and I listened faithfully to the tapes until by the time of my midsummer departure, I had learned some rudimentary conversational Spanish.

At the opening of the meeting, each person present introduced himself or herself. I was surprised that neither of the representatives of the American Bible Society (ABS) spoke any Spanish, since almost everyone else in the room was unilingually Hispanic. I was an instant sensation when I introduced myself with "*Mi nombre es Guillermo Russell!*" Little did I realize that I had already upstaged the general secretaries of ABS, who never quite forgave me my unintended affront.

This was my first real exposure to the worldwide scope of the United Bible Societies (UBS), and I learned a lot. In Canada, our emphasis was on scripture translation projects into our own indigenous Cree and Inuktitut languages as well as stockpiling, producing, and retailing various scripture resources in as many as one hundred different languages and dialects. But in the Hispanic societies of the Americas region, I soon realized that there was much more emphasis on distribution programs involving literacy scriptures and inexpensive "missionary" editions of gospel portions and New Testaments. I heard about the difficulties in and importance of working with the Roman Catholic majorities in virtually every country and the distinctive UBS use of native speakers of the indigenous languages being translated as compared with the tradition of other Bible Societies (like the Gideons, for example) who trained North Americans and Europeans in the languages on which they were to do translations.

I also learned a lot about the robust camaraderie among the Latino general secretaries. The Puerto Rican general secretary had originally been a radio announcer and had perfected the deep-throated rapid-fire delivery of an on-air personality. Every evening, he emceed a Spanish-language revue of the day's events with hilarious results. On the very first day of our meetings, he approached me quietly and inquired whether I would be offended if they included me in the repartee, hinting that the ABS general secretaries had no sense of humor and were easily offended. Of course, I agreed enthusiastically, and thus was born "*La Cucaracha Canadiense*" (the Canadian cockroach), an identity that followed me throughout my Bible Society career. As expected, the ABS general secretaries were not amused!

On the return trip, I stayed in Miami for a couple of days to make the acquaintance of the UBS Americas regional staff and to learn even more about the multiple facets of our Bible Societies' work throughout the region. Given the importance of indigenous language translation in Canada, I was fascinated to learn about the Quechua and Aymara translation projects in Bolivia and Peru and made a promise of sorts to highlight these projects in Canada's direct-mail fundraising efforts for the UBS global mission budget.

Despite having been out of the office for so long, I really needed a bit of a break; so while school was out, we five Russells went to Rondeau to spend a couple of weeks at the Little Pink Palace. Our idyll was heartbreakingly interrupted by the sudden and unexpected death of Ann's father, who had been diagnosed the year before with an aneurysm of the aorta. Once his funeral and burial were over, so was our vacation, and I headed back to Toronto to pack my bag for wherever it was I was scheduled to be, leaving Ann and the children at Rondeau to console her mother, Mimi, and one another in my absence. It was the first of many occasions when the work of the Bible Society took precedence over the life of my family, and it was a mistake I came to rue for the rest of my life.

However, once back in Toronto with Ann also back at work, our attention turned to preparation for our first European factfinding travel. Over the summer, the UBS regional secretary for Europe and the Middle East had started pushing for us to extend our visit to include three or four countries behind the Iron Curtain in Eastern Europe. Eventually, we agreed to add Hungary, Romania, Poland, and Czechoslovakia to our original itinerary of England, the Netherlands, Germany, and France.

We flew to London in early October and spent time both with the British and Foreign Bible Society (BFBS) and the UBS regional offices in their historic building at 146 Queen Victoria Street in the city. We were surprised to learn that the very first BFBS translation project had been the Gospel of John into Mohawk for Canada's indigenous people in the early 1800s.

We also visited the proposed new location for the BFBS in Swindon, an industrial town some seventy miles from London in southwest England. There, away from listening ears in London, the BFBS general secretary spoke very frankly of the shift in Bible Society priorities from regional districts with localized staffs to a centralized effort, emphasizing a nationwide direct-mail fundraising effort and up-to-date publishing facilities housed in modern logistically sophisticated warehouse operations. I recognized immediately that the Canadian Bible Society was on the cusp of a very similar shift, which would certainly be accompanied by all the pains and intrigues about which our host was apprising us.

Back in London, we had a scheduled orientation with the western UBS world service officer and his staff, with particular reference to the second half of our trip into Eastern Europe. While we were in his office, a telex was received from the Polish general secretary, requesting that we procure two pounds of bone meal to carry with us until we reached Warsaw. Although she had no idea what bone meal was, Ann was dispatched to find and buy some and thus missed out on a part of the orientation that would prove crucial later in our trip.

We traveled by boat train from London to the Hook of Holland, then on to Amsterdam, only learning as we traveled that the Dutch railway system had gone out on strike, and the whole country was at a standstill. We were to be met in Amsterdam by a representative of the Netherlands Bible Society (NBS), but, of course, no one showed up! Eventually we procured some Dutch coinage, found a pay telephone, reached the NBS, and arranged to be picked up by automobile in the plaza outside the railroad station several hours thence.

While we waited, we wandered center-city Amsterdam. What a shock! We were totally unprepared for the rampant and open drug use, the storefront sex shops, the red-light district, and the general amorality of the city. When we finally reached Haarlem, the home of the NBS, it was like a total disconnect: a suburb of Amsterdam, it was nevertheless a charming, clean, medieval town of cobblestone streets and gabled houses. The NBS was housed in an ultramodern printing and distribution facility, where the general secretary and his associates were all laypeople totally focused on the business side of printing and promoting the sale of a wide variety of scriptures in many languages and formats, including a Bible in today's Dutch, a scholarly edition in several languages, and missionary editions for Africa, the East Indies, and Latin America.

We were surprised to learn that the NBS had been one of the national Bible societies instrumental in the organizing of the UBS in 1946 and had purposefully extended its efforts since in directions almost *opposite* to the traditional modus operandi of the British, American, and even Canadian societies.

It was all about business, and the gruff general secretary scoffed at the foolishness of our Canadian translation efforts to produce New Testaments in Cree or Inuktitut at a cumulative cost of hundreds of thousands of dollars and then to sell the publications to our native peoples for about $2.00 per copy! In the end, we agreed to disagree, and the rest of our brief stay in the tulip capital of the world went pleasantly enough.

Next stop on our tour was Stuttgart, the home of both the UBS and the German Bible Society (GBS). A large industrial center (think Mercedes Benz and Porsche) in southwest Germany, it did not surprise us that the Bible Society presence mirrored more of the Dutch and less of the British modus operandi. Like the Dutch, the Germans were heavily invested in large printing presses and worldwide distribution contracts: Bibles, New Testaments, and gospel portions were in production for every continent on the globe, and fundraising for the global mission of UBS was highly sophisticated and impressively profitable.

At the UBS headquarters, Uli Fick was on hand to greet us and introduce us to the surprisingly small global support staff. He invited us to dine at home, where we met his charming and understated wife, who made it very clear that she was tired of her husband's globetrotting job and was eagerly awaiting his scheduled retirement in a few years. Once again, we were given an orientation in preparation for our visit behind the Iron Curtain, quite different in tone from the experience in London a couple of weeks before and much more sinister in its frankness of the how's and whys of UBS involvement with the Communist governments in the countries we would be visiting.

Our last stop in Western Europe was *la Société Biblique Française,* located in a small village some thirty kilometers southeast of Paris, where the francophone *secrétaire général* maintained a home office and small book depository. Though he was surprised to learn that I spoke rudimentary French, he seemed more threatened than pleased. In fact, he was very defensive about his premier position in the *Alliance Biblique Française,* which was supposedly the alliance of all the French-speaking Bible Societies of the world of which *la Société Biblique Canadienne* was but one.

He was inordinately proud of having obtained a Roman Catholic imprimatur for *Bonne Nouvelles d'Aujourd'hui,* the French version of the contemporary simplified English New Testament published as *Good News for Modern Man* but was frustrated that he had thus far been unsuccessful in securing a similar imprimatur for the French equivalent of the complete *Good News Bible* published as *La Bible en Français Courant.* Surprisingly to me, he seemed almost mistrustful of the CBS for seeking to publish Canadian versions of both scriptures for Quebec and actually fearful that he would lose control of the worldwide copyright monopoly he had thus far enjoyed in printing the only available copies of these contemporary French versions of the New Testament and complete Bible, which was, of course, exactly what happened when CBS began printing and publishing editions of both scriptures that were better products at cheaper prices and making them available through UBS to French-speaking ministries in francophone countries all over the world!

Ann and I were scheduled to fly out of Charles de Gaulle

Airport for Budapest, Hungary, on October 24, 1983. The day before, a Turkish suicide bomber had killed 241 American military personnel in an Islamic terrorist attack on a US Army barracks compound in Beirut, Lebanon. We were blissfully unaware of this horror story until we received a frantic telephone call at our Paris hotel early in the morning: Sarah, Kirk, and Rebecca had managed to track us down and place a transatlantic phone call to plead with us *not* to go behind the Iron Curtain when we all might be on the verge of World War Three!

Despite the heartbreaking pleas and tears of our children, we determined to go ahead. The airport was a shambles. Everything had ground to a halt. As a few international flights began to board, long lines of travelers submitted to lengthy and total strip searches. Ann was in tears: "I'm willing to go with you wherever you are determined to go, Bill," she moaned, "but I am not willing to be strip-searched here and now! If that's what it takes to get to Budapest, you will have to go without me!"

God has a sense of humour! Almost immediately, an airline agent began calling out the number of our flight, ironically headed for Istanbul as well as Budapest. He whisked us through a rudimentary passport and ticket check and herded us onto a plane ready for take-off. Among other things, it was our first experience of the Eastern European way of dealing with no prearranged seat assignments: every man for himself and let the women beware of being trampled underfoot!

Arriving in Budapest, we immediately sensed that we were in a different world. Armed soldiers were everywhere. Even before we got to passport control, we were required to buy 5,000 Hungarian forints for each day of our visa's four-day stay. Under the watchful eye of the military, we cleared passport control, obtained our luggage, and passed through formidable barriers into the public area of the terminal. There we began the unsettling process of looking for a total stranger flashing the most recent issue of the UBS yearbook. Finally, we spotted a young man in a dark suit, shirt, and tie, who spoke English and turned out to be the comptroller for the Hungarian Bible Society.

We were taken to a guest house, clean and modern and operated under whose auspices we never did learn, where we were shown to a spartan room with two twin beds made up in the European way with fluffy duvets and mounds of pillows, a decor style that had not yet made its way to North America. Our young host waited for us while we unpacked, freshened up, and settled in and then took us to meet the Hungarian Bible Society's executive team for dinner.

Later, back at the guest house, I got out my little pocket tape recorder to record a detailed account of the day's activities, only to remember the severe warnings in our orientations both in London and in Stuttgart to the effect that we ought to assume that every room we stayed in in Eastern Europe would be bugged! With hand signs, I told Ann that I was going to go out for a walk, during which I would record my day's observations. But once outside and on a tree-lined street with only occasional dim streetlights and traffic slowly passing by, I realized that I might look incredibly suspicious walking around talking into a tape recorder! So I returned to our room, packed the recorder away and suggested to Ann quite loudly that I was going to write some postcards to the kids back home.

This became our euphemism for my daily bedtime note writing in one of the two steno pads I had thought to pack back in Toronto. The idea that someone—anyone—might be hearing every sound in our bedroom troubled Ann more than it did me: she developed a sick headache that never totally left her through the fortnight of our time behind the Iron Curtain.

The next morning, after a very odd breakfast of cold cuts, cheese, pickles, and rolls served with delicious (and very strong!) coffee, we were picked up by the trio of Bible Society executives and taken to the Hungarian Bible house. There we learned about the to us almost unbelievable situation in which the Bible Society was able to produce and distribute Bibles and New Testaments legally in an officially atheistic and anti-Christian country. Working with the government-owned and operated University Press, the Bible Society was currently committed to printing 50,000 Bibles in Swahili for distribution in various countries in East Africa in return for which the Bible Society was being allowed to print 10,000 Hungarian-language scriptures for legal distribution primarily through the Hungarian Reformed Church across the country. The key, of course, was hard currency: everything paid for in American dollars, British pounds sterling, or German Deutschmarks!

Armed with this knowledge, we were taken to visit the University Press, where we were received like visiting royalty. In fact, dressed in a smart gray wool skirt-suit and being (we learned later) the first Bible Society *woman* any of them had ever seen, Ann was escorted gallantly through the whole printing process, while I trailed along behind, feeling much like Prince Philip accompanying Queen Elizabeth II. I did step forward, however, when we spotted a pallet stacked with some of the 50,000 Swahili Bibles and took some pictures to show back home in Canada as proof of what we would be telling Bible Society supporters across the country.

The next day, we made an unforgettable trip eastward across Hungary, almost to the Romanian border of Transylvania, to the ancient city of Debrecen to visit Tibor Bartha, the presiding bishop of the Hungarian Reformed Church. For a brief period in the mid-nineteenth century, Debrecen had been the capital of

Hungary as well as the locale of the University of Debrecen, the Reformed Theological Seminary and the *Nagytemplom* (Great Calvinist Church). Bishop Bartha was at the time of our visit being vilified in the West as a traitor and a puppet of the regime for his leadership in what he called "Evangelical Calvinism." In truth, his skillful and at times wily compromises with the Communist reality in his country led to the eventual empowerment of the Reformed Church as a counterbalance to the constantly persecuted Roman Catholic Church and even the emergence of the Marxist recognition that

> religion is not merely a remnant from the ideology of the historic past, but religion is a process satisfying social needs, (and) for this reason its passing away cannot be forced into a short time prognosis.

While visiting the *Nagytemplom,* our Bible Society trio insisted on garbing me in one of the quaint and characteristic pleated robes of Hungarian Reformed clergy and photographing me in the church's historic pulpit, a singular honour bestowed on visiting Christian leaders of international distinction and renown!

Then we were off to meet Bishop Bartha. He was charming and gracious, with a gravitas that was at once overwhelming and intimate. Eventually, I felt comfortable enough in his presence to query his feelings about his vilification in the West versus the adulation in which the martyrs of the faith in Hungary were held. I shall never forget the pathos and the wisdom of his reply: "There are some things worse than dying!"

Our third full day in Hungary was spent visiting Reformed pastors who were actively involved in the Bible Society's various programs of scripture distribution and Bible teaching. Our trio of hosts were determined to send us back to Canada with living proof that with the financial backing of UBS and its global mission budget, the word of God was *actually* being printed, distributed, and read in Communist Hungary! Little did Ann and I realize at the time how invaluable that proof would be when we returned home and began to tell the story to skeptical audiences across Canada.

Throughout our stay in Hungary, our Bible Society comptroller host had footed the bill for everything we had done. I still had 20,000 forints burning a hole in my pocket and so I began to insist that on our last night in Budapest Ann and I would like to treat the trio and their wives to dinner at a *really* Hungarian restaurant, complete with authentic cuisine and gypsy violinists. Almost as insistently, the two married executives demurred, and so it went, back and forth, all day until finally they relented and agreed to meet us with their wives at just such a restaurant that night.

It was a fabulous occasion! The food was extraordinary, the wine flowed freely, and the gypsy music was heart-stirring. However, when I excused myself late in the evening to go to the men's room, the young comptroller followed me. "Don't you realize," he began as soon as we were in the restroom, "that you are *shaming* us by insisting on paying for this dinner? Don't you know that if we are ever allowed to visit you in Canada, you will have to pay for *everything* for *us* because we will not be able to bring any money with us?"

Truly abashed, I agreed to silence my insistence and allow the Hungarian Bible Society to treat us to this memorable night out. Once we returned to the table, the check was presented, and the whispering among the Hungarians began. The comptroller emptied his official purse and then his personal wallet. So did both of the general secretaries, then their wives until in the end they confessed that, among all of them, they barely had enough cash to pay the bill, let alone leave an appropriate tip! Happily, I assured them that I would gladly contribute a 5,000 forint bill if that was sufficient, or more if necessary. They looked at me as though I were mad!

But the next morning, at the airport, I learned one of the most important (although never mentioned by anyone anywhere) lessons in Bible Society protocol. With the trio crowded around us, we advanced in line toward the first security gate, where armed soldiers were questioning each departing traveler and pocketing money that was obviously being confiscated. When I asked our friends what was going on, they explained that no one was allowed to leave the country with any Hungarian currency. "Well, I don't want to give 15,000 forints to *them*! Can I give it to *you*?"

"That would be very welcome! Thank you!"

So, with that, I emptied my pockets, they recouped 15,000 forints of their expenses entertaining us, and we all left happy! I also realized that this was an unspoken arrangement to be respected in any country with currency regulations; so respect it we did throughout Eastern Europe and then later in most countries of Central and South America.

It was a relatively short plane trip from Budapest to Bucharest, but the heavy hand of the Russian occupation of Romania was even more evident. From our airplane window as we taxied to a remote far corner of the Bucharest airport, we could see two Soviet tanks patrolling the space between the tarmac and the terminal building. We deplaned between two heavily armed soldiers at the foot of the stairway and then went between two more to board a bus that carried us at least a half mile to the terminal where more heavily armed soldiers patrolled the roofline.

In fact, similarly armed military personnel were everywhere

in evidence, first as we exchanged US dollars for Romanian leu, then at passport control and finally at long tables set up for the thorough inspection of the contents of every suitcase, handbag, and other form of luggage. As we neared the tables for our turn at inspection, I kept noticing a little leprechaun of a man jumping up and down outside the glass partition that separated us from the waiting public, shouting something incomprehensible, presumably in Romanian. As I hefted our biggest and heaviest suitcase up on the table, Ann abruptly swung her almost-as-big-and-heavy suitcase into my rear end, thrusting me forward enough that she could put her luggage on the table at the same time.

The leprechaun kept jumping and shouting and evidently finally caught the attention of the soldier who was about to open our bags. Shouts of what we later learned had been "Guests of the patriarch! Guests of the patriarch!" resulted in his asking incredulously, "*Tourista*? *Tourista*?" and then heaving our luggage off the far end of the table for us to retrieve, unopened! The leprechaun turned out to be "Father George," a priest of the Romanian Orthodox Church, an aide to the patriarch, and our host and guide for the next few days.

In the "small world" department, Fr. George boasted that he spoke good English because he had for a few years served as a priest at St. George's Romanian Orthodox Church in Windsor, Ontario. When he overheard me asking Ann why she had goosed me with her suitcase back in the terminal and then heard her explaining that someone behind her in the line had whispered in her ear, "You carry package through for me?" he blanched and blurted out: "That would have been an agent provocateur, trying to make trouble for the patriarch and his guests. You might have ended up in prison!" Ann's headache that had started back in Budapest just got a whole lot worse!

No sooner had we checked into our hotel than Fr. George insisted that we leave at once to attend an event celebrating the climax of the feast day festivities honoring Bucharest's patron, Saint Dimitrie Bassarabov. We walked a few blocks from the hotel to a vast esplanade that reminded me of the Champs Elysées in Paris; not surprising, Fr. George commented, because before the ravages of the Second World War and the Soviet occupation of Romania, Bucharest had been known as the "Paris of Eastern Europe!" There we saw literally tens of thousands of Romanians, mostly babushka-wearing women, carrying candles and singing psalms as they surged forward toward a catafalque at the far end, where, Fr. George explained to us, the patriarch of the Romanian Orthodox Church waited to receive us and welcome us to his country and his church.

At the foot of the catafalque, we were instructed to climb the few steps to the platform on which sat a gold and jeweled chest with a large black circle in the center of the top. Each of us, in turn, was to kiss the black spot, descend another set of steps, receive a bouquet of flowers, and be escorted into the presence of the patriarch. Ann preceded me, did what she had been told, and disappeared as I climbed up the steps. When it came to kissing the black spot, I wondered how many thousands of Romanians had already kissed it that day, so my lips hovered just above the spot for a reverent moment and then I too descended from the platform, received my bouquet, and went inside a pavilion nearby to be received by the patriarch.

As we waited with Fr. George for our moment with the patriarch, I asked him what that had all been about. He explained enthusiastically that the bejeweled casket was believed to contain relics of St. Dimitrie, which were traditionally to be reverenced with a kiss on the back of the saint's mummified hand! I nearly gagged, took a deep breath, and greeted the patriarch.

Later, back at the hotel, we began the sinister routine of returning to our room. As we approached the lobby, the desk clerk never lost eye contact while he reached under his counter and produced a key attached to a large and heavy brass ball. The elevator was dimly lit, shaky, and slow. When it stopped at our floor, we stepped out into total darkness, save for a lighted toggle switch on the wall beside the elevator door. Thinking nothing ventured, nothing gained, I flicked the switch and a single light bulb illuminated a long hallway. Before we walked all the way to the end of the hall where our room was located, the bulb switched off, leaving us, again, in total darkness. Abandoning Ann in the dark, I retraced my steps to the elevator, flicked the switch, and ran to open our room door before the light would go out again. Eventually, we learned the Romanian trick of my staying at the light switch to flick it on as often as it took Ann to reach our room, open the door, and turn on the light inside.

We had been warned back in London that our hotel room in Bucharest would certainly be bugged, and it was not hard to believe. Signs of Soviet oppression and suspicion dogged us throughout our stay in Romania. Walking out with Fr. George the next morning, I wanted to cross the street to take a picture of our hotel as I had planned to do at each location throughout our trip. He did his best to persuade me that I did *not* want or need a photo of this elegant old hostelry, but I persisted. As I raised my camera to my eye, a uniformed soldier grabbed my arm and pushed it down to my side. Then he remonstrated angrily with Fr. George, who lamely explained to us that in Romania no photographs of sites necessary to national security were allowed but that he had persuaded our unofficial escort not to confiscate my camera.

Our morning was spent at the patriarch's printing press,

where we inspected shed after shed filled with already-printed sheets of Bible paper. We learned about the Bible Society's deal with the government of dictator Nicolae Ceauçescu, whereby the Romanian Orthodox Church was allowed to produce a limited number of legal Bibles and New Testaments each year on the conditions that all the raw materials were provided from the West and shipped in Romanian trucks with all the labour paid for in hard currency provided by UBS. At that time, the latest shipment of Bible paper had all been printed on to prevent its being confiscated for other uses and was being stored until supplies of cardboard, fabric, and glue would arrive to enable the press to complete the print quotas allowed for that year. I was permitted to take as many pictures as I wanted, for which I was doubly grateful when we got back to Canada and reported these details to skeptical and unconvinced Bible Society audiences across the country.

In the afternoon, our guide took us out into the countryside to visit a monastery where the monks were heavily involved in legal scripture distribution and teaching. It was a fascinating trip: we marveled at the lush beauty of the farmlands and the centuries-old techniques of planting and harvesting. We were promised dinner with the monastery's abbot; but when the time came, he never showed. Later we learned that he was afraid to meet us for fear that we would say something untoward about our afternoon's experience when we got back to our hotel room, and he and his monks would bear the brunt of Ceauçescu's displeasure!

The next day was spent in and around Bucharest, visiting various churches and ministries whose clergy were also involved in legal scripture distribution and teaching. For the first time, we began to hear about the problem of "Bible smuggling" from the point of view of those who were cooperating with the patriarchate and the United Bible Societies in the production and distribution of scriptures and testaments that were validated for use in Romania because of our contracts made with Ceauçescu's government.

At that time, Bible smuggling was all the rage in certain evangelical and conservative circles both in Europe and in North America. But most of the Bibles brought into Romania by well-meaning but ill-informed (or ill-intentioned) innocent tourists or professional smugglers were apprehended and confiscated by government agents. As shockingly but truthfully reported in the West, these scriptures were routinely trashed and recycled into toilet paper, which was bad enough; but far worse was the confiscation and desecration of the equivalent numbers of our "legal" scriptures as a deterrent to the smuggling in the first place! This was a part of the story no one in the West ever heard!

Time after time, those working with UBS and the patriarchate pleaded with us to go back home and do everything we could to denounce and discourage the Bible smuggling efforts that were actually hampering the free and legal use of our scriptures. Unfortunately, it was an aspect of our tour that did not resonate well when we spoke about it back in Canada and actually caused us angry disruptions at events in the Bible Society districts that we visited afterward along with unfavorable media coverage across the country.

On our final morning in Romania, the airport departure experience was much less nerve-wracking than our arrival experience. Perhaps we were just getting more used to the armed military presence everywhere? Perhaps we were less troubled by the constant sense of the authorities' intrusion into and observance of our private lives, supposedly without our knowing? As we approached the departure security gates, we unselfconsciously handed over our stash of unspent leu to our genial host, who equally unselfconsciously accepted the cash with a simple "Thank you."

Our third destination was Warsaw, Poland, where the work of the Polish Bible Society was in the hands of a remarkable woman, Mme. Barbara Narzinska, whose husband was at that time the presiding bishop of the Polish Lutheran Church. Barbara and Ann hit it off immediately as two of only a handful of women in leadership roles in the UBS worldwide. Barbara escorted us to Warsaw's beautiful and modern Hotel Intercontinental, where we were to stay for almost a week. Quickly she brought us up to date on the political situation in Poland. The rebellious union leader, Lech Walesa, was under house arrest; martial law was in effect across the country; and strict rationing of basic foodstuffs was enforced in all the major cities. Because the majority of Poles either were or had been traditional Roman Catholics, the Soviets were purveying their usual atheistic hypocrisy of religious "tolerance," suppressing the dominant Christian denomination and laying much looser restrictions on the lesser church bodies of which Barbara's husband's Lutherans were the largest and most influential denomination.

Under Barbara's skillful and diplomatic guidance, the Bible Society had established a respectful working relationship with the Communist Polish government and had successfully translated, printed, and published a Polish Bible—*Pismo Święte*, the Warsaw Polish Bible—for free and legal use in the various Protestant churches in Poland.

As soon as we were settled in our hotel room, Barbara whisked us away by car to a mysterious destination, a darkened and apparently deserted old cathedral-style church, which we entered stealthily by an inconspicuous side door. Once inside, she led us through a warren of darkened hallways until suddenly we entered a gorgeous and brilliantly candlelit Roman Catholic sanctuary full of Saturday night Mass goers. Sliding into a few spaces left at the end of one of the front pews, Barbara admonished us, "Just listen!" The celebrant priest was leading a lengthy litany of intercession, not a word of which could we understand until, without warning, Ann and I realized simultaneously that *we* were being prayed for *by name*! To this day, it remains one of the most poignantly memorable moments in all of our Bible Society travels!

It was now the end of October. On our way back to the hotel, Barbara explained that tomorrow would be a very special worldwide Reformation Sunday observance of the 450th anniversary of Martin Luther's posting of his Ninety-five Theses on the door of the Wittenberg Schlosskirche in Germany. To mark the occasion, her husband had persuaded the Polish government's minister of culture to allow for a nationwide live broadcast of the anniversary worship service from the Holy Trinity Evangelical Church of the Augsburg Confession—*Kościół Świętej Trójcy*—at which Dr. Narzinsky was to be the preacher and to which we were invited.

It was an incredible experience. Holy Trinity Church, built in 1777–1782, is a classical rotunda, based partly on the Roman Pantheon. Its central dome is 33.4 metres in diameter and fifty-eight metres in height, and its impressive double gallery encircles the whole interior. So finely tuned is its architecture that it has been a renowned site for musical performances from concerts by Chopin to performances of the Warsaw Chamber Orchestra. The service lasted an hour and a half, and we learned later that every moment of it had been broadcast across Poland by the Communist-controlled radio network.

Equally incredible, though, was the after-service luncheon hosted by the Holy Trinity pastor and his wife. Despite the stringent food rationing, twenty-four dignitaries, including Ann and me, sat down to dinner at one table in the magnificent dining room of the church's manse. The menu included twelve tissue-thin slices of cooked ham cut in triangles and twirled artistically on a platter, twenty-four deviled egg halves, an overflowing green garden salad, a bountiful bowl of mashed potatoes, and a baked apple dessert. The dinner conversation swirled around the table in Polish, German, Russian, and French and focused mainly on scholarly comments about Martin Luther, Protestantism, the World Council of Churches, and the success interdenominationally of the Bible Society's Warsaw Polish Bible. Ann and I were in awe: not a word of English was spoken, yet we were included in the conversation using our Québécois French. As we rose from the table when we were finished, several of the guests noted that there were still a half slice of ham and a half of a deviled egg left on the platters and remonstrated with the pastor's wife for her excessive generosity in having provided such a rich banquet that there were *leftovers*! Ann and I nearly wept in admiration and humility.

Monday was spent in by-now usual touring of the printing presses financed by UBS to produce a variety of scriptures in primarily African languages in return for a quota of "legal" scriptures in Polish and Russian. In a late-afternoon walk through a beautiful urban park, Ann finally got to ask Barbara about the bone meal she had been lugging around in her shoulder bag ever since the day of our first briefing in London.

"It was the price of your visas," Barbara explained. Her "friend," the minister of culture, had fallen off a street curb while walking his dog, and the bones of his broken ankle were not healing well. Bone meal from the West was demanded as the quid pro quo for our admittance into martial law-riddled Poland, and Ann was simply to lay the pouch wordlessly on

Barbara's desk when we got back to the Bible House.

At my request, we attended a performance of the Polish National Ballet that evening in the magnificent Warsaw Opera House. The production was sumptuous, the music was lush, and the dancers were . . . hefty! The difference between Western-style prima ballerinas and their Soviet-trained counterparts was at first amusing and then puzzling and finally symbolic of what we had been experiencing since we had crossed the Iron Curtain. In Warsaw as in Bucharest and Budapest, there were monumentally extravagant and impressive examples of culture, art, and architecture. But alongside them and grimly undercutting their grandeur were the Stalin-era replacements of other relics of the past that had been destroyed by World War II or the Soviet occupation itself, bunker-style buildings of drab concrete and rusting steel that were depressing even to look at, let alone to live or work or worship or play in them!

The next day was November 1—All Saints' Day in Roman Catholic countries worldwide—and we were to join an old Catholic bishop and his secretary on a day's outing to visit a rural parish only a few miles from the Russian border. Although she had not given me very clear indications of her expectations of me for the day, Barbara was obviously perturbed when Ann and I showed up outside the hotel in informal layers of clothing chosen to keep us warm. "Where is his collar?" the bishop asked in Polish on first meeting me. "Where is his cassock? This is All Saints' Day and we are going to offer a mass for the town's dead!"

And, sure enough, that's what we did! After driving about an hour and a half, squeezed into the back seat of a very small Eastern European-produced car, we arrived in a farming community, the center of which was obviously the local Catholic church. Inside the presbytery, which was warm and cozy, we were offered tea and sweet rolls—no rationing here! The bishop and his secretary chatted at length with the parish priest—a short, fat, jolly little man clearly in awe of his episcopal visitor—most of the conversation seemingly in reference to me. By this time, the bishop's amanuensis had learned that Ann and I spoke rudimentary French, and finally he began to explain that the priest was being instructed to lend me ecclesiastical accoutrements appropriate for participation in the All Saints' Day liturgy.

Once I was rigged out in black pants that were too short, a clerical collar that was too big, and a cassock that was too loose, we set off on foot for the church, which was filling up in response to the summons of an energetic bell ringer. Inside the church, it was as cold as a tomb—literally—and rudimentary in every respect. As we processed in, the bishop's secretary informed me that His Grace had arranged for me to offer the homily with Barbara Narzinska interpreting and also for me to concelebrate the Blessed Sacrament during the mass.

Fortunately, the outline of the liturgy was familiar, so I knew what was going on even if I could not understand a word. When the gospel lesson was read, I realized that it was the Beatitudes from the Gospel of Matthew. Immediately, I knew that my homily text had to be Matthew 5:4, "Blessed are those who mourn, for they will be comforted." With Barbara translating every sentence, I acknowledged the mournful aspects of the day for the people of the village who had lost loved ones. Then I explained that it was also a day of mourning for my wife and me, who had lost her father just a few months before. A collective sigh from the congregation assured me they were with me. I spoke of the universality of death and mourning for each and all of us, even for God and his Son. By this time, there were tears in many eyes, including Ann's, which nearly did me in, so I switched to the gospel promise of comfort in our mourning, a promise on which we could rely because it was made by God's own Son, who knew whereof he spoke.

When I finished, the bishop got up from his seat, crossed the chancel and embraced me with the words, "*Mon frère en Christ!*" (My brother in Christ!), to which the whole congregation responded, "Amen!" Then we proceeded to concelebrate the sacrament of Holy Communion—a Catholic bishop and a Presbyterian pastor—a circumstance that would not have been possible in Canada then or even now but which seemed perfectly right on the Polish border with Russia on All Saints' Day in the family of the Bible Society.

Following the Mass, there was a raucous parade through the town to the parish cemetery, where families decorated the graves of their loved and lost ones and left specially-made candles burning on each and every gravestone. Dinner was served in the presbytery afterward, amid a lot of coming and going to and from the kitchen and the back door. Once the parish priest retrieved his regalia from me and I was in my own trousers, shirt, and jacket, representatives of the parish presented three huge baskets of produce, eggs, and a freshly slaughtered and plucked chicken, one each for Barbara, the bishop, and Ann and me. We were truly overwhelmed. To this day, I cannot recall that gift of such rural plenty in the midst of such urban want without tearing up.

The drive back to Warsaw was made memorable by the sight of so many candles still burning on gravestones and monuments in the cemeteries of the nameless villages through which we passed. When we returned to our hotel and were saying goodbye to the bishop and his secretary, I was able to tell the latter how much his conversing in French had meant to us and that we wanted him to have our gift basket for his own use and enjoyment. He burst into tears and hugged me, saying, like his bishop, "*Mon frère en Christ*!" No accolade before or ever since has meant as much to me!

The next morning, we were surprised to find Barbara waiting for us at the entrance to the hotel dining room. Realizing that she had accompanied us to every meal since our arrival, I assured her that it was not necessary for her to devote so much time and hospitality to us. "But it is!" she insisted. "You see, the tourist hotels are not rationed. Every meal I eat with you here puts more food on my family's table at home!"

Before we left for the airport, there was one more thing Barbara wanted to show us. Returning to the neighborhood of her Bible house, she took us around the corner and down the block to see the blackened ruin of a wall that still stood as a reminder of what had been the Polish Bible Society before the devastation of World War II. Emblazoned on that wall for all the world to see were the prophetic words of Isaiah: "The grass withers, the flower fades; but the word of our God will stand forever" (Is 40:8).

The fourth and final destination in our tour behind the Iron Curtain was Prague, Czechoslovakia. Once again, at the airport we bought the mandatory daily requirement of local currency, cleared passport control and customs, and began to look for a stranger carrying the ubiquitous UBS handbook. Our stranger turned out to be a meek and mild little man whose name, he told us, was Mirek, a nickname for a full name he would not share with us but all we needed to know. Mirek bundled us into a taxi, gave instructions to the driver, and then sat mute all the way to the Hotel Prague International, a stunningly modern and beautiful Western-style hostelry. Once he registered us and got our room key, he insisted, much against our urging, to accompany us to our room "To make sure," he explained, "that everything was satisfactory."

In our room, Mirek began to extol the beauty and efficiency of the new Prague subway system. As soon as we had gone to the bathroom and before we could even begin to unpack our suitcases, he became insistent that we accompany him to see the particularly beautiful subway station underneath the park on which the hotel faced. I argued that I had already seen subway systems in Montreal, Toronto, New York, London, and Paris, but he would not be dissuaded. So off we went.

Inside the subway station, which *was* beautiful but not so extraordinary as to warrant all the fuss, Mirek seemed to be waiting for something or someone. All of a sudden, we could hear trains converging on the station platform from two different directions. The noise was deafening, and the confusion of passengers dashing back and forth across the platform from one train to another was bewildering. In the midst of all this, Mirek grabbed my suit jacket lapels, pulled my head down to the level of his mouth, and shouted in my ear: "Your hotel room is *bugged*! Do you *understand*?" I nodded, he released me, the trains departed in opposite directions, and Mirek smiled for the first time since we had met him as he said, "Now I think you would like to go back to your hotel and freshen up!"

Such was our introduction to Prague, certainly the most repressed and hostile environment we had as yet experienced. Eventually, we learned that because of his representation of the United Bible Societies, Mirek and his whole family had been labeled Christian malcontents and his son, a licensed pilot, had been fired from his job with the Czech national airline.

Everywhere we went, Mirek first paused outside in the open air to brief us on who or what we were going to visit. A highlight of our tour was a visit to the Bethlehem Chapel of the Charles University, the first institution of higher learning in Central, Northern, and Eastern Europe. As we crossed the magnificent Charles Bridge, lined with renaissance statues of Roman Catholic saints, Mirek told us that we were about to enter one of the most revered sites of the Protestant Reformation, the very sanctuary in which Master Jan Hus, the university's rector, had preached in Czech, not Latin, as he expounded the fundamental beliefs of what within a decade of his own martyrdom in 1415 became Protestantism. There we would also meet the presiding bishop of the Czech Reformed Church.

For me, it was one of the most moving experiences of the whole tour. Jan Hus's preaching in the vernacular of his nation had become the impetus behind the translation of the Bible into the languages of the world's peoples, a foundational principle of the United Bible Societies worldwide. But when I thoughtlessly asked the presiding bishop about the size of his denomination in an atheistic and hostile Communist state, he replied: "Yes, it is a nice day, isn't it!"

Somehow, Mirek contrived to have us visit several Reformed churches on the outskirts of Prague whose clergy were actively involved in the dissemination of the very limited number of Bibles and New Testaments the Czech Bible Society was allowed to import and distribute legally in batches of 20–25,000 every five years under a contract negotiated by UBS with the officially atheistic government. This five-year importation was due for renegotiation, one of the reasons Ann and I were there, and one of the issues on the table was the Czech government's demand for a promise that the United Bible Societies would actively discourage Bible smuggling on the part of European and North American evangelicals—a tall order as it turned out!

In one of the almost invisible house churches, we met a university student doing Bible study with his pastor. Proudly, he showed us his own personal Bible, which he had received three years before upon being baptized. The book was in tatters, the imitation leather cover falling away from the spine, loose pages held reverently in order. I was appalled to think that the UBS had provided such a shoddy piece of work even as a "missionary" edition and said so!

Mirek looked crushed until the young man spoke up defensively: "You don't understand! I study my Bible every day! All the members of my family study my Bible every day! Three of my university classmates study my Bible every day! Our pastor borrows it several times a week for Bible study classes here at our church. We have worn my Bible out!"

Parenthetically, when Ann and I returned to Canada, this conversation became one of the most powerful anecdotes in our speaking engagements across the country. Whenever we used it, our last words were "How many of *you* have *worn out* your Bible in the last three years?"

As the historic capital of the kingdom of Bohemia and later of the Holy Roman Empire, Prague had been one of the most beautiful cities in Europe. During the Stalinist era, however, the municipal administration had become effete and corrupt, and much of the Baroque and Renaissance splendor damaged during World War II was hidden behind scaffolding, camouflaging he fact that little or no actual repair or maintenance work was being done. The so-called Prague Spring of 1967 had been brutally suppressed, and the fearful violence of that period had left the citizenry intimidated and leaderless. The anxiety was palpable and, ironically, prompted a licentiousness that was dismaying, if not shocking, in a city with such a rich Christian heritage. In the end, we were refused any access to the Communist ministry of culture, where any decisions about the importation of scriptures would be made, and we left Prague disheartened and grateful to be gone!

Our Montreal friends, Albert and Rosemary Schnell, had arranged for us to spend a day in and around Zürich, Switzerland,
with Albert's brother and his family. We were utterly overwhelmed by the cultural shock of flying a few hundred miles
from Prague after spending so much time behind the Iron Curtain. I shall never forget our feelings as we strolled down the famous Bahnhofstrasse, one of the most exclusive and expensive
shopping streets in the world. From poverty, oppression, fear,
and godlessness, we were suddenly in one of the richest and
freest places in the Western world.

To our amazement, we did not enjoy it. The shop windows
were filled with the most luxurious and extravagant of things,
and we were almost physically revolted. The careless and in-
considerate rudeness of the pedestrians made us ashamed for
their arrogantly taking for granted the privileges of freedom and
prosperity. Even the memorials to Huldrych Zwingli, one of the
very first heroes of the Swiss Protestant Reformation, seemed
shabby and neglected in the midst of such spectacular largesse.
His monumental statue by the River Limmat outside his Gross-
münster Church paid lip service to his being the actual founder
of the Reformed—as opposed to the Lutheran, Anglican, and
Anabaptist—tradition in Protestant Christendom. But, sad to
say, the statue was actually overshadowed and obscured by a
huge old pine tree, and the interior of the historic sanctuary was
permeated by the stale smell of neglect.

For me as a Bible Society executive, Zwingli's theological insistence upon the primacy of scripture in defining the Christian
faith, his vernacular preaching of "true divine scriptures," and
especially his translation of a "native" version of the Bible—the
Zürcher Bibel in 1520—made him a true hero of the Protestant
Reformation, but you would never have known it in Zürich!

From the Communist rebuff in Prague to the disillusionment

in Zürich, our first Bible Society factfinding tour ended with a dull thud, and we flew back to Toronto heavyhearted.

In our absence, my support staff had lined up a few speaking and preaching assignments for me before the end of the year. But one of the unexpected benefits of Bible Society representation quickly became apparent. No one wanted or needed a Bible Society fundraising spokesperson during the holiday seasons of Advent and Christmastide, so we planned and eventually enjoyed a prolonged Christmas trip to Nana's Place near St. Petersburg, Florida.

The same could not be said of the winter ahead. As word spread through the Canadian Bible Society about our trip behind the Iron Curtain, *everyone* wanted me to speak at local and district annual meetings. To respond to the deluge of invitations, Ann and I agreed to split the country and to travel in opposite directions to offer the slideshow and speech presentation on which we had both been working ever since our return from Europe.

Thus was born the *real* Bible Society career of *Ann Trotter Russell*! Ann's charmingly understated and unexpectedly hilarious accounts of our adventures in Eastern Europe took the Maritime provinces by storm and then Quebec and then the Ottawa District! Meanwhile, I was delivering a more somber but, I hope, no less effective message in British Columbia and the Western provinces.

In Vancouver, the district secretary had wangled me an invitation to appear on *"Webster!"* a popular morning talk show with Jack Webster, one of the West Coast's most controversial broadcasters. For some reason, Webster seemed to take me in almost immediate dislike and kept interrupting, arguing, and belittling my standard media presentation. In particular, he took exception to my comments about the negative impact of Bible smuggling on the actual availability and distribution of scriptures in Communist Eastern Europe. Then listeners' telephone calls began to come in, and the dialogue became more and more heated until we were actually shouting at one another on the air. Later I learned that that particular segment of the program had one of the highest audience participations ever!

By this time, Ann and I had not seen one another in several weeks, and her scheduled speaking engagements had eased off so that she had a few days free. In what felt at the time like a terrible extravagance, she flew to Regina, Saskatchewan, to spend a night with me. On the spur of the moment, we decided to merge our two somewhat different presentations for the Saskatchewan annual meeting scheduled for our one night together. The result actually set a new standard for our Bible Society speechmaking, and we received the loudest and longest standing ovation of our combined tours.

The next morning, Ann was to return to Toronto, while I went on to Winnipeg. As I waited for my flight in the Regina airport, news flashed across the TV monitors in the seating areas that an Air Canada flight from Regina had skidded to a crash at the end of a runway in a snowstorm in Toronto. Initial reports indicated that there were no deaths but many injuries. I was beside myself with worry for Ann. Should I cancel my Winnipeg speaking engagement and fly back to Toronto, or not? Was Ann seriously injured, or not? In the end, I flew to Winnipeg as scheduled, figuring that if it turned out that Ann *was* badly injured, I could just get on another plane eastbound and if not, then I would complete my annual meeting tour and return home to stay for a while, which, in the end, is exactly what I did.

Looking back, I realize that this episode became a paradigm for our future in the Canadian Bible Society. The society's needs and expectations always trumped our own, and I, particularly, so often felt conflicted about what to do and when and why every time such a choice had to be made.

In fact, although Ann escaped the airplane accident relatively unharmed, it soon became evident that she was among the walking wounded emotionally and spiritually. She fell into a deep depression and had to be hospitalized in Toronto's Queen Elizabeth Hospital, where she remained comatose for several days. I was due to fly to Lisbon, Portugal, for a meeting of the general secretaries of the major UBS supporting societies. On the advice of Ann's doctors, I canceled my trip to remain at her bedside. Suddenly, one morning she awoke and, seeing me there, said, "Shouldn't you be in Lisbon?"

When I told her that I had canceled my trip to be with her, she became very agitated and insistent that I should have gone and still should! Her doctors agreed: the physical and emotional crisis seemed to have passed, and she was no longer in mortal danger. So my faithful secretary, Rhona, secured me the last seat on the next Air Canada flight to London, then on to Lisbon, first class all the way!

The meeting was, in many ways, inconsequential. But it introduced me to a unique echelon of United Bible Society leadership: the general secretaries of the *half-dozen* national Bible Societies which raised almost *all* of the UBS world service funding: the British and Foreign (BFBS), American (ABS), German (GBS), Dutch (NBS), Australian (AUBS), and Canadian Bible Societies. I realized for the first time that my predecessor had made little of the fact that even then CBS ranked fourth or fifth in the *world* in terms of financial support for all the worldwide translation, production, and distribution efforts undertaken by UBS and that became one of the primary emphases of my own Bible Society career. Over time, world service fundraising became such an integral part of our CBS efforts that one year, we outdid all but the American and German Bible Societies to become *third* in the world, an effort that spurred a healthy rivalry with the German and Australian societies but did not ingratiate me to the ABS and BFBS leadership.

Ironically, the most memorable part of the meeting came on the day when the Canadian Broadcasting Corporation (CBC) tracked me down in Lisbon for a live, over-the-telephone radio interview about the Bible smuggling controversy that was still simmering in Canada. My Bible Society colleagues, especially UBS General Secretary Uli Fick, were duly impressed that I had become such a star in the Canadian media!

Back in Toronto, the Canadian Bible Society was running along quite smoothly. In the negotiations leading up to my appointment as general secretary, I had insisted that as the price for agreeing to live in the society's manse on St. Leonard's Avenue, I would be eligible to avail myself of the low interest mortgage funding available to the district secretaries. Since there was no call for a Bible Society preacher on Easter Sunday, we Russells packed our Sunday best and drove down to Rondeau to spend a long weekend in the Little Pink Palace.

Alas, Easter Sunday dawned to a raging snowstorm that kept us indoors and away from church all day. Monday morning as we set out for home, we drove as usual along Lakeshore and Bates Drives, checking out the real estate offerings along the beach. A new listing caught our attention, and I made a mental note to contact the agent the next day. I did, only to learn that there was already an offer on the property. Disappointed, I mentioned to the agent that we owned a cottage on leased land within Rondeau Park but really wanted to buy a year-round home on Lake Erie, so could he keep us in mind if and when another listing came available? He scoffed at the idea:

"Do you realize how many people also want just that?" But a month later, on the Saturday morning of the Victoria Day national Canadian holiday weekend, he phoned to report the listing of a home we knew and would surely love to have.

Kirk had been out all night for Upper Canada's prom, but the minute he arrived home, we bundled us all in the station wagon and set out for Rondeau. On Sunday morning, we saw the house on seventy-five feet of lakefront and priced at $79,900.00. We made an immediate cash offer of $75,000.00 and called my parents in Windsor to see if they could come right down to check the place out with us. By the time they arrived, we had received a response from the sellers' realtor: they were holding fast at the original asking price. I shall never forget my father standing in the backyard, admiring the unobstructed view of Lake Erie and advising me, "Don't lose this for $5,000!" I immediately upped our offer to full asking price, the sellers agreed, and by suppertime we owned 11780 Bates Drive, RR#1, Morpeth, Ontario!

By the next day, the sellers' realtor was advising his clients that they had priced the property too low and should withdraw their acceptance of our offer. It turned out that the old couple were long-time Bible Society supporters, had recognized my name from the society's quarterly publication, and were proud to have us take ownership of their beloved home. At the Little Pink Palace, my parents astonished us by offering to forgive the mortgage indebtedness we owed them for the cottage and to buy it back for the same $10,000.00 we had paid for it originally. Back home in Toronto after the holiday weekend, the Bible Society's chief financial officer, the Reverend Dr. Russell T. Hall, made quick work of our mortgage application, and by June 1st we were able to close on the property, which I then owned for a quarter of a century!

Sometime in this period, Ann segued out of the financial department of the national society to become my administrative assistant to work with Rhona to support my increasingly heavy travel schedule and conflicting demands of being the CEO of a $10,000,000-a-year Christian charity as well as the head of one of Canada's largest book publishers and distributors and at the same time a major player in financial support for the United Bible Societies worldwide.

The one saving grace in this hectic schedule was the odd weekend when I would not have speaking engagements anywhere. Ann and the children would pick me up at the airport on Friday afternoon and drive us all to the lake house, where I would collapse with fatigue until Monday morning, when we would all head back to Toronto at the crack of dawn to take up the schedule again. With my parents just a mile away inside Rondeau Provincial Park enjoying the Little Pink Palace once again and my brother Tom and his family often at their cottage in the Bates subdivision halfway between the park and us, we had some wonderful family time together that summer. I particularly relish the memory of Dad's 70th birthday party around the big old picnic table in the Pink Palace backyard when all ten of us immediate family were in the same place at the same time.

Together, Ann, Rhona, and I strategized that Ann and I would make an international factfinding trip about once every eighteen months and that I would make at least one Canadian-based exploration of our society's work in between. The first such trip was to the Canadian Arctic Circle to visit the native translators who had been working without much recognition for many years on a New Testament in the Inuit language of Inuktitut. So, in the heat of a Toronto summer, I flew to Nunavit with my parka and snow boots to see firsthand what is involved in an authentic Bible Society translation project.

It was an incredibly interesting trip. The settlement known as Iqaluit is located on Baffin Island, just south of the Arctic Circle but in the permafrost tundra of the Canadian North. With every "mod con" known to man, the day-to-day life of the Inuit is astonishingly ordinary in many respects. Snug little homes perch on pilings high enough to clear the never-ending snowdrifts. The sidewalks are actually elevated boardwalks, hugging huge conduits that contain the community's utilities— electricity, water, sewage, telephone, cable TV, and (most important of all) the central steam heating system that warms houses, schools, churches, and stores while radiating enough heat upward to melt the constantly falling snow from the boards above.

In a modest home, a brief snowmobile's ride from "downtown," a half-dozen Inuit native speakers of their common language, Inuktitut, work under the supervision of the society's translation "guru" in Toronto. This arrangement is not only typical but actually fundamental to every UBS translation project around the world. Instead of training English-speaking people to parachute in and then work in the native language to be translated, the Bible Societies use only native speakers recruited from their homelands and communities and then trained to use the sophisticated translation resources developed by linguistic and theological mentors under whose supervision the work is carried out from beginning to end.

Explaining this system to Canadian donors and supporters of the Bible cause was what made Ann and me feel that we had to *go* to where the translators were and work alongside them for a while to get the feel of the various projects for which we were seeking Bible Society support. "Been there, done that" was our motto long before it became an English-language byword!

Inuktitut, for example, is an indigenous syllabic language in which words and sentences are formed by the combination of three-letter syllables based on the vowel sounds *a, e, i, u,* and rarely *o.* While I was visiting the Inuktitut project, they were working on a passage from one of the Pauline Epistles in which the phrase, "the throne of grace," occurs.

The Inuit live in a classless and virtually leaderless society: there is no hierarchical governing system, so there is no concept of "kingship" and no word even approximating the idea of a "throne." Eventually, we resolved the problem with a long and complex syllabic construction a full page wide: "the chair the big boss sits on when he is being the big boss!" How wide-eyed and satisfied were my translators when they finally realized what they had accomplished that day!

During the next year or so, I found this anecdote very helpful in explaining why the Inuktitut project was so important as well as so expensive. Our New Testament would eventually cost about a quarter of a million dollars spent over some twenty-odd years, but it would be the *first* piece of literature published in the Inuktitut language in a written form no native speakers outside of our translation group would ever have seen. That *the first words* the Inuit of Nunavit and the Northwest Territories would read would be the word of God seemed to me to be a priceless gift to the native people of Canada and to the little congregations of faithful Christians that had for so long struggled to make sense of the good news without any spiritual resources other than the oral testimonies of missionaries.

Although I was living quite comfortably in a small hotel "downtown," my translators wanted to treat me to an authentic and traditional Inuit dinner. Early in the afternoon on the appointed day, one of the men took a pickaxe and a shovel and went out onto one of the snowdrifts surrounding their house.

After a few minutes of studying the frozen terrain, he swung his axe, shoveled some snow, and produced a frozen shank of the deer they had hunted and killed in anticipation of my coming. While we continued to work on the translation project all afternoon, the meat defrosted on a pad of newspaper on the kitchen floor. About four o'clock, another of the men brought out a huge machete-like knife and began to slice the meat from the bone, dice it, and throw it into a stockpot of vegetables that had been simmering, unnoticed by me, all afternoon. Six o'clock was apparently time for a beer, after which the deer stew was served in what "down South" we might call deep round pasta bowls. With chunks of crusty bread to sop up the broth, we feasted on one of the most memorably delicious meals I have ever had!

On the last day before my visit was to end, my translators asked if I could pack my suitcase and leave it with them overnight. They had a farewell gift for me and wanted to have it ready for the flight home to Toronto the next morning. They wouldn't tell me what it was, no matter how I pleaded, threatened, and cajoled! "Wait until you get home," they insisted, "then unwrap it quickly and you will know what to do with it!"

So that's what I did: as soon as I got home, I opened my suitcase to find a big bundle of newspapers wrapped around a huge intact Arctic salmon, still frozen solid in its newsprint insulation and truly one of the best surprises ever in my Bible Society career!

Around this time, the Canadian printing and paper industries fell into a recession, which lowered production prices to a point that CBS began competing for Bible and New Testament projects globally. To my amazement and delight, we won a UBS contract to print 250,000 copies of the full-color edition of *Dios*

Habla Hoy, the Spanish common-language version of the *Good News Bible.* The result was that in 1985, the Canadian Bible Society was the second-largest book publisher in Canada!

The fall of 1985 was also the season for Ann's and my second Third World factfinding tour, this time to most of the Spanish-speaking national Bible Societies in Central America. We began with a few days' orientation in the regional offices in Miami, where firm friendships began forming with the regional secretary, Alberto Carcamo, and his associates, Luciano and Atalah Jaramillo.

Our first stop was San Salvador, the capital of El Salvador. We were met at the airport by a feisty little Spanish-speaking-only general secretary and his supposedly English-speaking son. We were immediately whisked somewhat urgently to a suburban motel where we were to have dinner and spend the next few nights. As we were preparing for bed and I was about to phone the front desk to try to arrange a wake-up call, the local skyline lit up with a series of explosions and every visible light in the neighborhood went out. It was eerie to be in a strange country in the pitch-black darkness and not have any idea what was going on! We decided that the safest thing to do was to get in bed and cover our heads until morning light.

At breakfast with our general secretary host and his son, we learned that the explosions had, in fact, been bomb blasts set off by the anti-government Salvadoran guerrillas. Under cover of darkness, the rebel soldiers went door-to-door through that part of the city, extorting money from every household. Trembling, our host described how he had answered a knock on his door only to find a bayonet at his chin and a demand for money. "Did you give any?" I asked incredulously.

"*Si!*'" was his laconic reply.

It had been arranged that I was to speak on behalf of the

Bible Society at eleven o'clock from the pulpit of one of the largest Pentecostal churches in San Salvador. We arrived while the ten o'clock service was still in progress. Over 1,000 believers packed an elegantly simple sanctuary, but the worship was remarkably subdued because, as we soon learned, most of the people present had been through the same harrowing extortion experience during the night.

What to say under such circumstances? I brought greetings from the global Bible Society fellowship and from the Canadian Bible Society, in particular. Then I recounted having been in Warsaw, Poland, two years before and described what I had seen proclaimed from the one wall still standing of the Polish Bible Society's bombed-out Bible house: "The grass withers, the flower fades; but the word of our God will stand forever" (Is 40:8). That brief citation evoked a chorus of "Amens," which segued into a spontaneous Hispanic outburst of the great hymn "To God Be the Glory," and my testimony was over.

After the service, our host suggested a Sunday afternoon drive up into the Salvadoran mountains. In my naïveté, I responded that having glimpsed an ocean shore from the plane on our approach to San Salvador, I would prefer to see the Pacific Ocean in person for the first time. It was agreed that we would go back to the motel to change, the general secretary would drive home and pick up his family, and we would go to the seashore.

It was not a very long drive, but once we approached a highway that obviously skirted the coastline, we began a long search for just the right place to stop. The general secretary would pull into a location, his son would leap out of the van and approach the nearest building, then come out shaking his head, and we would drive on to the next spot. Eventually, we ended up at a vacant church campsite. While we men changed into our bathing suits, the women, including Ann, sat huddled in the shelter of an abandoned pavilion, too modest, I assumed, to get into bathing suits in front of total strangers.

But as we started down a long path to the beach, Ann came hurrying after us: she wanted to see the Pacific Ocean too! On the beach, she sat on a driftwood log while we three men cavorted in the shallow breakers at the shoreline. Gradually, we wandered farther and farther from the shore until we were beyond the line of breakers. Suddenly, I heard the unmistakable crackle of gunfire apparently overhead. "Is that gunfire?" I asked.

"*Si!*"

"Where from?" I queried.

"*Ai,*" gestured our host, pointing to the mountainside paralleling the beach.

"Should we be here?" I was almost afraid to ask.

"No!"

"Then why are we?" I demanded.

"*Porque su queras!*" ("Because you asked!") the general secretary's son translated.

"*Ahora, vamos!*" ("Let's go, now!"), my limited Spanish vocabulary provided that much of an answer; so we ran to the beach, grabbed unsuspecting Ann by the hand, and fled!

On the drive back to San Salvador, we stopped at a roadside vendor's campsite to have something to eat. Still feeling pretty shaken but proud that my Pimsleur Spanish lessons were already beginning to pay off, I insisted on ordering my own meal from the menu board nailed to a palm tree, which both impressed and amused the cook as well as the general secretary's family. Ann joined the family in enjoying a small steak and salad meal, while I looked at what I *thought* was going to be *crabmeat* soup and saw a great big crab sitting in a bowl of broth, blinking at me!

To be honest, I had already learned two very valuable lessons that afternoon, and I do not remember much else of what went on during the rest of our Salvadoran stay.

The second stop on our Central American tour was Guatemala, where the general secretary was a tall, handsome Castilian Spaniard who spoke elegant English. Guatemala City was deceptively peaceful, even prosperous, and the Bible house was well-stocked with scriptures in several languages, including some of the *Dios Habla Hoy* Bibles we had printed in Canada. Proudly, I showed the staff the "CBS" imprint on the Bibles' spines, whereupon they insisted that I autograph a whole case of the Bibles and have my photograph taken with them as a special promotion.

The interior of Guatemala was a different story. The rebel "killing squads" were terrorizing the native population, especially any who abandoned the traditional version of Roman Catholicism for the evangelical faith of Protestant missionaries and also, of course, anyone promoting Bible knowledge through the use of our Bible Society literacy scriptures, many of which had also been published for UBS in Canada. We felt under constant threat and probably were, although the general secretary was a pretty savvy operative, and we survived unscathed.

A humorous anecdote: We visited Antigua Guatemala, the country's ancient capital, and its magnificent cathedral on whose front steps the local indigenous population had set up a makeshift mercado. Encouraged by our host, I haggled a bit with a native woman selling little cornstalk dolls in native dress, persuading her to sell me a doll for *tres dolares* rather than the starting price of *cinqo dolares*. Back in Canada as Ann and I were rehearsing our public speaking tour presentations, our younger daughter, Rebecca, scolded me ferociously: "Daddy, that woman needed those two dollars a whole lot more than you did!"

Another humorous—but pathetic—anecdote: Guatemala City had suffered a devastating earthquake in 1976, causing 23,000 fatalities, 76,000 casualties, and widespread damage to many of the most heavily populated areas. An estimated 10,000 Guatemalan Indians lived in a deep ravine in the shadow of *Volcàn de Fuego*, ominously smoking even while we were there. The Guatemalan Bible Society was partnering with a group of missionaries to sponsor literacy classes using scriptural materials CBS had produced, an obvious and compelling story for us to experience, photograph, and return to Canada to tell!

We spent an afternoon in the ravine with the missionaries, showing the native women our literacy scriptures and promoting the classes to be held at an open-air site nearby at the rim of the ravine. At one point, I realized that Ann was being besieged by a group of women who were demanding we knew not what. The general secretary none too gallantly suggested that perhaps they had never before seen a blond-haired, blue-eyed white woman! But I realized that they were snatching at Ann's glasses and suggested that she just take them off and hand them to one of the women. She took them off, helped a native woman put them on properly, and handed her a literacy pamphlet. The woman studied the pamphlet, then her face fell, and she handed the glasses to another woman to try on. Same routine, same reaction, same disappointment until one of the women explained to the general secretary that they had thought it was the *glasses* that enabled *la Norde Americana* to read and that if *they* put her glasses on, they too would be able to read!

Before we left Toronto, we had had a very frustrating time trying to obtain visas to visit Nicaragua. Eventually, I had gone to the home office of the Nicaraguan attaché in a Toronto suburb and literally stuck my foot in his doorway while insisting that I *had* to see the official in charge of visas. He was cold and austere and informed me that evangelical Christians were not welcome in Nicaragua under the Sandinista government. I responded that I would then also understand that the hundreds of thousands of dollars in hard currency we spent in the country every year supporting the Nicaraguan Bible Society and its ministries would also no longer be welcome!

"Es muy differente!" (That's very different!) he exclaimed and grudgingly issued the visas. "You will be admitted," he said in very clear English, "but you will not be welcome. You are forewarned."

At that time, Nicaragua was very self-isolated from the rest of Central America, and flights into and out of the country could only originate from or return to certain countries, one of which was Costa Rica. So at the end of our stay in Guatemala, we traveled to San José, home of the Costa Rican Bible Society, for a weekend. The local general secretary recognized that his society was almost as "Americanized" as was Canada's and was therefore of little interest to us for mission interpretation and fundraising back home. He also, wisely, recognized that having just experienced Bible Society work in El Salvador and Guatemala and heading next to Nicaragua and Honduras, Ann and I would actually benefit from a weekend's R & R!

So after spending Friday night in a modest hotel in downtown San José, we were picked up at dawn and driven to the airport for a quick flight over to the Pacific coast and a weekend at a resort known as Tamarindo. Before we left, we were puzzled by two things. First, the hotel did not check us out but kept our account open for our return on Monday. And second, at the airport, the general secretary handed me an envelope stuffed with 20,000 colones to cover our weekend's expenses. When I remonstrated that that was surely too much, he replied cryptically, "You never know!"

Our flight was a nightmare. The rickety biplane shook and shuddered both at takeoff and on landing, which it did often, for the twelve passengers were headed to four different destinations, ours being the last. As we took off after the third landing, we asked the pilot how he knew where to go, since there were obviously no navigation instruments on his dashboard.

"See that mountain up ahead? We fly to it, then turn left, and there we are!"

And there we were! To alert the resort that we were arriving, the pilot buzzed the main building before landing in a harvested cornfield, where a small pickup truck waited to take us and our luggage to the resort, which turned out to be one of the most luxurious and beautiful places we had ever been.

And one of the most isolated: there was no telephone service, no television, no flights in or out until our return on Monday morning. So Ann and I just gave in and enjoyed it. Until after wining, dining, and dancing under the stars on Saturday night, we returned to our room to find a handwritten note slipped under our door:

> Mr. Russell, Where are you preaching tomorrow morning?
> We are Bible Society supporters from Vancouver, and we
> recognize you from pictures in the quarterly newsletter, and
> we would like to attend!

As it turned out, our "supporters" were in the room next door, with which we shared a balcony! So much for R & R!

On Monday morning, the financial puzzlements from Friday began to become clearer. Being the most Americanized country in Central America, Costa Rica also had the most rigorous currency restrictions. Tourists were only allowed one transaction per venue, whether by cash or credit card. I paid our account in colones—others used credit cards—and then we sat and waited for the biplane to buzz the resort to tell us it was time to go to the cornfield.

We waited and waited for several hours, sitting on our luggage in a sunlit courtyard with no amenities. People began to be hungry and thirsty and needing *el baño*, but nothing was available to us because we had already paid—and closed—our accounts! When I realized that I still had over 5,000 colones in my envelope, I pleaded with the management to allow me to pay cash for some iced tea or lemonade for my fellow travelers, which was finally—and grudgingly—allowed.

Once a bathroom was opened for us, we few men allowed the ladies to go first. When our turn came, one of the American tourists approached me: "I'm a millionaire real estate developer here looking at properties and suddenly I have *no* money. You seem to have some: can I *borrow* a thousand *colones*?"

I agreed not to a *loan* but to a *gift*: "You can pay it back with a contribution to the American Bible Society when you get home!" At that moment, we became fast friends.

Still no airplane, and by mid-afternoon we were all famished and even the management was relenting in its strictness. "I have 3,000 colones left," I told the maître d', "what can I buy to give all twelve of us something to eat?"

He figured that the most nourishing thing he could whip up for twelve desperately hungry people was a dozen hot fudge sundaes! He took the rest of my colones, served us with a flourish, and left us to sit until just after 5:00 p.m., when our plane finally showed up. By the time we arrived back in San José, the Bible Society general secretary had given up waiting to meet us and had prepaid a taxi driver to look for us and drive us back to our hotel, where our room—and our open account—

waited for us.

As we checked in again at the desk, I spotted an English-language newspaper in a rack in the lobby. I told the night clerk that I would surely enjoy reading something in English after a couple of weeks in Latin America, but I literally had no money.

"*Firmar,*" (Sign for it) he said nonchalantly, and I did as the chief executive officer of a ten-million-dollar-a-year Canadian charity and totally broke!

Early the next morning, we were on our way to the airport again, this time to fly to Managua, Nicaragua. Our plane landed and taxied to a spot about a half-mile away from the airport, where we could just make out armed military patrolling the roof of the terminal and two full-size tanks tearing up the tarmac as they ground their way back and forth between us and the terminal. At the foot of the stairs from the plane stood two teenaged boys armed with Uzi submachine guns, urging us into waiting jitney buses for the short trip to the terminal entrance.

As predicted, we were not made welcome. Clearing passport control took longer for us than for anyone else on our flight. Our bags were the last to appear on the carousel, and we were (for a while at least) the last two people in a long line of passengers waiting to clear customs. As we moved forward, our hearts sank to see that customs agents were opening every suitcase and flight bag and rummaging through the contents. Nearing the head of the line, we noticed a man's head bobbing up and down and shouting something on the far side of the glass partition holding back the public. "Been here, done this!" I muttered.

When it came my turn to heave my suitcase up on the counter to be opened and inspected, the shouting head became more and more insistent. Suddenly, in an apparent fit of her own déja vu, Ann thumped my backside with her suitcase propelling me forward. The customs agent stopped opening my suitcase and asked "*Sociedad Biblica?*"

Somewhat bewildered, I responded "*Si!*" That was obviously the right answer because thereupon, to my amazement and relief, he waved us and our luggage through untouched.

Beyond the glass partition, we were met by the bobbing head—a short, stout, and very nervous civilian carrying the ubiquitous United Bible Society's yearbook, who turned out to be the general secretary of the Nicaraguan Bible Society. In very limited English, he escorted us to his van and drove us wordlessly to our hotel. We checked in without incident, only to discover that there was no running water in our room. Assuming that this was another bit of harassment, I went down to the front desk to demand that the water be turned back on. "*No ai!*" (There is none!) was the response we came to recognize as the explanation for every deprivation and indignity we suffered throughout our stay.

Eventually, we learned that the National Liberation Front Sandinista (FSLN) rebel government of Nicaragua had arbitrarily turned off the water supply for the whole city of Managua for the day, just to remind the restive population that it was in their power to do so. When we asked for enough water to at least to brush our teeth, we were directed to the lobby bar, where we could purchase two plastic cups of Coca-Cola!

Looking back on the few days we spent in Managua, we jokingly called it our time of heartburn and heartache. The food—what there was of it—was largely tasteless and mysterious. There were almost no dairy products to be had; garden vegetables were wilted and unappetizing even before they were cooked; meat, what little there was, was of dubious origin and unrecognizable as to flavor. There were virtually no toiletries to be had, and what were available for purchase were cheap and phony knockoffs of American products.

The Bible Society's *Casa de Biblia* was a cement-block roofed rectangle surrounded by chain link fencing topped by barbed wire and guarded by an armed private security mercenary. Nevertheless, we were greeted like conquering heroes because—coincidentally?—just days before our arrival, a shipment of Spanish-language scriptures we had printed in and shipped from Canada had mysteriously been "found" by customs agents after being unaccounted for for almost a year!

Our host, who appeared to be so nervous and fearful, had every right to be. Christian visitors, unless they were known to be radical leftwing American liberal clergy sympathetic to the Sandinista revolution, were kept under constant and hostile surveillance. Unbeknownst to us (at least at first), the Bible Society general secretary and his wife were hiding their teenaged daughter from the Sandinista army, which had already conscripted their three sons into the military. Days before our arrival, out host had been arrested and taken into custody, stripped naked, and interrogated until late in the night and then turned loose to find his way home with no clothes, no money, no documents, and no idea why!

Unlike every other venue we had visited, there were no fieldtrips to meet missionaries or pastors or translators during the whole of our stay. "*Demasiado pelligroso!*" (Too dangerous!) was the explanation. So we spent our days in the *Casa de Bibla* and our nights alone in our hotel room and were very, very glad to leave for Honduras!

Tegucigalpa, the capital of Honduras, was described in some travel manuals of the day as "dirty, dangerous, and expensive," and it was! Although not quite as militarized as Managua, throughout the city, armed soldiers were visible everywhere and shortages of everything seemed to be the order of the day. Once again, the Honduran *Casa de Biblia* was a crude cement block structure surrounded by chain-link fencing and barbed wire and guarded by an armed mercenary.

After visiting the Bible house, our host took us for a long, scenic, and relaxing drive up into the mountains surrounding the capital city. To a degree markedly more obvious than in the other Central American countries we had already visited, there was a startling contrast between communities where the Roman Catholic church and clergy were dominant as compared to others where evangelical missionaries and pastors had made their mark. Filth, poverty, drunkenness, and lethargy prevailed in the former; industriousness, cleanliness, sobriety, and pride had become normative in the latter.

Even now, I have hesitated to write the paragraph above. Certainly, in our travels and testimonies back in Canada, we never even hinted at this embarrassing—even appalling—fact of Latin American existence. The truth remained a burden on Ann's and my hearts for the rest of our Bible Society careers. The scriptural promise of our Lord, "You will know the truth, and the truth will set you free" (Jn 8:32, TEV), was proving it-self in the lives of both indigenous and Hispanic Christians in Central and South America and giving rise to the theology of liberation that eventually shook traditional Roman Catholicism to its core.

Nowhere was this cause and effect more evident than among the Miskito native population living along the Atlantic coast of Honduras and Nicaragua. Here, and in the nearby city of San Pedro Sula, Christian missionaries were using Bible Society scriptures and literacy materials to combat one of the most cor-rupt and conflicted areas on the North American continent. It was my privilege to preach in the largest evangelical church in Sula on the Sunday morning of our visit. My translator and I had met the night before and established a remarkable rapport; during my message, her Indo-Spanish translation was as rapid as my halting English extempore preaching, and the congregational "Amens" came almost as soon as I finished whatever point I was trying to make. I still tremble to remember the palpable dynamic tension the proclamation of the gospel of Jesus Christ produced in that troubled city on that tremendous morning!

Our return flights from Tegucigalpa to Toronto were broken by an overnight in Miami, where we took advantage to debrief the UBS regional staff. Ann and I were still particularly troubled by the situation in Managua and the atmosphere of hostility and deprivation in which the Nicaraguan Bible Society staff operated there. We wanted to know what *we* and the Canadian Bible Society could do to alleviate any of that distress. It was Atalah Jaramillo who suggested very practically that we might take up some sort of collection of toiletries and personal necessities on our return to Toronto and ship it all to the Bible Society personnel to divide the cache among themselves as most needed and best served.

And that is exactly what we did. Everywhere either of us were scheduled to speak during that Advent season, we asked in advance for a collection of toiletries and personal hygiene items for our brothers and sisters in Managua. The national Bible Society staff in Toronto caught the spirit and recast their traditional exchange of silly Christmas gifts into a giftgiving extravaganza of toothpaste, deodorant, cosmetics, ointments, bandages, and facial and toilet tissue, all to be packed and shipped to Nicaragua.

And then the trouble began. No international air freight carriers flew from Canada to Nicaragua. How to ship the cartons and cartons of gifts to Managua? Atalah Jaramillo asked whether there was any way we could deliver the shipment to the UBS regional center for transport under the aegis of the Bible Society. That suggestion segued into the strategy of a Russell family trip to Nana's Place in Saint Petersburg, Florida, for Christmas with the precious cargo strapped to the roof rack of our sturdy Chevrolet station wagon.

The day after Christmas we set out from Saint Petersburg for Miami, little realizing what a long and arduous journey it would be. We were exhausted when we reached the regional center but thrilled to learn that Alberto Carcamo, the regional secretary, who was visiting family in Spain over the holidays, had offered us the use of his townhouse for our stay. The next day was spent in dealing with our shipment to Managua and dealing with Sarah, whose twenty-first birthday it was, and who was feeling as though her coming of age was being ruined by our being far from home, family, and friends amid a bunch of Latino strangers in Miami.

Little did she know that the Jaramillos were putting together a Latino-style birthday party to which they invited a few of their own teenagers' friends. After a marvelous homecooked dinner of *pollo con arroz*, the younger Latinos set off with Sarah and Kirk for a night on the town, hitting all the Hispanic high spots in an adventure neither Sarah nor Kirk will ever forget!

Nor was that the end of our benevolent involvement with the Nicaraguan Bible Society folk. The regional center staff were concerned that the prolonged and escalating stress of the situation in Managua was undermining the health of the general secretary, who was becoming more and more frantic about the safety of his only daughter, Alma, for whom he desperately wanted to arrange an escape from Nicaragua to the relative safety of America.

Given the number of Central Americans already in exile in

and around Miami, there was apparently no safe place able to receive and care for Alma at that time until Ann stepped in with the suggestion that the Canadian Bible Society (meaning *we*!) could accommodate Alma for the duration until an appropriate long-term solution might be arranged. Alma's parents were contacted and agreed to begin working on getting their daughter out of Nicaragua safely and secretly. We Russells returned to Toronto and were amazed at how quickly and easily we were able to organize a place for Alma in one of Toronto's public schools with an ESL (English as a second language) curriculum. Before we knew it, we had moved Kirk into the guest room at the house on St. Leonard's Avenue and created a room for Alma under the eaves on the third floor.

We never did learn how her family smuggled Alma out of Nicaragua, but she arrived one wintry day and took up life in exile in Toronto early in 1986. She came with almost nothing, but Ann arranged a world service expense line in the CBS budget to finance clothing, medical care, and personal expenses for Alma.

It was a learning experience for all of us. Incredibly naïve and secretive, Alma found it very difficult to integrate herself into our busy and demanding lives. She had never eaten—and immediately disliked—butter and margarine, but she had somehow developed a taste for mayonnaise and spread it lavishly on everything she ate! She was shyly reticent about allowing anyone to do her laundry until one day both she and her room smelled so foul that Sarah insisted on finding out what was going on! And what was going on was that Alma was rinsing out her few pairs of panties in her bathroom sink and drying them draped over a lampshade in her bedroom!

Understandably, she hated cold weather; but unfortunately she had arrived in Canada in January, and it was cold and snowy; and many days it was a real effort to get her out the door in the morning and off to school. She was morbidly afraid of strangers and fearful that anyone she had not already met might be a Sandinistan agent come to take her back home. In the spring, we took her to the Rondeau lake house—her *casa del lago*—which she found frightening, never having seen such a large body of water as Lake Erie.

The longer she was with us, the more difficult things became. By the standards of her upbringing, our children's discipline seemed very lax, and she began acting out her fears and frustrations in behaviors that were rebellious and resentful. Fortunately, before the end of that summer, a supposed "uncle" in the Miami area agreed to take her into his home, and Alma left Toronto and us before everything fell apart.

It had not helped, of course, that both Ann and I were traveling a great deal and were away from home more than we should have been, leaving a lot of the coping with Alma to Sarah, the competent, willing, and motherly elder daughter on whom we relied too much. This period was particularly hard on Kirk and Rebecca, who both needed *present* versus *absent* parents. Looking back, I realize that many of the familial tensions that grew up between our two daughters were rooted in this extraordinary period in our lives.

By the time Alma left, Sarah had graduated with honours from the University of Toronto with a bachelor of commerce degree and had been hired by Shell Canada in the company's marketing department. She delayed the start of work to take a youthful grand tour of Europe and then moved to Ottawa to begin her career in the oil business. Ann had not realized, I think, how much she had come to count on Sarah's support and competence on the home front and how much time and energy she had been able to devote to her burgeoning career as a Bible

Society speaker and mission interpreter.

While I missed Sarah, too, I was into an incredibly demanding period in my Bible Society leadership. Our direct mail fundraising efforts were producing tremendous influxes of cash contributions, eventually eclipsing the combined efforts of the nineteen district secretaries and their staffs. In the districts, the retail aspects of Bible distribution were changing as more and more commercial bookstores were carrying ever-widening stocks of scriptures in many versions and presentations. The inevitable comparisons between the national and district fundraising statistics and the growth of the warehousing and direct shipping operations made possible by the move into and then the renovation of the Carnforth Road facility made for tensions that had simmered below the surface ever since the annual meeting in the spring of 1986.

At the same time, my involvements in the international aspects of the Bible cause were taking me to New York, Miami, and London with increasing frequency. These trips were added to a schedule that still involved guest appearances at district annual meetings and Sunday preaching commitments literally across Canada. At some point early in 1987, I hired an unemployed but capable clergyman from Hamilton as my personal assistant, partly to relieve some of the pressures my travels were creating for Ann and partly to facilitate my own functioning more effectively in the midst of so much travel. Before long, it became a standing joke at the national office that Ann and Blake would book an executive conference room at Pearson International Airport outside Toronto and meet me to exchange a suitcase full of dirty clothes for another full of clean clothes and a briefcase full of finished work for another, full of matters requiring my attention and all this as I passed through on my way from one side of Canada to the other or off to foreign parts.

One such trip came late in the summer of 1987, when Uli Fick, the UBS global secretary, requested that Ann and I attend as observers the UBS global executive meeting to be held in London, England. At this cluster of events for Bible Society representatives from many countries who served on the UBS global executive committee, Uli unexpectedly announced his intention to retire from his leadership role within the next year, by which time it was his determination to move the UBS global headquarters from Stuttgart to London or somewhere in the United Kingdom.

Ann and I were included in everything and went everywhere. One evening, we entertained the American Bible Society executives at the Army and Navy Club on Piccadilly Circus where we were staying. Throughout the gathering, we were encouraged to meet and get to know the Bible Society global leaders we had never met before. At the end of the meeting, we were asked, out of the blue it seemed, if we would be willing to host the next year's global executive meeting in Toronto, which we were certainly both honored and humbled to agree to do.

Right or wrong, Ann and I left London at the end of August, convinced that Uli Fick, at least, was grooming me to become his successor as the UBS global general secretary. This conviction colored just about everything we did for the next year. Unfortunately, I realized much too late that the prospect of taking on this global responsibility with all that it entailed—including leaving Canada and everyone and everything we knew and loved and making our home in the United Kingdom for the rest of my working career—weighed heavily on Ann's mind and then her body until she began to suffer some of the symptoms of illness we thought we had left behind in Montreal.

Ironically at this very time, Dr. Bryant M. Kirkland, the Fifth Avenue pastor under whom I had worked during the first four years of my ministry, had also announced his retirement. I was delighted to be able to combine a planned trip to the American Bible Society in New York with an appearance at the grand formal banquet to mark Dr. Kirkland's retirement. I met and enjoyed catching up with several members of the Fifth Avenue Presbyterian Church, two of whom happened to be serving on the pastor nominating committee to recruit Dr. Kirkland's replacement, and before I knew it, my name was under consideration.

This double whammy of potential career opportunities, so vastly different, so equally desirable, was too much for Ann. She fell gravely ill, was hospitalized in the Queen Elizabeth Hospital in Toronto, and took many months to recover. Sadly, while she was suffering so, I was informed that Dr. Kirkland, on learning of my potential candidacy, had insisted that none of his many former ministry assistants should be considered as his successor. I realized that I was both disappointed and relieved. In my heart of hearts, I had always hoped that the Fifth Avenue pulpit might one day be mine, but I discovered that instead the lure of a global Bible Society ministry held more powerful sway over my current aspirations.

While all this was going on internationally, back in Canada one of the members of the CBS executive committee got a bee in his bonnet about formulating a strategic plan for the future of the Canadian Bible Society at both the national and district levels. He had been active in the Nova Scotia District affairs for many years but had recently lost his job as a top executive for one of the province's power industries and was itching for something to do. He took up temporary residence in Toronto and began to spend all day every day at the national offices, interviewing staff and writing job descriptions and just generally getting in my hair.

Ann's slow recovery of health and strength caused us to postpone any plans for what should have been that autumn's major factfinding trip to some distant part of the UBS world. But in God's mysterious providence, before the end of the year there came to us an invitation to be present in La Paz in January 1988 for the presentation to the president of the Republic of Bolivia of the first published copies of the long-awaited and extremely costly translations of the New Testament into Quechua and Aymara, the native languages of the two major indigenous populations of the Andes Mountains. The Canadian Bible Society had been the major UBS source of funding for both projects over many years, and it seemed fitting, somehow, that CBS be represented by its general secretary on this auspicious occasion.

Of course, that one-day event was not sufficient to justify such a long journey, and before we knew it, we were engulfed in UBS-generated plans to visit the national Bible Societies in Colombia, Peru, and Ecuador as well as Bolivia. Ann's health seemed to have stabilized and so off we went!

Our first destination was Bogotá, the violence-ridden and drug-infested capital of Colombia. A diverse and culturally sophisticated city of some 5,000,000 inhabitants then, it ranked as the third largest city in South America but was at that time the focus of an "asymmetric low-intensity armed conflict between government forces, leftist guerrilla groups, and rightwing paramilitaries," some of which occurred nightly right under the street-side window of the guest house in which we were staying. By day, no mention was made of whatever had happened the night before, but the streets were full of armed soldiers, the Bible house in the heart of Bogotá boasted a heavily armed security guard visible at the door night and day, and the Bible house staff, including the general secretary and his wife, were discouraged and demoralized almost to the point of effective paralysis.

The constitutionally specified official language of Colombia is Castellano, a unique dialect of the Castilian Spanish brought to the Americas by the conquistadores of the sixteenth century. However, the everyday street language in Bogotá was what we came to think of as Latin-American Spanish, complicated by the approximately sixty-eight other ethnic Colombian languages, each of which had semi-official status in its own territory. Few of these languages had large enough speakerships to warrant the Bible Society's efforts to publish any scriptures in them, so the Bible Society was left to distribute and encourage the use of *Dios Habla Hoy*, most copies of which had been recently printed in Canada, which made Ann and me instant celebrities in the eyes of the very few Bible Society supporters we were allowed to meet.

Instead, we were taken sightseeing: to the Salt Cathedral of Zipaquira; to El Museo del Oro (the Gold Museum); to the Chingaza National Park; and to the spectacular mountaintop Cerro Monserrate at over 10,000 feet above sea level, a seventeenth-century pilgrimage destination shrine dedicated to *El Señor Caido* ("The Fallen Lord"). Though enjoyable, all this was frustrating as there seemed to be little if anything that might be of interest or inspiration to Bible Society donors back in Canada.

The same could not be said of our second destination. A bustling metropolis and one of South America's largest cities, with a counted population of over six million inhabitants, Lima, Peru, sits at sea level on a beautiful stretch of Pacific Ocean beachfront. Unfortunately, a stagnant economy, a corrupt political situation, and the rise of the *Sendero Luminoso* ("Shining Path"), a Marxist-Leninist-Maoist Communist revolutionary guerrilla organization, had left Peru, and especially the arid mountainside areas surrounding Lima, in a nearly catatonic state of functioning paralysis.

Of particular interest to the Peruvian Bible Society were the *pueblos jóvenes* (young towns) — actually huge shantytowns of unspeakable filth and deprivation — created almost overnight by the frightened migration of the indigenous Quechua-speaking natives whom the *Sendero Luminoso* had been massacring in the jungled Andes mountains surrounding Lima. Because of the longstanding work of Quechua translators and Bible Society promoters, many small portions and pamphlets of scripture and literacy materials were available to these indigenous people eking out a miserable existence in these slums.

Two experiences are indelibly imprinted on my memory bank. The first was attending a Sunday morning worship service in a primitive Quechua chapel on the edge of populated Lima. During the recitation of a responsive psalm, I began to recognize the syllabic structure of the Quechua words and phrases and to realize that — linguistically at least — this South American indigenous language virtually mimicked the syllabic structure of the Inuktitut language on which I had once been observing our Canadian Inuit Bible translators working in the Arctic Circle!

An aside: It was particularly gratifying, on returning to Canada, to learn from our own Bible Society translation experts that there was certainly anthropological evidence linking the migration patterns of North American and South American indigenous linguistic and cultural groups and that I was not way out in left field by theorizing that the two geographically isolated syllabic language patterns might have had a common aboriginal source!

The second memorable experience in Peru came on that very same Sunday afternoon as the Bible Society general secretary led Ann and me deep into the most notorious *pueblo jóven*, perched precariously on a steep but arid mountainside north of Lima. There, a pair of British missionary women had formed a Sunday school in the very heart of the slum and were using Bible Society scriptures and literacy materials to teach the indigenous women and children to speak and read both in Spanish and in their own language.

The living conditions were incredible. Shacks made of rusted metal signs and old scraps of plywood had neither running water nor even rudimentary sanitation. Electricity from the high-voltage metal pylons of the power grid running overhead through the community was literally *stolen* by intrepid young men who shinnied up the pylons with extension cords to wire into the high-voltage lines. Many were electrocuted in the attempt; many others fell to their deaths; not unexpectedly, there was a visible dearth of men and boys throughout the community.

The missionaries' Sunday school was "housed" (if I may use the term very, very loosely) in a shanty belonging to an industrious widow. Somehow, she had managed to gather together a few carpets, pillows, benches, and chairs for seating for the mothers and their children who came in droves to try to learn to speak Spanish or to read in their own native language. When one of the missionaries introduced us as coming from Canada and showed the women the CBS imprint on many of the materials they held in their hands, we were treated like visiting royalty.

The women were particularly fascinated by Ann, who, though petite in stature by North American standards, towered a full head taller than any of them and had naturally blond, curly hair and bright blue eyes like some of them had never seen before! Soon, Ann was seated on a low stool among the children to read to them a simple Bible story from one of their literacy pamphlets. While she read, one by one the children took turns crawling up onto her lap for a few minutes before ceding the most beautiful spot in the room to another child. Running sores showed through the hair on a number of scalps; yellowish-green pus oozed from several ear canals; the stench was overwhelming; but Ann persisted in reading on and on until every child had had a turn on her lap.

Then our proud hostess invited us to share a cup of tea and some cookies — extravagant hospitality for her, unspeakable danger for us — but with one glance back and forth between us we assured one another that this was one act of grace we could not refuse. Tea and cookies it was; but later that night, writing in my daily journal, I quoted Ann's frank assessment of the afternoon: "If we get sick after this trip, it will have been because we let down our guard for one gloriously God-filled act of sharing!"

Our third destination was, finally, La Paz, Bolivia, surely one of the most fascinatingly inhospitable urban centers in the world! Spiraling downward in an extinct volcanic crater from the Andes' *Altiplano* (high plain) altitude of almost 13,000 feet above sea level, La Paz is the seat of government and the de facto national capital of the Plurinational State of Bolivia. Ann and I were there as guests of the Bolivian Bible Society, ostensibly to present the first published copies of the whole Bible in Quechua and Aymara to the president of the republic, Victor Paz Estenssoro. The Canadian Bible Society — and we personally — had been largely instrumental in funding these hugely significant projects in the Bible Society world and in the political and cultural life of Bolivia.

As such, we felt like instant celebrities. From the moment we stepped off the airplane that brought us from Lima (at sea level) to *El Alto* Airport (at roughly 13,000 feet above sea level)—the highest international airport in the world—we were treated with embarrassing solicitude. Only later did we begin to understand that this standard of care was not due to our celebrity at all but to the life-threatening rarity of oxygen in the air and the constant threat of *soroche* (altitude sickness) with its sudden onset of dizziness, fatigue, headache, nausea, rapid heartbeat, and shortness of breath.

For our first day in and around La Paz, the Bible Society's general secretary took very good care of us, and we handled the altitude pretty well. But on the second day, we began a round of radio and television interviews, meetings with local clergy supporters of the Bible cause and had little to eat or drink as we moved from venue to venue until by late afternoon I began to feel *awful*! I begged to be taken back to our hotel and put to bed, but our host would have none of that!

We were due to descend down into the volcanic crater that is the actual city of La Paz, there to have dinner at the home of a pair of Canadian Baptist missionaries who were great Bible Society supporters as well as prominent Canadian expatriates. The Bolivian general secretary was confident we would have much in common with our hosts. Additionally, he explained, we would be descending about 5,000 feet as we traveled into the city, and I would actually begin to feel a lot better at that altitude.

So down we went with little evidence of a positive impact on my *soroche*! After meeting with the Canadian missionaries, I confessed that I felt truly ill and would probably not be able to eat a bite of the Canadian dinner they had so thoughtfully prepared. "*Soroche?*" they asked and immediately proffered a white paper packet of plain white tablets, looking a lot like aspirin, and insisted I take one, which I did.

The result was dramatic, to say the least, and I began to feel better almost immediately. Before we left to go back up to our hotel, the missionaries insisted that I keep the packet of tablets and instructed me to take one whenever I began to feel queasy. "If you run out," they counseled, "you can buy a refill at any drugstore!"

So I did and got through the rest of our rigorous schedule with only slight bouts of discomfort. In fact, I felt so well by the time of the scheduled presentation of the Quechua and Aymara Bibles to President Paz Estenssoro, broadcast live on the Bolivian national television network, that I made a short speech in pretty fair Spanish, which greatly impressed everyone (even me!) because I still felt that my spoken Spanish at that time was rudimentary at best.

From La Paz, we flew the next day to Cochabamba, Bolivia's fourth largest city at an elevation of only 8,392 feet and in the very center of the country, with a population of some 600,000 souls, many of whom were Aymara-speaking Christians. We loved the local indigenous people, whose colorful native dress and fervent evangelical Christianity charmed us at every event we had in the two days we were there.

Realizing that our trip through the Andes was coming to an end and that we had a heavy schedule of Bible Society district annual meetings awaiting us as soon as we returned to Canada, Ann suggested that instead of trying to rush to develop our slides and write a mission interpretation program about them, we ought instead to outfit ourselves in the native costumes of the Aymara and present ourselves so dressed to ad lib our way through at least the first such meeting, scheduled to be held in Ottawa thirty-six hours after our scheduled return to Canada. Aided by the Bolivian general secretary, who thought the whole idea uproariously funny, we scoured the native mercado for a woolen cap with earflaps for me, along with a colorful serape to drape over one shoulder and a bright red sash to tie around my waist. For Ann, we found a distinctive white plaster of Paris flat-brimmed hat, a sequined frilly blouse, and a bright blue full-circle skirt with several crinolines.

The Bolivian Bible Society's general secretary was a very articulate veteran of many years' involvement with the United Bible Societies' political structure, and he surprised us by speaking openly of the hopes—even expectations—throughout Latin America that I would be elected the next global general secretary. My Latino colleagues had apparently noticed—and admired—the occasions on which I had stood up to the American, German, British, and Dutch general secretaries during my short Bible Society career and felt that the Third World national societies would receive a much more sympathetic hearing from me than from a global executive from any of the other highly-developed nations.

The fourth and final destination on our tour of the Northern Andes was Quito, the capitol of Ecuador, constructed on the foundations of an ancient Incan city, at an elevation of just over 9,000 feet above sea level, the second highest official capital city in the world. We were there to open a new Bible house, for which (as elsewhere) the Canadian Bible Society had raised a lot of the required funding.

Unfortunately, the president of the republic was at that time enmeshed in a potential revolution involving his former head of the Ecuadorian armed forces. On a day trip flight to and from the Pacific coastal city of Guayaquil, our airplane was accorded a pair of jet fighters as escort to guarantee our safety. For the whole time we were there, there was nightly fighting in the streets, and each morning we waited anxiously to learn whether the president was still in power or had been overthrown.

As elsewhere, our itinerary included visits to groups of

clergy, native Bible translators, and media interviews both in the city and in the surrounding mountains. One memorable day, we took the requisite tourists' trip to the *Mitad de Mundo* ("Middle of the World") to straddle the equator with one foot in the Northern Hemisphere and the other in the Southern. By the time we returned to Quito from that excursion, I was beginning to feel the effects of *soroche* again and vowed to take it easy that evening so that I would be well enough to enjoy the Bible house dedication the next morning.

Unfortunately as we settled down to dinner in the formal dining room of the very grand Intercontinental Hotel, Ann thought she heard the hotel intercom page me. I left the table and hurried to the maître d's podium, which was unattended. So I hurried out into the hallway to find a house phone of which there were none nearby. Then I hurried all the way to the front desk to check whether there might be a message about the next day's events. There were none, so I hurried back to the dining room to enjoy the dinner that had just been served.

As I sat down and assured Ann that there had been no page and no message, I felt faint—so faint that I collapsed face first into my dinner plate. Providentially, there was a convention of emergency caregivers going on in the hotel, and in a moment two EMTs rushed to our table. One quickly found an oxygen canister conveniently attached to a wall nearby, secured the face mask to my food-encrusted face, and revived me. Though we all agreed that I had fallen victim to *soroche*, the hotel manager insisted that I be carried up to our room and examined by the on call hotel physician.

The doctor arrived promptly, examined me thoroughly, confirmed the *soroche* diagnosis, and recommended that I spend a few restful days before resuming my tourism pursuits. Ann quickly explained that rest was not possible, that we had to be ready to appear at a function in the morning with the president of the republic and that what I really needed was some more *soroche* medicine.

"What kind of medicine?" demanded the doctor.

Ann pulled the empty paper packet out of her purse, showed it to him, and explained: "We were given these in La Paz, and they have kept my husband well until now!"

"*Senora*," he responded somewhat testily, "these are pure *cocaine!*"

As you can imagine, I had a wonderful time recounting this incident during my travels back in Canada, especially when speaking in Baptist church settings!

On the day of the scheduled Bible house dedication, we were all on pins and needles, wondering about the current fate of the president of the republic until at the appointed hour a military staff car drove up with an impressive escort, and the president's loyal minister of defense stepped out with a reassuring smile on his face. "*El Presidente es OK!*" was what it sounded like he said, and the program proceeded as though nothing out of the ordinary was going on.

Our scheduled return to Canada from Quito was on a very tight schedule, since we had a longstanding appointment to speak at the Eastern Ontario district annual meeting in Ottawa on the Sunday evening after our return. We flew to Miami on Friday afternoon, had a hurried supper with the Jaramillos, gathered up the various gifts with which we had been presented during our South American travels, and returned to the Miami International Airport for our scheduled trip home. Unfortunately, a strong winter storm moving across the upper United States and the southernmost quarter of Ontario and Quebec was playing havoc with the day's flight schedules.

Suffice it to say that we landed in Toronto very late on Saturday evening, waited almost two hours for our "suspicious-looking" baggage to clear customs and immigration, and arrived home just after midnight. Our flight to Ottawa required us to be back at the airport by twelve noon the next day, so we barely had time for a few hours' sleep, a repack of our luggage, including the Aymara regalia we had bought in Cochabamba, and we were off on a scheduled two-week tour of Ottawa, Montreal, and the Maritime provinces.

During the district annual meeting dinner in the nation's capital, Ann and I were actually feeling quite giddy as we slipped away from the head table and found our way backstage to change into our Aymara outfits. As we were introduced, the stage curtains gradually opened to reveal us standing there in the getups I have already described. We were greeted with hoots, hollers, and hilarity, which eventually punctuated almost everything we tried to say. We finally gave up and said, "Amen," to tumultuous applause.

Afterward, the Eastern Ontario district secretary confessed "Bill, you *did* look like the village idiot—*any* village idiot!" Ann's costume drew kinder remarks overall, and everyone seemed to agree that it had been the most entertaining district annual meeting ever! At our hotel, we stripped off the Aymara-ware and fell into bed exhausted. The next morning, we awoke early to get packed up again for a brief flight to Montreal, where we were to repeat our hilarious performance that evening. As we showered, each of us realized that we were unusually itchy in our nether regions and upon closer examination discovered that we were blossoming with *flea bites* everywhere the Aymara outfits had touched our skin!

Hastily, I packed every Aymara garment and accessory into one small suitcase, locked it shut, and began to wonder what on earth we were going to say to what would be a very large audience of Bible Society and Church of St. Andrew and St. Paul friends and acquaintances that night. As soon as we got to our Montreal hotel, I went out in search of a big can of Raid bug spray and the largest available containers of Benadryl, anti-itch spray, and calamine lotion. Back at the hotel, I took the Aymara suitcase out onto the sidewalk and ignored the curious stares of passersby as I emptied the entire canister of Raid into every garment, every accessory, and every nook and cranny of that one piece of luggage, which we then toted firmly locked up throughout the Maritimes until we ended up in St. John's, the capitol of Newfoundland.

Honestly, I have little if any memory of that trip: so memorable was the beginning and so devastating was the end of it! St. John's was bitterly cold and buried under snowdrifts higher than the cars on what roads had been plowed. The Bible Society general secretary insisted that we stay at his home rather than at a hotel and so contrary were some of the members of his district board that we did not have the energy or the will to gainsay any of them. In a board meeting before the district annual meeting, they were very critical of what they perceived to be happening at the national offices and were unkind to the point of rudeness toward Ann and me throughout our stay. Somehow, we made it through the district annual meeting and back to the general secretary's home, where Ann cried herself to sleep, mumbling as she did that it was exactly three weeks to the day since we had partaken of tea and cookies in the *pueblo joven* in Lima, Peru, and now she was sick right on schedule!

Providentially, we were due to fly out of St. John's back to Toronto at around noon the next day. Ann awoke with excruciating pain in her abdomen, which she forbade me to reveal to our host and hostess. "Bill, please, don't say a word. They will insist on taking me to a hospital, and if I end up in a hospital here, I will *die* here!"

To our hostess I pleaded Ann's "exhaustion"—and my own—until we bundled Ann up as warmly as we could and made our way to the airport, where, mercifully, the piles of snow had made parking very difficult, and our host and hostess were content to drop us off at the departures doorway and head back home. I was able to secure a wheelchair for Ann and with the aid of a compassionate flight attendant, got her onto the plane and in a few hours off again in Toronto, where I hailed a cab and took Ann straight to the emergency entrance of the Queen Elizabeth Hospital, where she had been a patient on several previous occasions.

Within a day or two, I also fell ill, so ill that on most days I did not feel well enough to go either to the office or to the hospital, where Ann was too ill even to notice. One day, when I made it to the hospital to visit Ann, she was taken from her room for tests of some sort. Feeling faint, I crawled up on her bed, where a nurse found me and insisted on having me taken down to the emergency area where I was diagnosed with congestive heart failure. I was given medication to relieve the infectious congestion in my pericardium but allowed to return home, where I spent several days in bed.

In retrospect, I realize that this episode marked the beginning of the end of my Bible Society career. Ann remained in hospital for a few weeks while I recovered enough (I thought) to complete my scheduled tour of the western district annual meetings. By then Ann was home from the hospital and seemed better enough to accompany me to the annual Americas regional gathering of general secretaries and UBS staff in Cartagena, Colombia, at the end of February. In the midst of a frigid Canadian winter, Cartagena seemed to be just what we needed and was in a totally unexpected way.

The strategic planning process that I mentioned earlier was nearing completion and was scheduled to be presented to the CBS national annual meeting sometime in April. The one missing piece was my input of a draft strategic plan for the roles and responsibilities of the district secretaries, upon which I had really had little or no time to work during the first two months of the year. Ann's suggestion that we stay in Cartagena for a few extra days at the end of the regional annual meeting to allow me enough peace and quiet to work out the district secretaries' draft strategic plan seemed like an inspiration and that is what we did!

Back in Toronto, we plunged headfirst into preparations for the CBS national annual meeting. Ann was barely able to function at the office, so a lot of the preparatory arrangements fell to my secretary, Rhona, and my personal assistant, Blake, to handle. Truth to tell, Ann had always handled so much of this effort herself that Rhona and Blake were not really up to the task, and by the time district secretaries and delegates began arriving in Toronto things were in a shambles. The daily meetings were all held in the national office's facilities, including that conference room we had included in the renovation plans specifically for this purpose.

My "draft" of a proposed strategic plan for the district secretaries had been distributed ahead of the annual meeting, and I was totally blindsided by the vehemence with which my colleagues began denouncing almost every aspect of the draft document. My pericardium began to fill again, and the requisite medication was quite debilitating personally so that I began to have to spend a couple of hours in the middle of the day lying down in my office while the meetings went on without me. When I learned, accidentally, that the district secretaries had held a secret evening meeting at a local church to plan how to resist my strategic plan, I was flabbergasted and furious and frightened. By then, the scheduled meetings were drawing to a close, and I refused to meet with the district secretaries before they left town.

Hard on the heels of all this came the long-awaited UBS global annual meeting, for which Ann had been preparing for almost a year. She insisted on being discharged from the hospital and gamely oversaw all the arrangements for travel, housing, meals, and entertainments for the forty-odd delegates, most of whom we had met the previous year in London.

One of the highlights of the planned schedule was a chartered bus trip to Niagara Falls, which most of those present had never seen and eagerly anticipated. Ann wisely stayed home, but I accompanied the group, sitting in the front seat of the bus behind the driver and fielding questions over the loudspeaker system as we rode along. In the almost silent dark of the return trip to Toronto, I began to think—really for the first time in a while—about Uli Fick's retirement and the nomination and election of his successor and realized that there had never been a word said about it so far in the time the global representatives had been in Toronto.

The other highlight of the UBS occasion was a formal dinner hosted by Ann and me in the Governor General's Suite of the Toronto Hilton Hotel (*not*, incidentally, where the delegates were staying!) The hotel was by now the "home base" of our dear friend, Albert Schnell, the executive chef for the entire chain of Hilton International Hotels, and he and his Toronto colleagues pulled out all the stops to make this event truly spectacular. Every course was exquisite, and our guests were well and truly impressed.

Among the guests, invited by Uli Fick at the last minute, was a Philippine Bible scholar who was doing a semester as a visiting professor at one of the seminaries associated with the University of Toronto. He seemed like a quiet, dignified academic, and I remember thinking it odd that he was suddenly included in this particular group on this particular occasion; but all became clear the next morning, when he was introduced at the closing session of the UBS global annual meeting as the executive committee's nominee to succeed Dr. Fick as global general secretary.

I was devastated. The last item on the UBS agenda was a ceremonial tree planting on the grounds of the CBS national offices. I had to grin and bear it for an hour of smiling, handshaking, and "See you next year!" Uli Fick never came near me; neither did the American Bible Society general secretary, nor the world service officer stationed in New York, nor the regional secretary stationed in Miami. One of the Latin American general secretaries came to me in tears and said, "I don't understand!"

All I could say was "Neither do I!"

Ann was deeply troubled. On the one hand, she knew how much I had wanted the job and how serenely (and foolishly) I had expected it. On the other hand, she was personally relieved not to be having to cope with moving to the United Kingdom and was feeling terribly guilty about reacting that way! Her critical abdominal pains recurred, and I took her to Sunnybrook Hospital, where a member of the Central Ontario district board was a doctor who had taken an interest in her case and wanted her under his personal care.

Shortly thereafter, Ann's doctor took me for a long walk on the Sunnybrook grounds and explained to me that Ann's internal organs were so badly compromised by whatever strange virus she had contracted in Peru that she would probably never be able to travel with me again or be able to be left behind without care while I traveled as I must in my position. "Bill," he concluded, "it pains me to say it, but I really think you ought to consider a career change!" As things turned out, Ann never actually worked another day for the Canadian Bible Society and was eventually classified as vocationally disabled and began to receive a Government of Canada disability pension.

While I was reeling from all this, I was summoned by the president of the CBS national board of directors to a mysterious nighttime meeting in the local hotel where we billeted our out-of-town district secretaries and delegates for the annual meetings. As I walked into the room, I was shocked to see not only her but also the Saskatchewan district secretary, one of the Alberta delegates to the national board, and the Nova Scotia district board member who had been working on the CBS strategic plan for the past six months. Tersely, they informed me that my services were no longer required by the Canadian Bible Society because I had failed to fulfill one of the first duties listed in my own new strategic plan job description, some hitherto unknown (at least to me) jargon about maintaining peace and harmony between the district secretaries and the national administration. I was given the option of submitting my resignation willingly or being terminated by an action of the executive committee and dismissed.

I must have been in shock because I didn't weep or rage or unleash any of the negative emotions that I might have expected of myself. Instead, I felt strangely at peace! I thought of the old familiar William Cowper hymn, "God Moves in a Mysterious Way, His Wonders to Perform," and I *knew* that God's mysterious providence had intervened in my life at exactly the time when I was most in need. I went home and slept better than I had in months.

The next morning, I called my secretary and personal assistant and asked them to come to the house on St. Leonard's Avenue. I told them both exactly what had happened and swore them to secrecy. Then I called the labor relations lawyer the society had used in other executive terminations and made an appointment to see him the next day. Finally, I went to the office and asked to see the society's chief financial officer and told him the whole story. He was shocked—or at least appeared to be—and began urging me to "fight" this unjust termination or at least to demand a full year's severance package as the price of my resignation. Ironically, his "full year" suggestion became the bottom line when I spoke to the labor relations lawyer the next day.

Meanwhile, reports of what the foursome in the hotel room had done began to reach other members of the executive committee and national board, and the reactions were (as I learned later) almost all unsupportive of my abrupt firing. Within a few days, the national board president came to my office and retracted her demand that I resign or be terminated.

I just laughed: "No way! I'll stay on, and you'll begin to build a dossier against me until I either walk away emptyhanded or you terminate me 'for cause!' It's a 'no-win' situation for me, and I won't do it. But you'll be hearing from my lawyer".

The next two months were incredibly painful. On the advice of my lawyer, I went to the office every day, sat at my desk, answered my phone, and did what little I could to keep the society "afloat" day-to-day. I drafted a letter of resignation, undated, which offered my immediate resignation and citing Ann's disability as well as my own compromised health as the reasons for my decision. Eventually, the executive committee agreed to a severance package that included a full year's continuation of salary and benefits, and I "retired" with a small "farewell" reception in the staff lunchroom and a few tears and hugs from my still-bewildered closest colleagues.

To this day, I have never returned to 10 Carnforth Road.

* * * * *

FORTUNATELY, MY "BENEFITS" INCLUDED THE low-interest mortgage loan I had acquired to buy our Lake Erie home. Quite quickly, with Ann released from Sunnybrook Hospital, we organized a yard sale to get rid of a lot of the stuff for which we would have neither space nor need at the lake house. The remainder we moved into a storage unit just outside Ridgetown. With some trepidation on her part, we enrolled Rebecca in the Blenheim District High School for the one remaining semester of her high school career and settled into what we expected would be a "retirement" lifestyle at the lake.

On the Saturday morning of the first weekend of the rest of my life, I looked at myself in the bathroom mirror and decided that my full black beard had to go. Begun almost as a joke when I had had adult mumps in Montreal, its image had punctuated my Black Watch chaplaincy and had followed me to Toronto, to appear in every publication and promotional piece for the whole of my Bible Society career. In order not to make too much of a mess in the only bathroom in the lake house, I hung a little round shaving mirror on the window frame outside the kitchen, lathered up my chin, and bared my face for the first time in a decade.

A few minutes later, while I was washing the breakfast dishes, Rebecca came into the kitchen, took one look at me, and burst into tears: "You don't look like my Daddy anymore!"

Leading up to my departure from the Bible Society, I had started thinking about looking for a doctor of divinity program at a seminary within commuting distance of Southwestern Ontario but was repeatedly stonewalled by the late date of my inquiries and the start dates of the programs I had found. Then I came upon an advertisement in a theological journal for a DMin program at the Ecumenical Theological Seminary in, of all places, Detroit, Michigan. In quick order, I made an appointment to visit the seminary, housed at that time in Detroit's Marygrove College, met with the dean, and was accepted into a program that had just begun its new year of studies. In addition to monthly twenty-four-hour "colleague groups," the program offered week-long continuing education seminars throughout the year, six of which were required for graduation. I was off and running!

Ann was worried about what we would do for income when our year of salary and benefits came to an end. Jokingly, I suggested that I might become an "interim" pastor, a category of ministry just then coming into prominence in the United States. Soon, she was on the internet, researching the qualifications required for interim ministry. Within days, she discovered the Interim Network, operating out of Baltimore, Maryland, which offered twice-yearly certification programs at various places throughout the United States.

Even before this, I had mentioned to the dean of the faculty of religious studies at Immanuel College in Toronto that I might pursue a career in interim ministry. He responded: "Are you serious? I know just the place for you!"

It turned out that he was from the small town of Woodslee, in Kent County, about a forty-minute drive from the lake house. The United Church of Canada congregation there was in schism. The minister, organist, treasurer, and over half the membership had just walked out in protest over the denomination's recent approval of same-sex marriages. Would I be interested in serving the remnant on an interim basis, financed by the national denomination as a demonstration of its determination to

support and serve local congregations weathering just such circumstances? Would I ever!

So, my "retirement" lasted about three weeks. Ann began
to relax. The Woodslee congregation took us to their hearts
from day one, and our time there was an almost constant joy.
Because they suddenly had a vacant manse next door to the
church, they invited us to move our stored furniture into it so
that we could be comfortable there on the days and nights we
spent in the community. After the exhausting schedules of my
Bible Society years, Sunday preaching, hospital and nursing
home visiting, and occasional weddings and funerals regularly
reminded me of how much I had been missing the routine exercise of a pastoral ministry. Ann's dramatic restoration of health
and strength was an unexpected blessing.

The Interim Network held a weeklong training session in
Dayton, Ohio, at the end of October, which I attended. While
there, I met and became friendly with a Presbyterian synod executive from the American Midwest. When she heard a quick
version of my life story, she responded: "We need you back in
the States. Why don't you fill out a PIF and see what happens?"

Just before Christmas 1998, Ann and I were shaken to the
core by the disaster now known as Pan Am Flight 103! Back
when we had been anticipating the possibility that I might become the UBS general secretary and live in and work from
somewhere in England, we had planned that Ann and Rebecca
would stay on at the lake house for six months or so in order
for Becca to complete the final half-year of her high school education. Meanwhile, I would settle into my new job, find somewhere for us to live in England, and contrive to fly home for
brief visits as part of my constant worldwide travels. When we
heard about the Lockerbie bombing, we just *knew* that had I
become the UBS general secretary, I would have been *on* that

ill-fated flight from London to Detroit on the Thursday before Christmas 1988. As upset as we were to think of what might have been, the tragedy stamped a full *stop* to any lingering regrets I still felt about the end of my Bible Society career.

I had long since come to terms with the fact that I would never again be a "tall steeple" pastor; but over the Christmas holiday period at the lake house, Ann kept urging me to fill out that Presbyterian Church (USA) personal information form (PIF) just to see what would happen! So I did.

And what happened was a virtual avalanche of inquiries from pastor nominating committees of churches large and small all over the United States. Most of them I declined to pursue; but three church information forms (CIFs) intrigued me enough to want to follow them up. Interestingly, as I look back, they were from three of the *smallest* congregations that corresponded with me, which indicated, I think, how realistically I was considering a return to full-time settled pastoral ministry!

The first was from a congregation in a suburb of Cleveland, Ohio. Having spent many summers of my life directly across Lake Erie from Cleveland, I was curious to see what felt like it would be "familiar" territory. Ann and I drove clockwise around the eastern end of Lake Erie, found our way to the church and community in question, and were immediately and unanimously uninterested! Continuing our trek around the lake, we ended up in Dearborn, Michigan, the locale of the second church on my list.

The First Presbyterian Church of Dearborn was an imposing Georgian Colonial edifice in a very upscale urban/suburban neighborhood that had so far withstood many of the trends that had plagued other parts of metropolitan Detroit. On a lovely tree-lined street off Michigan Avenue, the church campus was very reminiscent of the Wyoming Presbyterian Church in Millburn, New Jersey. Ann and I agreed that I should send an encouraging response to the pastor nominating committee, and so I did.

The third church on my list actually got in touch with me. A representative of the pastor nominating committee of the First Presbyterian Church of Deerfield, Illinois, Ruthann Showerman, showed up one Sunday morning in the little church in Belle River, Ontario, that was the second "point" of the two-point Woodslee pastoral charge. Her parents lived in Grosse Pointe, Michigan, and she had made a visit to them specifically to drive over to Belle River to "spy" on me!

Apparently, she liked what she saw and heard, and soon I received a call from the cochair of the Deerfield PNC, Bob Crawford, inviting Ann and me to visit his church in the near future. Within days came a similar phone call from a representative of the Dearborn PNC, and thus began a months-long back-and-forth process involving both congregations to both of which we felt drawn, each for different reasons.

As we pondered the alternatives, we became increasingly aware of some fundamental difficulties in each situation. In Dearborn, a growing Middle Eastern—largely Arabic—population was beginning to "squeeze" the WASP (White Anglo-Saxon Protestant) community. The Presbyterian Church's congregation was dwindling as were revenues, and the PNC was unrealistically expecting the new pastor to be the "savior" who would turn things around. I was unsure that I was the person to do that until the issue of a housing allowance and low-interest mortgage loan raised its ugly head. In neither case was the board of trustees willing (or, indeed, able) to finance a package that would enable us to buy a home in the community unless we sold the Rondeau lake house to do so. For us, that was a deal breaker, and I withdrew my name from consideration.

Living full-time at the lake house with my parents nearby in the Little Pink Palace within Rondeau Provincial Park and my brother, Tom, and his family in the Bates Subdivision halfway between had made Ann and me realize that our hearts' true home was there and always would be.

Meanwhile, with each visit to Deerfield, we were learning more and more about the unhappy end of my would-be predecessor's twenty-seven-year ministry. Under the placid suburban surface, the congregation was bitterly divided between those who still loved and revered Dr. Bernard Didier and those who had forced his unwilling and unwelcome retirement. Ironically as we flew back and forth between Detroit and Chicago, Budget Rent-a-Car was offering a promotional rental rate on its new line of Lincoln Town Cars, and so I rented one each time. My choice, economical though it was, raised red flags among those who had come to resent Dr. Didier's alleged financial chicanery, and when push finally came to shove, one member of the PNC adamantly refused to support my "unanimous" nomination to become First Presbyterian Church's new senior pastor.

By now, summer was coming to an end and with it my year of Bible Society salary continuation. The Deerfield PNC wanted Ann and me to come for one more interview to try to resolve their impasse. I agreed on the condition that I be allowed to meet privately and face-to-face with the PNC hold-out. The invitation stood, we traveled once more to Deerfield, where Ann spent a tense afternoon with Bob Crawford and his lovely wife, Winnie, while I went to the home of the lady in question and knocked on her door. She was clearly unprepared for this gambit, but she invited me in and asked me why I was there.

"I want to know exactly *why* you refuse to support my nomination to become your minister!" She was obviously flustered and hemmed and hawed until I said: "I want the *truth* and then I will leave."

To my amazement, she blurted out: "You are just *too much like* Dr. Didier! You look like him, you talk like him, you even preach like him, and we have just gotten rid of him!"

Then began a long and frank conversation, during which I tried both to differentiate myself from the *person* of Dr. Didier, while at the same time pointing out that there were certain qualities and even characteristics that a successful "tall-steeple" *pastor* needed to have and that she should be *glad* that I had at least *some* of them! In the end, she grudgingly agreed neither to oppose a "unanimous" nomination from the PNC nor to work behind my back against my candidacy or my ministry if I were called and installed.

Years before, during another candidacy experience, my Princeton Seminary friend and mentor, Professor Donald Macleod, had warned me that no one gets a first-rate call after the age of fifty! Providentially, the Deerfield PNC held one more meeting to finalize the nomination process over a festive dinner early on Saturday evening, September 9, 1989—the day before my fiftieth birthday!

Back in Canada, the dear folk of the Woodslee pastoral charge had organized a surprise fiftieth birthday celebration following the Sunday morning service. Even though most of them realized that my year of interim ministry among them was coming to an end, it felt like a heartbreaking time for all of us when I announced that I had just the night before accepted a unanimous invitation to become the senior pastor of the Deerfield church. But they were gracious, nonetheless, and our last month among them was a chain of happy and grateful farewells.

* * * * *

IT TURNED OUT TO BE surprisingly complicated to obtain visas to return to the United States as resident aliens. Ann and I were required to make several trips to the American embassy in Toronto. None of our children were planning to emigrate from Canada with us, and eventually we were granted green cards around November 1st, the date on which I was supposed to begin my Deerfield ministry. Our worldly goods were packed in a moving van, ready to roll, but by now Ann's mother's throat cancer had begun spreading to different parts of her body; so Ann decided not to use her visa at this time because, once it was validated, there was a three-month period when new immigrants to the USA should not leave the country.

This decision caused a major case of "red-tape-itis" at the Detroit border, when US Customs and Immigration officers were, at first, not willing to let Ann enter the country with me as a "visitor" who actually held a permanent resident visa. After hours of back-and-forth with the US consulate in Detroit and the RCMP in Ottawa, my visa was accepted, and Ann was granted a temporary visitor's pass for only ten days before she had to leave the country and not return until she was ready to exercise her permanent residency visa. In truth, unnoticed by the customs and immigration establishment, she did return to Deerfield later in the month of November as a "visitor" in the company of our three children in time to participate in my formal induction by the Presbytery of Chicago.

Since all three of our children were planning to travel together to Chicago to spend Christmas with us in our new manse, Ann's mother insisted on traveling with them to spend the holiday together, which we did. It was a very stressful time. Everything at First Presbyterian Church was still new and unfamiliar; we had never really unpacked everything that had been in storage for the past year, so the house was a shambles; and

Mimi was clearly dying before our eyes. As soon as Christmas was over, Sarah and Kirk accompanied Mimi back to Windsor and then went on their way, Sarah back to Ottawa, and Kirk to the lake house, where he and Rebecca were living and attending the University of Western Ontario and the University of Windsor, respectively.

Almost at once, Mimi took to her deathbed. Rebecca, Ann, and I decided to take a few days off to travel back to Windsor so that Ann could care for her dying mother and Becca could resume classes on schedule. Within days, Mimi died. Caught between another rock and a hard place, I wanted to be with Ann, but I also felt that I ought to return to Deerfield to attend the church staff's traditional "Twelfth Night" party. In the end, Becca traveled with me to keep me awake on the long drive and to help me put together a wardrobe of funeral clothes for all of us to transport back to Windsor in forty-eight hours.

The Twelfth Night party was certainly an eye-opener! Held in the basement of the home of one of the staff members, where wine flowed freely and tongues wagged carelessly, I learned that: one of my colleagues was gay; another was a drunk; a third was being divorced by her husband; and the fourth had just that weekend separated from his wife! They all professed to loathe the recently retired senior pastor, and they had spent the past year reveling in the almost total lack of staff supervision exercised by the interim pastor appointed by the Presbytery of Chicago! It was not an auspicious start to my ministry!

As planned, Becca and I returned to Windsor for Mimi's funeral. Ann's brother, Tom Trotter, held his mother's power of attorney and designation as executor of her will, so within a few days, the way was clear for Ann to leave Windsor behind and exercise her resident alien visa to come into the United States legally, which she did to our great relief.

Saturday, July 4, 1981
At the Woodbine Race Course, Toronto, Ontario
Sarah and I with the Queen Mother's private secretary
and principal lady-in-waiting
Sir Martin Gilliat (left) and Mrs. Frances Campbell-Preston

October 26, 1983
Debrecen Theological Academy, Hungary
With the general secretary of the Hungarian Bible Society (left)
and Bishop Tibor Bartha of the Hungarian Reformed Church

February 1984
In Vancouver, British Columbia
Arguing with Jack Webster on the BCTV set of Webster!

September 1984
At the lake house on Lake Erie near Rondeau
Celebrating my 45th birthday in our new vacation home
with Sarah (left), Becca, and Kirk

August 11, 1985
At the Little Pink Palace, Rondeau Provincial Park
Dad celebrating his 70th birthday with his whole family

January 1988
Bible house, Bogotá, Colombia
With the staff of the Colombian Bible Society

January 1988
Bible house, La Paz, Bolivia
With a native translator of the Quechua presentation Bible

Saturday, September 17, 1988
At the lakehouse on Lake Erie near Rondeau
Shaving off my black beard outside the kitchen window

THE
NINETIES

To say that the Deerfield staff was dysfunctional would have been putting it mildly. Staff meetings were a shambles. Each staff member seemed intent on one-upping his or her colleagues. The church secretary was operating a new computer system that she did not understand and had no intention of mastering. The financial secretary was the sanest of the lot but had a very inflexible understanding of what *was* and what *was not* "her job!" At the very first meeting of the session's personnel committee, the two elders who comprised the committee confessed off the record that none of the church's employees could hold a job in either of the large corporations of which they were executives!

The bitterness over the forced retirement of Dr. Didier came to a head within a very few months, when one of the church's most prominent and powerful elders decided to marry another of the church's elders and invited Dr. Didier to come back to conduct the wedding. All hell broke loose at the next session meeting, when the currently serving elders collectively determined that Dr. Didier could *not* conduct the wedding but that I *must!*

My years of experience dealing with Dr. Berlis in Montreal stood me in good stead. I immediately agreed to officiate and then promptly wrote to Dr. Didier requesting that he "assist" me in conducting the wedding and in participating in the following morning's worship by reading one of the scripture lessons. Suddenly, everyone seemed satisfied.

Then people began to fuss and fret over whether Dr. Didier should be invited to *preach* on the Sunday morning after the wedding. I deflected that issue by explaining that I had already invited him to participate appropriately. But it was Ann who put the icing on the cake by inviting Dr. Didier and his wife, Leota, to come to the manse for Sunday dinner after church. She pulled out all the stops in her own inimitable way: china, crystal, silver, flowers, good food, fine wines, and an elegant dessert. The Didiers were absolutely disarmed by the hospitality shown them and told all their friends about what we had done to honor them on their first visit back to the church.

As the news spread through the congregation and the community, my stock rose perceptibly higher and higher. Those who loved and appreciated the Didiers were pleased and proud that the Russells had entertained them so graciously, and those who did *not* were almost as equally pleased and proud that their new pastor and his wife had conducted themselves with such wisdom and humility. In many ways, this little incident really marked the beginning of my coming into my own as the new pastor of the First Presbyterian Church of Deerfield.

Even for the 1990s, many in the congregation were surprisingly homophobic. This presented a real challenge when the Presbytery of Chicago determined that our associate pastor's call had been irregular and there would have to be an associate pastor nominating committee (APNC) formed and a series of congregational actions taken to regularize his ministry in Deerfield. When he and I conferred, he was ambivalent about the whole process. In the end, he sought and secured a call to another suburban Chicago congregation as their associate pastor. I hated to lose him, as did many in the congregation, but we remained friends throughout the remainder of my own Deerfield ministry.

Nevertheless, God's providence is powerful, and soon the APNC process brought to our attention an experienced pastor from the Presbytery of Detroit in the person of the Reverend David Eshleman, who accepted a call to become my colleague and associate. With his charming wife, Lorraine, David was warmly welcomed into the community and served with understated but effective service throughout the years of my ministry and far beyond until his own retirement.

The decade of my ministry in Deerfield was memorably punctuated by the weddings of all three of our children. Sarah's engagement to Kevin Crow in 1990 marked the beginning of the bridal seasons, first for her, then for Kirk, then for Rebecca and then, eventually, for Kirk again.

Sarah was determined to be married at, or at least from, the lake house. She had met her Kevin while working the gate at Rondeau Provincial Park, and all of their memories and fun times together centered there. The ceremony was set to be held at the dear little New Scotland United Church where we had worshiped off and on for many years. Although Sarah actually wanted a tent marquee reception in the backyard of the lake house, we persuaded her that an outdoor event in mid-October was really impractical and so we secured the use of Chatham's Maple City Golf and Country Club for the reception. With Sarah living in Toronto, Kirk and Becca at the lake house, and

Ann and me in Deerfield, the logistics were a nightmare, but in the end we brought it all off.

Sarah ordered and procured her wedding cake from a Toronto bakery near where she was living and working for Shell Canada. She found her wedding dress in Long Grove, Illinois; we imported her hairdresser from Toronto; some of the flowers for the church and the reception DJ were from Ridgetown; having no church organist available, we used a CD featuring the world-famous organist E. Power Biggs; and instead of a limo, we used my recently purchased navy blue Cadillac Sedan de Ville. Each bridesmaid made her own dress in a beautiful blue Waverly print fabric; Lex McCrindle appointed himself the official photographer; Kevin's parents generously footed the bar bill; and Kevin's mother and sister prepared an eye-popping sweets table to be served with coffee at 11:00 p.m. Much against her better judgment, Sarah allowed me to conduct the ceremony and asked her beloved "Papa Luc" to escort her down the aisle.

At 11:30 p.m. on Saturday, October 19, 1991, we were surprised to realize that the wedding reception was still going strong and asked the DJ if he could continue the music a little longer, which he could and would and did! Finally, sometime around 1:00 a.m., he told me that in his experience if the reception lasted this long, it would continue as long as he kept playing dance music. Eventually, we called it quits at 2:00 a.m. — "the best money," Sarah told me later, "you ever spent!"

But the biggest surprise of the occasion was Kirk's unexpected announcement that he was to marry his fiancée, Katy, in Toronto in the spring after he graduated from the University of Western Ontario Law School. So began the second flurry of bridal preparations. As parents of the groom, Ann and I had little to do other than travel to Toronto from time to time for prenuptial events. Rebecca, on the other hand, was to be one of Katy's bridesmaids, and the choosing, creating, fitting, and paying for her pastel pink silk gown proved to be a production on its own!

From the distance of over twenty years, I think it is safe for me to say that Ann and I had grave misgivings about this marriage and on several painful occasions tried to share our concerns with Kirk, but he would hear none of them. Eventually, the wedding was held in a beautiful little Anglican Church in Toronto in June 1992, and I was honored to be asked to share in the conduct of the ceremony. The reception was held at the prestigious Toronto Hunt on a bluff overlooking Lake Ontario. Unfortunately, though the date was late in June, a cold and gusty wind was blowing in off the lake, making the dancing held in a spacious marquee very uncomfortable.

Unbeknownst to Kirk, the emotional and physical strain of the wedding preparations had put Ann in the hospital in Lake Forest for about ten days prior to the wedding. Putting on a brave face, she traveled to Toronto, hosted a magnificent rehearsal dinner in the Governor General's Suite at the Toronto Hilton Hotel (prepared, of course, by our good friend, Albert Schnell), and got through the wedding and the sit-down dinner portion of the reception. But during a vigorous first dance with Kirk's new father-in-law, she caught the heel of her shoe in a seam of the temporary dance floor, fell, and collapsed in tears. With the help of some Deerfield couples who were attending the wedding, I got Ann back to our hotel for the night and next day drove all the way back to Illinois to readmit her to the Lake Forest Hospital.

Putting all this on paper—even twenty-some years later—is surprisingly painful as I know it will be for Kirk when eventually he reads it. Suffice it to say that the story of his first marriage is his to tell, not mine.

Various aspects of Christian education were at the heart of the Deerfield congregation's place in the broader community, and it had long been felt that a full-time director was needed to maintain and advance the many programs presently led by various part-time staff members. Another search committee was formed, and eventually one of its members brought forth the name of a recently ordained woman who lived with her family in Evanston. I was not keen to add another ordained minister to the staff, given all the hidden costs of such a position mandated by the Presbyterian Church (USA). However, the candidate suggested—and the Presbytery of Chicago agreed—that she be appointed as "Christian education director" rather than be called and installed as another associate pastor, and so she was.

She was a very strange woman as we soon learned. With her knack for rubbing people the wrong way except for those who carried the same "women's lib" chip on their shoulder as she did we never really got along. She insisted upon being treated "equally" to a male counterpart on the staff except when she demanded special treatment because she was a woman.

One of the saddest episodes of my entire ministry career involved her bringing charges to the session against me of "sexual harassment." When the session's executive committee summoned me to respond to her allegations, I was stunned! Somehow, I managed to respond to each and every charge, giving my version of what had actually transpired in each case. At the end of the interview, the members of the committee expressed their conviction that I had told them the truth and that she had misinterpreted or misunderstood every incident through the lens of her own preconceived ideas. Then they asked me if I would be willing to continue working with her once the air was cleared. I still remember my firm response: "I would not; and if I were forced to, I would immediately begin to seek another call!"

That settled the matter, so to speak. Her appointment was terminated, she left, but I was brokenhearted and never really recovered a personal sense of joy in my ministry in Deerfield. Ann was enraged and refused to attend church for a while until another of her health crises put her in the hospital for a week or so, after which she grudgingly returned to worship with a new twist.

Ironically, back in the day at Princeton Seminary, one of our ministry practicum sessions had been devoted to a greater sense of tactile freedom among the clergy. We learned non-invasive ways to *touch* parishioners, non-threatening ways to *hug* women, even non-suggestive ways to *embrace* men. Now, a generation later, the pendulum had swung the other way, and such tactile expressions of pastoral care were being experienced as "sexual harassment." Apparently, while Ann lay in her hospital bed, she gave this conundrum a lot of thought, so when she was released and returned to worship, she quietly left her pew at the benediction end of every service and walked with me to the door where I would stand to greet my exiting parishioners. She told me to greet no one with more than a handshake, then she began to *hug* every little old lady and lonely old man who came to the door! Thus began a personal tradition I have observed ever since, both with Ann as long as she lived, and now with Sherri whenever "Rent-a-Rev" guest preaches anywhere!

Sadly, from then on, Ann refused to accept any leadership roles in the women's association or the congregation at large. Instead, she turned her energies toward the Junior League and began to work in the charity's thrift shop, where she made friends and enjoyed whatever satisfaction she could derive. She also found support as part of a quartet of ladies from the Deerfield congregation, who met regularly to float together in one of their pools.

Truth to tell and as a result of my eventual open-heart surgery that erased so much of my memory bank, I do not have many more anecdotal memories of my Deerfield ministry. The days and nights and weeks and months and years were filled with services, meetings, weddings, funerals, successes, and sorrows. As I think back, I remember: the Fourth of Julys, when the Russell family served lemonade on the church lawn at the end of the annual parade route; the Sunday morning when the new organist, Bill Crowle, and I put on a show-and-tell and raised enough money over two services to pay for the complete overhaul of the organ so badly needed; the Presbytery of Chicago special meeting when the president of McCormick Seminary, Cynthia Campbell, and I debated the pros and cons of same-sex marriage.

Reflecting back on those years, I have come to realize that the very best thing about them was their *ordinariness*! After the turbulent decade of my Montreal ministry and then the exhausting travel schedule of my Bible Society service, there was an overweening *serenity* about a lifestyle that both personally and professionally was so mundane and predictable and *nice*!

On a personal note, I enjoy memories of Rebecca and Alex's friendship burgeoning into love. The second Christmas we were in Deerfield, Rebecca had a seasonal job at NBD and was being encouraged by her boss, Mike Kiss, to attend the company's big fancy Christmas party. Needing a date, Becca invited Alex to escort her. When he arrived at our house in his beat-up old Chevy Nova, I told him that he could not drive my daughter to an event at the Sunset Ridge Golf Club in that "heap" and handed him the keys to my navy blue Cadillac Sedan de Ville!

I still enjoy remembering: the Hallowe'en I dressed them as a priest and a nun in my various clerical garments; the ill-fated over-the-top birthday celebration that began with a chauffeur-driven limousine downtown to the Four Seasons Hotel and ended with the two of them breaking up *forever*, which turmoil lasted about a week; and their gentle friendship with Ann's dear ninety-something friend, Helen Hartz, which culminated in her attending their wedding and giving them a complete table setting of sterling silver flatware that had belonged to her long-deceased daughter, Phoebe. And because Becca spent almost every weekend of her college career and every seasonal holiday and then the first year or so of her banking career with us in Deerfield, I also have uniquely happy memories of our daddy and daughter dates, driving downtown in Ann's burgundy-and-white Chrysler LeBaron convertible.

For Ann and me, there were: wonderful evenings at Ravinia, the summer home of the Chicago Symphony Orchestra; occasional visits from Nathaniel and Cameron Trotter; and deepening friendships with Bob and Winnie Crawford, John and Odie Snyder, Ham and Bettye Traylor, Mike and Gail Kiss, and others too numerous to mention.

And there were the annual and unforgettable *Russellfests*, when "the whole famn damily" (as Ann often put it) gathered at the lake house for one of the summer holiday weekends. Other than Christmas, each Russellfest was Ann's favorite event of the year. Painstakingly, she planned every detail. She ordered Land's End golf shirts embroidered with each family member's initials and planned meals for some twenty-odd relatives and friends. Tom and Mary Beth and Paul (and soon Julie) always joined us as did the five Trotters. Johnsonville brats simmered in beer for a day before the big feast, and everybody contributed something to the food or the fellowship or both.

At some point in this period, Ann devised a birthday gift-giving system that became the highlight of every annual gathering. At the end of each Russellfest, every member of the immediate family drew the name of another family member, for whom he or she would provide *one* birthday gift worth $100–125 as if from us all. We were allowed to "suggest" what we would really like to receive, which, in Ann's and my cases, resulted in several of the framed Marie Spence and Janet Forsyth water-color sketches of historic Rondeau, which I prize to this day, and a full and ample tablesetting of the iconic blue-and-white "Willow" tableware that is now the envy of Vicar's Landing!

Probably the most memorable Russellfest, however, was "the year of the keg," when Becca and Alex smuggled a fullsized keg of beer from Deerfield across the border and down to Rondeau. With Kirk's help, they wrestled the keg onto our rickety old wheelbarrow and trundled it back and forth to and from the beach every day. As I remember, I spent more on ice cubes from the Bayview Market to keep the keg cold all weekend than Alex had spent buying the darn thing!

On the actual day of that Russellfest, Dad and Mom came over from Tom and Mary Beth's cottage and spent the afternoon and evening snuggled in Dad's favorite rocking chair, while the grandsons kept him well supplied with draft beer. Before the evening was over, he was regaling all and sundry with Scottish poems and songs, an occasion I think no one present will ever forget.

Meanwhile, not surprisingly, Rebecca and her "good friend," Alex, were developing wedding plans of their own. Alex's father had been on the PNC that brought me to Deerfield, and Alex was probably the first boy in the congregation she had met and got to know. Through the years of her attending the University of Windsor, she had contrived to have classes on Tuesdays, Wednesdays, and Thursdays and drove back and forth weekly to spend her weekends in Deerfield. Through the goodwill of two of our elders, she had secured a seasonal part-time position with the National Bank of Detroit (NBD) and, as I have already mentioned, had asked Alex to escort her to some of the parties and social functions at the bank.

In a memorable tale that is theirs to tell, they became engaged on Mackinac Island at the end of one of the annual Chicago-Mackinac sailboat races, and Ann and I were thrilled for both of them. They planned to get married in the following spring and, from the beginning, knew that they wanted a "big" wedding: an invitation to the whole congregation to attend, a black-tie dinner-dance reception, a bevy of bridesmaids and groomsmen — in other words, the works! So, one Sunday afternoon, Ann and I sat them down at the manse and offered them $10,000.00 in cash if they would just *elope*! Somewhat sobered, they went for a long walk, while Ann and I waited and hoped they would accept our offer.

No way! A big wedding it was to be, and it was! As they wished, we invited the whole congregation to the church ceremony on April 29, 1995, and hosted a punch-and-wedding-cake reception in the church's undercroft, attended by over 300 people. One of the most poignant of all our wedding moments was when Becca's "Papa Luc" proposed the toast to the bride: not a dry eye in the room!

The ceremony itself was "really big!" The one thing upon which Alex had insisted from the beginning was that he wanted to walk his mother down the aisle. Fortunately, Becca wanted for her processional music the magnificent organ toccata from Widor's Fifth Symphony, which our new organist had learned to play for his job interview a few months previously. Together, he and I choreographed a big — no, *huge* — processional with Alex leading off, escorting his mother; then Kirk, following with

Ann; then five bridesmaids, each escorted by a groomsman; until finally Rebecca sailed down the aisle on my arm. As if all this were not enough, I had procured an arrangement of the toccata with sung "Alleluias," which the whole chancel choir sang out robustly as we walked to the chancel steps. Part way down the aisle, Becca squeezed my arm and whispered, "Daddy, this is even better than Maria's wedding in *The Sound of Music*!"

Following the undercroft reception, we all traveled downtown to the Drake Hotel for the requisite black-tie dinner-dance attended by about 125 of Becca and Alex's relatives and closest friends. It was a memorable and magnificent party, although with a bittersweet undertone for Ann and me. My mother was, unbeknownst to the rest of the family, descending alarmingly into Alzheimer's disease, and this would prove to be the last big social event she would attend before being placed in a memory care facility in Windsor. Also, Kirk and Katy's marriage was clearly on the rocks, and, ironically, all of the photographs of the wedding party show our son with the woman who would soon *not* be his wife and the woman who would eventually *become* his wife standing side by side!

One of the perks I had negotiated into the terms of call when I first went to Deerfield was sufficient time off to continue my doctoral studies at the Ecumenical Theological Seminary in Detroit. My program included monthly overnight "colleague groups" and occasional five-day continuing education seminars. By then, Rebecca was studying at the University of Windsor and had "inherited" her grandmother Mimi's little Chevrolet Cavalier. At first, I flew monthly to Detroit, where Becca picked me up at the airport, and we drove back to Windsor so that I could drop her off at her dorm and use the car to go back and forth to Marygrove College. Sometimes I stayed with my parents in their small apartment in Windsor; other times, I crashed at the

Bloomfield Hills home of Chuck and Julie Greening, friends from Rondeau. As often as possible, I also managed a brief trip to the lake house. Usually, I only scheduled one—or at most two—week-long seminars per year, when, again, the use of the Cavalier came in really handy.

For one such seminar, I stayed with Mother and Dad in Windsor and managed to run afoul of the American Customs and Immigration Service. By the morning of my fourth trip across the border to my class in Detroit, CIS's computers had picked up on my daily commute. My being a Canadian (never mind a resident alien in the USA) made the folks at the tunnel suspect that I had a new commuter job in Detroit about which I had not informed the authorities, so they pulled me over. They found it hard to believe that I was a fifty-plus-year-old student, living in Illinois but staying in Windsor and attending classes in Detroit, while claiming to be a clergyman in a place called Deerfield; so it took much of the morning to persuade them that it was all on the up and up!

My doctoral dissertation was about "interactive preaching," which was the current buzzword in homiletics. I crafted several series of sermons for which I gathered a dozen or so volunteers from the congregation to be weekly focus groups, assisting me in preparing, presenting, and critiquing seasonal sermons on various subjects. The end product was a dissertation titled, "With a Little Help from My Friends," which I was scheduled to defend orally late in May 1995. Unfortunately, in the aftermath of Becca's wedding, Ann was in the midst of another of her health crises and had been transferred from the hospital in Lake Forest by ambulance to the Loyola Medical Center in suburban Chicago, where she lay for many days in a coma. On the day before my scheduled dissertation defense, she rallied a little, and by that evening her doctors were encouraging me that her crisis had passed and that I should go to Detroit as planned.

Late that evening, I set out to drive across Michigan on I-94, but by the time I reached Battle Creek, I was too exhausted to continue safely. I spent a few hours asleep in a Motel 6 (never again!) and then drove straight through to Detroit, where I just had time for a Big Mac and fries before my 1:00 p.m. appointment of which I have almost no recollection, save that when I told the ETS faculty about what I had left behind in Chicago, the dean recommended that my dissertation be approved "for determination if nothing else!"

The 1995 ETS convocation was held in the sanctuary of the historic old First Presbyterian Church on Woodward Avenue in downtown Detroit. Ann felt well enough to sign herself out of the Loyola Medical Center to attend. My parents came as did Tom and Mary Beth and Lex and Ann McCrindle. When the ETS dean put my new doctor of ministry hood over my shoulders, I allowed myself a moment of genuine pride. Earned doctorates in ministry were still a relatively new and rare thing, and I knew that I was among the first of my Princeton Seminary classmates to have achieved this distinction. I also remembered back to when I had been considered "too young" to receive an honorary doctor of divinity degree from the Presbyterian College in Montreal and grinned to realize that I actually preferred "earned" over "honorary!"

Later that year, I began to think about leading a Deerfield Church group on a tour to the Holy Land. A new parishioner, Richard Ricart, whose family ran *imagine Tours and Travel*, offered to include me in a group of Pentecostals from Dothan, Alabama, who were about to leave for Israel; so off I went! It was a great learning experience, and I came home determined to lead some of my church members on a similar adventure.

A Holy Land tour program, including a three-day extension

into Egypt, came together surprisingly quickly, and by February 1996, Ann and I headed off to Israel with twenty-seven church members and friends. We had an incredible range of experiences, from the Mount of Beatitudes north of the Sea of Galilee to the ruins of Masada overlooking the Dead Sea and culminating in an unforgettable celebration of the sacrament of Holy Communion at the garden tomb on the outskirts of Jerusalem. Lives were changed, leadership potential was unearthed, friendships were made, and I returned with insights to include in some of the finest sermons I ever preached.

The same could not be said, unfortunately, of the Egypt extension. Without realizing the impact that it would have on our travel, Rick Ricart had arranged for us to experience the Pyramids and Sphinx of Giza and the Valleys of the Kings and Queens near Luxor and Karnak at the very end of the Muslim month of Ramadan, and it was a disaster from start to finish. By the time we crossed into Egypt at the western end of the Gaza, I was a wreck and lay, exhausted, on the back seat of the bus all the way to Cairo. Meanwhile, Ann, similarly exhausted, began to weep as she visualized Mary and Joseph and the baby Jesus traveling the desert wasteland through which we were driving.

Everything we experienced was dirty, crowded, noisy, late, and frightening. Not to belabor the point, I will record only one brief anecdote. By the time we reached the incredible Temple of Karnak on the last full day of our tour, it was late afternoon, almost closing time. As we wandered, awestruck, among the symmetrical pillars of the temple, a wiry little Egyptian security officer approached us and asked if we would like to see the royal enclosure at the very heart of the ruins. Eagerly— naïvely!—we agreed, and soon we were far from the exiting crowds in a secluded vantage point from which we could see the pillars in horizontal lines spreading out in all directions.

"Would Madam like to climb up on this rocky outcropping for a better view?" our helpful guide asked, and, of course, Ann would and did, with the assistance of this wizened little man. Once she was up and teetering on the rock, our guide suddenly became sinister as he reached out to me rubbing his fingers and thumb in the wordless symbol for "baksheesh!"

I pulled out my wallet and offered him a $10.00 American bill. "No," he insisted, "more!" As I began to argue with him, Ann wailed "Give him whatever he wants!" So I gave him a $20.00 bill, and he helped her down from her perch.

Ann was red-faced—whether with fear or fury I could not tell. "Couldn't you see where his hand was?" she demanded.

"No," I admitted, bewildered.

"Up my skirt, between my legs!" she screamed and began to sob.

As cool as could be, our "security officer" led us through an unimposing doorway and back into the main corridor leading out of the temple.

Sadly, for many years our father had shielded the whole family from our mother's deepening descent into Alzheimer's until by the summer of 1996 the disease had become so dangerous not only to herself but to him and the whole apartment complex in which they were living that her doctor insisted she be placed in a memory care facility in Windsor. Ann and I were at the lake house at the time and were able to step in and handle a tremendously painful situation with which Dad simply could not cope. We dealt with the social worker and the lawyer and then the nursing director of Huron Lodge until finally we took Mom physically to live there. The last sane words she ever spoke to me were: "I'd rather be dead!"

In Deerfield on Thanksgiving Eve 1996, Ann and I received

a phone call from Kirk in Toronto, telling us that he was giving up his law practice, his marriage, and everything else and coming home! Stunned and bewildered, I asked him, "Kirk, where is 'home?'"

"Wherever you and Mom are," came the tearful reply.

Sorrow, disappointment, anger, concern were all in the mix of emotions with which we prepared ourselves to receive our son back into our lives. Our Deerfield manse was large enough to accommodate another adult, and our Deerfield friends were wonderful about welcoming Kirk into their lives too. After Christmas, he traveled to Steamboat Springs, Colorado, to ski for a while; when he returned, he had several job offers, one of which put him in the trading pit at the Chicago Board of Trade. He was a long time finding himself, and he was very leery of romantic entanglements. "I want to find a woman who will love me for *myself*," he confided to me, "not what I do or what I make or what I might become!"

All through 1997, every crisis involving my mother's care seemed to require me to jump in the car or get on a plane and hurry to Windsor to deal with whatever real or imaginary emergency had arisen. In early December, I drove from Deerfield to Windsor for Mom's eightieth birthday. I had planned a festive afternoon with balloons, a corsage, and a birthday cake to share with her fellow residents. As I arrived at Huron Lodge, everyone was in a tizzy. When Mom's caregivers had gone to dress her for the party, they could not lay their hands on any of her "good" clothing. Eventually, they started finding a piece in a dresser here, then another in a dresser there until they began to realize that she had been systematically visiting other rooms, where she would exchange a bit of someone else's clothing for whatever she had on!

The party seemed interminable. Watching Mom try to remember how to feed herself her dinner was even worse until at last the nursing staff had her undressed and tucked into bed. As I sat at her bedside and kissed her goodnight, I said, "Gee, Mom, it seems strange for me to be tucking you in when you used to do it for me."

"I did?" she queried, paused, then asked "Who *are* you?" It broke my heart.

I managed not to cry until I got out into my car, then the tears just spilled. I still had to drive home to Deerfield to preach the second Sunday of Advent the next morning, but I could barely keep from crying as I drove through Detroit on I-94. Somewhere near the city limits, I prayed to God: "Isn't there a little church around here that could use me?"

Within seventy-two hours, I received an unexpected phone call from the chair of the pastor nominating committee at the First Presbyterian Church of Royal Oak, an inner suburb of Detroit, and the rest, as they say, is history!

The search process was long, uncertain, painful, and, in the end, resulted in the worst career move of my entire ministry. I was almost sixty—too old—and too wanting—no, *needing*—to relocate for all the *wrong* reasons. Ann did not want to leave her tight little circle of friends in Deerfield. Rebecca did not want her mother to move so far away. Kirk did not want to be maneuvered into moving in with his new girlfriend too early in their relationship. And my father did not want me to forsake what he considered to be the best church I had ever served for his sake.

Meanwhile. I was actually feeling *desperate* to alleviate some of the physical and emotional stresses in my life. What I did not recognize but should have was that my sense of desperation was, in fact, an early warning symptom of the coronary artery disease that would play havoc with my life and my ministry once I got to Royal Oak.

In due course, the Royal Oak PNC and I came to terms, and I announced my departure from the Deerfield church to take place at mid-summer 1998. The congregation was in shock as was I, I think. For the life of me, I could not seem to see how wrong this move was—for me and for everyone else. Bless their hearts, the Deerfield folks gave us a memorable send-off, with farewell receptions and parties and a Sunday morning service I still remember as one of the most enjoyable experiences of my ministry there.

Unfortunately, Ann's physical and emotional health couldn't take it. She awoke the morning of our Sunday farewell feeling ominously unwell. She got through the farewell worship service sitting beside me but nearly collapsed on the church lawn during the after-service festivities and ended up in the emergency room of Lake Forest Hospital by mid-afternoon. One of our favorite couples in the congregation had scheduled one last party for that evening, which I attended alone, and that was that.

As part of my severance package from Deerfield, I was due a month's vacation before beginning my duties in Royal Oak. We had found a two-bedroom apartment in a twenty-story high-rise building in nearby Southfield to which all of our worldly goods had been shipped just before our farewell weekend. For the duration, we had been staying in Lake Forest as guests of Bob and Winnie Crawford, and the duration turned out to be an extended one as Ann continued to be very ill in the Lake Forest Hospital.

Finally, I had to leave the Crawfords' generous hospitality and was taken in by Ham and Bettye Traylor. When Ann was released from the hospital, we stayed a few extra days with the Traylors before heading off to Michigan. One of my most poignant memories of this difficult period was our last evening in

Illinois, when Alex and Rebecca came to say goodbye and to announce their first pregnancy. Ann was truly heartbroken: she had for so long looked forward to being a grandmother, and now we were leaving the area for good! I really thought Ann might end up back in the hospital before we ever got away, but she made the trip to Royal Oak and Southfield without a crisis, only to end up in Royal Oak's William Beaumont Hospital a few days later.

Meanwhile, Kirk's plaintive desire to find a woman who would love him for *himself*, not what he did for a living nor what he earned nor what he might become, seemed to be coming to fruition. In the previous summer, he had "accidentally" met Jennifer Moss, one of Becca's bridesmaids, on the Chicago waterfront, and their mutual attraction was immediately clear! Once my departure date from Deerfield became public, Kirk and Jennifer confessed that they wanted to get married while we were still in Deerfield. That proved impractical and so a mid-August date was chosen, and I negotiated with the Deerfield session to be allowed to return to marry them even after my actual departure date.

Ann rallied once again and was able to make the trip back to Deerfield with me. Kirk and Jennifer's small but memorable wedding took place outdoors in the church's garth on a beautiful warm August afternoon, followed by a drive downtown to board a Chicago River party boat for a sunset cruise reception out into Lake Michigan.

Therein is a story that has to be preserved. Kirk's grandfather Russell had traveled from Windsor for the wedding, and we were so glad to have him present. Kirk had thoughtfully hired a limousine to transport his new in-laws, his grandfather, and his parents from the church to the boat. But I was concerned that once we boarded the party boat for the reception,

Dad would never be able to make it down and up the narrow spiral stairs leading from the main deck to the restrooms.

So I directed the limo driver to take us downtown via the Drake Hotel, where I knew there were restrooms right inside the main entrance. As we pulled up in our stretch limo and the doorman grandly opened the back door for us, he was astonished to see Ann and me, whom he knew very well from previous visits. "Don't get excited, Carlos," I cautioned him, "we're just here to use the bathrooms!" Without missing a beat, he held the door open, pulled me out of my jump seat, helped Dad and the Mosses from the back seat, then grandly pulled Ann from the other jump seat, and instructed the limo driver to "stand by" for our return!

The cruise was sensational! Wine and hors d' oeuvres were plentiful. A small dance band held forth on the top deck dance floor. We sailed out into Lake Michigan, cruising northward as we watched a glorious sunset turn the Chicago skyline into silhouettes. We sailed back into the city aglow with its myriad nightlights, and Ann and I were so happy that things seemed to be turning out so well for Kirk at last!

* * * * *

I DID NOT HAVE AN AUSPICIOUS START TO MY LAST full-time senior pastorate. Our Southfield residence was in chaos as was my new "study," tucked into a far corner of the Christian education wing of the First Presbyterian Church of Royal Oak. My predecessor, the Reverend Dr. Thomas Kirkman, turned out to have been a seminary classmate of my Deerfield predecessor—cut out of the same cloth—and left behind a staff almost as dysfunctional as the one I had inherited there. The Presbytery of Detroit's interim pastor appointee had been a weak and spineless character, and the staff had grown used to little or no supervision in an ecclesiastical jungle where "all the people did what was right in their own eyes" (Judg 17:6*b*)

In fact, Dr. Kirkman wrote me a letter of welcome, in which he humorously sympathized with my situation, claiming "No man should have to follow *both* Bernard Didier *and* Tom Kirkman!" But I did, and I also had to deal with the legacy of Dr. Kirkman's powerful wife Ruth, an ordained clergywoman in her own right who had built up a personal following of ultraconservative and ultra-evangelical lay people, one of whom was the church secretary. In her eyes, nothing I ever did or said or believed was sufficiently biblically based as to be acceptable.

Given its history and heritage, it was not surprising that First Pres had only one ordained pastor on staff—me—but had several lay colleagues whose whole families were long-time members of the congregation. Supportive cliques had formed around most of them, and I soon learned that they were truly sacred cows! For example, the youth ministries director, during our initial one-on-one conversation, complained that she was very unhappy in her work and couldn't wait to get married and leave Royal Oak altogether. When I mentioned this comment in a session personnel committee meeting, one of the elders vehemently denied that this was the case and outright accused me of being a liar.

One of the aspects of life in Royal Oak that had originally intrigued me was the burgeoning renewal of the suburb's downtown area just two short blocks from the church campus. Restaurants, bars, chic boutiques, and upper-middle-class apartments and condos were being built, and I foresaw interesting possibilities for ministries that would draw a whole new demographic to First Pres. Naïve me! Once it became clear that the renewal was attracting some alternative lifestyles (primarily gay and lesbian), the church might as well have been in another town altogether. There was no interest in—truth be told, there was overt hostility toward—what was happening two blocks away, and that was that.

Not all was unpleasant or off-putting, despite the circumstances of my start. The church had an outstanding organist/choirmaster and a very fine music ministry. Liz Spry was open to new and innovative ideas, and we created some wonderful worship experiences together. We did some teaching services on Sundays when we presented a choral masterwork at the later service and wove into the earlier service excerpts of the same work along with explanations of the texts, the music, and, in the case of the several masses we included, the liturgical movements and their significance.

Another strength of the church's programming was its Christian education ministry for children. During the vacancy before my arrival, the CE director had prevailed upon the board of trustees to do a complete renovation of the second floor of the CE wing to accommodate the trendy and complex curriculum known as "Joyful Journeys." On Sunday mornings and Wednesday afternoons after school, our children worked through an ever-changing exploration of Old and New Testament themes. The program required constant recruiting and training of teaching assistants, which became my supporting role.

Yet a third successful innovation was "Wednesday Night Live," an after-school and early-evening midweek family-oriented event for all ages. This had long been a dream of one of the church's most prominent families, and I did myself a lot of good by getting behind it and immersing myself in its various aspects. As I write this book, it gives me continuing pleasure to know that "WNL" is indeed still alive and thriving at Royal Oak.

The highlight of our first few months in Royal Oak was the decision of two of our three children so spend the Christmas holiday with us. To make it possible, Ann and I took a room at a nearby hotel, and Kirk and Jen and Rebecca and Alex took over our two-bedroom home for a few days. Because Becca was *very* pregnant, she claimed the master bedroom for herself and Alex, so poor Kirk and Jen had to sleep on the hide-a-bed in the den. We had a marvelous time together, and, for a few days at least, I felt as though perhaps all would be well after all!

During their visit, Becca and Alex were quite insistent that they were going to handle the arrival of our first grandchild *themselves*! We would be allowed to visit for a couple of days when the baby was born in mid-February 1999 but that would be all. So when, in the wee small hours of the morning, the fateful call came that Becca was in labor, Ann and I threw a couple of changes of clothes and some basic toiletries into a duffle bag and set out to drive to Naperville, Illinois, where the Klopps were living by this time.

Halfway across Michigan on I-94, our new cell phone rang: it was Alex, tremulously reporting that Becca was going to have to undergo a cesarean section birth and so could Ann please plan to come and stay for a *few weeks* to help care for the baby until Becca could heal enough to care for the baby on her own? We continued to drive westward, realizing that I would have to drive back to Royal Oak to conduct Sunday services and pack up enough clothing, medications, and incidentals to see Ann through a month-long stay. Needless to say, Ann was *in alt*, the happiest I had seen her since we—no, in truth I—had decided to move to Michigan eight months before. She played her part well, Victoria was delivered safe and sound the day after Valentine's Day, and I commuted back and forth between Naperville and Royal Oak several times to do my part.

A charming footnote: As an expression of their gratitude to Ann for her unexpected help, Becca and Alex presented her with a gorgeous Royal Doulton figurine of "Victoria" (HN2471) serenely seated with her pink floral skirts ballooning around her. It was the first "family name" Doulton figurine added to our growing collection and prompted an inspiration to begin collecting other "family name" figurines, which I have appreciated and enjoyed to this very day!

Tori's baptism took place on Mother's Day in the sanctuary of First Pres. The whole family gathered for the occasion: Becca's parents and Alex's, Tom and Mary Beth, all the Trotters, and Kirk and Jennifer. In his customary fashion, Alex made sure that there were Mother's Day corsages for all the mothers present except, unfortunately, for the most important mother of all. As I remember, Rebecca was not amused!

By then, the coronary artery disease about which I had not known had begun to raise its ugly head. During a routine physical examination by our new female primary care physician, she discovered the condition when I complained of chronic fatigue and frequent dizzy spells as we settled into our new life in Michigan. I was soon in the hands of a remarkable interventional cardiologist, who promptly performed my first angioplasty and inserted two stents in my severely blocked arteries.

July 1999 was the occasion for my second and much more serious, cardiac event. During the summer months, we were holding the church's earlier Sunday morning services in a shaded courtyard off Kirkman Hall. As I preached my sermon, I began to feel lightheaded, enough so that I did not try to climb the stairs to the garden level to greet the congregation but rather stayed on the lower level until all the worshipers had dispersed, when I asked one of the elders to help me get back to my study. At the point of collapse, I asked the elder to call Ann at home and ask her to bring me my little vial of nitroglycerin. He wanted to call 911, but I assured him that even one little nitro pill would make me fine; and, at first, it seemed to be the case. Unfortunately, the second service that Sunday was to be the occasion for the baptism of the firstborn grandson of members of the congregation with whom we had become quite friendly. When the hour of the service approached, I determinedly got up to put on my summer robe and nearly passed out. I can still remember holding on to the leg of a conference table in my study for support as I tried to stand again. By this time, my stalwart elder was insistent upon calling 911, which Ann did, while he went to open the worship service in the sanctuary.

As soon as the EMTs arrived with lights flashing and sirens wailing, they administered more nitroglycerin, and my blood pressure dropped so dramatically that I can remember hearing one of them use the term "bradycardia" and shouting, "I'm losing him!" as I lost consciousness. I came to in an ambulance speeding south on Woodward Avenue heading to William Beaumont Hospital. Fortunately, my heart was not damaged during this episode, and with a second angioplasty and two new stents, I was soon released from the hospital to recuperate at home.

At the church as in the rest of society, much of 1999 involved the over-hyped lead-up to the end of the twentieth century and the inauguration of the twenty-first. It was a time of tremendous interest in end-of-the-world speculations of all kinds, and the Ruth Kirkman fanatics in the congregation were having a field day! No matter what the announced topic of any Bible study event, the questions inevitably came around to end times theories and threats. I consistently took refuge in Jesus's words recorded at the start of the Acts of the Apostles: "It is not for you to know the times or periods that the Father has set by his own authority" (Acts 1:7). Of course, this answer did not satisfy those who wanted a firm prediction about the end of the world, and it led to some strained relations with powerful members of the session and the board of trustees.

In the end, the millennium hoopla turned out to be a non-event. Everyone everywhere stayed home for fear of travel difficulties and so did we and all our family. Our residents' association organised a desultory New Millennium's Eve party, which we attended for a while; but when nothing unusual happened at midnight or shortly thereafter, we went up to bed!

Sunday, October 6, 1990
Deerfield, Illinois
My little family at the Deerfield manse:
(from left to right) Sarah, me, Ann, Rebecca, and Kirk

Saturday, October 19, 1991
Outside the New Scotland United Church, Ontario
Carrying Sarah's train as we enter the church for her wedding

Summer 1992
The First Presbyterian Church of Deerfield, Illinois
In the garth before a summer Sunday service

April 29, 1995
The First Presbyterian Church of Deerfield, Illinois
Rebecca marries Alex Klopp

April 29, 1995
The Drake Hotel, Chicago, Illinois
Ann and I at Becca and Alex's wedding reception

February 1996
On the old road from Jericho to Jerusalem, Israel
Astride a white camel

February 1996
At the ancient ruins of Masada, Israel
Overlooking the Dead Sea and Jordan

Reformation Sunday, October 27, 1996
The First Presbyterian Church of Deerfield, Illinois
Ann and I wearing the Russell tartan
for a "Kirkin' o' the Tartan" service

August 15, 1998
On Lake Michigan off Chicago
Dancing with Ann at Kirk and Jennifer's party boat wedding reception

Mother's Day, May 9, 1999
The First Presbyterian Church of Royal Oak, Michigan
At the baptism of my first grandchild Victoria Ann Klopp

THE TWO
THOUSANDS

I HAD NOT BEEN VERY LONG INTO MY ministry in Royal Oak until I had begun to recognize the old familiar patterns of a long-time successful pastorate conducted like so many were in that period as a benevolent dictatorship! Like his friend (and my predecessor in Deerfield, Illinois), Bernard Didier, Tom Kirkman personified the old Roman leadership model of divide and conquer.

Not surprisingly, the congregation of the First Presbyterian Church of Royal Oak was riven with longstanding conflicts: the session versus the board of trustees; the men deacons versus the women deacons; the Sunday school teachers versus the "Joyful Journeys" leadership; the "old guard" of Royal Oak's social upper crust versus the newer members from the surrounding suburbs—Huntington Woods, Berkley, Southfield, Birmingham, Troy, Grosse Pointe, *et cetera*. For years, Dr. Kirkman had kept all these factions in balanced tension; but after his retirement, the fissures were allowed to fester, deepen, and strengthen.

The most troublesome conflict of all, however, was between the theologically and socially moderate members of the congregation for whom the Royal Oak church was more of a *community* and *congregational* institution and that doctrinally ultraconservative and denominationally restive segment of the membership that had its origins in the Bible studies led by Tom's wife Ruth, and which, after the Kirkmans' departure, coalesced around the personalities of one particular couple.

In the lead-up to the millennial year of 2000, this couple in particular had made my life miserable with a constant barrage of "Left Behind" style questions and comments as well as thinly disguised suggestions of conspiracy theory attitudes within the Presbyterian Church (USA). Even more disturbing, they began alleging purposeful neglect of issues springing from the, to them, imminent second coming of Christ.

In anticipation of a year's worth of "millennial" celebrations, the Royal Oak Church had planned a number of special worship services, musical events, and fellowship opportunities, most of which occurred as "a dull thud" or never actually happened at all. However, one of the most impressive of these events turned out to be a pair of services with full choir, soloists, and chamber orchestra presenting Théodore Dubois' *Seven Last Words of Christ* in April 2000, for which, incidentally, my lifelong friend Lex McCrindle commuted from Windsor for rehearsals and the Sunday presentations in which he sang with the tenor section of the church choir.

Even before our departure from Deerfield, I had been working on organizing another group visit to the Holy Land. There were a dozen or so friends from that congregation who had continued to pressure me to make another trip possible, so I began to work with Rick Ricart on plans for a pilgrimage after the Lenten and Easter seasons of 2000. Ann's health was so uncertain—in and out of the hospital with episodes of excruciating pain—that I invited our daughter, Sarah, to consider accompanying me and acting as my "second-in-command" for the trip, which she readily agreed to do.

As our departure date for Israel drew nearer and nearer, Ann once again took ill and remained so for so long and with such severity that her doctors eventually advised me not to leave the country, lest she might be dead before I returned. In desperation, I turned to the church's director of music, Liz Spry, who had organized frequent choral trips abroad and agreed, very much at the last minute, to take my place as the tour leader.

From the beginning, the tour had been planned around a side trip to the Oberammergau passion play, which is staged once every decade in Germany's Bavarian Alps. Sarah was particularly keen to attend the passion play, and it was originally scheduled as the first stop on the tour. But a raging snowstorm in the Midwest grounded the group's planes both in Detroit and then in Chicago, so the passion play excursion was hastily rescheduled to come at the end of the tour.

Let me record that Liz Spry did a wonderful job of replacing me, and Sarah did superb work as her assistant. They came home with many precious memories, most of which they shared with me. It was a wistful time for me—Ann's health had improved in due course, and I *could have* gone after all—but that was not in God's providence. Sarah, bless her heart, brought home as a souvenir for me a signed and dated Swarovski crystal passion play memento of a cobalt blue globe surmounted by a dove of peace with a silver sprig of olive branch in its beak. As I write this almost twenty years later, it still holds pride of place on display in our home, and it still makes me sad to remember all the mixed emotions that kept my life in turmoil at that time.

Not surprisingly, I continued to suffer cardiac "incidents," none quite as dramatic as the first two, but each requiring a trip to William Beaumont Hospital and another stent—seven in all, the results of five angioplasties—at the end of which my cardiac interventionist warned me that there was no more room for another stent and the next time would require open heart surgery! In the goodness of God, I found, and the congregation called and installed, the Reverend Carl Eschenbrenner as my associate pastor. As it turned out, he proved a *"Godsend"* in many ways through the remaining months of my Royal Oak ministry.

On December 8, 2000, Ann suffered a terrible and mystifying seizure and ended up in the emergency room at William Beaumont Hospital. Coincidently, there had been some kind of catastrophe elsewhere, and Ann ended up on a stretcher on the emergency room floor because there was no place for her in what we recognized later was a macabre version of the Christmas story playing out in our lives. Whether it was a TIA or a stroke was never medically established; all I knew was that she could barely speak and could not use her right hand.

As I sat on the floor with her for the several hours it took to handle the backlog of emergency room patients and get Ann settled in a hospital bed somewhere, I realized that she was convinced that she was dying, and she wanted to plan her funeral! Once I caught the drift of her determination, I gave her the little notepad I always carried with me, and she began to print with her left hand the hymns and scripture readings that she wanted to be included in her service. It was all I could do to keep from weeping as I helped her with this heartbreaking exercise.

Ann's health, which had been fragile for decades, had taken a shocking turn for the worse, and I was, once again, being forced to devote an inordinate amount of time and energy to her care. Unfortunately, by the end of 2000 there was open conflict between two different women in the congregation, each of whom had set herself up as Ann's personal guardian and the gatekeeper of access to her hospital bed and both of whom were creating enmity for me among people who did not understand what was going on. Even worse, one of them, whose daughter and son-in-law were both highly placed in the church's power structure, began to complain that I was neglecting my pastoral duties in favor of my personal attention to my critically ill wife!

I spent Christmas Day at Ann's bedside and then as much of the holiday season as I could afford to be away from the church. Early in January, her doctors indicated to me that she had suffered some brain damage in the episode before Christmas, and they recommended that she be transferred by ambulance to the University of Michigan teaching hospital in Ann Arbor whence she could be admitted into an experimental brain therapy program to try to reverse the damage and restore her to a modicum of good health.

I agreed, and thus began a nightmare season of commuting back and forth between Royal Oak and Ann Arbor, trying to balance Ann's needs and those of my increasingly disgruntled congregation. I felt truly impaled on the horns of a dilemma: my parishioners publicly applauded my "devotion" as *Ann's* husband and privately complained that I was hardly ever available for *their* pastoral care. Just conducting Sunday services and monthly session meetings was rapidly becoming "not enough!"

Under the clinic's care, Ann's health made unexpected improvement, enough that by Easter of 2001 she was considered well enough to be allowed to go home. Her psychotherapist suggested that perhaps a "vacation" would do us both good. I agreed and asked my friend Rick Ricart to arrange something for us. He came up with a booking on a cruise ship, scheduled to sail from Fort Lauderdale, cross the Eastern Caribbean, traverse the Panama Canal, then end up in Acapulco.

On April 22, the Sunday after Easter, just before we left on our vacation, I had the privilege of baptising our first grandson,

William Ronald Russell, not only named for his two grand-fathers but also carrying on the family tradition of "William, son of William, son of William." Will had been born in Naper-ville the previous November, and once again the whole family gathered to honor his baptism. My most vivid memory of the event, however, is that Will started screaming the minute I took him in my arms and continued screaming as I baptised him and carried him up and down the church's center aisle introducing him to the congregation. Only as I handed him back to Kirk (or perhaps Jennifer?) did Will stop screaming and then the congregation burst into applause.

At the buffet luncheon Ann had organised back at our condo, I made a presentation to Kirk and Jennifer for Will of the gold and silver signet ring engraved with my initials W-R-R that my parents had given me on my sixteenth birthday. As I pointed out that the middle R could stand for "Ronald" as well as "Ray," the baby's two grandfathers welled up with sentimental tears. It remains one of the most precious memories of my lifetime!

The much-anticipated vacation trip was wonderful, probably our best cruise ever and did us both a world of good. I felt badly about leaving Royal Oak, though, when so much nasty criticism was swirling around my neglect of my job. Also, my strong and faithful clerk of session, Francis Luttrell, had been diagnosed with terminal cancer of the esophagus, and I was fearful that he might die while we were away.

We had a bit of a scare in Cartagena, Colombia, where, after a morning's tour of the charming old city and a lovely lunch shipboard, I collapsed on deck as we were sailing out to sea. A couple of stewards got me back to our stateroom; the ship's doctor paid a brief visit and determined that I had had too much wine at lunch and too much sun deck side. "A good long nap is all he needs!"

And it appeared to be so. I recovered, and we enjoyed the rest of the cruise without incident. I was fascinated by the transit through the Panama Canal and couldn't wait to get home to talk it over with my engineering friend, Lex. Together, Ann and I attended many of the art auctions held when the ship was at sea. Eventually, we got up the courage to bid on—and win—a stunning little original oil painting by an artist signed as A. E. Barnes. So enchanted were we by her work that when a framed pair of numbered still life prints came up for auction later in the cruise, we bought them too!

I remember that our debarkation at Acapulco was very hectic. Then we had a long layover, awaiting the plane that would fly us back to Detroit. Our luggage was numerous and heavy and had to be lugged from one part of the Acapulco terminal to another. I thought, *If this doesn't kill me, nothing will*!

We returned to Royal Oak just before the regularly scheduled May 2001 session meeting. At that time, the Presbyterian Church (USA) was in excruciating turmoil over a lay-led endeavor called the "Confessing Church Movement." The twin foci of the movement were (a) forbidding gay ordination and (b) opposing same-sex marriage. The thrust of it all was a demand that ordained pastors as well as non-ordained lay church workers must sign a pledge to live lives ordered by "fidelity in marriage and chastity in singleness."

Unbeknownst to me, several elders in the Royal Oak congregation had taken advantage of my absence and the clerk of session's by-now advancing cancer to persuade him to include on the session's docket a discussion of and vote on becoming part of the Confessing Church Movement. After the usual and routine session business was completed around 9:00 p.m., these elders began their presentation in support of joining the movement. I felt blindsided, and the clerk, Francis Luttrell, felt heart-sick that he had allowed this matter to be sprung on me as it was. A spirited debate ensued and raged for almost an hour and a half, at which point Francis stood up, slammed shut the session minute book, resigned as clerk of session on the spot, and walked out of the meeting and the church. It was the last time I saw him alive.

I felt it was finally time for me to intervene. Heretofore, I had desperately tried to moderate the meeting as evenhandedly as possible, but now things had gotten out of hand. Slowly and clearly, I indicated my opposition to the movement in general and in particular to its litmus test provision regarding sexual morality. I pointed out that the language used by the movement to preclude *homo*sexual ordination and behavior was so general as to apply equally to *hetero*sexual clergy and church staff members.

"Do you realize," I concluded, "that if you approve this resolution tonight and join this congregation to the Confessing Church Movement, tomorrow morning I shall have to fire at least three members of our staff who *I know* are not living lives that accord with its provisions?"

One still-alert elder moved immediately to end debate and put the question. Another seconded the motion, which passed on a voice vote. Much relieved, I put the main motion to a vote with a show of hands. Two elders supported the motion; all the others voted against it. Then I adjourned the meeting.

The next morning, all hell broke loose! Those members of the congregation who were in favor of the movement were infuriated and acted accordingly. Angry phone calls, shaking fists, threats to withhold pledged income, suggestions that the Presbytery of Detroit ought to be called in to consider removing me from my ministry punctuated the day and continued on into the evening. Ann became almost as angry as those who were raging against me. We barely slept that night.

The morning following, with the telephone turned off, I urged Ann to keep her scheduled doctor's appointment while I went back to bed. But soon after she left home, I began to realize that I was not feeling at all well. Finally, I called the church office and asked Carl Eschenbrenner to come over and drive me to our doctor's office, which he did. My doctor took one look at me, ordered an EKG, conferred with her office colleagues and with Ann, who was still there and then called an ambulance to take me to William Beaumont Hospital ASAP!

My history of cardiac incidents had finally caught up with me. Let me share the way I described it to my congregation on the Sunday in August when I first returned to the Royal Oak pulpit.

On the morning of my open-heart surgery a couple of months ago, I was pretty apprehensive. A couple of communications glitches resulted in my arriving in the surgical preparation room having had no premedication to calm me down. Then I overheard that due to a mix-up involving the blood they were to have on hand in the operating room in case I needed to have a transfusion, my procedure was going to be delayed an hour or so. I was agitated enough to ask if I couldn't have something, whereupon—and this I learned later in a hilarious note from Terry and Kay Farlow, whose son was a nurse on one of the surgical heart teams at the time—a big burly anæsthetist gave me an injection and said, "Just wanted you to know a *Catholic* is putting you to sleep!"

But all I remember is being in the prep room, reciting the Twenty-third Psalm in my head! I was out for the hour's delay and the trip to the operating room and the quintuple bypass surgery and the time in the recovery room and the trip to a cubicle in the ICU. The first thing I was aware of was this warm and wonderful sense of being with the Lord and the Lord being with me. And then I began to realize that I couldn't move my arms or legs, which were in restraints. I couldn't move my head. I couldn't swallow. I couldn't see. And I thought, *I must be dead; I really* am *with the Lord, and the Lord really* is *with me*!

In truth, it was a pretty *disappointing* experience. After forty years of preaching assurances of life after death in Christ Jesus, I had expected *heaven* to be much more wonderful than *this*! As I tried again to open my eyes, an angel appeared before me and began to speak: "Mr. Russell— Mr. Russell, don't try to move or speak. You are in recovery and intubated and re-strained and will be until more of the anæsthetic wears off and you are more fully aware!" Oh, what a relief that was!

My procedure had apparently gone well, despite my obliv-ion, and I was soon moved to the hospital's cardiac intensive care unit. When Ann was allowed to see me, I was horrified. My open-heart surgery had shocked and frightened her to the point that she was clearly—and, for the first time, clearly to *me*—mentally ill. She moved and spoke and looked like a *zom-bie*, and I was terrified for her and for me.

I was hospitalized for a few weeks, largely because I was ad-mitted to the hospital's in-house cardiac rehabilitation program. My memories of that time are few and unfocused. I remember getting a tearful telephone call from Sarah, out in Calgary, Al-berta, worrying whether to fly to my bedside or to fly to The Hague in the Netherlands for an important meeting in her new global IT capacity with Royal Dutch Shell. I remember that Becca and Alex came to visit from Naperville and, unprepared for Ann's fragile mental state, had a tremendous row with her and left town brokenhearted.

And I remember a surprising visit from Matt Schramm, a

young man of the Royal Oak congregation who, with my encouragement, had applied to Princeton Theological Seminary
in preparation for becoming an ordained Presbyterian minister.
He was at loose ends, having just graduated from Hillsdale College and was awaiting a mid-August Hebrew course in advance
of his seminary education. In conversation about my ongoing
needs for help with my projected three-month recuperation at
home, he offered to become my "manservant" until it was time
for him to head off to Princeton, and so it was!

Matt was truly a godsend, not only to me but even more so
to Ann, who was still barely able to function rationally. Every
morning, he arrived about nine o'clock to make our breakfast
and stayed through the day until about five o'clock when he departed, leaving the makings of dinner on the kitchen counter.
During the day, he helped me bathe and dress, tidied up, did the
laundry, and drove Ann to the supermarket and other errands.
He also—much more than I realized at the time—interfaced
with the church staff and elders to protect me from the rising
chorus of complaints about how long it was taking me to recover from my surgery.

My recovery *was* long but not as long as my surgeon had
recommended, for I was back in the pulpit—if not full-time in
the office—at the beginning of August. Bravely—well, perhaps
foolhardily—I picked up on my promised summer sermon
series, "Time and Eternity," based, as in the past, on the weekly
Time magazine cover story. My computer's trusty "Sermons by
Date" record indicates that I did not preach on the Sunday of
the 2001 Labor Day weekend. I know not why; perhaps a by-
now long-forgotten *Russellfest*?

I *do* know that on the following Sunday—September 9,
2001—the day before my sixty-second birthday, I preached one
of the most poignant and prescient sermons of my career:

"Death, Be Not Proud!" I have included it among the appendices at the end of this volume, for it is a powerful, passionate, and persuasive testimony to my personal faith about life and death, and I want my loved ones and friends to be able to read it and meditate upon it after I am gone.

Of course, the *prescience* of the message was that it came just twenty-four hours before the events that all the world now knows as 9/11, the day of the four coordinated terrorist attacks that destroyed New York City's twin World Trade towers and wrought havoc at Washington's Pentagon and a Pennsylvania cornfield, killing almost 3,000 people and changing forever the course of human history.

Ann and I were at our Canadian lake house, having quietly celebrated my birthday the day before. Just after 9:00 a.m., an alarming telephone call from Sarah alerted us to the horrors unfolding in America. Within minutes, it seemed, the world was galvanized in fear. The news media reported, among other details, that all border crossings into and out of the United States were closed until further notice. We were trapped in Canada and were not able to return to the USA for several more days.

In retrospect, I recognize now that September 11, 2001, marked the beginning of the end of my four decades in ministry. Back in Royal Oak, members of the congregation were clamoring for the church to "do something!"—*anything*—to mark the spiritual significance of this horrendous chain of events. Carl Eschenbrenner, bless his heart, tried to organize some sort of vigil, but I, their pastor, was not *there* and my absence, however unintentional and unavoidable, was never forgotten or forgiven.

Just as the Québécois quest for sovereign independence from Canada had become the defining theme in my early preaching ministry in Montreal, so the suicidal terrorist attacks of al Qaeda became the defining motif that ended my pulpit career in America. I have added the three Sunday sermons I preached in the aftermath of 9/11 as appendices at the end of this volume and as a fitting record of who, where, and what I was at this turning point in my life. That they were *controversial* cannot be denied. But I still think that they were among the best on-point messages of my career—certainly equal in strength if not in influence, to my Montreal preaching—and I will be proud to be remembered for them if nothing else.

As if dealing with the aftermath of these tragedies were not enough, I was still coping with the six deaths in three weeks that had befallen my congregation in the second half of August, including the eventual and heartbreaking loss of my erstwhile clerk of session, Francis Luttrell, who had been speeded to his own demise by the Confessing Church Movement fracas back in May. At the same time, my own mother's condition in the nursing home in Windsor was deteriorating rapidly, and her death was clearly imminent.

On top of all this, I was suffering increasingly intense lower back pain that had begun in the aftermath of my open-heart surgery. Week by week, I was experiencing more and more difficulty in walking until by the beginning of October I was virtually unable to walk down the church's center aisle and up the chancel steps without the aid of Carl Eschenbrenner at my right arm. In a consultation with an orthopedic specialist, I was told that I must have spine surgery in the very near future or run the risk of losing the ability to walk permanently, so a date was set for near the end of the month.

Before then, my mother died, and the date was moved back a couple of weeks into November to allow me to assist my father in all that needed to be done both before and after Mom's funeral. Her service was held in St. Andrew's Church, Windsor, the old family church in the heart of our old hometown, and I was truly heartened by the number of members of my Royal Oak congregation who made the trip across the still-heavily guarded border to support Ann and me at this difficult time.

Since this is meant to be an anecdotal autobiography, I feel compelled to record here an incident that, though trivial at the time, came back to haunt my memory on more than one occasion. When my mother's health began to fail so rapidly, Ann took it upon herself to spend more and more time with both of my parents in Windsor. After a couple of weeks of sleeping in the second twin bed in Dad's condo, she took herself off to Rondeau for a few days of what she laughingly called her R & R at the lake house.

Unfortunately, Mom's condition took a turn for the worse, and we were told that the end was very near. I called Ann at the lake house and urged her just to pack up and come back to Windsor, which she agreed to do. Many hours later, she had not yet arrived, when I received a telephone call from my dear friend, Lex, who, inexplicably, was with Ann at the lake house and wanted to reassure me that she was all right but that it would be a few more hours until he brought her to Dad's condo.

By the time they arrived, I was almost beside myself with anxiety. Ann was a wreck: grieving, frightened, lost. Eventually, Lex took me aside to explain. When she began to pack to leave the lake house, Ann discovered that she was missing one of her diamond ear studs—expensive jewels I had given her for her fiftieth birthday some years before. She wore them constantly— even when swimming in the lake or walking on the beach—and we had had words about my fear of her losing them in the sand. Now, apparently, she had indeed lost one of them and was so panicked that she could not find it that she had called Lex to come down all the way from Windsor to help her look for it. When she finally gave up the search, she was in no condition to drive herself back to the city, so Lex had transported her to me.

I confess that I was *furious* — unwarrantedly so — but my own grief and fear and pain were at work in me, and I was surely not myself! I berated Ann vehemently for insisting on wearing expensive jewelry on the beach; "I told you so!" probably figured frequently in my tirade until Lex stepped in and challenged me to cool it! Eventually I did, but, of course, even more damage had been done to Ann's fragile mental health, which I will regret to my dying day.

On the Sunday after Mom's death, I began a long-promised sermon series on "What Presbyterians Believe," confronting the aftermath of the Confessing Church Movement May ruckus and more recent General Assembly actions related thereto. My mother having died just a few days before, after each service that morning I was nevertheless required to remain in the sanctuary for a prolonged and largely hostile question-and-answer exchange with members of the congregation. I remember nothing of the sermon, or of the Q&A afterwards. I only remember that I was weary, heartsick, and just about at the end of my rope!

Sad to say, our second granddaughter's baptism took place in the Royal Oak Church on October 28th, the Sunday morning after Mom's memorial service. The whole family had gathered in grief; now we were rejoicing in the birth and baptism of Abigail Kenyon Klopp, who was born in Naperville, Illinois, on the Fourth of July earlier in the year. Once again, we gathered at home for a celebratory luncheon, none of us in much condition to celebrate.

Three recollections remain indelibly in my memory bank from that event. The first is that Abbi's cousin, Nathaniel Trotter, travelled from Georgetown, Ontario, to be present with his family for both the memorial service and Abbi's baptism, on both of which occasions he played "Amazing Grace" on his bagpipes, which was the theme of my brief meditation that Sunday morning.

The second memory of the occasion is that my father came from Windsor for the event. Afterward, he sat in his favorite chair by a window overlooking the golf course across the street from our high-rise home. As he got up to leave, he pressed not on the arm of his chair for some reason but on the little glass-topped round skirted table beside his chair. Unbeknownst to him, its base was a large speaker box, which he overturned, sending the glass top and a goblet of red wine crashing to the floor on our vanilla-white Oriental carpet. He was mortified, I was annoyed, Ann was on her hands and knees trying to wipe up the stain, so Dad left, never to return to our home again.

The third recollection of that fateful day is the memory that Alex's parents, Dan and Nancy Klopp, drove from Deerfield for the funeral and baptism. Less than two months later, Dan suffered a massive heart attack and died suddenly and unexpectedly. To my lasting regret, we never saw Dan again after that bittersweet visit, and I mourn that neither Ann nor I were well enough to travel back to Deerfield to be supportive of Alex as he buried his beloved father and coped with all the inevitable grief, pain, anger, and bewilderment that follow a sudden death in the family.

Bravely, perhaps—foolishly, more likely—I preached the second message in the announced sermon series: "What Presbyterians Believe about Evangelism" on Sunday, November 4th and then went into hospital for that postponed surgery to correct the spinal stenosis left in my back from my open-heart operation in May. My doctors had informed me that the surgery was routine and that I would be back on my feet in a couple of weeks.

Not so! The necessary surgery proved to be greater than anticipated and the recovery period longer and the side effects more worrisome, so I lingered in hospital, that sermon series forgotten, and my hopes pinned on returning to my pulpit for the first Sunday in Advent.

One day while I was still in William Beaumont Hospital, the lead doctor in our family medical practice took rounds and spoke to me unexpectedly about *testosterone*, of all things. "Your blood work shows that you have *none*, and frankly I don't know how you can even think about getting out of bed in the morning!"

I had no idea what she was talking about, but I soon learned that testosterone is an anabolic steroid and the primary male sex hormone and that a low level of this essential hormone is very serious indeed for a man's health. She immediately began a regimen of AndroGel therapy, and I was released from hospital just in time to prepare myself for that first Sunday in Advent service with its lighting of the first candle of the Advent wreath and its seasonal celebration of the sacrament of Holy Communion.

My brief meditation for the morning contained a charming vignette of Ann's and my personal life, which I think it is appropriate to share here:

> Ann and I, to tell the truth, have not much been looking forward to Christmas this year. Months of ill health and hospitalization and surgery for both of us have us worn down, too worn down to think about hauling out the boxes of our traditional and beloved seasonal decorations. The woes of our world and the worries of our congregation, the illnesses of our parishioners and the bereavements of our family and friends have made it all seem too frivolous somehow.

But without saying a word to me or knowing of my meditation theme for this morning, Ann has been quietly stock-piling—you guessed it—*candles*! Yesterday afternoon, she took me out and persuaded me to buy a dear little already-lit fully-decorated Christmas tree. We brought it home like a couple of newlyweds and set it on the server in our living room, and Ann began to surround it with her candles. "A thing of beauty is a joy forever," they say, and I don't think that I shall soon forget the deep joy and the abiding comfort we felt as we lit those candles and thought about what Christmas really means.

I made it through the early service pretty well—Advent wreath and Holy Communion included. But by the time we got to the Lord's table in the later service, I was well and truly exhausted and must have conducted the Communion liturgy on autopilot, because I had no memory of it afterward. The next morning, I made an urgent appointment to see my doctor, which visit resulted in three things. First, since the AndroGel therapy did not seem to be making any appreciable difference to my testosterone deficiency, she insisted on referring me to a world-renowned endocrinologist who had just come to practice at William Beaumont Hospital.

Second, as we chatted about all that had been going on in Ann's and my life over the past few months, she casually inquired whether I ever had thoughts of ending it all. I replied that indeed I did and that I knew exactly how I would do it. And so, not surprisingly, before I left her office, she set up my first appointment with a Jewish psychiatrist who specialized in treating cases with a spiritual (i.e., Christian) component.

Third, my doctor advised that I give it a rest for a couple more weeks before returning to my pulpit, to which I grudgingly agreed. For reasons that were not clear to me then, neither are they even now, Ann took it into her head that this respite would be the perfect opportunity for us to travel to Naperville to be with our family for their traditional mid-December pre-Christmas get-together. Because neither of us was in any condition to *drive* that far, we decided to take the train from Dearborn to Union Station in downtown Chicago, which we did and had a very enjoyable trip.

Not so enjoyable was our arrival in Chicago. It was the Christmas season, and the train station was very busy, with every passenger seemingly laden with gifts as well as luggage. On debarking the train onto a narrow cement platform, we were crowded into a glorified golf cart with a trailer hauled behind it. Ann was seated on the last seat at the end of the last row of the trailer. I was seated beside her. Suddenly and without warning, the golf cart driver accelerated and wrenched his steering wheel to the left to begin a U-turn back to the terminal. The trailer whipped hard to the right, and Ann fell off, landing on her back with the lower half of her body on the platform and the upper half hanging out over the train track, her head actually resting on the nearer rail.

Shaken but apparently unharmed, Ann insisted that she was all right. She neither wanted nor needed medical attention; she only wished to be on her way to the Klopps to celebrate our family Christmas, which is just what we did. We had a wonderful time together, despite a growing painfulness in the small of Ann's back. It was a happy time, although poignant, as were all our family gatherings it seemed, since they were always overlaid by a question of when—if ever—we would be together again. This precious time with Sarah, Kirk and Jennifer, and Rebecca and Alex and their families would have been even more poignant, indeed, if we had realized that all of us would never be together again this side of heaven.

By the time we returned to Royal Oak, Ann's back pain was growing worse and worse. After a couple of trips to her doctor's office, it was agreed that she needed to be admitted to the hospital—again! I did not return to my pulpit until Christmas Eve, when, assisted by the chancel choir, I wisely used an old meditation on the Christmas carol, "What Child Is This," sung to the tune "Greensleeves." At the end of the third service of the evening, just after midnight, I was so weak and weary that I could not bring myself to step down out of the pulpit. My last clear memory of being in the sanctuary of the Royal Oak church is of the chancel choir's tenor and baritone soloists practically lifting me out of the pulpit and down the chancel steps. How I got to Ann's hospital bedside in the middle of the night or back home even later, for that matter, I have absolutely no idea!

On Christmas Day, Ann was released from the hospital for a few hours, and I took her home to see and enjoy the little lighted Christmas tree and the bevy of radiant candles she had collected for the season. During the afternoon, we phoned Naperville, where Kirk and Rebecca's families were together. At the sound of their dear voices on the telephone, Ann and I both burst into tears and sobbed our way through what must have been the *worst* Christmas memory ever for our loved ones!

I know that I conducted worship and preached on the Sunday after Christmas, for I was told repeatedly in the weeks to follow that I had actually baptised the grandson of two of our favorite members of the congregation that morning. I must have been compos mentis enough to have located, printed, and read some old sermon manuscript for the single service that day; but there is no message included in my computer's "Sermons by Date" file, so there, for all practical purposes, my ministry ended.

By the end of the year, I had applied to the Presbyterian

Church's Board of Pensions for disability status, and I never resumed full-time ministry again even though church records will show that the pastoral tie was not actually severed by the Presbytery of Detroit until the following September.

Early in the new year, I requested the session's executive committee chair to come to me in order to explain that I had applied for "disability" status with the Presbyterian Church (USA) and therefore should not receive my monthly stipend while the claim was being processed. Against his strongly worded objections, I pleaded with him to accept that my ministry—at least in Royal Oak—was over and that I wanted to give up our apartment as Ann and I intended to move to our Canadian lake house to live there more economically. All of this he adamantly refused to consider.

Meanwhile, the Board of Pensions had required me to undergo a battery of psychological tests to support my application for disability status and, once that application had been approved, to remain in psychotherapy for an undetermined length of time, which turned out to be about nine months with the psychologist who had administered the board's tests. I was already also seeing the psychiatrist to whom I had been referred at the end of 2001 and continued with him for almost a whole year.

In January, I began regular appointments with the endocrinologist to whom my doctors had referred me because of my lack of testosterone. His first question to me at the start of my first appointment was a bit of a shock: "How long has it been since your last erection?" Once I assured him that *erectile dysfunction* was the least of my concerns at that time, we got down to the business of discovering—through another battery of physical and psychological tests—that my pituitary gland had ceased to function and that I was suffering from a long list of afflictions attributable thereto. Chief among these, we eventually determined, were my alarming thoughts of suicide and my almost total loss of short-term memory. But with regular super doses of injected testosterone, I began to make a remarkable recovery.

That rate of recovery was enhanced considerably when my own doctors recommended me to a wholistic medicine clinic whose female physical therapist took me on as a patient on two conditions. The first related to my stubborn and unceasing lower back pain: she insisted that I was never again to carry my wallet in either of my pants' back pockets, since she firmly believed that sitting on that lump of leather, plastic, and paper was exacerbating my recovery. The second condition was that I rigorously adopt the "Eat Right for Your Blood Type" diet, which was enjoying great popularity at that time. No pork, no potatoes, no pasta were the hallmarks of my dietary routine to counteract the extreme acidity of my bodily systems. Ann, bless her heart, tried to follow the precepts of the diet according to her own blood type, but the "dos and don'ts" were so utterly and diametrically opposed that she soon gave it up, and we ate fundamentally different meals for the rest of her life.

Cumulatively, it all began to "work!" We were thrilled to be able to drive to Naperville for the Memorial Day holiday weekend, for which Sarah traveled from the Crows' family cottage on Rondeau Bay to help Rebecca and Kirk and their families celebrate Ann's sixtieth birthday. By the end of July, Ann was remarking that I smelled sweeter, behaved sweeter, and *was* sweeter than I had been in a long time.

That summer, we were spending as much of our time as possible between doctors' appointments at the lake house, when Ann developed a large and nasty-looking "water blister" over her spinal column in the small of her back. Our local doctor, John Button, thought it alarming enough that he urged us to travel back to Detroit to see our doctors there. The trip was timely, since we were planning to vacate the lake house (as was our wont) to allow the Trotter family to enjoy a couple of weeks of vacation there on their own. In previous summers, our nephew, Nathaniel, had often spent time with us in Royal Oak, but this year for some reason Ann felt strongly that it should be his brother Cameron's turn, and so it was.

Ann's doctor in Royal Oak did not seem duly alarmed by the growing water blister but prescribed a course of prednisone as a matter of precaution. I had some misgivings about the drug, since Ann had suffered so many different side effects from previous courses of it, but her doctor insisted that it was really the only medical recourse for dealing with whatever the thing was that was still growing on her back.

On the August Sunday of Canada's Civic Holiday weekend, the three of us drove back to Rondeau, enjoyed a happy and homey dinner prepared by Tom and Nancy, and took a couple of snapshots of the whole famn damily, standing on the back deck of the lake house before the Trotters drove back home to Georgetown. After they left, Ann complained—uncharacteristically for her—that she felt too tired to tidy up from the Trotters' vacation, so we left the lake house as it was and went to bed early.

In the morning of Monday, August 5, 2002, Ann slept late while I got up and prepared breakfast. When she awakened, I fetched her batch of morning meds and prepared a tray to serve her breakfast in bed. When I returned from the kitchen to her bedside, she was gagging and finding it difficult to speak. I was sufficiently alarmed that I called 911 and asked for an ambulance. The dispatcher suggested that I try to ease her discomfort by sitting her up at the side of the bed, which I did to no avail.

Suddenly, Ann spoke, clearly and distinctly. Looking out the bedroom window that gave onto an enclosed screened porch that was in total darkness, she exclaimed: "Look at the light, the *beautiful* light!" and collapsed back into the bed. Propping her up with pillows, I put my arm around her to support her, kissed her on the forehead, heard one last light sigh, and she was gone.

I sat holding her until the ambulance arrived, plus the Ontario Provincial Police in two patrol cars, and the nightmare began! Against my frantic objections that she had already been dead too long and there would be severe brain damage if they succeeded, the EMTs insisted on trying to resuscitate Ann with their electric paddles—standard operating procedure, they insisted—but to no avail. Eventually they gave up trying, by which time I was almost out of my mind with grief and fear and anger. They loaded Ann's body onto a gurney and into the ambulance and took off for Chatham's General Hospital, leaving one of the OPPs to drive me to the hospital.

In the police car, I used my cell phone to call our eldest offspring, Sarah, in Calgary, telling her the horrendous news and asking her to call Kirk and Rebecca. Wisely, she also called our dearest friends, Lex and Ann McCrindle in Windsor and Alan and Maureen McPherson in Hamilton, all four of whom set out immediately to come to my aid and comfort. At the hospital, there was nothing to be done but contact a funeral director in Windsor and leave Ann's body in the care of the county coroner, since a forensic autopsy was determined to be necessary. By this time, Lex and Ann had arrived, and they drove me back to the lake house.

Alana and Maureen arrived soon thereafter. Maureen was terribly grieved, and it took all four of us to calm her down enough to persuade her that she and Alan should return to Hamilton, there to await the funeral plans my family and I would formulate the next day. Lex and Ann graciously offered to stay the night with me in the lake house, which kindness I readily accepted. I could not bring myself to sleep in the bed in which Ann had just died, so I bunked down in the grandchildren's twin-bedded room, with a fresh candle burning to keep me company all night.

In the morning as I awoke, I was startled to see that the candle had burned down and guttered out in its candle stand. I felt Ann's presence very near and almost heard her telling me that that candle had been the measure of my necessary grieving and that I should get on with living. This wisdom I just could not accept so that night I searched out a very large and elaborately carved candle we had acquired somewhere along the way. I vowed that I would continue to grieve as long as that great big candle continued to burn.

After breakfast, Lex and Ann set off for home, knowing that Kirk was well on his way. By the time Kirk arrived, he found me being interrogated by one of the OPP officers. Kirk's lawyerly instincts kicked in, and he objected to my being questioned without a lawyer present, since he immediately recognized that I was under suspicion as Ann's *murderer*. With Kirk present, the tone of the interview changed markedly, and before it ended, the police officer indicated that he was a Presbyterian elder from Wallaceburg, whose church had just lost its minister and might I be available to do some *supply preaching*?

That afternoon, Kirk drove me into Ridgetown to buy a new spring and mattress set to replace the one in our master bedroom, Fortunately, the local merchant was very understanding, delivered the new bedding that same afternoon, and took away the spring and mattress that I could not bring myself even to look at. That night, I slept soundly in my new bedding, my fancy big candle alight at my bedside to comfort me. But in the morning, I was amazed and bewildered to see that it, too, had burned down to nothing overnight. And, again, I felt Ann's presence very near, urging me not to grieve over her peaceful and painless passing but to rejoice that she was with her Lord and I was free to get on with my life.

When my mother had died a few months earlier, Ann and I discussed every imaginable funerary possibility for ourselves as well as her and had firmly settled on immediate cremation, followed by memorial services first in St. Andrew's Church in Windsor and eventually also in the First Presbyterian Church of Deerfield, where our ashes were to be interred in the columbarium in the bell tower.

Because Ann had died without medical supervision, a forensic autopsy was required by the Province of Ontario before her body could be released for cremation. This indignity was performed very promptly by the provincial coroner in Windsor, and Ann's body was returned to the Kelly Funeral Home, where I was required to view her remains and certify that this was indeed her body. Kirk very kindly accompanied me to the viewing, something both Sarah and Rebecca bitterly wished they had been able to do but which the timing of the week's events did not permit. Frankly, at the time, I was just glad to get it over with.

With the arrival at the lake house of Rebecca, Alex and Tori, plus Jennifer and Will, I was grateful that Sarah and Kevin could stay at his family's cottage on Rondeau Bay and that the Trotter family could stay at the b. & b. nearby. Nevertheless, the lake house was where everyone gathered, and before long I really felt the need for some alone time. Ann's memorial service was scheduled for Friday afternoon, with Alan McPherson conducting the worship and Lex McCrindle offering the eulogy. So after lunch on Thursday, I betook myself back to Michigan to spend the night alone at home.

While I was there, it occurred to me to search out the three valuable rings Ann had always intended to bequeath to Sarah, Rebecca, and Jennifer in order to present them to our daughters after the memorial service. Alas, I could nowhere find Mimi's beautiful starburst diamond cocktail ring Ann had designated for Sarah, but what I *did* find was that one lonely diamond ear stud over which we had had such an unnecessary row a few months earlier when my mother had died. Its discovery in Ann's jewel box prompted such a tearful torrent of guilt and shame that I eventually cried myself to sleep without ever lighting the candle I had put by my bedside.

By morning, I reconciled myself to the realization that Ann, in her failing mental health, had done something with the missing ring and that I would probably never find it again. So later on, I gave Sarah the pearl and diamond dinner ring that she as a little girl had helped us pick out at Saks Fifth Avenue in New York; to Rebecca, I gave the sapphire and diamond Princess Di ring I had bought for Ann many years before; and to Jennifer went the very tailored diamond ring I had purchased during our last cruise. The fate of the diamond ear stud remained to be decided.

The memorial service at St. Andrew's Church was well attended by friends old and new. Because the church did not have a regular organist at that time, Liz Spry came from Royal Oak and played the gigantic Casavant organ masterfully. The Royal Oak Church's baritone soloist sang; Nathaniel Trotter played his pipes; Lex spoke with moving intimacy; Alan conducted the whole service with reverent simplicity; many of my extended Russell family relatives attended; and many of my Royal Oak parishioners made the trip across the border (again!) to offer much-appreciated support. My children banded together to underwrite the cost of a fellowship meal at Windsor's Caboto Club afterwards. All in all, I could not have asked for a more fitting tribute for a much-beloved wife, mother, grandmother, and friend.

For my birthday in early September, Ann and I had been planning a long-awaited trip to Calgary to visit Sarah and Kevin. Although Sarah assumed that I would forego the trip, I decided to go anyway, and I had a wonderfully therapeutic time. The one touristy thing I had wanted to share with Ann was a visit to Lake Louise, which I remembered so vividly from that NFCUS tour back in 1960. So I borrowed Sarah's car and drove up into the Rocky Mountains alone to revisit the hotel over lunch. As a very special birthday gift, Sarah bought me a day at the Banff Springs Hotel, so the next day I was steamed, massaged, stretched, and groomed in sybaritic splendor. My most vivid memory of the experience remains that of having lunch in my bathing suit, sunning on a private hotel balcony, then driving back to Calgary, where, by dinnertime, snow began to fall!

After months of uncertainty and inaction, the Royal Oak Church's session finally petitioned the Presbytery of Detroit to sever the pastoral tie between themselves and me. The formal action had been scheduled to occur in mid-August; but with Ann's untimely death earlier in the month, the date was postponed until mid-September. And so, on a dreary September Sunday afternoon, my life's career in ministry came to an end with neither a whimper nor a bang—just a dull thud. The First Presbyterian Church of Royal Oak accorded me a farewell reception of sorts: various personages made brief expressions of appreciation and trivial gifts to accompany them, and I was allowed to make a brief farewell address.

On Monday afternoon, I submitted to an exit interview with members of the Presbytery of Detroit's Committee on Ministry.

There was really little to say. The committee had negotiated a surprisingly generous severance package, for which I shall always be grateful. Then it was all over.

* * * * *

After my exit interview, I packed up a few things and drove straight to the lake house to begin the rest of my life. In truth, that night I felt nothing but overwhelming emptiness. In the morning, however, I began to try to sort out what I was going to *do* with that life. As I stared at my image in the bathroom mirror, I realized that for the first time in almost forty years, I was totally free to be *me*! Throughout the decades of my ministry, I had always felt that I needed to dress and groom and *look* like a Presbyterian minister. But that morning, no one cared anymore. During the later years of my Montreal ministry and throughout my Bible Society career, I had worn a full black beard, which I had shaved off as soon as we had moved to the lake house in 1988. Ann liked the beard, and I missed it, and right then and there I decided that I would grow it out again.

Ann's single diamond ear stud winked at me from my dresser, daring me to do something with it to symbolize my guilt and shame over the way I had berated her upon the loss of its mate and my determination to rise above all that negativity and never to allow myself to be so angry again. A jewelry store advertisement in the weekly Ridgetown newspaper caught my eye with an offer of a free gold ear stud with every ear piercing, so after breakfast, I drove into town and had my *left* earlobe pierced, planning to replace the gold stud with my diamond one once the piercing had healed.

Recognizing that I needed some new clothing appropriate to my retired status, I went shopping in Chatham. As it happened, everything I liked and bought turned out to be black, and soon I was a walking and talking exemplar of a style the fashion magazines of the day were identifying as "metrosexual!"

Ann had had grand plans for celebrating our fortieth wedding anniversary in mid-November, but what was I to do alone? I did not want to burden my family or friends with another grief-stricken occasion, yet I did not want to be absolutely alone; neither could I just ignore the date; so I did what Ann had been intending for us to do: I went on a *cruise*! My friend Rick Ricart set me up in a single cabin on a Carnival cruise to the Eastern Caribbean; I drove my relatively new Cadillac Sedan de Ville to Miami; and I had another wonderfully therapeutic experience.

On the first night at sea, I donned my tuxedo, popped my diamond stud into my earlobe for the first time, and went to dinner. Earlier in the afternoon, I had sought out the maître d', explained my emotional fragility, and requested a table for one in an inconspicuous corner of the dining room balcony. When I was seated, I realized that I was sitting right behind a bandstand where a trio of young Canadian musicians was playing soft jazz dinner music. Even before my meal was served, I started to weep uncontrollably as I realized that this was the actual *day* of our fortieth wedding anniversary and that I was probably going to be alone like this for the rest of my life.

I could tell that the musicians, like everyone else sitting nearby, were troubled by my behavior. When they took a break, I got up, walked over, and quietly explained to them why I was so emotional. They were relieved to be assured that it was not their music that was driving me to tears, and when they took up their instruments again, they played "The Impossible Dream" for me and made me cry all the more! At the end of their set, they encouraged me to come to one of the ship's lounges at 10:30 p.m. to hear them play some more. It seemed like an unlikely thing for me to do until I remembered that I was free to be me, so I went to the lounge. After each set, the band members came and sat with me and began to teach me about jazz. We formed a powerful friendship, and I spent the week as their biggest fan!

One of their friends was the ship's assistant purser — a beautiful young Estonian woman, named Nadia — who joined us as often as her duties would permit. As it turned out, the ship's officers were permitted to dine with the passengers on our last night at sea, so I asked Nadia if she would like to dine with me. She would, and she did, resplendent in her white-and-gold dress uniform. When I informed the maître d' that she would be joining me, he insisted that we sit at a table for two right against the balcony railing next to the bandstand. Through the week, I had become acquainted with the passengers sitting at tables near mine. As I entered the balcony with Nadia on my arm, the men seated near us began to whistle, the women began to applaud, and I realized that I had begun to *date*!

The cruise ended on Thanksgiving Eve. Our dear Naples friends, George and Sally Wiley, had invited me to extend my "vacation" by driving over the Tamiami Trail to be with them for the holiday weekend. While in Naples, I spent some time with a real estate agent looking at modest properties I might be able to afford when things settled down, and I drove North, confident that I would soon be returning to spend my winters in Florida.

Becca had graciously invited me to spend Christmas in Naperville. To mark my getting on with the rest of my life, I decided to give each of my three children some of the most precious pieces in my collection of original oil paintings. To Sarah, I gave the Thomas Garside rendering of the Gravenors' property on the North River in the Laurentians. This was the painting I had received as an honorarium from the Nesbitt family after Deane's funeral. For Kirk, it was an easy choice to give him the A & P farewell gift painting of *Baie St. Paul* on the Lower St. Lawrence River by Marius Mauro, since Kirk already had a small Mauro in his own burgeoning collection. Rebecca received the bespoke John Little vision of the Church of St. Andrew and St. Paul on Sherbrooke Street "before [in the artist's own hand on the reverse of the canvas] they ruined it forever!"

While still in Naperville after Christmas, I took ill as was my wont every winter. I still remember lying in the Klopps' guest bed and receiving a telephone message that my Detroit psychotherapist had cleared me to return to work. In a panic, I telephoned the Presbyterian Church (USA) Board of Pensions to explain that I had no job to return to, and I was certainly in no condition to begin looking for a new ministry call. After several agonizing days of waiting, I received a phone call from the pension board, informing me that they had talked with both my primary care physician and my psychiatrist and were convinced that I needed to be confirmed as *permanently* disabled with regard to my church pension. Oh, what a relief that was!

The year 2003 marked the bicentennial of the founding of what eventually became Montreal's Church of St. Andrew and St. Paul. The church's new young minister, Richard Topping, very graciously invited me to return to preach on one of the anniversary celebration weekends, and I chose (for what reason I cannot imagine!) the February weekend. I really was not yet well enough to undertake such a commitment, but I did anyway. I flew to Montreal, was greeted by Richard, housed in a nearby hotel, and wined and dined for three days. It was a bittersweet experience from start to finish. The news of Ann's death had not reached Montreal, it seemed, and so every event was overshadowed by the shock and grief felt by those who remembered us best and the nonchalance of those who did not.

On Sunday morning, I gave a children's message in which I mentioned Ann's death in passing. There were audible gasps from the congregation, which affected me much more deeply than I had anticipated. I had not written a new sermon in over a year, and I knew that what I had prepared for this occasion was not among my best work. I struggled to finish the sermon; I felt very lightheaded as Richard and I recessed up the long aisle at the end of the service, and I nearly fainted while greeting old friends and new at the church doors.

Colin Gravenor, a good friend from of old, came to my rescue, sat me down in the last pew on the center aisle, and moderated the greetings from then on. Afterward, he invited me to come to his home for supper that evening. I was delighted to be with Colin again, and I enjoyed meeting his sons, now all grown up.

I left Montreal on Monday morning to fly back to Windsor, saddened by the realization that in the quarter-century since Ann and I left the A & P for the Bible Society, many of the people we had most appreciated in the congregation were either dead, elsewhere, or still feeling resentment at our departure. As things turned out, another emotional upheaval awaited me at home, and I never resumed any meaningful contact with anyone in Montreal again.

On the morning after my return, I received a telephone call from my father, asking if I could come right away to Windsor to take him to the doctor as he was experiencing terrible pain in his left shoulder. I agreed that I would come at once, but I insisted that he call 911 and ask for an ambulance to take him to Hotel Dieu Hospital. Eventually, I found him there in emergency care, where a young doctor was assuring him that there was nothing seriously wrong—just bursitis—and that he should take some prescribed pain medication and rest until he felt better.

That was not the end of it. On Thursday morning, Dad phoned me again, pleading with me to take him to a doctor because the pain in his shoulder was unbearable. Again, I advised him to call 911 and assured him that I was on my way to his apartment. I arrived just as the EMTs were moving him out to their ambulance on a gurney. In his own inimitable way as chairman of the board of directors of his condominium community, he was dictating to his secretary as he went!

This time, he was admitted to Hotel Dieu. Another young doctor, of Indo-Asian ancestry, agreed that something was seriously wrong and assured me that he would work through the weekend to try to come up with a diagnosis. Realizing that this was becoming ominous, I telephoned my brother Tom in Toronto. I could not reach him; as a national vice president of the Bank of Nova Scotia, he was responsible, among other duties, for the physical safety of the bank's Toronto headquarters and staff. As it happened, the international economic Group of Seven was meeting at that time in Toronto amidst protests and violence, and Tom was sequestered in the bank building incommunicado to deal with it all!

By Monday, Dad's doctor had identified his malaise as a form of the usually fatal flesh-eating bacteria that had recently been much in the news. Surgery to amputate his left arm at the shoulder might save his life; but given his lifelong disability in back and hip, he would probably never walk again with only one arm to aid his balance. I had less than twenty-four hours to make a decision whether or not to operate. Meanwhile, Dad was heavily sedated; but every time he became aware that I was there, he would plead with me, "Let— me die, Bill . . . just let me die!"

Again, I phoned Tom and got through to him. The situation in Toronto was still critical, and he could not leave; so he gave me full authority to do whatever I thought was best. I warned him that I would probably opt for palliative care to keep Dad comfortable and allow the disease to take its course, which the doctor estimated might be only a matter of days. Tom concurred and promised that he would come to Windsor the very moment he was free to do so. In the end, he arrived in Windsor a few days later, just in time to have Dad realise that he was there, and by morning our father joined our mother in their eternal home.

Another family funeral in St. Andrew's Church. Providentially, the church's new minister, in whom Dad had taken an immediate and intense dislike, was away at the time, and the church's associate minister, a young woman Dad had opposed at first and later had come to appreciate, conducted the service with grace and empathy. Tom and I both spoke; our cousin, Carol Ann, sang a solo; a surprising number of Royal Oak parishioners attended; and the kirk session processed as a body to honour the humble man who had become the congregation's senior elder. Tom was to be the executor of our father's estate and carried out the arduous responsibilities of that role with sensitivity and thoroughness for which I shall always be grateful, for by then I was in just about as bad shape as I had been when we laid Ann to rest.

Kirk and Rebecca suggested that I go somewhere warm for a while, so I booked two weeks at the modest little beach club in Destin, Florida, that Ann and I had discovered the previous year when a member of the Royal Oak congregation had given us a week's timeshare at a high-rise condo there. Becca, Alex, Tori, and Abbi came to be with me for one week; Kirk, Jennifer, and Will came for the second week. "Somewhere warm" was just what I needed, and it did me a world of good.

In the spring, I was back and forth between Rondeau and Naperville several times. On one of these trips, I took it into my head to trade my second big beautiful old Cadillac Sedan de Ville for something smaller and sportier. I was dismayed to learn that the Cadillac had very little trade-in value, but Kirk and Alex made the astute suggestion that I just keep it for as long as it did not cost me much money and use it for big trips—and big loads—once I had a much smaller car. In the end, I purchased a barely used silver Mercedes Benz 2003 C-class hatchback with a *Kompressor* engine. I loved that car: it was for me a symbol of my newfound freedom, and I appreciated every moment I spent driving it!

Someone who did *not* love it was my improbable new special friend, Barbara, the widow of my late clerk of session, Francis Luttrell. She had befriended Ann in the months after her husband had died and continued to befriend me after Ann's death. It was from start to finish a rocky relationship. I was emotionally vulnerable and very, very lonely except when I was in Naperville. Barbara was attentive, especially when I underwent hip replacement surgery; but she was devoted to her family, most of whom lived nearby, and also to her cluster of long-time friends with whom she was used to spending a great deal of time. For a while, she insisted on keeping our friendship secret. Even when our "dating" became a public thing, she seemed insistent on keeping it separate from her other friendships and relationships. We frequently argued about my feeling like a fifth wheel, and although she often hinted at our getting married, I knew that there would never be enough room in her life for me on a full-time basis.

Ironically, it was my personal physician who set in motion

the life changes that resulted in our going our separate ways. In the fall of 2003, my personal physician told me that I should not spend another winter up north but should go somewhere warm for a few months. I opted to return to Destin, to the modest little beach club condo I had so enjoyed the previous winter. I invited Barbara to accompany me. She was scandalized and vehemently refused! So I went to Destin for the winter alone, thank God!

On the first Sunday in December, I attended morning worship at the dear little old Episcopal Church of St. Andrew By the Sea in downtown Destin. As I have recounted many times since, during the passing of the peace, a cute little blonde cheerleader approached me out of the congregation and welcomed me to St. Andrew's Church. It was as though God tapped me on the shoulder and whispered, "Bill, pay attention!" which I did!

After worship, the congregation gathered in their fellowship hall for a light luncheon. I went along, hoping to spot my cheerleader at one of the tables. For the longest time, she was nowhere to be seen. Suddenly, having completed her altar guild responsibilities in the sanctuary, she appeared and went to sit down next to an older woman with frizzy grey hair. I immediately joined them at the table, whereupon "Ms. Frizzy" zeroed in on me and dominated the conversation for so long that eventually God's intended gift got up and left.

I followed her out into the church parking lot, where I introduced myself as a "snowbird" in Destin for the winter and asked if I might take her out to dinner some evening. Grudgingly, she wrote her name—"Sherri"—and her telephone number on a scrap of paper, gave it to me with not a word of encouragement, and left.

When I got to my own car, there was an urgent cell phone

message from Kirk, reporting that Jennifer, eight months pregnant, was in hospital and about to undergo surgery. There was some danger that the anæsthetic might bring on a premature delivery. Since I had long ago promised that I would travel to Naperville for the Christmas holiday season in order to care for grandson Will while Kirk and Jennifer were dealing with the birth of their second child at New Year's, I called Kirk back and offered to come at once. At first, he demurred, not wanting to intrude upon my winter vacation so recently begun; but eventually he admitted that he was feeling pretty desperate and my being there would be a great help.

So I hurried back to my condo, threw a couple of changes of clothing into a duffel bag, drove to the Fort Walton Beach airport, parked my car in the full price lot, bought a full price return plane ticket to Chicago's Midway Airport, and flew off to the rescue.

Needless to say, Jennifer's operation was a complete success: there was no premature delivery; in fact, she did not deliver Ryan Campbell Russell until New Year's Eve, by which time I had been in Naperville for nearly a month. True to form, right after Christmas I became ill with my usual mid-winter bronchitis-threatening-pneumonia and spent most of a day in the emergency room of a local hospital. Kirk, realizing that I would be of no use caring for Will for the next few days, called Jennifer's mother in Arizona and begged her to come to their aid, which she was delighted to do. Long distance from Canada, where the Klopps were visiting the Trotters for a few days, Rebecca organized a car and driver to take me back to Midway, and I flew out to Fort Walton Beach as Ryan was being born.

When I got back to my condo, I found Sherri's scrap of paper on the kitchen counter, but I felt too ill even to call her for a few days. On New Year's Day, though, "Ms. Frizzy" turned up at my door. She tracked me down and had come by the beach club every day looking for my car. She wanted me to go to a movie with her, which I declined probably none too graciously.

On the following Sunday, I dragged myself out of bed and went to church, hoping to find Sherri to apologize and explain why I had not called her until then. She was a no-show, and I was surprised by how disappointed I felt. When I returned to my condo, I took a deep breath and telephoned the number on the scrap of paper. Sherri was not particularly pleased to hear from me after more than a month of silence. However, after I explained all that had gone on in that period, she relented and agreed to have dinner with me that very night.

I had never been to Kelly Plantation, one of Destin's high-end gated golf communities, and it was a challenge even finding Sherri's home. She had rescued a big black Labrador retriever from the middle of a road the day before and was too anxious to get the new dog settled with her two other little doggies to leave them in the morning to go to church, but she felt confident that they would be all right for an hour or so while we had dinner.

During our meal at Fisherman's Wharf, Sherri told me the sad stories of her previous marriages: the first ending in divorce and the second in the death of her "true love," Bob Fuss. "So I'll be straight with you, Bill," she insisted. "I have had the love of my life, and I am not looking for another."

To which I replied, "Well Sherri, I, too, have had the love of my life, but I *am* looking for another!" And so began what turned out to be a winterlong courtship! It certainly was not love at first sight, but it was not long before we both began to feel that God had given each of us a rare and wondrous gift of friendship.

Needing health insurance in her widowhood, Sherri had taken a thirty-hour-a-week part-time job as the weeknight evening receptionist at Destin's newly opened Sacred Heart Hospital. It was from there, most nights, that we went to the only place open 24/7 in Destin, a Waffle House not far from Kelly Plantation. It got to be a joke of sorts that when the Waffle House staff saw two pairs of headlights drive into their parking lot just after midnight, they put on a fresh pot of decaf coffee and started a couple of crispy waffles for us. We found it so easy to talk to one another that our Waffle House "dates" often lasted a couple of hours, after which we both headed "home." Little did we realize until much later in the spring that a couple of the old biddies in my beach club were keeping track of my nighttime comings and goings, which they characterized to one another as my "catting around!"

Some weekdays, we participated in the activities of the snowbird programs at the local senior citizens' center. In particular, we learned to line-dance, an accomplishment we eventually put to good use at our wedding. At first, Sherri kept trying to distance herself from me, reminding me that I was "only a snowbird" and would leave in the spring, so I should go out dining and dancing with other women rather than devote myself exclusively to her. So I would do as she suggested and then turn up at the hospital at about 11:45 p.m. to regale her with stories of what a good time I had had earlier that evening. This routine got pretty old pretty fast for both of us. I was still in my metrosexual mode with my black wardrobe, grizzled beard, and diamond ear stud until the night Sherri told me that she really liked me and really enjoyed going out with me *even if* I was *gay*!

My immediate response was, "Sherri, give me half an hour, and *I'll show you how gay I am*!" That night, back at my condo, the diamond ear stud came out for good, and the next day we went shopping at Dillard's for some brightly colored shirts.

After about a month, Sherri confessed that she had some concerns about her financial affairs and asked if I would look over her most recent monthly investment statement. I did, and I was shocked to realize that I was falling in love with a very wealthy woman. At first, I was really troubled by the disparity between her financial situation and mine. But she put things into a perspective that was totally new to me: "Bill, if you let my money come between us, you're a fool!"

When the lease on my beach club condo was nearing its end, Sherri invited me to move my stuff into the guest suite at the back of her house on Leaning Pines Loop in Kelly Plantation. "Only if we get engaged," I countered, and she agreed! To make it official, I took her to dinner and dancing at the Ocean Club, where I was by this time a well-known patron. We were seated at a table for two, right at the edge of the dance floor, in full view of the whole crowd. Ahead of time, I had persuaded the club's entertainer to sing *our* song, "At Last." During the song, the maître d' appeared, carrying a silver tray on which was a small velvet box. I got down on one knee, opened the box, and formally asked Sherri to marry me. When she said, "Yes," the audience erupted in applause!

As we began to make wedding plans, Sarah, Kirk, and Rebecca were apparently having fits about what was happening to dear old dad. They began a race to see who could get down to Destin first to check out this obvious "golddigger," who had her claws in their father. Rebecca won, and came to visit ASAP. Her visit was brief and punctuated with whispered telephone conversations with her siblings, reporting on whatever was going on in Kelly Plantation. When I pointed out that I was sleeping in the guest room at the opposite end of the house from

Sherri's bedroom, Rebecca's only response was, "*Sure*, Dad!" Finally as she was packing to leave, Becca confided that she had come to check out a "golddigger" and had realized that it was probably *me*.

Once we were engaged, Sherri and I began to make plans to travel up to Canada for our first summer at the lake house. In the week between Canada's Victoria Day and America's Memorial Day holiday weekends, we packed into our two vehicles three dogs, Sherri's trousseau, and all the "odds 'n' ends" she was uncertain whether she would find when she got there. Finally, we set off for the two-day trip northbound on I-65 and I-75 to Detroit and then on Ontario's infamous Highway 401 to the exit for New Scotland and Rondeau Provincial Park.

The lake house certainly looked disappointing on arrival: the grass was long and uncut; the shrubbery was overgrown and ugly; the beach was littered with dead fish and a winter's worth of debris; and there was not a springtime blossom in sight! Most disappointing of all, spring had come early and warm to Southern Ontario that year, and eager gardeners had already bought up most of the flats of pretty annuals we had looked forward to planting around the place. We vowed that next year we would make the trip earlier and only in one vehicle.

Near the middle of June, we made a quick trip by car to Naperville, where I was honored to assist the pastors of Knox Presbyterian Church in the baptism of my fourth grandchild, Ryan Campbell Russell. As usual, the Klopps provided excellent hospitality for an after-church reception, during which I was delighted to introduce Sherri into my friendship with Jennifer's parents, Ron and Diane Moss.

Before we got to the lake house, we had been sorely tempted to *elope*, just the two of us getting married, until we began to realize how many loved ones and dear friends we would disappoint and perhaps even alienate if we did so. Sherri wanted to get married on a significant date, one she would always easily remember, and I wanted to be married at the lake house because it was the most convenient destination to which most of my loved ones could travel. Finally, we settled on the Fourth of July on the beach at the lake house in the late afternoon with a simple reception on the deck and in the backyard to follow. Rebecca had already created a charming wedding invitation. Alan McPherson agreed to conduct the ceremony. Nathaniel Trotter promised to play his bagpipes. A florist, a caterer, and a disc jockey were found in Ridgetown. And we were actually all set.

Or so we thought! Who could have foreseen that shortly after the Klopp family arrived two days before the ceremony, the lake house's always temperamental septic tank would overflow all over the front yard!? Fortunately, I knew whom to call, and a sewage tanker truck and driver soon appeared to dig up and drain the system, eventually leaving smelly mud all over the front lawn right up to the front door.

By the time the Kirk Russell family arrived, the lake house was getting crowded, so Sherri and I removed ourselves to a well-recommended bed and breakfast accommodation in Ridgetown. Sad to say, it was significantly *not* what we had been led to expect, so the next morning we moved out and took refuge in that log cabin bed and breakfast establishment at the east end of Rondeau Bay so familiar to my family.

The day of our wedding dawned bright and beautiful and continued so until nightfall. Everything went off as planned: a sunset service on the beach, conducted by Alan with Sherri and me in bare feet; a bridal processional played by Nathaniel on his pipes; darling flower girls (i.e., granddaughters) distributing small wrist corsages to all the ladies present; about fifty guests in total with food and drink sufficient for all; and Sherri and I line-dancing together to "Could I Have This Dance for the Rest of My Life?"

We spent our wedding night in the b. & b. with several sets of our wedding guests. After a festive brunch at the lake house provided by our children, we took off for the traditional honeymoon Sherri wanted to spend at Niagara Falls. Our "honeymoon suite," complete with a red heart-shaped jacuzzi tub (!), overlooked the falls. Because it had rained out the Fourth of July fireworks displays in all the cities and towns on the American side of the falls the night before, every community within sight across the horizon provided us with a progressing panoply of fireworks, which we watched from the comfort of our hotel room.

We spent the next day doing the touristy things Niagara Falls had to offer and realized that one full day there was *more than enough*! So the following morning, we set off in torrential rain to visit Niagara-on-the-Lake—too wet even to get out of the car!—and then drove on to Guelph because Sherri remembered that some of Rich Speer's relatives had lived there. We found a place to spend the night, then got up the next morning and decided to head back to the lake house by way of Stratford. Thus ended our brief honeymoon.

It gladdened my heart to see how much Sherri enjoyed being at the lake house. She loved learning about the local agriculture and the out-of-the-way antique shops and the distinctively Canadian products available at the big new Sobey's supermarket in nearby Blenheim. She also loved charming the local gentry with her southern accent and walking the sandy beach in her bare feet and positioning in the gardens across the front of the lake house, created by the renovations I had continued even after Ann's death, the new flowering shrubs and foundation plants Tom and Mary Beth had given us as a wedding gift.

One of the things Sherri did *not* love about being in Canada was the distance we were from her Destin home, especially when a mid-summer hurricane began to threaten the Emerald Coast. When it looked as though the storm might make landfall right near Destin, we hurriedly packed the dogs in the car and drove straight south to make sure her house was safe. In the end, the storm missed Destin altogether, and we returned to the lake house weary but relieved and convinced that we would not make the trip again in two cars as we had done this first year.

In the fall, we returned to Florida and settled into a new "retirement" life pattern, centered largely on St. Andrew's by-the-Sea Episcopal Church and Sherri's friends there. I connected with the PC(USA) Presbytery of Florida and made my "rent-a-rev" persona available for some emergency and interim supply preaching. Early in 2005, I began to work with a couple of local "destination wedding" planners and found much pleasure in pastoring families far from home for one of the most important occasions in their lives. Prolonged interim ministries in Lynn Haven, a suburb of Panama City, and Niceville, across Choctawhatchee Bay from Kelly Plantation, provided Sherri with the new experience of being a minister's wife, a role she claimed that she had always wanted.

During the winter and spring of 2006, Sherri and I enjoyed a season of interim ministry at the Shalimar Presbyterian Church. Out of the blue, I received an intriguing request from the First Presbyterian Church in Fort Walton Beach, asking if I would be willing to conduct their Saint Andrew's Society's biennial "Kirkin' o' the Tartan" service in the absence of a settled pastor. Having led just such services in Deerfield and Royal Oak as well as elsewhere, I knew that I already had all the necessary ingredients for a "Kirkin'" in my laptop computer, so with the enthusiastic consent of the Shalimar congregation, I agreed to lead the service on Sunday, February 16, 2006. As it happened, our longtime friends Lex and Ann McCrindle were visiting from Windsor at the time and attended the service, Lex wearing his tartan trews! Dear neighbors from Rondeau, Jim and Sheena Ladouceur, were in Destin for the winter as snowbirds, and Jim filmed the whole service very professionally, then produced a DVD to preserve the event as a cherished memento.

The summer of 2006 provided an unexpected preaching opportunity when the pastor of the First Presbyterian Church of Chatham, Ontario, tragically lost his wife to cancer and begged the session to give him the whole summer off to regroup his young family and restore his own pastoral equilibrium. I was invited to become the church's summer pulpit supply, a gift I was glad to give to a congregation that had played occasional and important parts in my life-long spiritual journey. Deciding to use my "barrel of soliloquy" sermons over the summer, I began to organize them into a preaching series that would span the life and ministry of Jesus Christ from the prophecies of Isaiah to the writing of Luke's Gospel. Incredibly, the series was enthusiastically received by the congregation, particularly the message of Martha, which Sherri delivered on my behalf with a powerfully "southern Israel" accent!

For as long as we had been married, Sherri had been pestering me to write a book—*any* book! By the end of that August, I realized that I had more than enough material for a book comprising the full collection of the twenty-one sermon soliloquies and monologue meditations I had been working over all summer; and thus was born *If Only I Had Known . . .*, to be published in 2010 by Parson's Porch Books in Cleveland, Tennessee. Meanwhile, the annual rhythm of summers in Canada and winters in Florida, as wonderful as it was in its own way, had eventually begun to pall, especially as the post 9/11 security measures on both sides of the border at Detroit/Windsor became more and more intrusive and prolonged. Add to those experiences the difficulties we encountered every summer obtaining our prescription medications by mail, let alone the complications of moving money back and forth among our bank accounts in both countries, plus the annual worrying threat of a hurricane hitting Destin while we were gone, and Sherri and I began to wonder if maintaining our Canadian home and lifestyle was worth it!

Our return trip to Florida that October turned the tide. With a fully loaded cartop carrier strapped to the roof of my new Cadillac SRX and three dogs plus our "overnight" luggage squeezed into the back, we were flagged at the Windsor/Detroit Tunnel for a customs inspection. "Pull over here," bawled a burly Customs and Immigration officer, "roll down your windows, turn off the ignition, and step out of the vehicle!"

Whereupon our two little doggies, Bogey and Kelsey, began to bark and dance and try to jump out of the open windows. "If either of our dogs gets loose, it will be your responsibility to catch it and return it to us," I informed the officer in my most stentorian pulpit voice.

"Okay, then. Just roll up the windows and step out of the vehicle!" As we did so, another burly C & I officer, this one a statuesque woman of African-American descent, marched up to the back of the SRX and lifted the tailgate to be confronted by our big, black Labrador retriever, Rocky, who was instantly very much in her face.

"Uh, I guess everything is okay back here!" she shouted as she slammed down the tailgate. And we were free to go but badly shaken as we thought about how laboriously I had packed every inch of available space with everything that we had accumulated over almost six months in Canada and how impossible it would have been to put it all back together if the C & I officers had been determined to rummage through everything.

By the following spring of 2007, I was *dreading* the return trip to Rondeau as was Sherri it turned out. "You know," I confessed over breakfast one morning, "the lake house has been my heart's true home for twenty-five years, and I don't want to start hating it now!" Before long, we had arrived at the shared conclusion that the time had come to sell the lake house that summer if possible. I began to make plans to drive up to Canada by myself to put the house on the market then return to Destin to drive Sherri and the dogs north for what might be our last summer at the lake.

Sherri, however, was already looking ahead and was determined that if I had had lakefront property in Canada, then I must also have lakefront property in the United States. She began researching lakes within one day's driving distance from Destin. Eventually, she zeroed in on a huge lake one of our Kelly Plantation neighbors knew about in southcentral Kentucky and started to check local real estate listings in the area. By the time I set out to drive northward, she had seen several attractive listings in a place called Somerset and had identified the realty firm whose listings we most admired. Armed with this information as I drove, I telephoned the realtor and inquired whether an agent might be willing to spend a day showing me around if I detoured from I-65 across Kentucky on the Cumberland Parkway. Of course they would and did, and I fell in love with Lake Cumberland and Somerset.

To make a long story short (as one of Sherri's Speer in-laws used to say), the lake house sold within days. With the help of my friendly Kentucky realtor, I found a spectacular mountainside home just outside Somerset for almost exactly the same amount of money. By mid-August we had moved all my earthly Canadian goods to 425 Woodside Drive, and my Canadian life was virtually over.

A red brick Georgian two-story home on almost two acres in the foothills of the Great Smoky Mountains, "Cardinal Crest" was wonderful, to say the least. Fortunately, we had moved my John Deere riding mower with us from Rondeau, for it took the better part of a day to mow the property. Once Sherri got over the shock of it all, she loved it as much as I did. In addition to the family antiques and heirlooms we had brought from the lake house, we scoured the antique mall at the edge of town for furniture and accessories and made an impressively homey home.

As it turned out, several of our new neighbors were members of the First Baptist Church in downtown Somerset so that is where we began attending church. We found the congregation and its pastor, Dr. French Harmon, and his staff very welcoming and soon became active in several aspects of the congregation and community life. Among the latter, we particularly enjoyed the monthly Somernites Cruise Saturdays, when the downtown streets were filled with as many as a thousand vintage and show vehicles on display.

To help me with caring for Cardinal Crest, I was fortunate in hiring a jack-of-all-trades named Mike Christian. Starting out with a few hours a week, Mike became essential to the maintenance of our Kentucky home. With Mike's help, we enjoyed many happy visits to Cardinal Crest and became more and more involved in Somerset life.

As the winter of 2007–2008 segued into spring and our trips back and forth between Destin and Somerset increased, we began to think seriously about selling Sherri's Kelly Plantation house after all and replacing it with an easy-to-care-for condo somewhere along the Emerald Coast.

In April, Sherri launched her career as a retailer with "Somerset House Fine Finds," an elegant little booth in an antique mall of 150 dealers just north of Somerset. Her "inventory" began with the accumulated but no longer wanted or needed treasures of our combined seventy years of married life. Then, to maintain a well-stocked booth, we began to haunt auctions, thrift shops, and yard sales, looking for unappreciated items that, washed and polished, might appeal to our rural Kentucky clientele.

As we spent more and more time in Somerset, my friendship with French Harmon deepened, especially after one of his sermon references prompted me to ask whether he had ever visited the Holy Land. He had not but wished he could, and by the end of the summer we were actively recruiting participants for a ten-day pilgrimage being organized by my friend, Rick Ricart.

With another Advent and Christmas season approaching, we found ourselves reluctant to return to Destin even though we knew we *ought* to! Learning that our three faraway families were planning to be together for a pre-Christmas weekend in Illinois, we began to drop not-so-subtle hints that we would gladly prolong our stay in Somerset if we were invited to drive up to Naperville to share the family festivities. We finally realized that either we were being too subtle or the family just didn't want us there, so we gave up hinting.

We had so enjoyed the lifestyle of our year and a half in Kentucky that we decided to spend Christmas 2008 and the New Year's of 2009 at Cardinal Crest with an eye to perhaps making Somerset our full-time home until we were able to sell Sherri's Destin property and figure out where we were going to spend the rest of our lives.

Our first Christmas at Cardinal Crest put a full stop to all that! On what to me was still Boxing Day, we experienced our first typical Kentucky winter ice storm. What started out as rain soon coated *everything* with an inch or so of solid ice as the temperature plummeted, and we were virtual prisoners in our own home. The driveway was so steep and slick that it would have been dangerous to try to drive *down* it, and even Mike's old four-wheel drive Dodge Ram truck could not make it *up* to the house! As the temperature began to rise and the ice began to melt, we packed up what we did not want to leave in the house and prepared to drive down to Destin, leaving Mike responsible for the maintenance of the property while we were away and abandoning any thought of *ever* living in Cardinal Crest full-time!

By June 2009, a group of twenty pilgrims, mostly from the First Baptist Church of Somerset, set off for the church's first-ever trip to Israel. Assisted by David Pendley as staff liaison and accompanied by Dr. Harmon as "just one of the pilgrims," we enjoyed a memorable ten days touring sites in Galilee, at the Dead Sea, and in and around Jerusalem.

On our very first day of touring in a typical last-minute change of plans due to one unforeseen factor or another, our Israeli guide, Isaac, and our Palestinian driver, Ramses, took us to a recently developed site that I had never before visited. "The Mount of Precipice," just outside Nazareth, is the traditional spot from which angry Nazoreans tried to throw Jesus over the edge of the cliff, accusing him of blasphemy (Luke 4). To my surprise and delight, I discovered that the development of this mountaintop overlook had been financed by an interfaith group of my family's long-time friends and neighbors back in Windsor, Ontario.

As we were preparing for a baptismal reaffirmation ceremony at the Yardenit baptismal pools at the southern end of the

Sea of Galilee, one of the site directors asked if a small group of Nigerian Christians could join us, since they had no pastor with them and fervently wished to affirm their baptism at such a holy site. A life-long Southern Baptist with all the "baggage" that that implies, Dr. Harmon nevertheless graciously agreed and assisted me in immersing four very black Africans in the River Jordan in the midst of our little group, and (to the best of my knowledge) no one thought or said anything amiss!

One of my most enduring memories of that first pilgrimage was the sight of Dr. Harmon at the Church of All Nations adjacent to the Garden of Gethsemane, weeping as he prostrated himself at the rock traditionally identified as the place where Jesus prayed, "My Father, if it is possible, let this cup pass from me; yet not what I want but what you want" (Mt 26:39).

About half the group had opted for an extension of the original tour in order to spend three days in Egypt. Having been there, done that, I bade farewell to both halves of our pilgrim band at the Ben-Gurion Airport in Tel Aviv and flew alone to Athens.

For some time, Rick Ricart at *imagine Tours and Travel* had been trying to persuade me to lead a church group tour to Greece, Turkey, and the Greek islands in the "footsteps of St. Paul." I had finally relented to the point that I agreed to extend my trip by traveling on to Athens once the rest of the group were on their way — some to Egypt, others back to the USA.

After a day spent in and around Athens with the wife of Rick's counterpart in Greece, I boarded the *Aquamarine*, a midsize, shabby old ship, for a three-day cruise of the Greek islands. It proved to be a dismal experience. Accustomed to the everyday luxuries of travel in the Holy Land, I found the "footsteps of St. Paul" to lead to poorly maintained sites with poorly planned amenities. The cruise ship experience was also eye-opening with its huge gambling casino and nightly Las Vegas-style nightclub revues featuring scantily-clad showgirls and double-entendre comic routines. At the end of the cruise, I reported to Rick that there was no way that I could ever lead a bunch of Southern Baptist pilgrims from Somerset, Kentucky, through such an experience.

Back in Somerset, in a classically "it's a small world" happenstance, Somerset's First Presbyterian Church celebrated an historic anniversary by inviting as the weekend's guest preacher none other than the Reverend Dr. John Killinger, who, with his wife Anne, had been very hospitable to my Ann and me during our Princeton Seminary days, when John was the teaching assistant to my preaching professor, Dr. Paul Scherer. Recognizing one another at the end of the anniversary service, John and I were delighted to renew an old acquaintance and remain in touch with one another.

Keeping in touch eventually led to an email exchange in which John asked why I had never been published. That query, in turn, led to his introducing me to his friend, David Tullock, the owner and publisher of Parson's Porch Books, located in Cleveland, Tennessee. "All things working together for good" resulted in a contract to publish *If Only I Had Known . . .*, for which I finally got down to work organizing, editing, and writing brief introductions to each of the twenty-one soliloquies that would make up the book. What a tremendous amount of work that turned out to be!

For my seventieth birthday on September 10, 2009, Sherri organized a totally surprise birthday celebration. Sarah flew in from Calgary, Kirk and Rebecca came with all their children, plus Tom and Mary Beth, Lex and Ann, and Alan and Maureen to spend the Labor Day weekend at Cardinal Crest! It was an incredibly generous gift on Sherri's part, for in addition to the

party itself to which a number of our local friends were also invited, she paid for all the hotel accommodations for our out-of-
town guests. At one point, during a hilariously wet game of
water polo in a pool full of children, grandchildren, close relatives, and dear friends, I thought to myself, "It doesn't get
much better than this!"

The family's birthday present literally took my breath away
and explained something that had been bothering me since the
previous Christmas. The surprise gift was a handsomely framed
24" × 20" photographic portrait of *the whole family*, taken
when they were all together in Illinois in December. Sarah, Kirk,
and Rebecca had all known how much Sherri and I had wanted
to be with them, but they were afraid that the little grandchildren might give away the secret of the photoshoot and spoil the
planned birthday surprise! That photo portrait remains one of
my most prized possessions and hangs now in our hallway
where I pass it and nod to my dear ones many times a day.

Earlier in the year, unbeknownst to any of my family other
than Sherri, I had applied to the United States Department of
Homeland Security for naturalization as an American citizen.
Throughout my decades of ministry in both Canada and United
States—with the notable exception of the years we lived in
Montreal—I had remained determinedly noncommittal about
controversial political and social issues that might have divided
my congregations. Now, finally, married to an American citizen
and planning to spend the rest of my life somewhere in Kentucky or Florida, I decided that it was time to pledge allegiance
to the land that had been so good to me in so many ways over
so many years.

At the First Baptist Church in Somerset, I had become
friendly with the Honorable Harold "Hal" Rogers, a long-serving member of the US House of Representatives. Hal enthusi-

astically sponsored my citizenship application and tasked his local administrative assistant to do whatever might be appropriate and helpful to speed my application to a successful conclusion. With that savvy young man's help and advice, the process did move forward very quickly. Among the "hoops" through which I was required to jump were two brief trips from Destin to Citizenship and Immigration offices in Jacksonville, which afforded me unexpected opportunities to visit and learn about Westminster Woods on Julington Creek, one of the premier life care retirement communities in the Presbyterian Church (USA)'s denominational sponsorship.

In an impressive ceremony at the federal courthouse in downtown Pensacola on November 20, 2009, I became a naturalized citizen of the United States of America. It was a proud yet poignant occasion for both Sherri and me. She was (and is) by nature very patriotic, so she was sublimely proud of me and my decision. At the same time, we had loved spending time together at the lake house in Canada and this felt like a very final step in a process that seemed like a *renunciation* of my birth, my background, and much of my life.

With another winter ahead, I was becoming more and more aware of how dependent Sherri and I had become on Mike Christian to help maintain our Kentucky home and lifestyle. After consulting with a building contractor, I offered to create for Mike a fully self-contained one-bedroom apartment in the spacious basement of Cardinal Crest, where he could live rent-free in return for becoming our live-in "project manager." Mike happily agreed and was able to move into the apartment at year's end.

October 27, 2001
Southwinds, Windsor, Ontario
Four generations of William Russells:
William, William Kirk, William Ray, and William Ronald

Sunday, June 13, 2004
In Knox Presbyterian Church, Naperville, Illinois
"Grampa Russell" after baptising his youngest grandchild,
Ryan Campbell Russell

Sunday, July 4, 2004
At the lake house on Lake Erie near Rondeau
With Matt Schramm (left) and the Reverend Dr. Alan M. McPherson
relaxing before the wedding

Sunday, July 4, 2004
At the lake house on Lake Erie near Rondeau
Sherri and I barefoot and just married

Sunday, February 16, 2006
At Fort Walton Beach, Florida
With my lifelong friend Lex
after the Presbyterian Church's Kirkin' o' the Tartan

August 2006
At the lake house on Lake Erie near Rondeau
"Farmer Bill" with his new John Deere mowing tractor

June 2009
Atop the "Mount of Precipice" near Nazareth, Israel
*A site recently developed thanks to some of my family's
friends and neighbors in Windsor, Ontario*

June 2009
At the Yardenit baptismal pools in Galilee, Israel
Pastor French Harmon about to immerse me in baptismal reaffirmation

June 2009
At the Yardenit baptismal pools in Galilee, Israel
Pastor French Harmon watches
as I pronounce a "Presbyterian" benediction

June 2009
On the Mount of Olives, Jerusalem, Israel
My First Baptist Church, Somerset, KY, pilgrim band

June 2009
In Athens, Greece
At the Acropolis

September 10, 2009
At Cardinal Crest in Somerset, Kentucky
My 70th birthday party with Sherri and my grandchildren:
(from left to right) Tori, Will, Abbi, and Ryan

November 20, 2009
Federal Courthouse in Pensacola, Florida
Introducing myself to the immigration judge
at my naturalization as an American citizen

THE
TWENTY-
TENS

DURING THE WINTER MONTHS OF 2010, Sherri had the good sense to remain in Destin. I made several trips back and forth to Somerset, during one of which the Cardinal Crest HVAC boiler gave out, and I spent nine days huddled in the master bedroom with its electric fireplace, while the outside temperature hovered in the teens and Somerset enjoyed a record seven-and-a-half-inch snowfall.

In March though, Sherri and I drove down to Satellite Beach to attend a revue performed by Sherri's best friend Bunny Adams' tap-dancing "Golden Steppers." On the way back to the Panhandle, we detoured up I-95 to Jacksonville to introduce Sherri to Westminster Woods on Julington Creek, that beautiful old Presbyterian Church-related life care retirement community about which I had been in correspondence for some time. We were sufficiently impressed that by the end of that September I invested in a new independent living neighborhood to be built there sometime in 2011.

In early May, I flew from Lexington, Kentucky, to Jamaica

to assist in the destination wedding of my only niece Alexandra Trotter and her long-time beau, Matthew Terry. An unexpected highlight of the trip was the pleasure of spending an hour sailing on Montego Bay with my nephew, Nathaniel, whom I had not seen in several years.

Against my better judgment, 2010 brought with it plans and preparations for a second First Baptist Church pilgrimage to the Holy Land. I had been opposed to the idea from the beginning, feeling that it was too soon to sponsor a second trip, and I was proved right. Even though David Pendley was enthusiastic about the venture and eager to learn more about being a pilgrimage tour leader, Dr. Harmon realized that he could not be out of the country for a prolonged period again that late winter, so he pulled out of the planning, thereby removing one of the real incentives for his parishioners to sign up for the trip.

Unfortunately, he boasted to another local Baptist preacher about the benefits both spiritual and financial of such a tour, and before long we had a few of that second congregation's members signing up to travel with us. Their pastor expected his wife and son to travel with him for free and for himself to become co-leader of the group. It turned out that he was not as popular as he thought he was, either in his own congregation or in the community at large. Only a handful of his members actually paid deposits, and a couple of First Baptist's members withdrew when they learned he would be co-leading the tour.

As the departure date drew nearer, we barely had enough participants to warrant a typical Israeli tour bus. Almost at the last minute, our tour broker, Rick Ricart, suggested that we include a half-dozen pilgrims and their pastor from a small Presbyterian congregation in San Diego, California, so as to make our tour economically viable. We agreed—I with many misgivings—and off we went.

From the start, it was clear that the three groups would not meld very well. Social, political, economic, and spiritual differences dogged every decision and made the exercise of any leadership an uncomfortable effort. Our familiar and much-appreciated tour guide, Isaac, was not accustomed to dealing with a troika of pastors, each vying for control of the itinerary, and kept turning to me for decision-making, which naturally affronted the others and isolated me.

The absolute nadir of our tour came on the way back to Jerusalem from Bethlehem on the second-last full day of our trip. Rushing to get back to the Temple Mount in time for our early evening appointment to walk the Western Wall Tunnel, we neglected to take time for a bathroom stop en route. There were no facilities at the Western Wall, so by the time we traversed the tunnel and made it back to our tour bus, some of our pilgrims were quite desperate to relieve themselves.

On the bus, Isaac suggested that we backtrack to the Mughrabi Gate entrance to the Temple Mount, where there were public restrooms. As our bus pulled up into the nearest parking space, the "other" Somerset pastor pushed the emergency switch to open the rear door and shouted, "I've been here before. Follow me!" He jumped off the bus, followed by about a dozen of our pilgrims, and set off to the *left* up the hill toward Mount Zion. Unfortunately, the public restrooms were about fifty feet to the *right*, down the hill, where David Pendley led everyone else to their relief!

Startled by this unexpected exodus of our pilgrims, Isaac and I remained on the bus for a moment until we both realized that our group was now divided in two, with half of them heading in the wrong direction. I said that I would chase down the errant bunch headed toward Mount Zion if he would stay with the bus until the other group returned, then have the driver pull ahead until the bus caught up with us.

Clearly, I made the worse choice. I was nowhere near to catching up with those I was chasing when I began to huff and puff and nearly passed out due to shortness of breath. I sat on a low stone wall until our tour bus hove into view, and David and Isaac helped me onto the bus and into my seat. Eventually we caught up to the other half of our group, many of whom had desperately relieved themselves in the low bushes in front of the Mount Zion retaining wall. Once all were safely aboard the bus, I was so relieved that I began to sob and then gasp and then faint.

In retrospect, I realize that this was a classic example of my medical tendency to overproduce adrenaline during a crisis and then lapse into adrenal shock once the crisis is past. At the time, however, all I could think of was that I was dying and would have to be cremated in Jerusalem and shipped home in an urn.

I spent the whole of the next day resting in bed at our hotel but felt well enough on the following afternoon to accompany the group to the Garden Tomb, one of my most favorite sites in the Holy Land. There, David Pendley and I led a farewell celebration of the sacrament of Holy Communion. That evening, we all shared a final meal together, where the atmosphere was very tense. Concern for my health, anger and embarrassment at the foolishness of the pastor who had led so many on a wild goose chase, wistfulness that the tour was over and some of our new San Diego friends would never be with us again made it a bittersweet experience for us all.

Every visit to the Holy Land proves memorable in many and unexpected ways. This one happened to take place during an international terrorist-inspired UPS/FedEx bomb scare. The security at Tel Aviv's Ben-Gurion Airport was truly horrendous. From the time our tour bus dropped us off in Tel Aviv until I walked out of the regional airport in Lexington, Kentucky, I had spent a total of twenty-three hours in transit, and I was very ill. Thus ended my Holy Land tour guide career.

In the second week of January 2011, a new and energetic realtor unexpectedly sold Sherri's Destin home in twenty-four breathtaking hours. By then, we had researched the Jacksonville area pretty thoroughly and were looking forward to relocating there. Sadly, though, when I telephoned Westminster Woods to report the sale of Sherri's home and our need for somewhere to live within the next two months, the administration had nothing to offer but a one-bedroom apartment in the assisted living neighborhood of the community.

That was not what we had in mind. However, we decided to set out eastward across I-10 to Jacksonville to spend a day with a realtor, looking at real estate in every gated community from Queen's Harbor in Atlantic Beach to the TPC and Sawgrass Country Clubs in Ponte Vedra Beach. Weary and discouraged by the end of the afternoon, I grudgingly accepted our realtor's offer to show us just one more house in a high-end gated golf course community known as "The Plantation."

As we turned off Highway A1A toward the forbidding-looking plantation gatehouse, Sherri spotted huge old live oak trees festooned with Spanish moss and said, "This is it. This is where I want us to live!" The last house we were to see became the house on which we made an offer, which was accepted and into which we moved early in March.

For Mother's Day weekend, we drove to Naperville, Illinois, to celebrate daughter-in-law Jennifer's post-graduation from Saint Francis University in Aurora with a well-earned doctorate in educational administration. Armed with the prospect of this new and distinguished credential, Jennifer began the search for a full-time teaching position at the university level and eventually accepted an appointment to the faculty of Barton College in Wilson, North Carolina. With his "executive placement" business flourishing in a way that enabled him to work from anywhere, Kirk and family had departed Illinois for Clayton, North Carolina, where grandson Will took up year-round golf, and grandson Ryan began a very promising career as an equestrian.

Jennifer had worked long and hard for this recognition, and we were very proud of and for her. Rebecca and Alex hosted a wonderful celebration in their backyard after the graduation ceremony, and I rejoiced to observe how my four grandchildren had taken "Nana Sher" (as they chose to call her) to their hearts, and them to hers!

We truly loved living in the Plantation except for the realization that we had moved ourselves another 200 or so miles farther away from Somerset and Cardinal Crest. I doggedly made a number of trips back and forth, each trip requiring an overnight stay en route. Soon, and sadly, I decided to list the property for sale with the same realty firm through which I had bought it four years before but now with no results.

On one of my midsummer visits to Cardinal Crest, Mike Christian and his new wife alerted me to the news that her mother was terminally ill with a rare form of cancer, and she really wanted to leave our little apartment in the basement and move downstate to care for her mother until her death. I was torn: on the one hand, I could not begrudge Becky the opportunity to care for her mother; but on the other hand, I could not imagine how we were going to maintain Cardinal Crest if our caretakers moved out!

God moves in a mysterious way—at least we thought so at the time—when, on my birthday on September 10, 2011, our next-door neighbors in Somerset urged a young family renting the house across the street from them to call me to inquire whether I might consider a lease-to-own deal. I would, and I did with the help of John Prather, a distinguished Somerset lawyer who, with his wife, Hilma, had been pilgrims on my first First Baptist tour to the Holy Land.

By Thanksgiving, Sherri had successfully liquidated her stall in the antique mall on the edge of Somerset, selling off many of the precious furnishings and accessories for which we would clearly have no room in our little retirement cottage in Retreat Place at the Plantation. The family antiques we had brought from Rondeau were moved: some to Ponte Vedra Beach; some to Naperville, Illinois, where Becca and Alex still lived; and others to Clayton, North Carolina, where Kirk and Jennifer and their boys were making a new life around her professorship at Wilson College nearby. The remainder we consigned to a local auctioneer, who carted everything away and eventually sent us a check for the proceeds of a long evening's sale.

We spent the Advent and Christmas season experiencing the worship life of St. John's Epsicopal Cathedral in downtown Jacksonville, where the dean and I had hit it off from our very first visit. In fact, she invited me to preach the sermon at the cathedral's annual St. Andrew's Day festal choral evensong at the end of November and to lead the "Dean's Forum" adult education classes on the Sunday mornings in Advent.

The Kirk Russell family had planned to stop by Ponte Vedra Beach for a pre-Christmas visit on their way southward for a Christmas cruise. Unfortunately, Ryan became very ill while traveling from North Carolina, and they passed us by, promising to visit on their return trip, which they did. Bob and Diana Kesler drove down from Atlanta to spend New Year's Eve with us. Jim and Sheena Ladouceur joined us for a raucous game of *Strategy* during the countdown to midnight.

Unfortunately by the end of winter, we were realizing that the commute to downtown Jacksonville from Ponte Vedra Beach was seeming longer rather than shorter and that we were missing out on most late Sunday and midweek evening events at the cathedral because it just seemed too far to drive, especially in the dark. Regretfully, we shopped churches nearer to the Plantation, and by Easter 2012 we ended up at Christ Episcopal Church in the heart of Old Ponte Vedra. In the fall, we joined the "Mallory Episcobells" and had some wonderful times with that welcoming and talented bell-ringing group.

During the year, Sherri committed to funding a scholarship for needy education majors at the University of Georgia. In celebration of her renewed connection with her alma mater, she took me to my first ever American college football game, homecoming "between the hedges" at Athens, Georgia, where the Bulldogs won so decisively that even I understood it!

If Queen Elizabeth could proclaim 1992 her "annus horribilis," 2013 was certainly *ours*! A yearlong struggle with aches and pains and hospitalizations and surgeries for both of us culminated in our accomplishing one of the things we had intended in our move to the Jacksonville area: we transferred all our medical care to the physicians, surgeons, nurses, technicians, and support staff at the East Coast outpost of the world-renowned Mayo Clinic. Mayo is about a twenty-minute drive away across the Intracoastal Waterway that separates Jacksonville from the barrier islands of which Ponte Vedra is a part. Collectively, the Mayo Clinic began to make our lives worth living again and our health issues more bearable, inspiring in us a confidence that their diagnoses, treatments, and prognostications were "right on!"

As a part of this major readjustment in our lives, we sold our little retirement cottage on Retreat Place in the Plantation at the beginning of December 2013 and bought a somewhat larger home better suited to the aging-in-place lifestyle pattern we were gradually adopting. With a large pool and an even larger screened lanai overlooking the eleventh tee box of the Plantation golf course, it was meant to be our "last" move this side of heaven!

At some point during the travels of my Bible Society career, I had read that if one wanted to be remembered as a good tipper, one ought to tip consistently with $2.00 bills! Once we began to avail ourselves of the valet parking service offered at Mayo, I consistently tipped the valets from my stash of $2.00 bills. Eventually, the valets began to recognize my black Mercedes Benz E350 and began calling me "Two-Dollar Bill." When I mentioned this to my Mayo primary care physician, Dr. Lee told me that I should consider my nickname a singular honor at Mayo, which I did!

Prior to our going to the Mayo Clinic, two years of too many prescription steroids and antibiotics had wrought havoc with my immune system, so my new medical care team forbade me to travel by air or to attend crowded events or large worship services. After months of consultations and arguments pro and con, I underwent a still-experimental LINX procedure, which basically would prevent me from aspirating my own acid reflux and causing recurring cycles of infection. At first, Medicare refused to cover the novel procedure. The Mayo Clinic offered me a protocol by which if I would pay the purchase price of the $1,200.00 magnetic beads appliance, Mayo would cover the $20,000.00+ costs of the procedure. This we did, and Mayo pursued the claim with Medicare for many months until the obvious and remarkable success of my operation became so compelling an argument that Medicare relented and approved the LINX procedure, not only for me but for every Medicare patient after me!

2014 marked not only Sherri's and my tenth wedding anniversary but also my seventy-fifth birthday, the fiftieth anniversary of my graduation from Princeton Seminary, and the centennial of the First Presbyterian Church in Royal Oak. Respecting Mayo's total travel ban, I missed both the Princeton and the Royal Oak milestone celebrations. Fortunately, Sherri and I were very content just to stay at home, enjoying our pool and lanai and the much-welcomed visits of Alan and Maureen, Lex and Ann, and the Alex Klopp and Kirk Russell families.

In many respects, 2015 was more of the same old, same old. We were delighted that Sarah was able to extend an end-of-summer trip to Houston for a weeklong Royal Dutch Shell conference into a long weekend visit with us. Unfortunately, soon after she returned to Calgary, she suffered a stroke and was hospitalized with worrisome neural damage. Calgary has a world-class stroke clinic, where she was enrolled in an experimental heavy-duty home therapy program and soon reported significant progress toward her return to work in full vigor.

We were truly aging in place as we had intended, enjoying our Plantation home, pool, and lanai. But as I wrote in our "Christmas letter" at the end of the year:

Sad to say, we are learning day by day that "aging in place" is not all it's cracked up to be! Anecdotal evidence, plus the recent firsthand experiences of loved ones and friends, have convinced us to do something that wasn't even on our radar six months ago: we have become "Associate Members" at Vicar's Landing, a life care retirement community (LCRC) nestled on the grounds of the TPC Sawgrass Players Club just a couple of miles north of us here in Ponte Vedra Beach. Our names are at the bottom of a very long waiting list for residential accommodation, but in the meantime we are availing ourselves of fitness training, fine dining, and frequent worship opportunities on the recently renovated and beautifully landscaped campus.

In the spring of 2016, anticipating our eventual move to Vicar's Landing, we listed our Plantation home for sale with our realtor friend, Doug Mathewson. For the Plantation's big spring real estate open house, Sherri staged our home creatively—so creatively that we removed enough stuff to fill a 15' × 15' storage locker with things we *might* want in our eventual Vicar's Landing apartment.

At the end of June as if by way of strengthening our resolve to move into a life care retirement community, I suffered a cardiac incident, the first hint of recurring heart disease in over a decade, and underwent angioplasty and the insertion of a stent to open one of my arteries. Ironically, the *incident*—not a true heart *attack*—began on our way from the Plantation to Vicar's Landing for a strength and balance exercise class. Following my hospitalization, I began a course of cardiopulmonary rehabilitation at the Mayo Clinic which, conveniently, segued into a prescribed set of exercises I was able to undertake three times a week in the well-equipped fitness facilities at Vicar's Landing.

Following upon a very well-received line dancing performance in a Vicar's talent show, Sherri volunteered to teach a weekly line dancing class, which immediately attracted a dozen women aged seventy-two to ninety-six. For my part, I began to sell at auction on eBay some of the higher value treasures that members and associates contribute to the annual Boutique.

An unexpected and alarming prayer focus at midyear was the news that my brother, Tom, had been diagnosed with an inoperable brain tumor. By Christmas, we learned that the mass had responded well to chemotherapy and radiation, and we looked forward to visiting with Tom and Mary Beth when they traveled down to Clearwater from Canada for their annual winter vacation.

That Christmas, Alex Klopp succeeded in tracking down one of the last *Nirvana* radio-controlled model sailboats available in North America and bought it for me in anticipation of my joining the "Royal Vicar's Yacht Club" when we moved into Vicar's Landing. I took the boxed kit with me when Sherri and the doggies and I drove over to Clearwater to visit Tom and Mary Beth at their Bay Aristocrat Village winter home. Although he was clearly ill, Tom persisted in helping me assemble and rig the *Nirvana* while we were there. That proved to be the very last time we were together before he died, and I honor him wistfully every time I race *SH-BOOM II* in a RVYC regatta.

By early in the New Year of 2017, it was becoming clear—even to me—that the lease-to-own contract on our Cardinal Crest property was not going to survive the financial irresponsibility of our tenant family. Upon the advice of John Prather, I initiated eviction proceedings, which for a while, were thwarted by the chicanery of the tenants' lawyer. But, in time, we secured from the Pulaski County court a final eviction date of May 20, 2017.

On May 18, Sherri and I set off from Ponte Vedra Beach to drive north to Somerset with our two little doggies to be present for the actual eviction process. At midday on the 19th, news of our impending arrival reached our tenants, who were busy packing to vacate the premises. In apparent panic (the reasons for which became clear the next day), the family literally and immediately fled the state in a convoy of vehicles, leaving behind a refrigerator and freezer full of food, dirty laundry littering the whole house, and a pair of feral cats they had been feeding for some time.

When we finally gained admittance to Cardinal Crest the

next day, the house was in a shambles. While we awaited the arrival of a locksmith to change all the exterior door locks, we discovered that most of the appliances had been removed, along with a large-screen television system, two electric fireplaces, and the beautiful hot tub we had installed in a screened porch off the master bedroom.

A team of cleaners started to work on Monday and began revealing to us evidence that the family had been growing, packaging, and dealing marijuana from the garage. A pair of holes in the master bedroom wall across from where the bed had sat, augmented by some local gossip and authenticated by the suspicions of the county police, indicated that the couple had, indeed, been producing pornographic videos *on site*!

Heartbroken even more than incensed, we met with a realtor recommended to us by our lawyer, John Prather, and immediately listed the whole property for sale, although at an asking price the realtor warned us was probably unrealistic. And so it was, for despite all we tried to do to make the place attractive, there was no buyer interest. After two weeks, we gave up, lowered the price as our realtor recommended, and returned to Ponte Vedra Beach.

While puttering around the Somerset property, I had been experiencing some light-headedness and shortness of breath, which I put down to the extreme emotional distress under which I was working. However, within twenty-four hours of being home in the Plantation, I suffered a second cardiac incident and was rushed by ambulance to the Mayo Clinic. Another angioplasty, another two stents, and another warning that the next time might mean open-heart surgery if not death!

Literally as Sherri was driving me home from the hospital, my cell phone rang, and the realtor who had helped me buy Cardinal Crest ten years before asked pointedly "Why is your

Woodside Drive property listed at such a low price?"

When I told her the long sad story of the lease-to-own deal ending in eviction and the distressing condition in which we had found the house when it was restored to us, she confessed "I have always wanted to live in that house. Would you be willing to sell it to me?"

I certainly was and did, effectively striking a big chunk from the net worth statement we had submitted to the Vicar's Landing administration when we signed on as associate members. I began to wonder whether we would still qualify for admission.

I need not have worried. Early in July, a phone call from Tess Crosby, the Vicar's Landing marketing director, informed Sherri and me that there was an apartment becoming available that she thought might suit our needs. And indeed it did: with 1,500 square feet of space, including two bedrooms, two bathrooms, a den opening onto a sprawling lawn, and an open-concept living room/dining room/kitchen, it was (to our amazement) eligible for a "total rehab!"

It took until the end of October to complete the renovations required and requested, but the results were sensational. With the enthusiastic cooperation of teams of carpenters, electricians, plumbers, and painters, our new "forever home" so recreated the ambiance of our Plantation house that we—and the doggies—immediately felt at home. Having graphed to scale the floorplan well in advance of moving, I was confident that everything we wanted to move would actually fit in, and it all did with the energetic assistance of Kirk, who drove down from North Carolina to be of help and encouragement!

Providentially, while there had been little or no realtor interest in our Plantation home for a year and a half, a couple from Minnesota came on very short notice to see it one Saturday morning in early November. By the end of the afternoon, we had a mutually acceptable offer and a perfectly timed closing at the end of the month.

"Amesbury," the "A" in our new address, is a pair of three-story apartment blocks surrounding two beautifully landscaped open-air atria. Our home is on the ground floor, which provides us with not only a "back door" leading from the den to a spacious lawn but also almost fifty feet of outdoor foundation plantings, in the middle of which we have had a paved patio laid. Seven palm trees grace the property, plus three crape myrtles, a swath of jasmine groundcover, a bed of Indian haw-thorn, a privacy screen of blue-flowering plumbago, accents of red salvia, and a perfect spot for our beloved wine-red porcelain birdbath!

As we moved in, Kirk, on behalf of the whole Russell family, presented us with a handsome bronze-and-black oval plaque to be mounted under our "A-109" address at the atrium doorway. Above and around an impressive "R," it prays God to "Bless This Home and All Who Enter It." So every time Sherri or I come or go through our front door, we are reminded, not only of the blessings that are truly ours in living here but also of the generous understanding with which our loved ones have sup-ported our decision to secure our places in this life care retire-ment community for the rest of our days.

Our first holiday season at Vicar's Landing included a sump-tuous Thanksgiving buffet, two trips downtown to hear the Jacksonville Symphony's "Holiday Pops" and *Messiah* concerts, a gala Amesbury house dinner, a candlelit Christmas Eve service and then a mind-boggling "British" New Year's Eve festivity featuring a live TV feed from London, England, with Big Ben ringing in the new year at 7:00 p.m. local time.

As has been the case so often over the decades-long course of our friendship with Alan and Maureen McPherson, they were our very first visitors in our new home. In our downsizing, we have designated as our "guest rooms" the nearby Hilton Garden Inn and Marriott Sawgrass Resort, both just outside the Sawgrass Players Club security gates. Since then, in addition to Alan and Maureen, Bob and Diana Kesler, daughters Sarah and Rebecca, and granddaughter Abigail have all made good use of these hostelries' convenient locations.

2018 has seen Sherri's line-dancing troupe grow in size and accomplishment. One of their favorite endeavors is putting on half-hour shows for the residents of *The Stratford*, Vicar's Landing's assisted living residence. My involvement in selling high-end contributions through *The Boutique* on eBay has flourished and has thrown us together with a whole new group of friends.

Summertime brought an unexpected pleasure, with a long weekend's visit by our daughters, Sarah and Rebecca. We also spent a couple of weeks in a rented cabin in the North Georgia mountains and made a sentimental journey back to Destin for a week in September. In mid-October, Vicar's Landing celebrated its thirtieth anniversary with a gala black-tie dinner dance, for which I had served on the planning committee. We felt pretty spiffy as Sherri complimented my new Black Watch kilt outfit with a sparkling royal blue evening gown.

I made my pastoral debut on Thanksgiving Eve, when I led an interfaith chapel service with a mix of seasonal hymns and old-fashioned patriotism. The next week, our neighbor, Bill Ross, and I hosted the first-ever St. Andrew's Day dinner. Ten days later, I was privileged to perform a small family wedding in the chapel for a young couple of our dining room waitstaff. Christmas Day was made memorable by the visit of Kirk, Jennifer, Will, and Ryan Russell. Once again, New Year's Eve was celebrated "British" style.

Now, in 2019, I am looking ahead to my eightieth birthday

on September 10, and, I hope, finishing up this anecdotal auto-biography before it becomes an over-long obituary. In February, Sherri and I "starred" in a special Valentine's Day play reading, written and directed by our friend and neighbor, Ken Gorman. It was a light romantic comedy, and we were accorded a standing ovation, the first time anyone present could remember a play reading being so well received.

It is always a delight to welcome the visits of family and friends. In March this year, we enjoyed a spring break visit from daughter, Rebecca, and granddaughter, Abigail, who will be a freshman at the University of Alabama in the fall. It is hard to believe that our eldest grandchild, Tori, will be a junior at Kansas University this fall. Thanks to Wi-Fi, we get to enjoy many of trumpeter Tori's KU band performances.

In May, I directed and Sherri and I acted in Vicar's Landing's first-ever murder mystery dinner. A cast of thirteen thespians interacted with an audience of 170 mystified diners, spreading real clues and red herrings throughout the crowd. The highlight of the evening was certainly *The Vivacious Vicarettes*, a dozen of Sherri's line-dancing ladies dressed as flappers and doing the Charleston and three other numbers as the floor show in a pretend 1920s Chicago speakeasy. Sherri literally brought down the house with a scream as she interrupted the *Vicarettes*' encore number by spotting her "lover" lying dead at the foot of the auditorium stage!

The Royal Vicars Yacht Club has turned out to be a real delight. Weather permitting, we hold monthly regattas on Sunday afternoons, when seven or eight radio-controlled *Nirvana* model sailboats compete around a figure-eight racecourse in the little pond at the center of the Administration/Activities/Health Center buildings. With Rebecca and Abigail to join with Sherri in cheering me on, I won the first race of the March regatta! At the midsummer hiatus, I am excited to be tied with our commodore for second place in the overall standings.

In August, Sherri and I planned to celebrate our fifteenth wedding anniversary and my eightieth birthday "off campus" in another rented cabin near Ellijay in the North Georgia mountains. Unfortunately as the renowned Scots poet Robbie Burns once put it so succinctly, "The best-laid schemes o' *mice* an' *men* gang aft a-gley." During the second night of our ten-day vacation, Sherri stumbled in the dark on the bottom step of the front porch, fell onto a stone slab and badly hurt her ankle. When the emergency room doctor in East Ellijay assured us that it was "only a sprain," we agreed to give it a rest and sit out the remainder of our stay on the cabin's screened porch watching the white-water river flow by. However, when we returned to Ponte Vedra Beach, our primary care physician at the Mayo Clinic insisted on a second look and with the help of more X-rays and an MRI determined that her ankle was indeed fractured and her Achilles tendon was torn.

As I write the last few pages of this collection of anecdotes, poor Sherri is confined to a wheelchair for another eight to ten weeks, after which her doctors will decide whether or not her torn tendon needs surgery. Meanwhile, line dancing is out of the question for a while; but nevertheless, come September 24, Sherri and her wheelchair will "star" in another Vicar's Landing play reading written and directed by our friend Ken Gorman.

If a hurricane should result in "mandatory" evacuation from Ponte Vedra Beach (as has happened twice in the past three years), we may flee to the Kirk Russells' new home in Clayton, North Carolina. Kirk assures us of a bed, since grandson Will will be "away" as a freshman at William Peace University in downtown Raleigh, where his mother Jennifer is now dean of the education faculty. While there, it would be a special thrill to get to watch grandson Ryan and his horse, "Clem," in equestrian training.

As always, we still have a great deal to which to look forward. Eventually, Sherri will be able to resume her line dancing classes with a half dozen newcomers attracted by the popularity of the *Vivacious Vicarettes*. With playlists stored on her iPad, I get to be "Mr. Music" for the dancers. On November 1st – All Saints' Day – I hope to conduct a first-ever memorial celebration of the "saints" we have all "loved and lost awhile" during the past year at Vicar's Landing.

The annual *Boutique* in mid-November is a weeklong effort on the part of many, many residents and associates to raise funds to support the Members' Association Scholarship Fund for our student employees. In truth, Sherri actually works all year long receiving, sorting, primping, pricing, and packing away contributions for her *Christmas Boutique*, where she and her team turn the fitness studio into what one old codger last year described as "an eyeful of eye candy!"

As November segues into the holiday season, many members expect me to lead another interfaith Thanksgiving Eve chapel service as I did this past year. My distinguished Scots neighbor, Bill Ross, talks about our forming a "St. Andrew's Society" in time for the Patron Saint of Scotland's holy day dinner at the end of the month. December has its own momentum of cocktail and dinner parties, special entertainments, a candlelit Christmas Eve service and another rollicking "British" New Year's Eve dinner dance.

Already, plans are afoot for another murder mystery dinner around St. Patrick's Day 2020, again to feature Sherri's *Vivacious Vicarettes*. The Members Association's Dining Committee, on which I serve, will be working with Chef Martyn Carré and his staff to plan and present sumptuous holiday buffets for New

Year's Day, Easter, Memorial Day, the Fourth of July, Labor Day, Thanksgiving, and Christmas. The recently gifted jukebox in the auditorium is being programmed for occasional hour-long impromptu before-dinner dances.

And . . . just let me catch my breath . . .

October 2010
Near Capernaum, Israel
Aboard a "Jesus Boat" on the Sea of Galilee

Mother's Day, Sunday, May 8, 2011
Saint Francis University, Aurora, Illinois
Sherri and I with Doctor Jennifer Moss Russell,
having just received her doctorate in educational administration

Mother's Day, Sunday, May 8, 2011
Naperville, Illinois, in the Klopps' backyard
"Nana Sher" with my four grandchildren
Will (left), Abbi, Tori, and Ryan

January 2014
The Plantation, Ponte Vedra Beach
Offering to blow some heat northward
to our Canadian friends in deep midwinter

March 2017
At Bay Aristocrat Village, Clearwater, Florida
With my brother Tom after rigging SH-BOOM II

Wednesday, October 17, 2018
Vicar's Landing auditorium
Sherri and I at the Vicar's 30th Anniversary Gala

November 2018
In the fitness studio at Vicar's Landing
Sherri and her line dancers in rehearsal

Christmas Day, December 25, 2018
On a terrace overlooking the pond at Vicar's Landing
With my grandsons Ryan (left) and Will

Wednesday, February 13, 2019
Vicar's Landing auditorium
Sherri and I in "A Special Valentine" play reading

Sunday, March 24, 2019
Royal Vicars Yacht Club Regatta
With granddaughter Abigail, helping me launch SH-BOOM II

Tuesday, May 14, 2019
Vicar's Landing auditorium
Sherri (as Mona Crawfish) and I (as Beanie O'Bannon)
with Gordon West (as Chuck Limburger)
at "The Grand Gatsby" murder mystery dinner

AFTERWORD

And if by reason of strength they be fourscore years, yet is their strength labour and sorrow; for it is soon cut off, and we fly away (Ps 90:10).

DURING MY ANNUAL PHYSICAL AT THE MAYO Clinic this year, my primary care physician, Dr. Gary Lee, told me: "Bill, if you can make it to eighty, I can almost guarantee that you will live to eighty-eight!" And based on actuarial statistics for octogenarian men, he *meant* it!

Living in a life care retirement community like Vicar's Landing, we learn early and are reminded often that *longevity* is a "two-edged sword" (Heb 4:12). On the one side, we rejoice in the health and happiness of friends and neighbors, many of whom are well into their nineties, and some who still thrive at a hundred and older. And we realize that we may be so blessed as to do likewise.

But, on the other side, our mortality is brought home to us every time a fresh rose appears on that sinister little round table across the hall from our mailboxes, discreetly announcing the death of yet another member of our close-knit community. Others in our little circles of friendship, and eventually we ourselves, live in fear of falling, of outliving our money, of slipping into senile dementia, of having a stroke, or a heart attack or a diagnosis of cancer or Parkinson's or Alzheimer's or *whatever*.

As Bishop Bartha of Hungary confessed to me so many decades ago, "There are some things worse than dying." He was right as I thought I understood back then, but I understand much more fully as I live and breathe here and now. So I want my family and friends to know and appreciate and respect that Sherri and I are neither afraid to live nor afraid to die: not now and not whenever God invites us to heaven.

If there is one last thing I want to leave with my loved ones and friends and anyone who happens to read my life story, it is what I said to my Royal Oak congregation in that prescient sermon titled "Death, Be not Proud" some eighteen years ago (see Appendix VI):

Friends, I've told you before—and, sad to say, I'll probably have occasion to tell you again—I believe in "the resurrection to life everlasting" with all my heart and soul and mind and strength. I couldn't do what I do for a living if I didn't believe in life after death and in the inseparability of our eternal destiny from the love of God we know in Christ Jesus our Lord (Rom 8:38–39).

In my "old age," I recognize that I am—and probably always have been—a true Calvinist Presbyterian at heart, for I find "amazing grace" and "blessed assurance" in St. Paul's predestinarian admonition:

> We do not live to ourselves, and we do not die to ourselves. If we live, we live to the Lord, and if we die, we die to the Lord; so then, whether we live or whether we die, we are the Lord's (Rom 14:7–8).

William R. Russell
Vicar's Landing, Ponte Vedra Beach, Florida
September 10, 2019

APPENDICES

APPENDIX I

A Sermon Preached by

The Reverend William R. Russell, BA, MDiv

in

The Church of St. Andrew and St. Paul

Montreal, Quebec

Palm Sunday, April 3, 1977

M Y ANNOUNCED SERMON TOPIC AND TEXT FOR this morning reflected my intention of completing my Lenten sermon series on Revelation's Seven Cities with a study of St. John's letter to the church at Philadelphia (Rev 3:7–13).

But during the past forty-eight hours, I have become convinced that the completion of a sermon series is not as compelling a concern in the minds and hearts of my parishioners today as is the consternation caused by the provincial government's publication on Friday of its White Paper on Language Policy. Oblique, if not direct, political comment has been an important part of this winter's sermons drawn from the apocalyptic books of the Bible; perhaps the time has come for a frank and forthright application of what I have been preaching to the developing political and cultural crisis in Quebec.

* * * * *

I HAVE FOUR MAIN THINGS TO SAY THIS MORNING, and each can

be summarized in a word and each word begins with a "c."

First, we must be calm. Friday's White Paper should not have come as a shock to any well-informed Quebecker: but *it did* because so many of us, both in the French majority and in the English and ethnic minorities, hoped for something more temperate, more reasonable, more conciliatory. Already, many people are responding very emotionally—even irresponsibly—to the news reports of the government's purported intentions, and high emotionalism is not going to help!

If you have not read the White Paper in its entirety, I urge you to do so. It may take you an hour or more, but I guarantee that the time and energy spent on studying the original—albeit "unofficial"—English text will prove both rewarding and re-assuring. There are some deeply disturbing attitudes and aspirations held by our present government; but I, for one, find it strangely calming at last to know where we all stand.

* * * * *

SECOND, WE MUST BE COMPASSIONATE. Had I preached this morning's scheduled sermon, I should have spoken about "the positive power of brotherly love." Never has that characteristically Christian motive been more important to the future of our country, our province, our city, our way of life.

We need compassion toward our francophone fellow citizens. Many of them—I am convinced *the majority* of them—are as troubled as we are by the repressive implications of the White Paper. Many of them are, indeed, victims of a centuries-old situation rife with injustices and inequalities—as often as not the legacy of their own political, social, and religious leadership—and today they find their legitimate expectations being exploited to accomplish the ideological ends of politicians elected in good faith, only months ago, to give our province "good government."

And we need compassion towards our anglophone friends and neighbours. These are trying times for many of us, and they are beginning to take their toll in terms of mental strain and emotional upheaval and physical exhaustion. Whether we are aware of it or not, few of us are at our best these days, and we must remember to treat one another with extra patience, extra sensitivity, extra encouragement, extra compassion. These "extras" become particularly important when we get into the complicated business of *staying* versus *leaving*. We all have different concerns and commitments, different problems and pressures: some of us are determined to stay, others anxious to leave. Let us not be too hard on one another, too judgmental of each other's motives, whichever choice we think we must make!

* * * * *

THIRD, WE MUST BE COURAGEOUS. Throughout this season's sermon series from Revelation and, indeed, in the earlier passages from Daniel, we have heard the Bible's reiterated encouragement to "hold fast," "stand firm," and "be of good courage." Jesus Christ is *still* King of kings and Lord of lords; God's will *will* be done—on earth as it is in heaven!

Congregations, communities, whole cultures have passed through dark and difficult days before in human history. Our accustomed and comfortable way of life may be threatened; our beloved and respected business and medical and social and religious institutions may face a pinched and problematical future; our options may be reduced to leaving with what we can or learning to live as a minority people in an alien nation. But others have weathered the same storms and discovered a God-

given strength and a glorious self-awareness that have brightened their troubles and blessed their distress.

On this Palm Sunday, of all Christian festival days, we can
take heart from the gospel record of our Lord, Jesus Christ, who
entered a troubled and threatening city, knowing full well that
the cries of "Hosanna!" would soon become the clamor of
"Crucify him!" In his calm nobility, his compassionate ministry,
his courageous sacrifice are surely to be found our comfort, our
inspiration, and our peace.

* * * * *

FOURTH AND FINALLY, WE MUST BE COMMUNICATIVE. Up until
now, many of us have felt that our best interests—and the best
interests of all Quebeckers—were best served by a low profile
and a faithful silence. Others of us have opted for shrill and im-
passioned outbursts, which have had little more effect than
"sound and fury, signifying nothing." A few of us have had the
privilege of direct access to officials of the present government
and have tried our best to make known the convictions and concerns of the people we represent.

Obviously, these strategies have all proven insufficient to
deflect the powers-that-be from their present hardline thinking.
What to do next? I am not sure, and others will doubtless come
forward in the days and weeks ahead with wise and useful suggestions. For the immediate present—today, during Holy Week,
certainly before Easter—I want to urge an outpouring of communication, particularly in the form of well-thought-out, well-
written letters from well-informed, well-prepared people like
yourselves, letters addressed to the premier, the minister of state
for cultural development, your local MNA, or whomever.

Because I like to practise what I preach—whenever possible—I have already written my letter. I plan to read it to you from this pulpit, in order that you may all know what I have said and where I stand. I have *not* consulted the kirk session or the board of trustees as to its contents; there has not been time since Friday; and besides, I do not want to implicate them directly or officially in what must be an intensely personal and uniquely difficult exercise for us all.

Because it may prove *too* difficult for some of you and because I realize that—like it or not—my writing to the provincial government as I have *does* somehow reflect upon this church and its congregation, I thought it might be well to provide an opportunity for a few of you to associate yourselves with me and my letter in a supportive way. (I also know full well that those of you who *do not* support my position will each be strongly motivated to write a letter disavowing it!) I have therefore left some blank sheets of church stationery on the tables in the narthex: if there should happen to be any signatures on any of them after service, I shall attach them to my letter before mailing it.

I have chosen to write to the Honourable Camille Laurin, minister of state for cultural development not only because it was he who chiefly drafted the White Paper but also because it was he who included me in a small group of anglophone Protestant clergy invited to his office to represent our constituencies' convictions and concerns before he prepared this infamous document. It is clear that our conversation had precious little impact on his thinking—all the more reason for me to write to him now in the following terms:

Palm Sunday, April 3, 1977
The Honourable Camille Laurin
Minister of State for Cultural Development
800 Victoria Square
Montreal, Quebec

Dear Dr. Laurin:

I am one of those Quebeckers who "momentarily feel per-
plexed" by the publication of your government's White
Paper on Language Policy.

Having read the "unofficial" English translation carefully in its entirety, I must compliment you on the document's clear and uncompromising presentation of your
government's ideas and intentions concerning the legislated
priority of the French language in Quebec. At the same
time, I must confess that I find the document's arguments
unconvincing and its conclusions unsupported even by the
evidence quoted.

More importantlly, I must protest the very spirit and sub-
stance of what is self-admittedly "a restrictive law," one
which less charitable commentators are already labelling
the repressive and coercive legislation of a totalitarian regime.

As a Canadian, I protest the White Paper's flagrant disregard of relevant provisions of the British North America
Act on the pretext that bilingualism has not been fully realized in Canada's other provinces: their wrongs do not
make you right!

As a Quebecker, I protest the White Paper's blatant assumption of the eventual separation of Quebec from the
rest of Canada and its withdrawal into what you describe
accurately but unintentionally as "the linguistic ghetto of
a small North American nation"; your much-promised referendum on independence has not yet been held!

As a Montrealer, I protest the White Paper's shortsighted
disregard of the adverse effects of such language policies

upon the "quality of life" in our city. The depression evident in the business community is matched by deteriorating morale within our medical, educational, social, and
religious institutions, caused in large measure by deeply-
felt doubts about the very future of those institutions, and
by the almost-daily departures of friends, neighbours, colleagues, and competitors to less threatening environments
in other Canadian provinces or the United States. With the
White Paper's language-of-education provision virtually
guaranteed to discourage immigration on other than a
short-term basis and the steady emigration of businesses
and individuals from the city and province, it is little
wonder that many non-francophone Quebeckers are increasingly convinced that your government's "hidden
agenda" is the elimination of all those you choose to think
of as "minorities."

As an anglophone, I protest the White Paper's pious as-
sertion that "there can be no question of abolishing English
education nor of rejecting the cultural tradition which has
inspired it until this day," when, in fact, the obvious intent
of the proposed legislation is to exert upon the English minority's institutions the very pressures towards extinction
about which the document complains in Chapter I concerning the situation of the French language in Quebec. Apparently, your government, despite its protestations, has
decided that it is English Quebec's turn to feel "insecure,
threatened, and vulnerable to attack"; surely you cannot
be surprised that, to paraphrase your own words, "this
chronic insecurity has bred legitimate feelings of distrust
which . . . give rise to an incurable xenophobia."

As a Christian, I protest the White Paper's warlike overtones in such phrases as "a reconquest by the French-speaking majority in Quebec." I protest the coercive implications
of recurring language about penalties, sanctions, fines, public denunciation, enforced compliance, etc. I protest the
equation of a "moral" response to this document with the
statement that "the essential thing is to accept it and apply

it." It is a noble aspiration to seek the "solidarity" of our traditional "two solitudes": the gospel of Jesus Christ teaches that reconciliation comes not through recrimination and repression but through forgiveness and forbearance.

As the pastor of a large and active congregation, I protest the complete absence from the White Paper of any reference to, or review of, the role of the churches or the requirements upon the churches, in your government's proposed legislation. Not only are we the keepers of civil registers for the Province of Quebec and thereby your colleagues in the recording of the most intimate human "rites of passage"; but we shall also, obviously, bear the same brunt of enforcement as other institutions directly associated with public administration. Have you no word for the churches? Or has your government already consigned us to the oblivion apparently awaiting all institutions not in eager compliance with your particular vision of the future?

At the outset of the White Paper, your government declares that it "wants the people to use this means to assess their rights and the tasks suggested for them." I regret to inform you that I assess my rights—and the rights of all Quebeckers, whether French- or English-speaking—to be unarguably and unacceptably abrogated; I assess my tasks to be not bland acceptance and meek application of your threatened legislation but open opposition and unstinting struggle against the enactment of the unfair and unwise language policies of your government as presently published.

Respectfully yours,
William R. Russell

* * * * *

IN ONE SENSE, I ALMOST FEEL AS THOUGH I ought to apologize to the congregation for having laid on you so weighty and controversial a subject on what has traditionally been a happy and festive church occasion. But in another—and more theological—sense, Palm Sunday has always been the most bittersweet of liturgical festivals: the "last hurrah" that introduces Holy Week and the poignant acclamation of a King whose crown is to be of thorns and whose enthronement is to be on a cross.

On the night in which he was betrayed, our Lord spoke long and hard to his disciples about the imminent ordeal of his passion and death. His last recorded words on that occasion are ones we might well carry into this ominous Holy Week, with its ever-intensifying approach to Easter: "I have said this to you, that in me you may have peace. In the world you have tribulation; but be of good cheer, I have overcome the world" (Jn 16:33).

Let us pray:

Blessed be Thou who hast come—and dost come again and again—in the name of the Lord! May our "Hosannas" be heartfelt not only on this festive day but on every occasion of our spiritual pilgrimage with Thee; that, knowing the Easter glory of Thy victory over sin and death, we may indeed and always be of good cheer; for Thy name's sake. Amen.

One Year Later . . .

A Sermon Preached by

The Reverend William R. Russell, BA, MDiv

in

The Church of St. Andrew and St. Paul

Montreal, Quebec

Sunday, April 2, 1978

Happy the man who stands firm when trials come. He has proved himself and will win the prize of life, the crown that the Lord has promised to those who love him (Jas 1:12).

D URING A WEDDING RECEPTION RECENTLY, an acquaintance whom I had not seen in a long time spoke to me appreciatively about the "Open Letter" I had written to Dr. Camille Laurin right after the publication of his White Paper on Language Policy. Her comments prompted me to go to my files to reread the sermon of which that Open Letter was a part and to discover that as unbelievable as it may seem, it was a year ago—exactly one year ago today—that I spoke to you about what I then called "the developing political and cultural crisis in Quebec."

A lot has happened in that year—some of it encouraging, some not so encouraging—and I thought it might be worthwhile to take a fresh look at the concerns and convictions that were foremost in our hearts and minds then. I want to do so in the particular context of the Presbyterian Church in Canada's Special Committee on National Unity, which I have chaired since last year's General Assembly. The committee met for two days here in Montreal at the middle of last month to finalize its report to the next General Assembly; and, while I am not at liberty to divulge the details of that report, I think you may be interested in knowing its general point of view and recommendations to the whole Church.

* * * * *

In the sermon that accompanied my Open Letter to Dr. Laurin, I appealed for four things from this congregation and from the English-speaking community of Montreal: that we be calm, compassionate, courageous, and communicative. In large measure, I think we have achieved those goals—not necessarily as a result of my sermon and letter—but because of the faithful determination and forthright leadership shown by many people from different sectors of our society.

In terms of communication, we have succeeded almost too well. After the initial shock of last April wore off, it seemed that everyone wanted to have something to say about Quebec separation or minority language rights or the unity of Canada. The federal government's Task Force on National Unity revealed just how diversely and passionately Canadians feel about the issues affecting the future of our country; the news media have featured the story so insistently that we are all growing tired of reading, hearing, or even speaking about national unity; and yet we remain almost morbidly fascinated by the possibilities of the dissolution of our nation and the disappearance—at least in Montreal—of our accustomed way of life.

Nevertheless, all this communication has served the useful purpose of informing all Canadians of the gravity of the issue confronting us. Within the Presbyterian Church's Special Committee, the degree of concern and the depth of informed opinion increased markedly between October, when first we met, and March. The rest of Canada evidently cares as much as we in

Quebec do, and that fact has been lost on neither those most stridently seeking separation, nor those feeling most beleaguered in their linguistic and geographical isolation from their fellow citizens in other parts of the country.

In terms of calm, compassion, and courage, however, I am not sure that, collectively, we are doing as well as we think. During my winter's illness, I became—of necessity—somewhat out of touch with how my parishioners and their families and friends and neighbours, were responding emotionally to the ongoing political and economic and cultural tensions in which we all live these days. Since my recovery, I have been trying hard to catch up, while at the same time trying to maintain some of that valuable objectivity my months of noninvolvement had given me.

What I see—or think I see—is a surface calm beneath which lurks a turbulence of anxiety and suspicion. Many people are not being honest with their friends and families—let alone with themselves—when they pretend that everything is more or less "business as usual," while they actually plan and prepare their escape should things get much worse. I say this to you quite plainly: my greatest fear for the future of this congregation— and of the English-speaking community in Montreal—is that so many of you are now so well-prepared to go that an unexpected or unfortunate turn of events may precipitate an "exodus" out of all proportion to the events in themselves.

* * * * *

As I reread my "Open Letter" to Dr. Laurin one year later, I was intrigued to realize how the issues and emphases it contained have become resolved or realigned with the passing weeks and months. In the opening paragraphs, I spoke of what some people were "already labelling the repressive and coercive legislation of a totalitarian regime." The words sounded harsh at the time—and still do—but their charge has been increasingly confirmed by the legislative programme of the present provincial government, and the anglophone minority in Quebec is clearly no longer alone in its concerned opposition to our government's intervention in so many aspects of public and private life, like, for example, its meddling in so serious a business as the planning of »*la fête de St. Jean Baptiste*«!

A year ago, bilingualism and biculturalism were bêtes noires—both within Quebec and beyond. Today, if my special committee's report is right, Canada's unique linguistic and cultural heritage is increasingly being perceived and appreciated—at least in the other provinces—as one of her greatest strengths and as one of her best bulwarks against assimilation into an ever-threatening North American political and economic entity.

A year ago, we were all aghast at the *Parti Québécois*' blatant assumption of the "eventual," indeed inevitable, "separation from the rest of Canada." The "inevitability" of that "eventuality" seems much less certain today. But more importantly the resolution of the question is now seen much more clearly to be a political and economic one, rather than a moral and spiritual one. My special committee may draw down the ire of Presbyterians on its head for reminding us that, and here I quote from our report: "no Christians have the right collectively to assert that any specific constitutional arrangement past, present, or future, possesses divine approval: all constitutions are basically human inventions." The quest for Canadian unity must be undertaken primarily in terms of political and economic considerations, and we Christians will do well to see to it that the basically constitutional battle is fought fairly, frankly, and fearlessly—whatever the outcome!

A year ago, the "warlike overtones" and "coercive implications" of the provincial government's cultural policies were frightening many Quebeckers. Today, the strident vocabulary has softened a little—just a little—and the government's coerciveness is being felt, as I have already suggested, by every sector of the Quebec community. In my opinion, this is an encouraging—albeit unpleasant—development in that it is making repression a political and economic issue, rather than a racial and cultural one, and will be dealt with, in due course, by tax revenues and poll results, effecting in the meantime, I hope, a genuine possibility of reconciliation among the mutually oppressed language and culture groups in the province.

A year ago, I spoke of the evident depression and deterioration in Montreal's "quality of life" as a result of the government's language policy. That sad state of affairs continues and hardly needs comment except that it is now out in the open, thanks, in large measure, to the directors of Sun Life putting it on the front page of everyone's mind! But, whereas *Parti Québécois* spokesmen used to claim that no economic sacrifice was too costly to make in the quest for political separation, an aide to the provincial minister of finance recently admitted to my special committee that the economic plight of the average Quebecker has long since replaced cultural sovereignty as the key preoccupation, behind the scenes, of the PQ cabinet. Here again, reality seems to be asserting itself encouragingly against theory in issues that affect the future of us all.

A year ago, it seemed that only English-speaking Quebeckers and French-speaking Canadians outside the province were much concerned about so-called "minority language rights." Now, my special committee seems convinced that the larger issue of minority rights in general has impressed itself strongly on the Canadian mind and that the time has come to press—and here I quote again: "all majority groups in all parts of our nation so to conduct their affairs that due recognition be given the rights of minorities within their bounds, to the end that all minority groups may exercise fully the rights and privileges of citizenship, within the inevitable limitations of their situations." To paraphrase St. Paul, *our* present sufferings may be as nothing compared to the greater weight of good that may come to all Canadians as a result of their determination to do away with the indirect causes of our distress!

And finally, a year ago, I questioned the role of the churches under the linguistic and cultural restraints about to be imposed by the provincial government. When he visited this congregation six weeks later, Dr. Laurin assured me that "nothing would change" as far as the churches were concerned; and so far, in a sense, nothing has. Some congregations and their ministers are taking refuge in that fact and are preparing themselves for a future as dwindling but determined repositories of the way things are.

But, Christian friends, continuing change—perhaps even accelerated change—is inevitable—separation or no—for our country and our province and our city and our people. Things will never again be the way they were. The future belongs to those who will prove themselves willing to adapt and advance, rather than resent and retreat. Our 175th Anniversary motto is ". . . to be continued." The cost of continuing, I insist, is going to be a fearless and faithful acceptance of the future far exceeding our proud and grateful appreciation of the past.

*   *   *   *   *

IN HIS GENERAL EPISTLE, ST. JAMES SPOKE OF THE happiness of those who stand firm when trials come. Our trials are upon us, and so far we have proven ourselves steadfast of spirit and firm of faith. I pray that that resolve may not weaken in trials yet to come but that our love of Christ and of his community here may open us eagerly to whatever God's future has in store so that the prize of life may indeed crown our continuing work and worship and witness in Christ's name.

Happy anniversary of our yesterdays! Happy anticipation of our tomorrows!

Let us pray:

> For the happy privilege of serving Thee, O God, in whatever circumstances Thy providence provides, we give Thee thanks and praise; praying only for such firmness of our faith and perfection of our patience that we may grow wise in waiting for Thy future and mature in meeting it for the sake of Jesus Christ, Thy Son, our Lord, in whose name we ask it. Amen.

Positively "No"

A Sermon Preached by

The Reverend William R. Russell, BA, MDiv

in

The Church of St. Andrew and St. Paul

Montreal, Quebec

Sunday, May 18, 1980

All you need say is "Yes" if you mean yes, "No" if you mean no; anything more than this comes from the evil one (Mt 5:37).

THE LAST THING I EXPECTED TO SEE ON THE third page of yesterday's *Gazette* was a photograph of our church's signboard announcing my sermon topic for this morning, let alone to hear from Herb Luft this morning asking permission to film part of our service for Pulse News! (If I could manage this kind of publicity every week, we would never have to advertise!)

At first, I was dismayed. I had promised the kirk session that I would keep "a low profile" during the Referendum debate, and I really thought that I had. My family and friends have been nervous about the possibility of retaliation against both individuals and institutions prominently associated with the "No" position, should it win by a narrow margin, and I had not intended to do anything to raise their anxiety level.

But then as I read the church advertising page further back in the same paper and thought about the sermon topics I had seen announced on other church signboards around town for today, I realized that most preachers apparently intend to act and speak as though it is "business as usual" this morning, de-

spite our being at the climax of perhaps the most serious political decision thus far in our nation's one hundred and thirteen
years' existence. Somewhere between page three and page thirty,
I decided that it is not such a bad thing that as the *Gazette* put
it, "concern about the referendum will find its way into *at least
one* of Montreal's churches this weekend" (italics mine).

Because I am concerned—as I know you are—about the referendum and about its present and potential impact on our lives
and the lives of our families, friends, and fellow Canadians. We
are all tired of hearing about the subject, and some of you may
have come to church today hoping to get away from it all, but
we are still preoccupied with the issues and questions and allegations and insinuations around which the debate has raged all
these weeks, and I wonder whether anyone can responsibly resist bringing it all to God in thought and prayer today.

* * * * *

I WANT TO ADDRESS THE FIRST PART OF MY concern to any
members or adherents or friends—or strangers for that matter—
in the congregation who support the "Yes" option. I am going
to vote "No" on Tuesday, and I hope that you can and will understand my motivation and respect my right to do so as much
as I understand and respect your quest for sovereignty association or even outright separation for Quebec.

I do not believe that I am a mindless federalist or an insensitive supporter of the status quo. Seven years ago, almost on
this day, I decided to accept the call of this congregation and to
move my family to Montreal from the United States because, in
part, my wife and I wanted our children to grow up in Canada
and in the best bilingual, bicultural context Canada had to offer.
We still want that for our children; we still enjoy it for ourselves.

My vote has to be "No"— *Positively* No!"

At the same time, I can accept that, for some of you, being *Québécois* is more compelling than being Canadian and that your definition of "homeland" is more closely drawn, geographically and culturally, than mine. I do not doubt the fervour of your patriotism, the attractiveness of your options, the courage of your convictions. Neither do I expect you to doubt mine.

What I hope you and your confrères beyond these walls and others far beyond the English-speaking community can understand is that my "No" is truly *positive*. It says "Yes" to Canada, my country; "Yes" to a federal political system which, though perpetually in need of renewal, is still more appealing to me than any other option presented thus far; "Yes" to a way of life that I find abundant, prosperous, optimistic, and diverse, especially in terms of bilingualism and biculturalism that is uniquely to be encouraged and enjoyed.

Unfortunately, my "Yes" to all that means a "No" on Tuesday—and, more than that, a "No" to every nationalistic political aspiration that would weaken or endanger Canada as I know it. But I am not saying "No" to you as a person or as a people. I am not saying "No" to the French language, the French-Canadian culture, the French-speaking majority impact on my life and my family and my work and my future.

* * * * *

IN HIS SERMON ON THE MOUNT, Jesus advises his followers: "All you need say is 'Yes' if you mean yes, 'No' if you mean no; anything more than this comes from the evil one" (Matthew 5:37).

After the outpouring of oratory from both sides during the past weeks and months, we can all agree with the second part of our Lord's observation! But the first part—about a simple "Yes" or a simple "No"—just is not that simple. Our Lord was talking about the extravagant oaths by which his countrymen would traditionally affirm their honesty or integrity and the impossibility of their ever fulfilling those oaths should their claims be proved false and so the meaninglessness of making such oaths in the first place.

Our Lord was not talking about referenda when he pleaded for a simple "Yes" or "No." In that sense, his words are a *pretext* rather than a text for my remarks this morning. Would that a simple "Yes" or "No" suffice on Tuesday as a simple answer to a simple question! But that is not the case; and so, the second half of my pre-referendum message is to those of you who will mark your ballot *pour le "Non."*

* * * * *

I PRAY YOU EACH AND EVERY ONE TO resolve to make your "No" a *positive* one. For too many years, we English-speaking Montrealers are perceived to have said too many "Nos" to too many things so that by now we are thought to be a bloc of obstructionists in the way of every legitimate French-Canadian aspiration. Should the "No" win on Tuesday, all that will be said again—as it has been said over and over in the weeks past—perhaps it will be said even more aggressively in a violence born of frustration.

Then we anglophones shall need to listen to some of Jesus's other bits of advice from the Sermon on the Mount: "If anyone hits you on the right cheek, offer him the other as well . . . love your enemies, and pray for those who persecute you . . . you must be perfect just as your heavenly Father is perfect" (Mt 5:39, 44, 48).

To bring reconciliation out of recrimination and peace out of prejudice and friendship out of fear, we should all make sure that our "No" says "Yes" — not only "Yes" to Canada and its federal system, renewed or otherwise; but also, and even more importantly, "Yes" to Quebec; "Yes" to its French-Canadian majority; "Yes" to its unique cultural blend and balance; "Yes" to its people's longing for a better definition of their constitutional place in the whole of Canada; "Yes" to Montreal, and our significant community within a community; "Yes" to the survival and strengthening of our institutional and personal way of life; "Yes" to our future and Montreal's and Quebec's, no matter what the results of Tuesday's vote.

Because come Wednesday, it is more likely that nothing will have changed. We shall be the same people with the same problems and opportunities, with the same neighbours and associates, with the same fears and frustrations, with the same economic and social and cultural and moral and political problems to address.

* * * * *

EVEN MORE IMPORTANTLY, God will not have changed or Jesus Christ or their Holy Spirit. The same "Lord of hosts is on our side our safety to maintain," of whom we sang but moments ago. The same Jesus Christ is with us who taught that God is love and that those who love God must love one another too. The same Holy Spirit is at work in our world who has turned the tide of human history again and again towards God's will and God's way.

Positively know that God has a hand in all this — though what his purposes are may not be clear to us or anyone else and may, in fact, be thwarted for a time by the ill-will and disobedience of those who love him not. God is still sovereign, still strength and refuge to those who trust in him, still "in straits a present aid!"

"Therefore, though the earth be moved, we will not be afraid!"

* * * * *

INSTEAD OF A PRAYER WITH WHICH TO CLOSE, I have asked Wayne Riddell to be prepared to play Canada's not-yet-official national anthem, "O Canada." I ask you to sing it and the hymn to follow immediately not as a national anthem and hymn but as a tribute and a prayer and an affirmation of faith:

From ocean unto ocean our land shall name you Lord
and, filled with true devotion, obey your sovereign word.

There may be some among us who feel that they can no longer sing these words this way: I hope that they will feel that they can at least stand silently at attention out of respect for a country that has given us all so much, even the freedom to vote on whether or not we want to destroy it.

When next we sing "O Canada" together, we shall at least know the outcome of the referendum vote. Let us each and all do our part: by voting "Yes" or "No" as conscience and conviction guide us, then let us trust the rest to God's unfolding providence.

Amen.

"*Merci*"

A Sermon after the Referendum

A Sermon Preached by

The Reverend William R. Russell, BA, MDiv

in

The Church of St. Andrew and St. Paul

Montreal, Quebec

Sunday, May 25, 1980

Let us come into his presence with thanksgiving,
and sing his psalms of triumph (Ps 95:2)!

A s WE STOOD SINGING "O Canada" at the start of this morning's service, I could not help thinking how differently we sang it at the end of worship last Sunday before the referendum.

Then, we sang it prayerfully with concern and apprehension and tears of heartfelt loyalty welling up in our eyes. Today, we sang it jubilantly with pride and confidence and sighs of relief coming deep from within.

The past seven days have seen such a surprising mix of unexpected events and unaccustomed emotions. So much has happened—so much has changed—since last Sunday's worship was intruded upon by the lights and distractions of a television news camera. I was a wreck, wondering whether I had done the right thing in letting the newsmen come and what their selective editing might do—for good or ill—to my congregation and my community. (Let me say, parenthetically, that I was more than pleased by the coverage CFCF-TV gave the service and the sermon last Sunday night, and I commend Herb Luft for the sensitivity and balance with which he reported our worship and my words on that occasion.)

On Monday, the tension across the city and province was made eerie by the complete blackout of media coverage on the referendum. Tuesday was unbelievably beautiful but electric with emotion as people crowded to the polls then waited for the results. It was not long into the evening before the trend of the voting became clear. Yet no one wanted to trust the computer forecasts: the *oui* side hoping it would not be so striking a defeat; the *non* side unable to believe that the victory could be so decisive.

By Wednesday, a strange calm had settled over the city. The violence so many feared in the aftermath of a *non* win was limited to a few minor and well-contained incidents, deplorable though even they were! Both Premier Levesque and Mr. Ryan were statesmanlike in their post-referendum public remarks as a collective shudder of relief went up from both sides that the months of argument and tension and waiting and uncertainty were finally at an end.

On Thursday, it was "back to normal"—the "normal" I remember from five or six years ago when we first lived in Montreal. Then on Friday, the tourists came to town, and I noticed more license plates from Ontario and New York and elsewhere than I can remember seeing in our streets on any weekend in years. (And if any of those tourists are in the congregation this morning, let me assure you that we *love* having you back!)

By today, the referendum seems for many like a bad dream to be quickly forgotten in the thrill of victory and the relaxation of anxiety too long lived with. For others, the focus of concern has already shifted to the rush for constitutional reform at the federal level and the fear that too little eventually too late may put us right back in the separatist situation from which we have but so recently escaped.

* * * * *

BUT IN THE BRIEF, precious interval between the euphoria of victory and the letdown of facing up to the problems and divisions that still beset our province and our nation, I hope we can have the grace to stop and say a few well-chosen words of thanks—*Merci*!— Thanks!" for all that went into what many of us now see as a second chance for Canada and Quebec and our role as a congregation and community in both.

First, I think we should say thanks to all those people in Quebec's English-speaking and ethnic communities who have remained courageous and strong and positive during these months—and, indeed, years—of anxiety and pressure and change. For a lot of us, it has been hard to stay and to stay confident of an acceptable outcome. We miss loved ones and friends who have moved away; we realize that everyday life has irrevocably changed, never again to have things as they were; we still face a future fraught with economic uncertainty and social unrest and political manoeuvering.

But so many of our relatives and friends and neighbours have risen magnificently to the challenge of the recent referendum, setting aside the usual divisions of partisan politics, perhaps even overcoming a lifelong aversion to becoming actively involved in the political process at all! They have written lists and made telephone calls and gone door-to-door and run errands and put up posters and served as agents and poll clerks and drivers on voting day, and the victory of the *non* is at least in some measure theirs.

To each and every one of you who actively worked to make the referendum a fair and full expression of public opinion, I say, "Thank you!" And to those of you who are now sitting back enjoying the fruits of others' labours, I voice the hope that you will find opportunities to say a few "Thank yous" too!

Next, I want to express a personal—and, I believe, a corporate—*Merci*! *Merci beaucoup à nos amis et voisins Québécois qui nous ont donnés, mardi passé, un beau cadeau—la vraie bienvenue à leur Québec dans notre Canada.*

The size of the *non* plurality leaves no room for doubt that at least one out of every two French-speaking Quebeckers feels about Quebec—and about Canada—pretty much as we English-speaking Quebeckers do and that is a statistic few of us would have really believed a week ago.

It is also a statistic upon which we can all begin to build the positive spirit of reconciliation and respect and renewal about which I preached and for which we fervently prayed last Sunday. In the first flush of winning the referendum, let us never forget that what we have really won is the opportunity to trust and be trusted in a milieu in which we are—and shall always remain—a minority: the freedom to remain proudly Canadian in a proud and aggressive Québec, the chance to help build a just and tolerant and righteous and godly community that transcends language and culture and ethnicity and fear.

Third, I want to say a similar "*Merci!*"—and one in which I hope you will join just as wholeheartedly—*Merci beaucoup aux Québécois pour le Oui, qui acceptent gracieusement la décision democratique du peuple de Québec, et qui éspèrent, comme nous, l'avenir d'une nouvelle histoire Québécois—une histoire d'amitié, et de progrès, et de fierté pour notre province et pour notre pays.*

That last Tuesday night's incalculable defeat for those who would divide Quebec from Canada passed as uneventfully and peacefully as it did is another great gift for which we should all be profoundly thankful, for it offers real hope that friendship and mutual respect and common interests now have a chance to rebuild so much of what has been destroyed over the past few years of animosity and suspicion and restriction.

Finally, I want to give God glory for his providential part in the events of the past week. Last Sunday, we prayed for a fair and peaceful and happy outcome from the referendum, whatever the actual results. That we have had, and more!

It is sometimes easier to pray when things look bad than when they look good. Fear and uncertainty seem to lend prayer a certain eloquence and fervency. But if we really beseeched God last Sunday to guide and guard our people and our province through the dangers of the past seven days, ought we not to give him the praise—and the credit—now that things have worked out so well?

And by that I do not mean the vote. I would never presume to suggest that God is on the side of the *non* as over against the *oui*! God is "on the side" of *all* his people and only "has his hand in it" (as I put it last Sunday) to help *us* work out *our* problems freely and fairly and faithfully. We and our fellow Quebeckers and our fellow Canadians will need all kinds of providential power in the months and years ahead: thanks be to God for showing us so triumphantly this week what his goodwill can do!

* * * * *

TODAY IS PENTECOST—the birthday of the church—and we have made only passing reference to it in our hymns and anthems and prayers.

Yet this *is* a real *birth-day* for *our church* at least. We have had added to our strength today these eleven fine new friends: I wonder how many other churches in Montreal are celebrating

Pentecost—let alone the referendum victory—as positively as that! We have received great gifts of love and trust and affirmation from the French-speaking majority in whose midst we live and work and witness and succeed. We have seen the hand of God at work for good in our world and have found fresh hope and reassurance in the evidence of his power. We have received the fire of the Holy Spirit from a strange and un-expected source this week, and we are aglow with a quiet confidence and an inner peace.

We have much for which to say "Thanks!"—"*Merci!*"—thanks to one another—*merci l'un à l'autre—merci à Dieu*—thanks be to God. Amen.

Let us pray together, using the words of the Unison Collect for Pentecost Day printed in the order of service:

> Mighty God: by the fire of Thy Spirit Thou hast welded disciples into one holy Church. Help us to show the power of Thy love to all people, so they may turn to Thee, and, with one voice and one faith, call Thee Lord and Father, through Jesus Christ. Amen.

The "No" That's a "Yes"

A Sermon Preached by

The Reverend William R. Russell, BA, MDiv

in

Knox Presbyterian Church

Windsor, Ontario

Sunday, June 1, 1980

On the day of the opening of the 1980 General
Assembly of the Presbyterian Church in Canada

*And now faith, hope, and love abide, these three: and the
greatest of these is love* (1 Cor 13:13).

I N OUR CHURCH IN CENTER-CITY MONTREAL, we have sung "O Canada" during morning worship on the past two Sundays.

Two weeks ago—just forty-eight hours *before* the Referendum—we sang it prayerfully with concern and apprehension and tears of heartfelt loyalty welling up in our eyes and a genuine question in our minds as to whether or not we would ever be able to sing it again quite that way in the Province of Quebec.

Last Sunday—in the unexpectedly peaceful and overwhelmingly positive *aftermath* of the Referendum—we sang "O Canada" jubilantly with pride and confidence and sighs of relief coming deep from within and a genuine gratitude to God for so happy an end to the months—and even years—of tension and uncertainty and grief and fear through which we English-speaking Quebeckers and our French-speaking friends and neighbours and, indeed, the rest of Canada have come.

Yet, ours was not—even on the night of the Referendum results—the noisy, boisterous, exultant celebration of "victory" that I gather broke out in other parts of Canada. Those of you who watched the television coverage and saw the half-empty arena of the "No" committee during M. Claude Ryan's long speech that night may have been surprised at an apparent lack of enthusiasm; but we English Montrealers were not. Many feared violence in the streets and stayed home to be safe, a fear which, I am glad to say, proved ill-founded, largely, I believe, due to the overwhelming plurality for the "*Non*," and the realization by even the most ardent separatists that over fifty percent of the French-speaking voters that day had chosen not to approve a process of negotiation that might have led to the breakup of Canada.

But, even more than fear, it was fatigue and frustration that kept Montrealers—French and English—from feeling too exuberant about the Referendum results. We have already lost so much because of Quebec separatism, and many of us suspect that there may be still more losses ahead. We have lost relatives and friends who have moved away to other parts of Canada; we have lost jobs and income and future prospects as companies large and small have fled the economic and political uncertainties of our province; we have lost the excellence we can no longer maintain in our depleted and demoralized schools and hospitals and churches and clubs; we have lost the faith that the rest of Canada ever really cared about us as individuals and families and congregations and communities caught in the separatist storm. We remember and we grieve that until a few short months ago many, many Canadians outside Quebec virtually abandoned us loyal Canadian Quebeckers—English as well as French—with a contemptuous "Let them go!" At such high cost, there is little joy in winning, only profound relief that the worst may be over.

Maybe! But we cannot help wondering—and worrying—whether the extravagant promises of constitutional reform and renewed federalism can ever be kept, given the attitudes and aspirations of the other nine provincial governments and the fact that Quebec still has a separatist premier for whom the only political gain in the process will come from subtle obstruction of every effort to negotiate a "new" Canada. Nor should the rest of Canada be fooled into believing that the defeat of "sovereignty association" means the inevitable defeat of the *Parti Québécois* in our next provincial election.

Political thinking in Quebec has a logic all its own: the *Péquistes* have given us good government, all things considered; and M. René Lévesque made a gracious—even magnanimous—speech on the night of his defeat, and a sympathetic backlash to the referendum results may well sweep him back into power when he next goes to the polls. Should that happen and should the projected constitutional conferences fail to offer a renewed federation acceptable to all the provinces, we may well see separatism raise its ugly head again—and worse—not only in Quebec but elsewhere in Canada too!

My mood, post-referendum, may be subdued, but it is not pessimistic. Contrary to our Lord's injunction in the Sermon on the Mount that we *"just say 'Yes' or 'No'—anything else comes from the evil one"* (Mt 5:37)—which was my sermon text (or, rather, *pretext*) on the Sunday before the Referendum—French and English Quebec has spoken a resounding "No" that is a profound "Yes!" A careful reading of the Referendum results suggests that better than one out of every two *Québécois*—evenly distributed all across the province—feels about Canada pretty much as we English-speaking Quebeckers do. That is a statistic we could not have believed two weeks ago and that is a statistic the rest of Canada can never again dismiss with contempt!

Quebec's "No" says "Yes" to Canada: now we wait to hear Canada say "Yes" to us. We wait to hear Canada say a genuine "Yes" to our unique cultural heritage and language problems. We wait to hear Canada say a gracious "Yes" to our efforts to resume our rightful and loyal place in the mainstream of Canadian life. We wait to hear Canada say a generous "Yes" to certain political and economic and social aspirations which, though often uttered in French, are not really very different from those being articulated in an oily Western accent or a salty Maritime one! We wait to hear Canada say a Godly "Yes" to the efforts at reaffirmation and reconciliation that are so desperately needed not only within our province but between Quebec and the rest of Canada.

Gerry Doran promised you a Christian perspective on the Quebec Referendum, and after these ten minutes or more of other stuff, here it comes. Last Sunday, I urged my congregation to give God glory for his providential part in the referendum process through which we have come. In the weeks preceding the vote, we prayed faithfully "for a fair and peaceful and happy outcome from the Referendum, *whatever* the actual results," and that's a direct quote from one of my previous sermons.

Our prayers were certainly answered and more! And, by the way, I do not mean the vote itself. No one inside of Quebec or out should ever presume to suggest that God is on the side of the "*Non*" as over against the "*Oui*," that God is *for* national unity and *opposed* to political separation. I believe, and have repeatedly reminded my people, that God is "on the side" of *all* his people and only exercises his providence to give us the best possible chance to work out our problems freely and fairly and faithfully.

There can be no gloating among Christians that one side has

"won" and another "lost," in Quebec or anywhere else. We have *all lost* in this struggle: lost precious relationships and proud reminiscences and personal respect. And we have *all won*: a new opportunity, a second chance, to prove what the grace of God and the love of Christ and the goodwill of the Holy Spirit can do to heal a nation and bless its people and up-build the Kingdom in our midst.

The opportunities for personal reconciliation and public affirmation are "fields white unto harvest" for the Christian churches not only in Quebec but in the rest of Canada. The francophone vote in our Referendum last week is a great gift for which we should all be fervently thankful. For us English-speaking Quebeckers, it is, at last and at best, *une vraie bienve-nue*—a real welcome—into the new Quebec in which we have for so long been made to feel an unwelcome, unwanted minor-ity; for all of Canada, the "No" that's a "Yes" holds out real hope that by God's grace, friendship and mutual respect and common interests now have a chance to rebuild so much of what has been destroyed over the past few years of animosity and suspicion and resentment on both sides.

Seizing these opportunities may not be easy. Our French-Ca-nadian friends and neighbours are in worse straits than we An-glophones. Families, parishes, and communities have been split in two by the arguments *pour le Oui ou le Non*; political dreams and economic hopes have been blasted, especially for many young Québécois, by the defeat of their option and the defection of their employers; fear, envy, anger, and violence seethe, sup-pressed beneath the outward calm in the streets of Montreal. Things can never again be the way they once were, and English Canada—inside the province and beyond—is seriously mistaken if it thinks that everything is settled now that the Referendum is a thing of the past.

But *love can* work wonders, and the love of our Lord Jesus Christ that compels us Christians to "turn the other cheek" and to "walk the second mile" (or "kilometre" as the *Good News Bible* corrects us!) and to pray for those whom yesterday we thought to be our enemies—*that* love can win where our politics have proven a dead loss!

And *faith can* move mountains, especially the faith of men and women of goodwill that God is still at work in human history and by his grace can guide us to equitable solutions and honest compromises and just provisions for our future as a nation under his hand.

And *hope can* conquer all, when it is the hope enflamed by the Holy Spirit to encourage the faint-hearted and uphold the weak and comfort the distressed and reassure the suspicious and calm the violent in every segment of our society.

"Now faith, hope, love remain, these three, but the greatest of these is love." We who live as an English-speaking minority in the Province of Quebec love Jesus Christ and his church and the relatives and friends and neighbours and enemies he has given us who happen to speak French. We believe that by his grace they love us, too, and are prepared to walk faithfully and hopefully into the future he is preparing for us together.

We dare to ask that those of you who love Jesus Christ and live as an English-speaking majority in the rest of Canada will remember to love us and our *Québécois* colleagues and the minorities in your midst who happen not to speak English as their mother tongue and that you will join us in the faithful, hopeful quest for God's good purposes for our Canada 'til Christ's Kingdom comes.

Let us pray:

Certain that nothing can separate us from the love of Christ—neither death nor life; neither angels nor heavenly rulers nor earthly powers; neither the present nor the future; neither the world above nor the world below—nothing in all creation—we give ourselves gladly, faithfully, hopefully to that love and glorify the God who does all things well through Christ Jesus, his Son, our Lord. Amen.

APPENDIX VI

"Death, Be Not Proud"

A Sermon Preached by

The Reverend Dr. William R. Russell

in

The First Presbyterian Church of
Royal Oak, Michigan

Sunday, September 9, 2001

O death, where is thy victory?
   O death, where is thy sting? . . .
   But thanks be to God who gives us the victory through
our Lord Jesus Christ (1 Cor 15:55, 57).

WHEN I FINALLY TOLD HER WHAT THIS Sunday's sermon was going to be about, Liz Spry's shoulders slumped.

Earlier in the week, I had told her that, depending on the subject of the cover story in this week's issue of *TIME Magazine*, I hoped I might extend the summer season one more week and do a sermon based on whatever *that* would turn out to be. Well, it turned out to be an assessment of whether or not General Colin Powell is doing a good job as the US Secretary of State—and I couldn't readily see a preaching theme in that!

What I did feel a burden of soul to deal with this morning even though it is the start of a new school year and the beginning of a new church program season and a Sunday on which there may be many first-time visitors in worship, and what I still feel heavily on my heart, is the extraordinary pain of the past three weeks in which so many families of our congregation have shared the faith-challenging experiences of death and burial, bereavement and mourning, sorrow and relief, and pride and joy.

Death is never an easy sermon subject, and it's certainly not so today of all days. But six deaths in three weeks in a family of faith the size of ours is felt by almost everyone somehow, at some level in some context of personal grief or loss or sympathy or identification.

Death itself is never easy to deal with, whether it's the "long goodbye" of Alzheimer's or the sudden shock of a heart attack; the lingering indignity of cancer or the "tough love" of turning off a respirator; the heartrending loneliness of an old person who has outlived mind as well as body, family as well as friends; or the heartbreaking untimeliness of a too-young husband, father, brother, son; the losing of a loved one or the facing up to our own mortality.

In the past month, some of us have been through it all. Others of us have suffered *other* griefs and losses: the diagnosis of an incurable illness, the accidental death of a loved one or friend, the failure of a business or a career or a marriage or a dream.

All of us know someone, like someone, care about someone, who has recently felt sad or mournful or aggrieved or lost. And we've done what we do at times like these: we've baked casseroles or made cookies or sent flowers or prayed prayers or signed guest registers or hugged one another or cried in private or worshiped in public to give God the glory for the loved one or friend we have loved and lost awhile.

It's the *worship* that has impressed me the most: the funerals and memorial services, whether packed and powerful sanctuary worship punctuated by grand anthems from our chancel choir or king's men or whether private and poignant chapel services with only the nearest and dearest (who sometimes number very few), this family of faith has reached out with its rich architectural, liturgical, and musical resources to serve grief-stricken families and far beyond to the community at large in ways that have been wonderful and memorable and comforting and inspirational.

One of the funeral prayers I often use thanks God for "the unquenchable trust deep in the Christian heart that life does not end with death," That's what our mutual ministry has been about these past weeks in particular and much of the time in general. Stripped to its essentials, we preach and proclaim that God loves us and that Christ died for us and that

> neither death, nor life, nor angels, nor rulers, nor things present, nor things to come, nor powers, nor height, nor depth, nor anything else in all creation, will be able to separate us from the love of God in Christ Jesus our Lord (Rom 8:38–39, NRSV).

That's a marvelous message too many of us take too much for granted until its power and promise become abruptly relevant to our own lives or the lives of those we love and respect and admire and depend on. "Life does not end with death," and whether that thought strikes terror to your conscience or produces "peace that passes understanding" for your heart and mind and soul, it's what our Lord Jesus Christ lived and taught and suffered and died and rose again and ascended into heaven and reigns at the right hand of God the Father through time and eternity to tell us and to call us to *live* each and every day of our lives as though it were *true* because it *is*!

When I went back to school for one last year—the infamous "Grade 13" once offered in Ontario—I had to memorize a lot of poetry. (Do kids today still memorize poetry? Or do they just call it up on their computers?) One of the most memorable poems—it has stuck with me all these years—was a sonnet by the sixteenth and seventeenth-century English cleric, John

Donne. It begins:

> Death, be not proud, though some have called thee
> Mighty, and dreadful, for thou art not so;
> For those, whom thou think'st thou dost overthrow,
> Die not, poor Death, nor yet canst thou kill me.

And it ends:

> Why swell'st thou then?
> One short sleep past, we wake eternally,
> And death shall be no more. Death, thou shalt die.

"Death, be not proud, . . ." I say those words to myself as I enter the sanctuary or chapel for every one of the funerals or memorial services we do. "Death, be not proud, . . ." for this beloved one, "death shall be no more . . . nor yet canst thou kill me."

We have a Lord of whom to be proud. We have a gospel in which to be confident. We have a faith through which to find peace. We have a family of faith amongst whom to find solace and support and strength. We have a tradition of praise and prayer that puts even death in its proper perspective.

I have been tremendously proud of those we have loved and lost awhile who went to meet death knowingly, courageously, fearlessly, faithfully. I have been tremendously proud of the bereaved families who have planned their departed's "final offices of faith and love" with such care and compassion and concern to make a mighty witness to our faith in the resurrection to life everlasting.

I have been tremendously proud of my colleagues in ministry, both staff and lay, for their untiring efforts to assist me in ministering to the spiritual and practical needs of the families who have lost loved ones. I have been tremendously proud of our chancel choir and king's men and their conductor, Liz Spry. They have been profoundly affected by three of these recent deaths, and they have literally sung their hearts out for the comfort, encouragement, and inspiration of those who had gathered to pay final tribute to Francis Luttrell, Charlotte McCray, and Jeff Jarman.

I have been tremendously proud of our congregation as it has closed ranks like a true family of faith to surround these various bereaved families with affection and admiration and assistance. To each and all, "well done, good and faithful servants" (Mt 25:21)!

And, above all, I have been tremendously proud to be able to read and interpret old, familiar, comforting, inspirational passages of scripture that proclaim our resurrection faith, like that one from 1 Corinthians 15, and undergird our confidence that "life does not end with death" and that "one short sleep past, we wake eternally, and Death shall be no more."

Friends, I've told you before—and, sad to say, I'll probably have occasion to tell you again—I believe in the resurrection to life everlasting with all my heart and soul and mind and strength. I couldn't do what I do for a living if I didn't believe in life after death and in the inseparability of our eternal destiny from the love of God we know in Christ Jesus our Lord.

When times are toughest, I meditate upon the "suffering servant" foretold in the prophecy of Isaiah: "despised and rejected . . . a man of sorrows and acquainted with grief . . . stricken, smitten by God and afflicted."

Sometimes, I can't help identifying the suffering servant with myself or someone to whom I am trying to minister, but I always end up remembering to whom the passage is *really* testifying. It was *our Lord Jesus Christ* who was "wounded for our transgressions . . . bruised for our iniquities; upon him was the chastisement that made us whole, and with his stripes we are healed" (Is 53, selected references).

It was his death that robbed Death of its pride and power; it was his resurrection that opened the way for me, for you, for all believers, into life everlasting; it is his living presence in which we face life and death and dying and rising and eternity; it is his love, sacrificed on a cross, raised from a tomb, ascended to the right hand of God the Father, in which I have confidence and through which I commend my spirit and yours to the everlasting arms of the Almighty.

"Death, be not proud . . ." Oh no!

"O death, where is thy victory? Thanks be to God who gives us the victory through our Lord Jesus Christ" (1 Cor 15:55, 57)!

Amen.

"Even Though . . ."

A Sermon Preached by

The Reverend Dr. William R. Russell

in

The First Presbyterian Church of
Royal Oak, Michigan

Sunday, September 16, 2001

Even though the fig-trees have no fruit
  and no grapes grow on the vines,
even though the olive-crop fail
  and the fields produce no grain,
even though the sheep all die
  and the cattle-stalls are empty,
I will still be joyful and glad,
  because the Lord God is my savior (Hab 3:17–18, TEV).

A*UNQUE.*"

"*Aunque.*"
"*Aunque.*"

I first heard this plaintive-sounding Spanish word years ago during worship in the Central Baptist Church in the heart of La Paz, Bolivia. I had been told that this was the largest Protestant congregation in an overwhelmingly Roman Catholic country and that I was to represent the United Bible Societies as the guest preacher—through an interpreter, I hasten to say—on the occasion of a very special anniversary.

As my wife Ann and I arrived on a hot, humid Sunday morning, we bypassed a splendid stucco-and-stained-glass church façade and stumbled through a dark, narrow, rough stone-paved passageway between two high walls and under a plywood canopy of sorts, into a large, plain, even ugly multipurpose room packed with smiling, singing, swaying Bolivianos obviously energized by their worship and their fellowship and their faith.

As the service progressed inexorably toward the sermon, the way Baptist services all over the world tend to do—and Presbyterian services, too, for that matter—the pastor and people took up a haunting litany of prayer and praise, each exchange beginning with the repeated word "*Aunque.*" From the printed-in-Spanish order of service, I figured out that the litany was based on a passage of scripture from the Old Testament prophecy of Habakkuk and eventually I fumbled with my ever-ready *Good News Bible* to find the English equivalent upon which, perhaps, to base my sermon's opening remarks.

Now, the book of Habakkuk is usually regarded as the work of a very minor Hebrew prophet about whom we know almost nothing except the surmise that he lived and witnessed to the word of God around the end of the seventh century and the turn of the sixth century BC, during the height of the rise to world prominence of the Babylonian empire, masterminded by Nebuchadnezzar, the Chaldean military genius who besieged and eventually destroyed Jerusalem in 597 BC and took the elite of the Jews into forty years of captivity in Babylon.

Habakkuk was a very unpopular prophet, for he saw clearly but unwillingly that God was somehow at work for good—for judgment and redemption—in Nebuchadnezzar's attacks and sieges and victories:

> O Lord, how long must I call for help before you listen, before you save us from violence? Why do you make me see such trouble? How can you endure to look on such wrongdoing?...
>
> But how can you stand these treacherous, evil men? Your eyes are too holy to look at evil, and you cannot stand the sight of people doing wrong. So why are you silent while

they destroy people who are more righteous than they are (Hab 1:2–3, 13)?

Habakkuk climbed into a watchtower to await God's reply. It was not long in coming:

> But the time is coming quickly, and what I show you will come true. It may seem slow in coming, but wait for it; it will certainly take place, and it will not be delayed. And this is the message: "Those who are evil will not survive, but those who are righteous will live because they are faithful to God" (2:3b–4).

This was, of course, the same prophetic voice that spoke so powerfully to Martin Luther two millennia later, and became the basis for the Protestant Reformation's doctrine that "the just shall live by faith."

But the main point of Habakkuk's prophecy was that the people of God were *not* as righteous as they thought they were: wealth and greed were the standards of their society; crime and murder were commonplace; drunkenness, lust, violence, rape of the environment and of the impoverished went unchecked and unchallenged; thievery, shame, deceit, and idolatry had at last brought terrible judgment on God's chosen people. And, at the end, the voice of God thundered: "The Lord is in his holy Temple; let everyone on earth be silent in his presence" (2:20)!

* * * * *

SISTERS AND BROTHERS IN THE LORD, I don't think I have to labor the point. The word of God is as ageless as eternity and as up-to-date as tomorrow.

We mourn the innocent victims of last Tuesday's atrocities: the men and women (and probably children) buried in the rubble of the World Trade Center; the service personnel blasted into a crater in the Pentagon; the passengers and crews of the hijacked jetliners; the police and firefighters and rescue workers lost to the implosion of the twin towers; the bereft families back home; the now-homeless neighbors of the blasts; the about-to-be-laid-off employees of firms already gone out of business or soon to cut back drastically. We grieve the suddenness, the untimeliness, the senselessness of their deaths, and we honor the courage and sacrifice and selflessness of those who are working so hard to rescue any who may still be alive and to recover the remains of those who are in the embrace of the Almighty.

And surely as individual victims of these unspeakable acts of terror they *were* "innocent": innocent of any particular sins or crimes or secrets worthy of such a horrendous end.

But America as a whole is not so "innocent," not so "righteous" as we would like to think. Last night, as I was getting ready for bed, I flipped through the channels offered by my cable company, at once a little relieved and a little repulsed at the rapidity with which things were getting back to normal on TV. The commercials seemed more squalid, somehow, the humor more coarse, the violence more ludicrous, the sex more gratuitous, the corruption of virtues and values more pervasive and more appalling than I had noticed before.

Wealth and greed, crime and murder, drunkenness, lust, cruelty, rape, theft, shame, deceit, idolatry. My heart grieved anew, my spine quivered with apprehension, my head bowed in repentance for the *un*righteousness I have seen and done and ignored and allowed and been party to, and my prayer echoed Habakkuk's "O Lord, how long?"

Biblical history is full of the disturbing truth that the God and Father of our Lord Jesus Christ—the God who is at work in everything for good, the God of love—is also the God of truth and justice, of righteousness and judgment, of the beginning . . . and the end.

In Washington's National Cathedral on Friday, Billy Graham called for a spiritual revival in America. Though no one will notice—or care—I'm going to go him one better: I think the United States of America—and certainly its neighbors to the north and south—need a spiritual *revolution*! Vengeance is not God's will for us: repentance is! Military strikes against the perpetrators of these atrocities will not strike out the pernicious evils at the very heart of America's values and vices. Reasoned justice, genuine mercy, deep humility (the prophetic virtues proclaimed by Micah) will serve our nation and our world better.

* * * * *

AND FAITHFULNESS, ABOVE ALL, FAITHFULNESS.

"*Aunque*" is Latin-American Spanish for "even though." The litany I heard all those years ago in La Paz was based on the closing verses of Habakkuk's heart wrenching prophecy:

> *Even though* the fig trees have no fruit
> and no grapes grow on the vines,
> *even though* the olive crop fails
> and the fields produce no corn,
> *even though* the sheep all die
> and the cattle stalls are empty,
> I will *still* be joyful and glad,
> because the Lord God is my Savior (Hab 3:17–18 TEV).

"Even though . . . even though . . . even though. . . ."

And the *anniversary* they were celebrating with such exuberance? Theirs had been a large, prosperous, self-satisfied, cantankerous, judgmental congregation until two years before, when the roof of their sanctuary had collapsed during Sunday school before morning worship, leaving only the front façade standing and twelve little children dead in the rubble. From that tragedy they had learned much about themselves and their faith and their Lord; and they were celebrating that *revolution* in their spirituality and the news that, after twenty-four months of struggle, the insurance companies and the city bureaucracy had finally agreed to let them *tear down* their false front and *build* a *new* church.

"Even though . . . even though . . . even though . . .

I will *still* be joyful and glad because the Lord God is my Savior."

And the "*still*"? That's the *Good News Bible* translation of the same Hebrew word that appears in the Greek New Testament on our Lord's lips in the Garden of Gethsemane and that we read in English as "*nevertheless.*"

Friends, I daren't say more. I believe with all my heart that a life of faithfulness is stretched constantly between "even though" and "nevertheless," and never more so than for America and Americans in these days of grief and loss and anger and uncertainty and fear and turmoil.

God is *good* and with Jesus Christ as our Lord and only Savior, God wants *us* to be good. God is *loving* and with Jesus Christ as our Lord and only Savior, God wants *us* to be loving. God is *faithful* and with Jesus Christ as our Lord and only Savior, God wants *us* to be faithful.

Even though . . . even though . . . even though . . . I will still be joyful and glad, because the Lord God is my Savior.

Amen!

"Freedom and Fear Are at War . . . And God Is not Neutral Between Them!"

A Sermon Preached by

The Reverend Dr. William R. Russell

in

The First Presbyterian Church of

Royal Oak, Michigan

Sunday, September 23, 2001

Beloved, let us love one another because love is from God; everyone who loves is born of God and knows God. . . . In this is love, not that we loved God but that he loved us and sent his Son to be the atoning sacrifice for our sins. . . . God is love, and those who abide in love abide in God, and God abides in them. . . . There is no fear in love, but perfect love casts out fear. . . . We love because he first loved us (1 Jn 4:7, 10, 16b, 18, 19, NRSV).

I AM NOT AN AMERICAN.

As most of you realize, I am a Canadian by birth and by citizenship, and through two "tours of duty" ministering to congregations in the United States—the first for nine years right out of seminary in churches in New York and New Jersey and the second now for almost twelve years on Chicago's North Shore and here in Royal Oak—it hasn't made much of a difference one way or the other.

I pay taxes just like other Americans; when I was younger, I registered for the draft and carried my card diligently in my wallet until I was about forty; now that I'm getting older, I look forward to Social Security staying solvent long enough to finance my eventual retirement. The main thing I can't do as a resident alien—an immigrant without citizenship—is vote, and that right withheld has always made me very cautious about speaking out on issues of American politics over which I can exercise no influence at the ballot box and therefore prefer to remain silent. And *that* determination has saved me many a squabble over the past thirty-seven years of ordained ministry.

But if ever there has been a moment in my almost twenty years of living in the United States when I truly wished I were an American, it must have been last Thursday night when President Bush spoke to the nation. I was so proud of the president and of the show of unanimity in the Congress and of the patriotism waved and shouted and sung and prayed across the country.

*   *   *   *   *

AMERICA IS AT WAR WITH TERRORISM, and America has challenged its allies to declare themselves at war with terrorism, too, or be regarded as at war with us.

As the TV talking heads have been reminding us for days now, this will be a war unlike any other in which the United States has fought. There will be new rules of engagement, like whether defenders of our homeland may shoot down a commercial airliner full of innocent passengers because a few suicidal terrorists have hijacked it and may divebomb it into a building full of people and kill thousands more victims than the airplane itself holds. There will be strange alliances: suddenly, countries and regions we've never heard of and know little about are strategically vital, and the goodwill of Pakistan is the diplomatic focus of the secretary of state. So far, it seems, nothing has happened: no retaliatory air strikes, no televised minute-to-minute land invasions, no missiles launched from offshore naval vessels, no proven enemy, no declaration of war as such!

Media pundits speculate about when (and whether) the president will act, especially now that Congress has given him such sweeping authority and an initial forty billion dollars to bankroll the effort! And act he will, says President Bush:

We will direct every resource at our command—every means of diplomacy, every tool of intelligence, every instrument of law enforcement, every financial influence and every necessary weapon of war—to the destruction and the defeat of the global terror network

We will not tire, we will not falter, and we will not fail.

And I think he *means* it!

I'm more concerned about how *the rest of us* will act as our nation goes on a war footing against an unnamed enemy in an unknown wilderness on an unprecedented search-and-destroy mission that may end up killing as many "innocent" people as the attacks on the World Trade Center and the Pentagon and leave America looking as bloodthirsty and irresponsible as the terrorists we seek to eradicate.

Our president has urged us to "live our lives" and "hug our children," to be "calm and resolute, even in the face of a continuing threat," to live by the same principles for which we claim to fight, and single out no one "for unfair treatment or unkind words because of their ethnic background or religious faith," to continue to be generous in contributions, patient with the delays and inconveniences of tighter security confident in the strengths of the American economy, and prayerful "for the victims of terror and their families, for those in uniform and for our great country."

But even now, the media are full of reports of criminal scams to divert the funds contributed by well-meaning but ill-advised donors supporting every kind of spontaneous appeal for aid. The families of victims are being deceived and defrauded by heartless crooks playing on their fears, their hopes, and their posted information about those they have "loved and lost awhile." The high-end retail shops at the base of the twin towers of the World Trade Center have somehow been looted already, even before the bodies of the victims have been found and removed! Arab-Americans—Christians as well as Muslims—are being harassed and hurt by ignorant racists who can't differentiate between an enemy and a lookalike. And to add insult to injury, it appears likely that terrorist "insiders" here in the United States and abroad manipulated the financial markets to reap huge cash benefits because of their foreknowledge of the disaster to come!

Our president has said that freedom and fear are at war. And he is right. A great statesman in declaring another great war advised that the only thing we have to fear is fear itself. Today he would not be right. We have as much to fear from our own apparently inalienable freedoms as we do from the Taliban and Osama bin Laden.

We are free—too free—to do shameful things in the name of "freedom." And, I fear, we are edging into a time when having invoked the name of God in so many devout "God bless America" prayers, we may start to do some truly wrongheaded things in the name of God.

"God" isn't just "any old god." The God in whom we trust is the God and Father of our Lord Jesus Christ, the God of unfailing mercy and amazing grace, the God of love who is love and who, through his Son, our only Savior, commands us to love one another and not just "any old other," but the "other" who is our enemy as much as the "other" who is our friend.

This is truly "tough love," my friends, for it flies in the face of all that we are feeling as a nation—and as a world—right now about vengeance and retribution and the "destruction and . . . defeat of the global terror network" Our president has assured us—and the world—that America will "meet violence with patient justice, assured of the rightness of our cause and confident of the victories to come."

"Freedom and fear are at war . . ." "have always been at war . . ." the president said last Thursday night; "and we know that God is not neutral between them." That may end up being the defining quote of George W. Bush's presidency; for he knows the gospel of our Lord Jesus Christ as well as I do, and understands that God is not neutral about love, either.

Jesus infuriated his enemies as well as, I suspect, some of his friends, with teachings like, "Love your enemies and pray for those who persecute you so that you may be children of your Father in heaven." Or, "You have heard that it was said, 'An eye for an eye and a tooth for a tooth.' But I say to you, do not resist an evildoer" (Mt 5:44, 38–39).

The spontaneous student "peace movement" that has sprung up in the past week or so is getting pretty unfavorable press coverage and public reaction across the nation. But, sisters and brothers in Christ, a lot of what these young people are saying sounds a lot more like what Jesus would say than a lot of the rhetoric coming out of some of the supposedly "religious" spokespeople on the radio and TV talk shows.

"God is *not* neutral" about the outcome of this warfare. But God cannot "bless America" if America does not trust and honor and live out who and what God really is and *that* is *love*.

In his first epistle to the early Christian church—in times of terrible persecution of and suffering by believers in Jesus Christ—John wrote that "perfect love casts out fear" (1 John 4:18). What he meant—and what I believe—is that when we live in love as individuals, as families, as congregations, as communities, as nations; we live in God; and God lives in us, and where or what could be safer?

We may love justice, but we must love mercy more. We may

love freedom, but we must love responsibility more. We may seek vengeance, but we must love God and not overstep his prerogatives, for "Vengeance is mine," says the Lord (Romans 12:19). We may fear the future, but we must love Christ, who reassures us that our futures are already bought and paid for through his sacrifice on the cross. We may not know what to do next, but we must love God's Holy Spirit, who will "teach (us) everything and remind (us) of all that (Christ has) said to (us)."

"God is not neutral," but "God is love," and "there is no fear in love, but perfect love casts out fear."

And the perfect love of God is this: "that we obey his commandments . . ."

We love because he first loved us . . .

And this is the victory that conquers the world, our faith" (1 Jn 4:16b, 18b; 5:3; 4:19; 5:4b).

Amen!

"God Only Knows!"

A Sermon Preached by

The Reverend Dr. William R. Russell

in

The First Presbyterian Church of

Royal Oak, Michigan

Sunday, September 30, 2001

I have seen the business that God has given to everyone to be busy with. He has made everything suitable for its time; moreover he has put a sense of past and future into their minds, yet they cannot find out what God has done from the beginning to the end. That which is, already has been; that which is to be, already is; and God seeks out what has gone by (Eccl 3:10–11, 15, NRSV).

NOT SINCE THE SEPARATIST CRISIS IN French Canada nearly a quarter-century ago has my preaching caused the outburst of comment—pro and con—that has been provoked by my sermons on the past two Sundays.

I have been profoundly impressed by and am deeply grateful for the thoughtful responses—and even the apparently thought-*less* ones—that so many have shared with me in letters, emails, phone calls and face-to-face conversations these past two weeks.

During my first preaching pastorate in New Jersey (now a very, very long time ago!) I learned the bitter lesson to dread it if someone in the shake-my-hand line at the door at the end of a service said, "That was the *best* sermon I've ever heard on *whatever*!" Because I knew for sure that, five or six handshakes later, someone else would invariably say "That was the *worst* sermon I've ever heard on _____!"

And so it's been since September 11th. Emotions are running high across America and here in metro Detroit and right within our own family of faith. I've conducted nine public worship services since the terrorist attacks upon our country—two spontaneous prayer services, a funeral, two memorial services, and four Sunday services—and each in its own way has occasioned far more comment than usual and across a far wider than usual spectrum from appreciation to animosity. America is looking to its houses of worship and to its spiritual leaders for comfort, reassurance, strength, and vision: we are in the midst of a crisis of faith of unimagined proportions and unmeetable expectations, which only proves again the age-old maxim that even we preachers need to be careful about what we pray for, for we may get it!

Early in the week, a neighboring clergyman, who has been experiencing as much intensity of emotion in his congregation as I am feeling here, asked me what I was going to preach about today. I shrugged and said, "God only knows! The situation changes so fast and the news coverage is so relentless and the needs of my people are so varied and so volatile, I can't imagine what God's Holy Spirit will require of me and inspire in me come Sunday morning."

As the week wore on and I listened to so many different points of view from so many different people on so many different aspects of "America's new war" (as CNN has unofficially identified it), I began to realize the unexpected insight of my original admission. "God only knows" what's going on and why and where it's heading and when it's going to be resolved and how it's going to end.

To many, that may seem a disappointing—even disturbing—admission on my part. I am sorry not to have any easy answers to your hard questions.

But to some—and, I pray, in this spiritually discerning and disciplined family of faith, to more than a few—it will be *enough*: to affirm that *God knows*—even if *only God knows*—

what's actually going on and when and where and why and how
God's going to work in and through and around and over and
under and in spite of it *for good* may be as far as Christian faith
can take us at this moment (Rom 8:28).

* * * * *

BUT THERE ARE THREE SIGNIFICANT AND REPEATED ISSUES that
some of you have raised about my last two sermons and even
about the scripture passages I have chosen to read or have read
in our eight recent worship services that are troublesome
enough that I want to address them, at least briefly, to clarify
any misunderstandings about what I have said or taught or implied in response to this national tragedy of unprecedented horror.

First of all, I have often addressed the theme of bad things
happening to good people, and I have always tried to stress the
point that they *do happen*! In God's infinite wisdom and unfailing providence, the price of freedom is permissiveness: for individuals, for families, for communities, for nations, for all. God
created us to be free and permits us to be free, both when we
use our freedom to launch life-changing research, push frontiers
farther out into space and under the sea, create new artistic im-
agery of self-disclosure, and even when we *abuse* our freedom
for the most perverse, evil, and destructive purposes imaginable.
The victims of such perversity, evil, and destruction as human-
kind are free to work upon themselves and upon one another
are just that: *victims*, often as "innocent" as anyone else of the
terrible fate that befalls them and "unprotected" by the hand
of God so many seem to think somehow God ought to use to
intervene and arrest our freedom, willy-nilly, with miraculous
caprice to spare those who don't deserve to die.

There's an email making the rounds this week recounting the stories of some of the lifesaving coincidences that spared people from dying in the implosion of the twin towers of the World Trade Center, the ramming of one façade of the Pentagon, and the crashes of those three jetliners with suicidal maniac extremists at the controls. Missed flights, missing baby-sitters, illness, distraction—you know the sort of thing—and the tearfully grateful non-victims attributing the miraculous coincidence to God's individual and immediate intervention in their personal lives. Such stories may make great reading in *Guideposts* or *Reader's Digest*, but they make very bad theology about how God respects and sustains human freedom and they make very cruel presumptions about the victims whom God apparently did *not* find worthy of lifesaving coincidences or death-defying miracles.

I insistently believe that God was just as much "with" the men and women who got to work on time and died as "with" those who came in late and were spared. God cared just as much about the people who kept their appointments that day and died as about those who did not and lived. God honors the self-sacrifice of the police officers and firefighters and rescue workers who happened to be outside of the twin towers when they collapsed and did not die as he honors those whose lives were snuffed out in the smoke and flame and dust and rubble.

And I just as insistently believe that God did not cause these horrors to happen as occasions of judgment upon Jews or gays or capitalists or any other identifiable minority targeted by America's religious right: what an utter fool Jerry Falwell made of himself with his bitter, judgmental, off-the-cuff remarks right after the tragedies! And what a poor excuse of an apology he offered later!

And I even more vehemently insist that God will somehow

be *at work for good* in all this. God has already done great things by inspiring the heroism of the countless men and women who have given their time and energy and emotion and even life itself to the rescue work in New York, Virginia, and Pennsylvania. God has already done great things by uplifting the patriotism of a nation that had almost forgotten how to wave the Stars and Stripes and sing "God Bless America." God has already done great things by unleashing the generosity of a great nation and the echoing offerings of an awestruck world to provide aid, comfort, and relief to the victims of the United States' unforgettable 9/11 day of death and destruction.

* * * * *

SECOND, THE PERMISSIVENESS THAT PROVIDES REAL freedom must be tempered by the sense of responsibility that undergirds true liberty. Americans are more enthusiastic about "freedom" than they are about "responsibility." Ann and I went over the border last night to the debut concert of the Windsor Symphony Orchestra's new conductor, who is terrific by the way. The border crossing through the tunnel into Canada was almost routine, but the return trip across the bridge into the USA took well over an hour of bumper-to-bumper creeping and crawling through Customs and Immigration. Already, one can see and feel—and regret—the difference: the cars jockeying for position is intensifying, the patience of the travelers is wearing thin, the attention of the surveillance officers is less intensive and more going-through-the-motions. North Americans want convenience, and we want it now, and terrorists be damned!

Between the civil libertarians and the folk united to separate church and state, you'd think that the American Constitution proclaimed freedom *from* responsibility rather than *through* it.

If we are to wage war against terrorism, then we all have to play a part and pay a price and sacrifice some personal freedom for the sake of preserving "liberty and justice for all."

And speaking of "justice," one of my friends in the congregation told me the other day—with some asperity in his voice—that he was waiting for my sermon on "justice" in all of this as opposed, I gathered, to that "love your enemies" stuff I was preaching last Sunday. I hinted he might have to wait a long time; then I thought that maybe I ought to give that some more thought. A lot of people are clamoring for "justice" right now: "justice," that is, for Osama bin Laden and the Afghani Taliban leaders who are allegedly harboring bin Laden and his terrorist cells and camps and campaigns. By "justice" they really mean *vengeance* and, in fact, *death* for what some are calling "the incarnation of Satan" and his minions of an unspeakably evil holy war, ridding the world of terrorism once and for all, the "final solution" for this frightening turn of events.

The trouble with "justice" as a sermon theme for an evangelical Christian preacher is that it is so "Old Testament." The word itself, according to my computerized Bible search program, appears 115 times in the Old Testament but only fourteen times in the New Testament, and of those, only six appear in the teachings of Jesus. And even that is misleading, for two of them are doublets of the same event reported in both Matthew (23:23) and Luke (11:42), in which Jesus quotes the prophecy of Micah about "what does the Lord require of us" and then complains that the scribes and the Pharisees, the self-appointed, self-satisfied, self-righteous leaders of the Jews under Roman occupation, were *neglecting* "justice and mercy and faith."

The only other time the four Gospels show Jesus as speaking about "justice" is in the eighteenth chapter of Luke as our Lord told the parable of the needy widow and the unjust judge, the point of which is that God will mete out justice even when a corrupt judicial system won't, and the question at the climax is, "And yet, when the Son of Man comes, will he find faith on earth" (18:8)?

* * * * *

YOU SEE—AND HERE IS MY THIRD POINT—in the Gospels, in the recorded teachings of our Lord's own words, living a life responsive to the Good News of God's salvation and responsible for sharing that good news with a waiting world is more defined by forgiveness, mercy, grace, and love than by justice. The word "forgive" appears twenty-two times in the New Testament, seventeen of them in the Gospels; "mercy" fifty-four times, almost half of them in the Gospels; "grace" shows up 108 times in the New Testament versus three times in the Old Testament; and "love" tops the list with forty-four appearances in the Gospels, 182 in the New Testament as a whole, and, surprisingly, 302 times in the Old Testament.

"Reducing Kabul to rubble," as some have been urging loudly this past week, may be satisfying public policy for some Americans but not for Christians. "Slaughtering every Afghani who aids and abets terrorism" may be a winning TV soundbite solution for this crisis but not for Christians. Hunting down and doing away with Osama bin Laden and his followers may slake America's bloodthirst for vengeance but not for Christians.

There is only one death that absolves the guilt and assuages the grief over 6,000 deaths or 3,000,000 or the whole world's, and that sentence was executed 2,000 years ago on a cross outside Jerusalem. "For God so loved the world. . . ." [You know the rest by heart, or you can look it up in the Gospel of John, chapter three, verse sixteen.]

*   *   *   *   *

AT A TURNING POINT IN HIS PUBLIC MINISTRY as Jesus was sending his disciples out to spread the gospel throughout Jewry, he
warned his nearest and dearest not to think that he had come
"not to bring peace to the world, but a sword" (Matthew
10:34). He knew that his message would mean division between
father and son, between mother and daughter, amongst in-laws
and households, and certainly within the church and without.

As puzzling as this prediction has always been, I believe that
Jesus spoke of such times as these: when men and women of
good will and high ideals disagree fundamentally about what
has happened, who is responsible, how we should respond and
when and where. War as we have known it may be the president's policy option, and it may not; either way, Americans
need to support the commander in chief and defend the national
security and integrity whichever way he leads.

For Christians, this part of patriotism is potentially very
difficult and personally very divisive. We think of America as a
"Christian" country and of ourselves as "Christian" citizens.
Yet as several of you have confessed to me in the past two
weeks, "Maybe it isn't 'Christian' to feel the way I do."

Maybe it isn't; maybe it is. Christ's gospel is good news of
love, grace, mercy, and forgiveness; that is clear. Justice—certainly vengeance—is/are God's to dispense; that is equally clear
in both the Old Testament and the New.

Freedom demands responsibility, and responsibility rests on
humility before God and man. I pray us each to be humble
enough to be wise and wise enough to be Christ's and Christlike
enough to entrust our very lives to the love of God, now and
for all eternity.

Amen!